STRANGERS TO THE CONSTITUTION

STRANGERS TO
THE CONSTITUTION

IMMIGRANTS, BORDERS,
AND FUNDAMENTAL LAW

GERALD L. NEUMAN

PRINCETON UNIVERSITY PRESS

PRINCETON, NEW JERSEY

Library of Congress Cataloging-in-Publication Data

Neuman, Gerald L., 1952–
Strangers to the Constitution : immigrants, borders,
and fundamental law / Gerald L. Neuman.
p. cm.
Includes bibliographical references and index.
ISBN 0-691-04360-4 (CL : acid-free paper)
1. Aliens—United States. 2. Emigration and
immigration law—United States. 3. Civil rights—
United States. I. Title.
KF4800.N48 1996   342.73′082—dc20   [347.30282]
95-39587 CIP

This book has been composed in Times Roman

Princeton University Press books are printed
on acid-free paper and meet the guidelines for
permanence and durability of the Committee on
Production Guidelines for Book Longevity
of the Council on Library Resources

Printed in the United States of America
by Princeton Academic Press

10 9 8 7 6 5 4 3 2 1

CONTENTS

PREFACE

THE PURPOSE of this book is to explore the constitutional foundations of immigration law and aliens' rights in the United States. Despite the United States' identification as a country of immigrants, immigration law has long been treated as outside the constitutional mainstream. Hesitancy to enforce constitutional limits has reflected the special character of the phenomenon of immigration: it involves foreign individuals crossing the border from foreign or international territory into the domain of the United States' territorial sovereignty. Both of these reasons for uncertainty about constitutional protection—the personal status of the individuals and their geographical location—will receive close attention.

The ultimate goal will be to find persuasive contemporary answers within the framework of U.S. constitutional practice. The inquiry will be historical as well as theoretical, for several reasons. First, the U.S. system of constitutional law operates through precedent, and so consistent prior judicial decisions have presumptive authority. Second, history also serves a critical function. Aspects of current constitutional rules that appear perplexing may be illuminated by their historical antecedents. Sometimes outdated background assumptions and forgotten political movements have produced constitutional interpretations that persist after the structures that supported them have vanished. If these interpretations have no convincing contemporary justification, they should be replaced. Third, courts often invoke the historical practices of the other branches of government directly in constitutional interpretation. False or oversimplified representations of the past can have negative consequences for the present, whether they result from inadvertence or from ideologically inspired wishful thinking.

Accordingly, this book proceeds in two parts. Part One, consisting of Chapters Two through Five, investigates underexamined aspects of constitutional history that provide the necessary background for the normative constitutional analysis of Part Two. The historical chapters offer interpretations of the events they relate, while recognizing the complexity of the past and the ongoing competition among differing ideologies. Part Two is more argumentative than descriptive, seeking the best resolution of contemporary questions in light of U.S. constitutional tradition.

More specifically, Chapter One explains the problem of defining the scope of U.S. constitutionalism, which determines where, when, and in whose favor constitutional limits on government action apply. The chapter introduces some possible approaches to the personal reach of constitutional rights and their geographical field of application. It also recalls the social contract background of the Constitution and demonstrates how ambiguities within that tradition set the stage for future disagreements, including the anomalous treatment of immigration in modern constitutional law.

Chapter Two develops the historical context for the early evolution of aliens' place in U.S. constitutionalism, by portraying the forgotten period of state immigration regulation. Contrary to popular myth, the borders of the United States were not legally open prior to the federalization of immigration law in the late nineteenth century. Instead, immigration regulation was conducted primarily as an exercise of the "police power" at the state level, and it involved qualitative restrictions on undesired migrants rather than the quantitative restrictions on the volume of migration that have characterized modern federal immigration law. Although the dominant reality for social historians may be the ease of immigration (evading these restrictions if necessary), legal historians cannot overlook the maintenance of such regulations. By analogy, social historians might properly regard the Prohibition era as a period of widespread drinking, but a legal history of the period owes some emphasis to the fact that speakeasies were not legally open.

Chapter Three then addresses the constitutional legitimacy of the state restrictions on migration. Prior to the adoption of the Fourteenth Amendment, which protected individual rights against the states, the major basis for objection to state restrictions was federalism. In fact, antebellum assumptions about freedom of interstate migration differed greatly from those prevalent today. Some of the state regulation enjoyed express legislative support from the federal government, and nearly all categories enjoyed federal judicial approval before the Civil War.

Chapter Four analyzes the historical episodes crucial to the evolution of the rights of aliens within the borders of the United States. The terms of the debate were set in the controversy over the infamous Alien Act of 1798. Many Federalist defenders of the act denied the rights-bearing capacity of aliens, invoking a membership account of the Constitution as a social contract. The Jeffersonians offered a competing interpretation of social-contract theory and the Constitution, under which the subjection of aliens to United States law entitled them to the protection of the Constitution, as a result of the mutuality of legal obligation. This opposition of membership and mutuality approaches provides a principal theme of the book. The constitutionality of the Alien Act was never tested in the courts during its brief life, but subsequent history offers a positive lesson in the consistent recognition of aliens' rights, according with the Jeffersonians' mutuality approach. The chapter also shows how the relation of aliens to the body politic was complicated by the practice in some states and territories of enfranchising unnaturalized alien residents as voters. Some politicians criticized this practice on membership grounds, and others championed it on mutuality grounds, but the courts of the period regarded alien suffrage as constitutionally optional, neither forbidden nor required.

Chapter Five turns to the geographical scope of constitutional rights, their extension beyond the borders of the states, first to other federal territories and later to U.S. government action in foreign countries. Here as well, membership and mutuality theories can be distinguished. The competition between these theories resulted over time in a wavering among dominant approaches. It also produced an intermediate approach, which I label "global due process," under which nontextual principles of fundamentality determine which rights are available to persons in exotic locations. This checkered history provides resources of argument, but not definitive resolutions, for guidance in future disputes. Unsettled issues have multiplied since the 1950s, when the Supreme Court overthrew the former assumption that constitutional rights were territorially limited and therefore never available, even to citizens, outside the borders of the nation. Although the new assumption corresponds more accurately to modern understandings of the geographical consequences of sovereignty and the international behavior of the United States, constitutional law has not yet fully assimilated this tranformation.

Part Two then employs the insights gained from the historical inquiry to address the most important questions in contemporary constitutional law concerning immigration. Chapter Six presents an argument that modern uncertainties should be resolved in favor of a modern form of the mutuality of obligation approach, making constitutional rights available extraterritorially to all U.S. citizens and to those aliens on whom the United States seeks to impose legal obligations. The chapter contrasts this approach with the alternative extremes of universalism and a Hobbesian membership approach. It also compares the mutuality approach with the middle ground emerging in the Supreme Court's few cases on the subject, the global due process methodology of Justices Kennedy, Frankfurter, and Harlan, which extends some constitutional rights to aliens abroad.

Chapter Seven explores the proper role of constitutional rights in constraining immigration policy. It elaborates the consequences of both the mutuality of obligation approach and global due process for aliens' rights to enter or to remain in the United States. It argues that the recognition of extraterritorial constitutional rights not only reinforces the current trend toward limited judicial review of immigration policy, but supports a stronger presumption that constitutional constraints on immigration policy are fully enforceable by the courts.

Chapter Eight deepens the analysis by pursuing the example of aliens' political rights in the United States. It first probes the current constitutional viability of alien suffrage, finding that modern doctrines remain consistent with the historical practice of permitting the states to enfranchise their alien residents. This conclusion underlines the importance of aliens' political speech, focusing critical attention on the United States' most controversial immigration policy, the exclusion and deportation of aliens on ideological grounds. The chapter investigates the circumstances under which the exclusion of aliens from initial entry to the United States on grounds of political speech might be reconciled with First Amendment constraints, within the mutuality of obligation and global due process approaches. It also determines that under either approach resident aliens can never be deported from the United States on the basis of speech for which citizens could not constitutionally be punished.

Chapter Nine considers an issue of great political salience today: whether children born in the United States to illegally present alien parents should be U.S. citizens. That question turns first on the interpretation of the citizenship clause of the Fourteenth Amendment and second on whether that clause will itself be amended. The chapter discusses current proposals to reinterpret the citizenship clause to exclude illegal aliens' children and shows that the revisionist proposal is not a defensible substitute for the traditional meaning, which is supported by both history and reason. The chapter then confronts the policy arguments for amending the Fourteenth Amendment, and it concludes that the Constitution's traditional shield against the emergence of a hereditary caste of denizens should be preserved.

The constitutional arguments presented in the second part of the book may not persuade all readers, but the book will not fail of its purpose if it succeeds in two lesser respects: first, to confront participants in current debates with the complexity of the past, and second, to insist on normative perspectives that these debates must take into account. Readers who follow that far are encouraged to pursue further investigation themselves.

ACKNOWLEDGMENTS

THE RESEARCH for this book has occupied me, in parallel to other projects, for several years, and the debts of gratitude have grown accordingly. It is a pleasure to recall the benefits I have gained, jointly and severally, from T. Alexander Aleinikoff, Debra Anker, Nadine Baker-Barrett, Barbara Black, Richard Briffault, Lea Brilmayer, Stephen Burbank, David Cole, Lori Damrosch, Hilda Daniels, Erhard Denninger, Alexia Dorszynski, John Dugard, Maryellen Fullerton, Lani Guinier, Patrick Gudridge, Louis Henkin, John Honnold, Daniel Kanstroom, Andrew King, Harold Hongju Koh, Seth Kreimer, Friedrich Kübler, Noyes Leech, Howard Lesnick, Lance Liebman, Daniel Malone, Bruce Mann, David Martin, Eben Moglen, Henry Monaghan, John Mulkern, Subha Narasimhan, Bradley J. Nicholson, Thomas Odom, Jamin Raskin, Carol Sanger, John Scanlan, Michael Schill, Peter Schuck, Rogers Smith, Margaret Ulrich, and Alan Watson. I am glad to thank them again. Ed Baker has been tireless in criticism, and Carol Jones Neuman has been tireless in consolation.

I have been touched by and am grateful for the support of the University of Pennsylvania Law School Institute for Law and Economics, the Ida Russell Cades Memorial Fund, and the Dean's Fund of the University of Pennsylvania Law School; the John M. Olin Foundation; and the Samuel Rubin Program for the Advancement of Liberty and Equality through Law and the Walter E. Meyer Research in Law and Social Problems Fund of the Columbia University School of Law.

Although the book was conceived as a whole, earlier versions of several chapters were previously published as articles as phases of the research were completed. I thank the copyright holders for permission to reprint as follows:

Chapters Two and Three and portions of Chapter Nine derive from the article "The Lost Century of American Immigration Law (1776–1875)." This article originally appeared at 93 Colum. L. Rev. 1833 (1993).

Chapters One, Five, and Six and portions of Chapter Four derive from the article "Whose Constitution?" 100 Yale L.J. 909 (1991). Reprinted by permission of The Yale Law Journal Company and Fred B. Rothman & Company.

Portions of Chapters Four and Seven derive from the article " 'We Are the People' ": Alien Suffrage in German and American Perspective," 13

Mich. J. Int'l L. 259 (1992). Reprinted by permission of the Michigan Journal of International Law.

Portions of Chapter Nine derive from the book review "Back to *Dred Scott?*" 24 San Diego L. Rev. 485 (1987). Copyright 1987 San Diego Law Review Association. Reprinted with the permission of the San Diego Law Review.

STRANGERS TO THE CONSTITUTION

Chapter One

WHOSE CONSTITUTION?

T HE CONSTITUTION begins with "We the People." Where does it end?

Constitutional argument serves as the nation's preeminent vehicle for asserting constraints of fundamental principle. Eligibility to participate in constitutional discourse confers an opportunity to influence the shaping of the framework for government action. Conversely, one strategy for silencing objections to government policy has been to deny that the Constitution affords any protection to the objector. The critic is a stranger to the Constitution and should not meddle with it.

That strategy has been employed repeatedly throughout the two-hundred-year history of American constitutionalism. Notorious examples include the definition of slaves as lacking legal personality and devoid of rights, the Supreme Court's characterization of free African Americans in the Dred Scott case as having "no rights which the white man was bound to respect,"[1] and the treatment of Native American tribes as "domestic dependent nations" having neither all the privileges of a sovereign nor all the rights of a corporation.[2]

The domain of U.S. constitutionalism has always been contested, and it has grown as the nation has grown. The disputes no longer relate directly to questions of race but prominently involve distinctions of citizenship, distinctions of geography, and the interaction of the two. The reach of the Constitution to government action on the high seas and in foreign countries is highly uncertain, and even the Constitution's effects in island territories of the United States, like Puerto Rico and Guam, remain unsettled—a relic of colonialism. The availability of constitutional rights to aliens outside the United States and the impact of constitutional rights on government regulation of immigration are currently in flux.

Some scholars have suggested that the rising trajectory of constitutional protection points to its universal application to all forms of government action, regardless of person, place, or context.[3] The courts have not reached that point yet, and other scholars argue that they never should.[4] Defining the domain of constitutionalism has major practical implications for immigration policy, the conduct of foreign affairs, military action, and the participation of American citizens in an increasingly global society. In recent years, claims of constitutional right have been raised by Englishwomen living near American overseas missile sites, United States investors dispossessed by American-influenced takings for Salvadoran land reform and for training Nicaraguan contras, American and foreign organizations tied by financial strings to restrictions on overseas abortion counseling, and Haitian refugees held by the United States at the Guantánamo Bay Naval Base after being captured on the high seas.[5] Similar issues arise routinely in transnational civil litigation and criminal prosecution, especially in this age of massive narcotics smuggling. They arose less routinely when the United States invaded Panama to arrest General Manuel Noriega.[6] Perhaps not everyone, everywhere in this dangerous and unstable world, should be shielded against government action by the standards of U.S. constitutional rights.

THE SCOPE OF THE CONSTITUTION: LOOKING FOR QUESTIONS TO THE ANSWERS

I emphasize at the outset that the major object of inquiry in this book is United States *constitutional* rights. An individual's constitutional rights do not always coincide with her subconstitutional statutory or common law rights available at a given time within the United States' domestic legal system, her human rights recognized under international treaties or customary international law, or her moral rights independent of any legal system. Constitutional law is one among a plurality of normative systems, which interact in complex ways.

It is therefore helpful to recall some positive data supplied by the legal system before looking for the theoretical constructs that might enable us to understand them. United States citizens within the borders of the states possess the full complement of constitutional rights; that is the core situation for which constitutional rights were created. The Supreme Court has also held for more than a century that aliens within the United States are persons entitled to constitutional protection.[7] That includes aliens who are unlawfully present, although recent Supreme Court dicta suggest that intensified concerns over both drugs and migrants penetrating the border may put pressure on that commitment.[8] Moreover, the Court has further held that aliens not present in the United States are entitled to constitutional protection with regard to actions taken within the United States against their property rights.[9]

The situation becomes more complicated with regard to government action outside the borders of the States. In the nineteenth century, the Supreme Court generally maintained that government action outside the borders of the *nation* was not constrained by anyone's constitutional rights.[10] In the once-famous Insular Cases (1901), the Supreme Court held that the

Constitution does not even "follow the flag," that is, the United States may acquire sovereignty of "unincorporated" possessions where it will be bound only by those provisions of the Constitution that the Court deems "fundamental"; these cases have never been expressly overruled.[11] However, in *Reid v. Covert* (1957), the Supreme Court held that even in foreign countries, the requirements of trial by jury and indictment by grand jury must be afforded when United States authorities prosecute United States citizen civilians for capital crimes.[12] Since *Reid v. Covert*, it has generally been recognized that the Constitution as such "applies" wherever the government of the United States may act, and provides the source of the federal government's authority to act there—the disputable question is whether a particular constitutional limitation on the government's authority to act should be regarded as including within its prohibitions unusual categories of places or persons. In 1990 the Supreme Court held that the Fourth Amendment's warrant clause placed no restrictions on searches of nonresident aliens' property located in a foreign country.[13]

From its inception the very text of the Constitution has suggested inconsistent readings of its intended scope. The Preamble arguably speaks the language of social contract, perhaps even narrowing the provisions that follow by emphasizing that "We the People of the United States, in Order to . . . secure the Blessings of Liberty *to ourselves and our Posterity*, do ordain and establish this Constitution *for the United States of America*" (my emphasis). On the other hand, the supremacy clause gives a different characterization of the document—"This Constitution . . . shall be the supreme Law of the Land"—and Article III appears to "establish Justice" for foreign citizens, subjects, and even ambassadors by designing tribunals that will decide their cases impartially. We will later see that social-contract and law-of-the-land interpretations can be easily reconciled, but the contrast illustrates the Constitution's susceptibility to diverse conceptualizations.

Four kinds of approaches have emerged in the course of American constitutional history, which might assist in resolving these problems of interpretation: universalism, membership approaches, mutuality approaches, and "global due process." I will introduce them in that order.

Universalism

Universalist approaches require that constitutional provisions that create rights with no express limitations as to the persons or places covered should be interpreted as applicable to every person and at every place. The precise commands of the provisions, especially of those creating rights subject to balancing tests, may vary from place to place, but one can never simply dismiss the provisions as inapplicable.

The argument for universal application may rely upon the natural rights background of the American constitutional tradition, possibly reinforced by contemporary conceptions of human rights. Or it may proceed simply by literalism, observing that some portions of the constitutional text limit their protection expressly to certain places or persons, and others do not.

Some have also argued for universalism by replacing its natural law foundation with the argument that because the Constitution is an "organic" act giving "life" to the federal government and providing its only powers, the federal government cannot exercise powers withheld by the Constitution anywhere or with respect to any person. This organic argument has force when offered in response to claims of inherent extraconstitutional power free of all constitutional restriction. But when offered as a rule for determining the personal or geographical scope of constitutional restrictions, the argument frequently becomes circular. For example, understanding the Constitution as an organic act establishing the federal government is wholly uninformative as to whether the freedom of speech and association protected by the First Amendment includes the political activity of Nicaraguans in Nicaragua or even the political activity of Americans in Mexico.[14] Application of the organic principle presupposes an interpretation of the pertinent constitutional restriction and does not in itself supply one.

Although the universalist approach has significant support among modern commentators, it has played almost no role in American constitutionalism until recent years. It did surface in one dissenting opinion by Justice William Brennan, but even there it appeared only as an alternative.[15]

Membership Models

Social contract rhetoric has played a significant role in American constitutionalism. Social contract theory seeks to legitimate government through the idea of an actual or hypothetical agreement embodying the consent of the governed, who have established the state and empowered it to govern. Some accounts of social contract theory identify a limited class of "members" as the proper beneficiaries of the contract. The beneficiaries have rights based in the contract; nonbeneficiaries are relegated to whatever rights they may have independent of the contract. A skeptic who did not ascribe normative force to social contract arguments could still invoke the idea of a social contract as a historically grounded tool for interpreting American constitutionalism.[16]

If the restriction of constitutional rights to members is to be justified by characterizing the Constitution as a social contract, then it becomes necessary to identify the set of parties to the contract. As we will see later, advocates of restrictive membership approaches have argued for widely varying descriptions of the parties: they may include all the citizens of the nation "the United States," the subset consisting of those who are citizens of the various states, or some intermediate group including citizens of some, but not all, of the territories. During certain periods of American history, it has been claimed that the parties to the Constitution were not individual citizens, but rather the several states. Moreover, even if individuals are parties to the Constitution, that document reserves sovereign political power to the people of the states alone, and only they have given their consent to it at the time of each state's accession to the union. Accordingly, some supporters of a membership model have argued that constitutional protections should be available only within the geographical limits of the states (plus or minus the District of Columbia, which was formerly part of Maryland), and *not* in the territories.

Mutuality of Legal Obligation, Including Strict Territoriality

Under a strictly territorial model, the Constitution constrains the United States government only when it acts within the borders of the United States. Strict territoriality prevailed as dogma for most of American constitutional history, until the Supreme Court overturned it in 1957 in *Reid v. Covert*. During that period, courts rarely saw any need to justify it.

For nineteenth-century American law, this model made sense as a reflex of the territorial sovereignty of the nation-state.[17] Chief Justice Marshall had asserted as a basic principle that "[t]he jurisdiction of the nation within its own territory is necessarily exclusive and absolute."[18] To a territorialist, a law is binding of its own force only within the territory of the nation-state that promulgates it. If the Constitution is viewed as a law or legal norm, then the territorialist would conclude that the Constitution has power to bind only within the nation's borders. Extending the Constitution over the entire territory then gives it the maximum geographical scope that it can have of its own force.

Thus rationalized, strict territoriality may be seen as a special case of a more general approach that focuses on a sphere in which American municipal law operates.[a] Rather than define that sphere solely in terms of ge-

---

[a] The term "municipal law" is used here in accordance with its use by writers on international law to designate the law of a given nation-state, in opposition to international or natural law. In an earlier version of portions of this book, I used the label "municipal law approach" for what I describe in this book as the "mutuality of obligation approach." See Gerald L. Neuman, Whose Constitution?, 100 Yale L.J. 909 (1991). The substance of the argument has not changed, but the new label may be more helpful to the reader and echoes the emphasis on mutuality in Justice Brennan's dissenting opinion in United States v. Verdugo-Urquidez, 494 U.S. 259 (1990).

ography, one may define it in terms of a broader range of factors. The Constitution, as fundamental municipal law—"the supreme Law of the Land"—also operates within that sphere and constrains the actions of government. When the government acts outside the sphere of municipal law, it enters a field where its actions do not impose obligations. Individuals are not bound there by the United States government; nor does the Constitution bind the government to respect what would otherwise be the individuals' constitutional rights.

Both the narrow territoriality approach and the broader approach can be derived from a social contract understanding of constitutionalism that differs from membership approaches in its account of how one becomes a beneficiary of a social contract. Under this understanding, rights are prerequisites for justifying legal obligation. The historical investigation later in this book will associate the mutuality of obligation tradition with, among others, James Madison, John Marshall, John C. Calhoun, Roger Taney, the first Justice John Marshall Harlan, Hugo Black, William Brennan, and Harry Blackmun. In Chapter Six, I will argue that it represents the best account of American constitutionalism.

Balancing Approaches, or "Global Due Process"

Extending to an individual abroad the full complement of constitutional rights that she would enjoy within United States territory may seem too generous a compensation for subjecting the individual to only some of our laws. If one views a constitution as a contract designed to create a balance of power between the governors and the governable, then the government's reduced right to obedience and reduced means of enforcement might be thought to call for a reciprocal reduction in individual rights. Universalism is often criticized for the danger that would be posed to the United States if it unilaterally renounced powers that other nations freely exercise.[19]

This emphasis on the countervailing necessities of overseas action may suggest that all of these models can be collapsed into a brand of harmless universalism: recognize constitutional rights as potentially applicable worldwide, and then permit them to be outweighed by countervailing government interests through a balancing process. One might engage in ad hoc balancing in the individual case, or balance more categorically; this balancing process may be intrusive or highly deferential. This approach suggests that, ultimately, extraterritorial constitutional rights boil down to a single right: the right to "global due process." Historically, this approach has been associated with Chief Justice Edward Douglass White, Felix Frankfurter, the second Justice Harlan, and Anthony Kennedy.

THE SOCIAL CONTRACT BACKGROUND

The linked traditions of social contract theory and naturalist international law played an important role in both the creation of the United States Constitution and the early debates over its applicability to noncitizens and to government action outside the states. One representative of both traditions, Emer de Vattel's *Law of Nations*, requires particular notice because of its great prestige in post-Revolutionary America, also reflected in these debates.[20] Because these debates framed the issues for future reconsideration, it is necessary to give closer attention to these traditions if we wish to understand the ideas that the debaters were invoking, as well as to gain insight into what a serious commitment to a social contract view of constitutional rights might entail. It will appear that the traditions contained serious ambiguities concerning the personal and geographical scope of a social contract, ambiguities that provided alternative orientations for American constitutionalism.

The central problem that the social compact tradition sought to address was the legitimacy of government—how the duty of the subjects or citizens to obey the laws could arise, and what limits there might be, the transgression of which would release them from obedience. The theory has ancient roots, but one medieval form particularly deserves mention here: the idea of a contract of government between the monarch and the people, articulated in an oath or charter at the time of accession.[21] This description, however, presupposes the people as a unity capable of making an agreement that binds its members. Later thinkers explored the relationship between individuals and society that could support such a binding agreement.

The social contract analysis was motivated by the view that an individual obligation to obey must be grounded in individual consent, either actual or justly presumed. The authors imagined individuals in a "state of nature," without the protections of a common earthly authority. Whether solely from a desire for greater security, for cooperation toward material improvement, or out of an inherent sociability, they came together and agreed to form a polity. This collective agreement may be called the social contract proper, in contrast to the contract of government between the ruler and the ruled. For most writers, the contract extended itself to the descendants of the original members by means of tacit consent deduced from their acceptance of its benefits.[22]

The number and content of the original agreements varied from author to author. These variations were crucial because they determined who was bound to what. Thomas Hobbes, for example, eliminated the contract of government. In his vision, competitive, self-interested individuals, rationally seeking escape from the universal warfare that characterized the state of nature, agreed to join together and to submit to whatever particular individual or group the majority would select as an absolute sovereign. No contractual limitations or conditions on sovereignty existed, and the sovereign could not be accused of breach, although sovereign failings might lead to the commonwealth's dissolution through external conquest or other social breakdown.[23]

Most later writers in the social contract tradition sought to restore the limitations on the sovereign. Samuel Pufendorf included both the social contract proper and the contract of government in a multistage description of the origin of the state.[24] For Pufendorf, the power of government was limited by the explicit terms of the agreements, the ends for which government was instituted, and the laws of nature.[25] John Locke followed Pufendorf in subjecting governmental power to natural law, but for reasons of his own he replaced the contract of government with a "fundamental positive Law" establishing the government.[26] The powers of government were held in trust, and breach of this trust justified the people's resuming their natural liberty. The trust analogy "fitted Locke's intention admirably, for unlike the contract of government, in which rights and duties were reciprocal, it left the duties on the side of the government, and the rights on the side of the people."[27]

The idea of a fundamental law establishing the form of government held greater prominence in later writings, including Vattel's *Law of Nations*.[28] Vattel was a disciple of Christian Wolff, who agreed with Pufendorf in viewing humans as naturally sociable.[29] Vattel explained the creation of the state as the product of an act of association, or social contract, followed by a fundamental regulation or constitution, which set forth "the organization by means of which the Nation acts as a political body; how and by whom the people are to be governed, and what are the rights and duties of those who govern."[30]

The notion of a written and binding fundamental law, of course, became the great vehicle for American constitutionalism.[31] Because the notion had previously existed more in theory than in practice, the authors did not fully anticipate the questions that would arise in its implementation. Two points on which they were susceptible to opposing interpretations were the rights of aliens under the fundamental law and the extension of the fundamental law to newly acquired territory.

Aliens and the Social Contract

The social contract analysis places primary emphasis on the relationship between a state and its subjects or citizens. What then does it tell us about the rights of aliens? By definition, aliens began as outsiders to a particular social contract; they were either isolated individuals or members of another polity. The members of a given society remained in a state of nature as to outsiders. The consequences depended on one's understanding of a state of nature.

For Hobbes, continuing in the state of nature left outsiders in the condition of war. Thereafter, any outsider who sought to enter the country must submit to the sovereign and become a subject, unless the outsider or his own sovereign had managed to gain a contrary promise from the local sovereign.[32] In the latter case, the outsider's security rode on the terms of the promise, for "the Infliction of what evill soever, on an Innocent man, that is not a Subject, if it be for the benefit of the Common-wealth, and without violation of any former Covenant, is no breach of the Law of Nature."[33]

The notion of an alien's entering the country requires a shift of attention from the society as a union of individuals to the occupation of territory by a society. For Hobbes, the territory of a commonwealth simply consisted of those places where the commonwealth succeeded in exercising power. No property rights existed in a state of nature, and property was distributed by the sovereign after the institution of government. Hobbes had no scruples about conquest, so the territory could be consolidated into the sort of country an alien might think of entering. But those who ascribed a fuller set of duties to the law of nature, identifying a natural right in the possessor of the soil, should have had more difficulty explaining why nations do not interpenetrate one another, like the weave of a cloth or a checkerboard, or at least like "a slice of Swiss cheese."[34] Instead, they simply assumed a domain or a country voluntarily assembled.

The assumption of a non-Hobbesian universal natural law also made an alien's life less cheap. A sovereign sometimes had a natural obligation to permit aliens to enter the territory, particularly when the alien's need was great or the entrance could be permitted without significant disadvantage.[35] Adherents of the natural law school also limited the conditions the sovereign could justly attach to an alien's entrance.[36] They agreed that a sovereign had the right to insist on the alien's subjection to its laws as a condition for permission to enter the territory.[37] Thus entrance by an alien entailed tacit consent to the laws, restoring the consensual basis of obligation. This led some to the semantic question whether the alien became a subject, or a temporary subject, or even a temporary citizen, though it was clear that an alien's admission and submission to the laws did not empower the alien as a full member of the body politic.[38]

The strength of natural obligations, however, should not be overestimated. For Vattel, as for Wolff, most natural obligations bound only "internally," in the sovereign's conscience, and were not "perfect" obligations. That is, they had not been recognized by the nations as rules whose violation justifies the use of force.[39] Except in cases of absolute "necessity,"[40] Vattel and Wolff regarded the sovereign's obligation to admit aliens as internal and imperfect. The sovereign had the "external" right to decide for itself whom its interests enabled it to admit and under what conditions.[41]

What does it mean to say that an alien is subject to "the laws"? That became the crucial question in the debates on aliens' rights. Wolff and his disciple Vattel discussed at length the character of the laws to which aliens must submit, but they were ultimately unenlightening. Vattel maintained that "[b]eing thus subject to the laws, foreigners who violate them should be punished accordingly," and that the sovereign "agrees to protect them as his own subjects."[42] These were only natural obligations, but the foreign state was entitled to intervene

> in cases where justice has been denied or the decision is clearly and palpably unjust, or the proper procedure has not been observed, or finally, in cases where his subjects, or foreigners in general, have been discriminated against.[43]

Nonetheless, Vattel stated that resident aliens "have only certain privileges which the law, or custom, gives them,"[44] and Wolff explicitly mentioned the sovereign's right to "pass laws which hold foreigners alone."[45] Vattel excepted them from certain laws that were "operative only in the case of citizens or subjects."[46] Vattel and Wolff criticized as unjust the confiscation of aliens' movable property on their death, but neither saw cause for complaint in uniform laws denying aliens the right to possess immovable property or to marry local women.[47]

Thus, the natural law tradition supported the notion that the externally binding law of nations required at least some minimal level of justice to aliens.[48] At the same time, it suggested that many legal discriminations against aliens were consistent not only with externally binding law, but also with internally binding natural obligations. Not even Wolff, who labeled aliens "temporary citizens," thought they were naturally entitled to equal treatment with citizens in all things. The tradition provided no unambiguous criteria for deciding which discriminations were permissible, either internally or externally. Vattel and Wolff said nothing about whether fundamental laws were included among those to which aliens were entitled.

Territorial Expansion and the Social Contract

Vattel and the naturalist school of international law discussed not only aliens who entered a sovereign's territory, but also the extension of sovereignty over new territory. The naturalists generally argued that the acquisition of inhabited territory must be founded in consent. European practice led them to recognize a category of "patrimonial" monarchy subject to the monarch's disposition, but the naturalists sought to limit this doctrine.[49] The social contract was a bond of unity, and a nonpatrimonial state could not alienate a portion of its members without their consent, at least not without compelling necessity.[50] Some of the naturalists, however, presumed the tacit consent of those defeated in a just war to the government of the conqueror.[51]

The naturalists did not contend that a state must extend its own fundamental laws over new territory. They assumed that natural rights should be respected in any constitution, but there were many different ways of achieving this. Several of them, including Vattel, wrote approvingly of a conqueror in a just war who rules the conquered territory under its prior form of government.[52] They did not view monarchy as necessarily inconsistent with natural law, nor the rule of one territory by another, so long as it was grounded in original consent.[53] However, Vattel briefly observed that when the political laws of a nation do not draw express distinctions, they also extend to its colonies.[54]

Thus, as in the case of aliens, the lessons of the natural law school for the scope of the Constitution were equivocal. The sovereign should conform to positive fundamental laws in all of its territory, but Vattel and the other naturalists did not require that the fundamental laws of a state be uniform throughout its territory, and they did not discuss which departures from uniformity were appropriate. Presumably a sovereign whose fundamental law placed restrictions on the conditions of acquisition was bound by those restrictions, but their content was a local and not a universal question. Some basis for universal principles, however, may be seen in the requirement that any fundamental laws adopted must respect natural rights, and in the alternative means of legitimation provided by giving the acquired territory the fundamental laws that its own population prefers. It should be noted for future reference that nothing in this tradition makes the convenience of the acquiring power a sufficient justification for the content of fundamental laws imposed on the new territory.

THE IMMIGRATION ANOMALY

Vattel's description of a sovereign's responsibility to aliens has also influenced the constitutional treatment of immigration in the United States. Immigration law has become an isolated speciality within American law, where normal constitutional reasoning does not necessarily apply. This anomalous state of affairs, which has been widely recognized and often deplored, resembles Vattel's account of the external international law of migration. Although Vattel contended that a nation was morally (or "internally") bound to admit aliens when it could do so without causing substantial harm to its own interests, he also observed that nations reserved the right to make the evaluation of harm for themselves. There were no enforceable external norms declaring that a nation must admit aliens in particular circumstances.

In the late nineteenth century, the Supreme Court transformed this characterization of international law into a constitutional doctrine of Congress's "plenary power" to exclude or expel aliens, unconstrained by any judicially enforceable constitutional limits.[b] As a result, the substantive criteria for entry to the United States, whether for temporary visits or for indefinite residence, became immunized from judicial review. Even the criteria for the deportation of alien residents from the United States received no constitutional scrutiny from the courts.[c] The exclusion of aliens from the United States on grounds of their political views or their race formed a central feature of immigration policy in the first half of the twentieth century.

Nonetheless, aliens were not read out of the Constitution altogether. The Supreme Court condemned racial discrimination against aliens by the individual states, confirming that an alien was clearly a "person" protected by the Equal Protection Clause.[55] The Court held that the procedures by which the federal government implemented the deportation of aliens who had already entered the country must satisfy the requirements of due process of law.[56] Even the minimum of procedural protection, however, may be denied to aliens seeking to enter the United States for the first time or to return after an extended absence. The Supreme Court applied this harsh doctrine most spectacularly in 1953, holding that the government could bar an alien's return to his citizen family in upstate New York without giving him any explanation of its reasons for considering him a security risk, even though the consequence appeared to be that the alien would spend the rest of his life trapped on Ellis Island.[57]

Justice Felix Frankfurter, confronted with yet another peculiar example of the inapplicability of normal constitutional reasoning to immigration legislation, once observed:

> [M]uch could be said for the view, were we writing on a clean slate, that the Due Process Clause qualifies the scope of political discretion heretofore recognized as belonging to Congress in regulating the entry and deportation of aliens. . . .
>
> But the slate is not clean. As to the extent of the power of Congress under review, there is not merely "a page of history," but a whole volume.[58]

[b] It is unclear whether this doctrine should be considered as denying that constitutional limitations on Congress exist at all, or only as impairing their judicial enforceability. See Chapter Seven.

[c] For readers not accustomed to the terminology of immigration law, "deportation" means the removal outside the country of an alien who has already entered it, lawfully or unlawfully; "exclusion" means the rejection of an alien who has arrived at the border but has not yet entered the country, at least as the law defines entry.

This book is more open-minded. First, scholarship is not bound by unclean slates. Second, the Supreme Court itself began the process of cleaning—or cracking—the slate in the 1970s. In *Kleindienst v. Mandel* (1972) and *Fiallo v. Bell* (1977), the Court began to accept "a limited judicial responsibility under the Constitution even with respect to the power of Congress to regulate the admission and exclusion of aliens."[59] Although the Court restricted itself in those cases to ensuring the minimal rationality of federal immigration policy, the existence of what it termed a "facially legitimate and bona fide reason" for the policy,[60] the reaffirmation of constitutional constraints on exclusion and deportation gives hope for future development. Turning the pages of history and reason together not only may enlighten, but may yet have practical effect.

PART ONE

THE PAST

Chapter Two

THE OPEN BORDERS MYTH AND THE LOST CENTURY OF AMERICAN IMMIGRATION LAW

TOO OFTEN, legal discussions of immigration regulation in the United States rest upon a myth, the assertion that the borders of the United States were legally open until the enactment of federal immigration legislation in the 1870s and 1880s. The myth is a pleasant one, and it may seem ungracious to contradict it. It reinforces the identification of the United States as a nation of immigrants and provides a historical basis for criticizing later policies of immigration restriction. It is embodied in Emma Lazarus's poetic fiction that the Statue of Liberty once welcomed the "tired and poor" and the "wretched refuse" of teeming shores,[1] an ideal that some writers have seen as betrayed by the *subsequent* federal immigration policies.

Moreover, the myth has a substantial foundation in fact: U.S. legal policy warmly welcomed certain kinds of immigration, and restrictive laws were often poorly enforced.[2] Neither Congress nor the states attempted to impose *quantitative* limits on immigration.

Nonetheless, the borders were not legally open. Regulation of transborder movement of persons existed, primarily at the state level but also supplemented by federal legislation. Some of this legislation is immediately recognizable as immigration law; other legislation is less easily recognized because it applied to the citizens of other states as well as to foreign immigrants.

Historians of immigration have not been wholly unaware of the existence of these laws, but in recent decades they have focused primary attention on the experience of the immigrants who arrived. Immigration lawyers and judges, however, have been accustomed to accounts that suppress the pre-1875 regulation.[3] This misimpression is not harmless, because inattention to the early history of immigration has distorted debates on the solution of current problems.[a] The purpose of this chapter is to recover the

[a] For example, the long history of state regulation of migration on local police power grounds undercuts the argument for applying the political question doctrine and related forms of extraordinary deference to all federal immigration rules. See Chapter Seven. This history

legal history obscured by the open-borders myth, so that the constitutional issues of that period can be understood in a more accurate context.

This chapter examines the five major categories of policy implemented by state immigration legislation: regulation of the movement of criminals; public health regulation; regulation of the movement of the poor; regulation of slavery; and other policies of racial subordination. Aside from slavery, as I will show, all of these policies continued into the second, federal century of immigration law. The illustrations here are drawn largely from the states of the Atlantic Coast, from Maine to Texas, which include the states under greatest pressure from European immigration. A comprehensive picture of immigration regulation in all the states awaits further research by others. The chapter also gives brief notice to two policies that played a minimal role before 1875 but were more prominent in the later federal law: ideological restriction and alien registration.

Questions of categorization arise when we look in the past for immigration laws. For example, both state and federal governments enacted prohibitions on the importation of African slaves; there are plausible reasons for and against characterizing such laws as regulating immigration.[4] Other statutes may not be immediately recognizable as immigration laws because their sanctions were aimed not at the immigrants, but rather at the persons responsible for transporting them. Moreover, when states are the regulating units, migration controls may apply equally to international and interstate migration, or to United States citizens as well as aliens. Yet even if such controls do not reflect policies specifically directed against immigrants, they do not produce a regime of open borders.

Although these distinctions may explain why an older immigration law may not have been categorized as such by indexers or codifiers, and may be hard to find or even to recognize once found, they should not deflect attention from the substance of the regulation. If we are interested in probing the myth of legally open borders, then we should be looking for valid laws prohibiting the movement or transportation of an alien across a portion of the United States border.[5] For purposes of this inquiry, a statute regulates immigration if it seeks to prevent or discourage the movement of aliens across an international border, even if the statute also regulates the movement of citizens, or movement across interstate borders, and even if the alien's movement is involuntary.[6]

---

refutes the claim that various constitutional provisions were never intended to apply to illegal aliens because the borders were open until 1875. See Chapter Nine. With further research by others, aspects of this history might also illuminate the perennial problem of the allocation of power over immigration between Congress and the president.

CRIME

Keeping Out Convicts

Outrage over foreign criminals is a recurrent theme of immigration policy. Antebellum states' opposition to the immigration of persons convicted of crime continued a long-standing dispute of the colonial period. The sentencing of felons to transportation to America and their shipment to the colonies as indentured servants had sparked repeated protests, including Benjamin Franklin's famous proposal to ship rattlesnakes to England in return.[7] Several colonies attempted to pass restrictive legislation, but after the enactment of the Transportation Act of 1718 such legislation was frequently vetoed by the British government.[8] Independence released the states from that control but also widened the field by tempting other European nations to dump their convicts in the United States.

The outbreak of the Revolutionary War immediately obstructed the British policy of penal transportation to America. When peace came in 1783, the British made some attempts to send convicts to the United States secretly as ordinary indentured servants. One shipload was successfully landed in Baltimore in December 1783, but a second ship, in 1784, was refused permission to enter United States ports and ended up in British Honduras.[9] The British then abandoned their efforts and established the penal colony at Botany Bay in Australia.[10]

Meanwhile, the states began enacting legislation to make certain that penal transportation to the United States would not be resumed. Georgia enacted a statute in 1787, directing that felons transported or banished from another state or a foreign country be arrested and removed beyond the limits of the state, not to return on penalty of death.[11] More important, the Congress of the Confederation adopted a resolution in September 1788, recommending that the states "pass laws for preventing the transportation of convicted malefactors from foreign countries into the United States."[12]

Within a year, several states responded to the Congress's call, although by varying modes of implementation. Connecticut limited itself to the Congress's recommendation by banning the introduction of convicts sentenced to transportation by a foreign country.[13] Massachusetts, Pennsylvania, South Carolina, and Virginia more broadly prohibited the importation of persons who had ever been convicted of crime.[14] Some of these statutes also prohibited migration from sister states, and others limited their bans to convicts from abroad. All the states except Georgia directed their sanctions toward those responsible for bringing the convict into the state. The remedial provisions of Pennsylvania's statute went beyond deterrence, expressly requiring persons responsible for bringing a convict into the state from abroad to remove the convict from the United States at their own expense.[15] Massachusetts integrated its convict statute with its poor laws, and indeed, to draw a clear-cut distinction between the exclusion of criminals and the exclusion of the undesired poor would be anachronistic. Massachusetts criminalized the knowing landing of persons who were convicted in another state or country of infamous crime, who were sentenced to transportation, or who were "of a notoriously dissolute, infamous and abandoned life and character" and required masters of arriving vessels to file passenger manifests including a report of the "character and condition" of each passenger.[16]

In later years, after the federal Constitution had taken effect, further states enacted similar legislation, and states that already had such legislation reenacted or amended their provisions.[17] Maine, Maryland, New Jersey, New York, and Rhode Island borrowed statutes from other states or devised their own.[18] Strangely, New York seems not to have passed a convict exclusion statute until 1833.[19] Although the indentured servant system declined,[20] incidents of European nations' sending foreign convicts to America continued and excited protests. The exclusion of convicts became a relatively uncontroversial element of nativist demands for immigration restriction from the 1830s until the Civil War.

The federal government was slow to take action to exclude foreign convicts.[21] On several occasions before the Civil War, houses of Congress requested information from the executive on the shipment of convicts and paupers by foreign governments.[22] According to the information provided, the United States' diplomatic protests to Switzerland and various German states did meet with some success.[23] In 1866 Congress took a further step by enacting a resolution "protesting against Pardons by Foreign Governments of Persons convicted of infamous Offenses, on Condition of Emigration to the United States," labeling them "unfriendly and inconsistent with the comity of nations" and requesting the president to insist that such incidents not be repeated.[24] Finally, in 1875, a prohibition of convict immigration was included in the first federal statute restricting European immigration.[25] The exclusion of aliens who have previously been convicted of crime has continuously remained an important focus of federal immigration policy.[26]

Methods of Banishment

In 1917 the federal government also began deporting aliens from the United States for committing crimes of moral turpitude after their arrival.[27] The state law precursors of this technique were two institutions of the criminal law: banishment and conditional pardon. To the best of my knowledge, no state statutes singled out aliens for expulsion from the state or the

United States as punishment for serious crime,[28] but aliens were subject to these generally applicable sanctions.

The archaic punishment of banishment survived into the first century of American independence.[29] Indeed, the period began with the massive banishment of British loyalists, a practice whose soundness as a matter of political theory was endorsed by Supreme Court dicta in *Cooper v. Telfair* (1800).[30] A number of states adopted constitutional provisions prohibiting the "exile" or "transportation" of persons from the state, though in some instances the prohibition applied only to citizens of the state.[31]

More significantly, a functional equivalent of banishment could be achieved through the grant of a conditional pardon, a form in which banishment persists to this day.[32] State governors were often expressly or impliedly empowered to pardon offenders on condition that they leave the state or the United States, for a period of years or forever.[33] (This was the very practice that the states protested, when European countries engaged in it, and the criminal predictably emigrated to the United States.) Because so many crimes were capital in the eighteenth and early nineteenth century,[34] many defendants were likely to accept such a pardon and to comply with it.[35]

A state governor's pardon that was conditioned on the defendant's remaining permanently outside the United States threatened execution of the original sentence if the defendant reentered any of the states.[36] Now that the federal government actively deports aliens, twentieth-century courts have had some difficulty sorting out which forms of banishment of an alien defendant from the country usurp the attorney general's deportation power,[37] but in the nineteenth century this conflict had not yet arisen.

POVERTY AND DISABILITY

Perhaps the most fundamental function of immigration law has been to impede the movement of the poor. In neither the eighteenth century nor the nineteenth century did American law concede the right of the needy to geographic mobility. At the time of independence, the states took with them the heritage of the English poor laws, which made the relief of the poor the responsibility of the local community where they were legally "settled."[38] These laws gave localities various powers to prevent the settlement of persons who might later require support and to "remove" them to the place where they were legally settled. Accordingly, some of the most important provisions of state immigration law are sprinkled through the state poor laws.

This limited conception of the rights of the poor was expressly articulated in Article 4 of the Articles of Confederation, which excepted "paupers, vagabonds and fugitives from justice" from the equal enjoyment of the privileges and immunities of citizens.[39] Although the 1787 Constitution omitted this qualification from its Privileges and Immunities Clause, the courts continued to assume that paupers had no right to travel.[40]

The history of state measures against "foreign paupers" from 1776 to 1875 is complicated by the development of the poor law generally in the same period. The rough similarity among state laws at the beginning of the period was disrupted both by varying conditions and by the uneven pace of evolution from the traditional system of local fiscal responsibility for transfer payments (or "outdoor relief") to a more centrally financed system that relied more heavily on institutionalization. Modern scholarship has devoted much attention to David Rothman's thesis that almshouses became more prevalent in the nineteenth century because the poor came to be seen as deviants in need of control rather than neighbors undergoing misfortune.[41]

The high incidence of pauperism among immigrants raised concern and hostility. Many Americans viewed their country as a place where the honest, industrious, and able-bodied poor could improve their economic standing, free from the overcrowding and rigid social structure that blocked advancement in Europe.[42] Failure to become self-supporting was seen as evidence of personal defects.[43] Many feared that European states were sending their lazy and intemperate subjects, as well as the mentally and physically disabled, to burden America.[44]

State and local efforts to avoid these burdens had very limited results.[45] The states were more successful in raising money to defray the expense of supporting impoverished immigrants than in preventing their landing, although at some periods financial disincentives may have led carriers to screen their passengers. I give particular attention here to the states of Massachusetts and New York, before discussing the situation in some other states, and the federal responses. This attention is justified by the circumstances that New York City and Boston were the two leading immigrant-receiving ports and that their efforts to deal with foreign paupers provoked three of the five leading Supreme Court cases on state immigration law.[46]

Massachusetts

Like other states, Massachusetts built on the English poor law system of settlement. The 1794 poor law eliminated the earlier practice under which towns could disclaim financial responsibility for undesired newcomers by giving them a pro forma "warning" not to remain.[47] After 1794, persons newly arriving in a town became settled inhabitants either by meeting certain criteria such as property ownership or by receiving the express permission of the town government. Until 1868, however, virtually all of these statutory criteria included citizenship requirements.[48] A town was initially responsible for relief of any poor person found within it, subject to rights of reimbursement from the town where the individual had his legal settlement, or from the Commonwealth if the individual had no legal settlement in any Massachusetts town.[49] Alternatively, instead of seeking reimbursement, the town could have the individual "removed" to his place of lawful settlement, or "by land or water, to any other State, or to any place beyond sea, where he belongs."[50]

The legislation included measures to prevent the entry of persons who would become chargeable. The 1794 poor laws imposed a penalty on any person who knowingly brought a pauper or indigent person into any town in the Commonwealth and left him there.[51] This provision applied to intrastate and interstate, as well as international, dumping of the poor. As interpreted by the courts, the crime involved an element of bad intent to foist the expense of the pauper onto the public and did not cover innocent transportation of the poor.[52] The 1794 poor laws backed up this prohibition with a requirement that masters of vessels report the "names, nation, age, character and condition" of passengers brought "from any foreign dominion or country without the United States of America," but placed no other special burdens on the vessel.[53]

Beginning in 1820, however, Massachusetts returned to the colonial system of demanding security from masters of vessels when their passengers seemed likely to become paupers.[54] The 1820 statute required a bond to indemnify the town and the Commonwealth for expenses arising within three years with respect to any passenger lacking a settlement in the Commonwealth whom they considered liable to become a public charge.[55] In 1831 this provision was amended to apply only to alien passengers, and the master was given a choice between posting security for those alien passengers whom the town officials thought might become public charges and paying the sum of five dollars per alien passenger landed.[56] Reportedly, masters usually preferred to give bond rather than pay; experience later demonstrated that the state had difficulty collecting on these bonds.[57]

Faced with an increase in the number of indigent immigrants in the 1830s, Massachusetts eliminated the master's choice between bond and payment. The 1837 law bifurcated the obligations instead. First, the master was forbidden to land without bond any alien passenger found upon examination to be within a group of categories of persons presenting a high risk of becoming a public charge, including those with mental or physical disabilities.[58] Second, the master was required to pay two dollars per alien passenger who was *not* in the high-risk categories.[59] This payment was rationalized as commutation of a hypothetical bond, compensating the state for the risk that the passenger would later become a public charge.[60]

A bare majority of the United States Supreme Court invalidated the two-dollar payment as an impermissible head tax on alien passengers in the *Passenger Cases* (1849).[61] By the time this decision was finally announced, the numbers of impoverished immigrants arriving in Massachusetts had been magnified by famine in Ireland. The state responded to the Supreme Court's decision first by repealing the head tax, and then by the subterfuge of requiring bonds for *all* alien passengers, while permitting the master to make a "voluntary" commutation payment in lieu of bond for those passengers who were not in the high-risk categories.[62]

Initially the commutation payment was a flat two dollars, but in 1852 the state authorized officials to demand bond or a higher commutation payment to cover passengers whom they judged to present an intermediate risk of future indigency.[63] This system remained in force until 1872, when the state abolished all bonding and commutation for passengers outside the high-risk category.[64] The bonding of high-risk passengers continued, however, as did a newer requirement of bonding by corporations importing labor into the state.[65]

In 1851 the state exempted from the bonding requirements those vessels on purely interstate routes but subjected them and land carriers to liability for the support or removal of foreign passengers who became a public charge within one year of arrival.[66] In succeeding years, this provision was successfully invoked for the removal of paupers to other states and to Canada at the expense of railroad companies.[67] Eventually, however, it was undermined by the Supreme Judicial Court's refusal to construe it as applying to common carriers who transported passengers without reason to know that they were likely to become public charges.[68] The same liability was extended to "any corporation or party" bringing strangers into the state.[69]

Because aliens were not entitled to "settlement" under the poor laws, unnaturalized immigrants remained permanently subject to deportation under the provisions of the poor laws empowering local officials to seek an order causing paupers without settlement to be sent back where they "belonged" at public expense.[70] In practice, however, local officials had little incentive to take trouble to remove paupers for whom they would otherwise be paid—perhaps overpaid—by the Commonwealth.[71] In the 1850s, the nativist reaction to heavy Irish immigration led the Massachusetts legislature to address this problem.[72] It created state workhouses and required the towns to send paupers without a settlement in the Commonwealth to those workhouses in lieu of state payments for their support in the town. State officials were authorized to initiate proceedings for the removal of paupers "to the place or country from which they came."[73] These interstate and international removal activities were documented in annual reports to the state legislature and applauded in the nativist press.[74]

New York

The post-Revolutionary poor laws of New York State also began as variations on the classical eighteenth-century form.[75] As revised in 1788, the statute decreed that strangers who gave notice of their arrival in a city or town would acquire a legal settlement if they remained twelve months without being ordered removed. If during that period a justice of the peace found the strangers likely to become a public charge, he could order them removed.[76] Until 1813, paupers who returned after removal were subject to severe corporal punishment as well as retransportation.[77]

Removal at first was accomplished by the cumbersome process of "passing on": officials of each town along the path of migration conducted the stranger to the town from which she had come until they reached a town where the stranger was legally settled or passed the stranger on across the border of the state.[78] For paupers who had entered the state through New York City, later provisions authorized removal to that city, by passing on or otherwise.[79] A further amendment in 1817 provided for removal directly to places of legal settlement in other states or in Canada.[80]

New York fundamentally revised its poor laws in the 1820s, partly from dissatisfaction with the costs and complications of removal and partly from a desire to deter pauperism by replacing outdoor relief with a system of county workhouses.[81] The revision abolished the practice of removing indigents from one county to another. Instead, persons were to be supported in the county where they fell into need, with the expense to be shared between the town and the county.[82] The revision also eliminated removal out of the state, a procedure that, the reformers had noted, had often been impeded by the danger that the officials performing the removal would be punished by the receiving state.[83] At the same time, New York preserved its own penalties on any person who brought a pauper into the state and left him there, and it further obliged the offender "to convey such pauper out of the state, or support him at his own expense."[84]

Meanwhile, special provisions addressed paupers arriving by sea. The port of New York became, after all, the principal port of immigration to the United States. The 1788 poor law required masters of vessels arriving at New York City to report within twenty-four hours the names and occupations of all the passengers whom they had landed. If a reported passenger could not "give a good account of himself or herself" or appeared likely to be a charge to the city, the vessel was required either to return the passenger to the place of embarkation within a month or to enter into a bond with sufficient surety that the passenger would not become a charge.[85] This system was modified in 1797 by requiring the vessel to give bond *before* landing emigrants from foreign countries.[86] Thereafter, no provision required the removal of alien paupers coming from Europe who had been permitted to land.[87] Instead, the legislative efforts were directed primarily toward imposing financial responsibility on vessels for their passengers.

The 1797 statute had required the bonding of only those passengers deemed likely to become chargeable to the city. The officials' discretion was rechanneled in 1799 by authorizing them to demand a bond for any alien passenger in such amount (up to $300) as they considered proper to indemnify the city against the risk that the passenger would become chargeable within two years.[88] For most passengers, the officials developed the practice of permitting the master to commute the bond for a few dollars.[89] The 1799 statute also attempted to prevent evasion by imposing penalties on vessels that put ashore within fifty miles of the city alien passengers who intended to proceed to the city.[90] When this regulation proved ineffectual, the reporting and bonding requirements were revised to include the passengers who had been landed outside New York City with the intention of proceeding to the city.[91]

If the bonding requirements were intended to deter the transportation of indigents, the lawmakers failed to anticipate the opportunities for profitable evasion created by the massive increase in immigration in the 1830s. Some bondsmen sought profit by taking on enormous, and therefore uncollectible, liabilities at a trivial per-passenger price. Worse, some bondsmen actually accepted responsibility for the support of bonded immigrants who fell into need, and the city found itself confronting a vicious system of private poorhouses. The administration of the bonding and commutation system was itself plagued by embezzlement.[92]

In 1847 the state reformed the bonding system by creating a board of Commissioners of Emigration, including as ex officio members the presidents of the German and Irish emigrant aid societies.[93] They were made responsible for overseeing a more effective and discriminating system of passenger reporting and bonding, as well as the protection of immigrants from fraud and abuse. Bonds were required for certain categories of alien passengers deemed likely to become a public charge, including those with mental or physical disabilities, the elderly, and even single mothers.[94] Otherwise, one dollar was charged per alien passenger in lieu of bond.[95] When the Supreme Court invalidated head taxes in the *Passenger Cases* (1849),[96] the New York legislature reformulated this charge as a voluntary option to the giving of an actual rather than a hypothetical bond.[97] (Ultimately, the Supreme Court was unimpressed with this designation and invalidated the commutation charge for solvent passengers in *Henderson v. New York* (1876),[98] one of the cases that brought to an end the era of state immigration law.)

To prevent the types of abuse that had occurred earlier, the 1847 statute addressed the capitalization of the bonding companies and made the Commissioners of Emigration responsible for the maintenance and support of passengers who would otherwise become a public charge. The commissioners were also empowered to apply their funds "to aid in removing any of said persons from any part of this state to another part of this, or any other state, or from this state, or in assisting them to procure employment, and thus prevent them from becoming a public charge."[99]

Unlike the nativist officials of 1850s Massachusetts, New York's Commissioners of Emigration were not hostile to immigration, and they expressed their preference for helping immigrants find work.[100] The inclusion of representatives of immigrant communities on the board and its combination of regulatory and social service functions reflected a more hospitable intention. Nonetheless, the annual reports of the commissioners indicate that they also used their powers to facilitate the voluntary return of alien passengers to Europe,[101] and sometimes used their discretion in setting commutation fees to induce the vessel owner to return passengers at his own expense rather than bond or commute for them.[102]

In their 1857 report, the commissioners noted with satisfaction the "improved character and condition of the emigration," which they attributed to a number of causes, including "the more stringent legislation, and the action under it, of the officers of the Commission, aided by the co-operation of the consuls and diplomatic officers of the United States abroad, thus excluding, in a great degree, the most worthless class, sent by local or State authorities abroad, to be thrown upon our shores for support, or to live by worse means."[103]

Other States and Federal Responses

Other states dealt with the legacy of the English poor laws in different ways. The settlement-and-removal system remained strong in New England. Maine, like its parent Massachusetts, continued to provide for removals out of state.[104] Bonding was imposed for out-of-state passengers in 1820, although officials were given the option of accepting commutation payments in 1838.[105] Rhode Island towns could not physically remove an out-of-state person themselves but could order him to depart; between 1803 and 1838, he was subject to whipping if he failed to depart or if he returned.[106] Rhode Island later made railroads financially responsible for the passengers they brought into the state and adopted a bonding and commutation system for passengers brought by vessel.[107]

Pennsylvania's poor laws, prior to 1828, provided for out-of-state removals or carrier liability only after the passengers had been landed.[108] If the "importer" of "infant, lunatic, maimed, aged, impotent or vagrant" persons were identified, he could be required to give security "to carry and transport such [persons] to the place or places whence such [persons] were imported or brought from, or otherwise to idemnify" the town for any charge.[109] An overhaul of the poor relief system in 1828 emulated contemporary changes in other states by emphasizing almshouses and by adopting a bonding and commutation system for arriving passengers.[110] In practice, one historian notes, the officials preferred head money to bonding, but he also reports several cases "in the 1850's where persons were allowed to bring infirm relatives from Ireland only if sufficient bond was given."[111] Maryland, in contrast, contented itself with a $1.50 head tax, disguised after 1850 as a commutation payment.[112]

Farther south, the English tradition of settlement and removal seems to have weakened in practice, if not on the books. A recent study concludes that the evidence "strongly suggests that the settlement provisions went largely unenforced."[113] One cause of the relaxed attitude may have been that "[t]he great waves of pre–Civil War immigration largely bypassed the region."[114] Nonetheless, some states were "watchful to avoid being burdened with imported paupers."[115] In South Carolina, a colonial poor law of 1738 remained in force throughout our period, requiring masters of vessels to give security for any passengers found to be "impotent, lame or otherwise infirm, or likely to be a charge to the parish."[116] In addition, Charleston required bonding or commutation for all out-of-state passengers, at regressive rates.[117]

New Orleans, in contrast to other Southern cities, became an important immigrant port, primarily for passengers intending to proceed up the Mississippi in the years before railroads linked the Eastern ports with the Midwest.[118] Louisiana had a statutory vehicle for regulating these arrivals in its vagrancy laws, which required an examination of all alien passengers and empowered city officials to require the vessel to give security that the passenger would not "become a vagrant . . . or be found guilty of any crime, misdemeanor or breach of the peace" within two years.[119] Louisiana also imposed a head tax for revenue purposes in 1842, which was disguised as a commutation payment after the *Passenger Cases*, and which was in fact enforced.[120]

The concern that paupers were being sent to the United States as a matter of official government policy by European countries led the states to call for federal action. In the 1830s and 1840s, congressional resolutions sought information from the executive regarding foreign government assistance for the emigration of paupers.[121] In 1855 efforts to enact a bill to prevent the immigration of criminals and paupers triggered states' rights objections in the Senate and rejection by the House of Representatives.[122] Meanwhile, the executive responded to some incidents with diplomatic protests, which may have induced caution on the part of foreign governments.[123] These protests continued after the Civil War,[124] and finally in 1882 a ban on the landing of any "lunatic, idiot, or any person unable to take care of himself or herself without becoming a public charge" was included in the second federal statute regulating European immigration.[125] The public charge provision has played an important role in federal immigration law ever since.

CONTAGIOUS DISEASE

Another traditional function of the regulation of migration has been the protection of public health by limiting the exposure of the local population to contagious diseases. Exclusion on grounds of contagious disease was not added to the federal immigration laws until 1891, somewhat later than the exclusion of Chinese laborers, convicts, and persons likely to become a public charge. This delay does not indicate that public health regulation of migration was a novelty, but rather reflects the strength of the tradition of federal deference to state regulation of migration in that area, exercised for most of the nineteenth century through the mechanism of quarantine.

The term "quarantine" derives from a forty-day period of isolation and cleansing imposed on arriving travelers and their goods to make sure that they were not infected; the practice originated in the fourteenth century as a measure against the plague. Quarantine measures were later applied to other acute diseases with high mortality rates, especially smallpox, yellow fever, typhus, and cholera.[126] Passengers and crew could be isolated on board the vessel or removed to a quarantine station, hospital, or lazaretto. Asymptomatic passengers were isolated for observation; those already infected would either die or recover, and in either case they would cease to spread the infection. (In the meantime, however, they might infect quarantine personnel or other passengers detained in quarantine.) During quarantine, the vessel itself, its cargo, and the personal possessions of the passengers might also be subjected to treatment intended as disinfection.

Quarantine practices should be distinguished in two respects from the federal immigration exclusions that began in 1891. First, quarantine usually targeted acute diseases, but federal immigration exclusions extended to chronic diseases, whose victims were not likely to recover or die after a limited period of isolation. The federal medical exclusions were adopted in addition to, not instead of, a quarantine system.[127] Indeed, the emphasis on *nonfatal* chronic diseases at the turn of the century reflected a desire to be more selective in the choice of immigrants, not merely the need to protect the resident population from infection.[128] Second, quarantine laws applied to a state's own citizens as well as to aliens and citizens of other states. This feature is underscored by the common provision that unauthorized persons going aboard a vessel in quarantine or entering the quarantine grounds rendered themselves subject to detention in quarantine.[129]

Some state laws went beyond quarantine measures by providing for the punishment or expulsion of travelers from proscribed places. In some instances, officials were authorized to suspend commerce with infected locales by proclamation.[130] In Massachusetts, town officials could warn any person coming from an out-of-state place where "small-pox or other malignant distemper" was prevailing to leave the state within two hours or "be removed into the State whence he or they may have come," unless disabled by sickness.[131] In New York,[b] town officials had the authority to examine a person who had come from an infected place and to send him out of the state if they had good cause to suspect that he was infected, unless he was an inhabitant of New York.[132]

As for actual quarantine, state legislation in the period before 1875 exhibited numerous variations. There were quarantines at seaports and, less commonly, quarantines at interstate borders.[133] Some legislation delegated broad discretion to local authorities,[134] and other legislation prescribed a framework of more and less stringent quarantine measures depending on such factors as the ports from which the vessel arrived, the occurrence of illness among the passengers and crew, and the date of arrival.[135] Quarantine was often more exacting in the hot months, because it had been observed that yellow fever outbreaks followed seasonal patterns.[136]

The particular ports of embarkation were taken into account at several levels of regulation. The international maritime quarantine regime included the issuance of "bills of health" to vessels by officials at the ports from which they embarked, certifying the state of public health at the time of departure.[137] Some legislation specified geographic zones for which more stringent quarantine was required regardless of the bill of health.[138] Executive officials were often authorized to proclaim a foreign or domestic port infected on an emergency basis.[139]

Those who found it impossible or inconvenient to comply with quarantine laws sometimes resorted to evasion, corruption, or violation.[140] Travelers to Philadelphia and New York, for example, sometimes tried to evade quarantine by landing in New Jersey, and legislation was occasionally passed to close this loophole.[141] Local officials might also be bribed; it has been observed that, "[f]ortunately for New York City, forcing vessels to unload their cargoes and undergo the contemporary cleansing proce-

---

[b] Passing mention should also be made of New York's head tax for the support of the marine hospital; beginning in 1797, the state levied a tax on the crews and passengers (regardless of nationality) of vessels entering the port of New York, to defray the expense of caring for patients in the lazaretto. See Act of Mar. 30, 1797, ch. 67, § 5, 1797 N.Y. Laws 93. In later years, excess revenues from this tax were diverted to other uses. This was the head tax invalidated by the Supreme Court on commerce clause grounds in *Smith v. Turner*, one of the *Passenger Cases*, 48 U.S. (7 How.) 283 (1849).

dures presented more opportunities for enriching the officials than simply permitting them to land. In consequence, the enforcement of the quarantine laws, for its day, was relatively effective."[142] Masters of vessels who failed to submit to quarantine and passengers who eloped from quarantine were usually subject to criminal prosecution.[143]

Both facially and as applied, quarantine regulation went through cycles of tightening and relaxation, even to the point of abandonment. As one historian noted, "The history of all quarantine laws shows that their enforcement varied in direct ratio to the recency or imminent threat of a major epidemic disease."[144] Moreover, throughout the nineteenth century, the practice of quarantine was bound up with a scientific controversy over the causes of the relevant diseases.[145] Quarantine measures reflected a "contagionist" theory of the disease, which held that the disease was spread geographically by infected persons or things. "Anticontagionists" maintained that the disease had local environmental origins (possibly in "miasmas") and was not spread by travelers; quarantines were therefore useless, expensive, and cruel distractions from more appropriate local sanitary measures. The predominant influence of anticontagionists in Boston, for example, prevented quarantine there against the cholera epidemic of 1866.[146] Historians have noted an ideological aspect to the popularity of anticontagionism in the mid-nineteenth century, when the substantial interference of quarantines with free trade chafed against laissez-faire economics.[147] Toward the end of the century, advances in bacteriology both vindicated the contagionist theory and reinforced some of the local sanitary practices of the anticontagionists. Improved diagnostic techniques also reduced the inefficiencies of quarantine.[148]

In the mid-nineteenth century, contagionists and anticontagionists carried on their debate in national and international conferences aimed at uniformizing (or relaxing) quarantine practices.[149] Within the United States, proposals for a federal quarantine law had a heavy burden of tradition to overcome. State authority over quarantine legislation had long enjoyed the unequivocal endorsement of the federal government. The issue first arose in 1796, when a representative from Maryland proposed that the president be authorized to regulate the quarantine of foreign vessels arriving in United States ports.[150] The bill provoked a debate in the House on the locus of authority over quarantine, with the proponents (mostly Federalists) contending that quarantine laws were regulations of commerce and therefore beyond state authority.[151] The bill's opponents defended state authority on various grounds, including the right of self-defense, varying local conditions, characterization of quarantine as an internal police regulation, and denial that pestilential diseases were objects of commerce.[152] The proposal failed by a large majority,[153] and Congress instead authorized the president to direct federal customs officials to aid in the execution of state quarantine and health laws.[154] Congress reiterated these instructions in an act of 1799, designed to harmonize quarantine and customs enforcement.[155]

These statutes contributed to John Marshall's recognition in *Gibbons v. Ogden* (1824) that "quarantine laws [and] health laws of every description" formed part of the "immense mass of legislation, which embraces everything within the territory of a State, not surrendered to the general government."[156] At the same time, Marshall observed that "Congress may control the state laws, so far as it may be necesssary to control them, for the regulation of commerce."[157] Even after the Civil War, in anticipation of the cholera epidemic of 1866, Congress rejected a proposal to substitute uniform federal regulation of quarantine for the traditional system of cooperation with state laws.[158]

After 1875, the states continued to regulate quarantine with federal cooperation, and the Supreme Court continued to reaffirm state authority in the field.[159] Meanwhile, scientific support for the contagion theory helped build a consensus in favor of national quarantine enforcement. Starting in 1878, federal health officials became more actively involved in quarantine.[160] Then, in 1893, federal legislation authorized the imposition of nationwide minima for international quarantine and invited the states to make voluntary transfers of their quarantine establishments to the federal government.[161] Concurrent regulation lasted until 1921, when New York became the last state to surrender its international quarantine functions.[162]

RACE AND SLAVERY

A far more controversial category of state immigration legislation concerned the movement of free blacks.[163] In the antebellum period, there was no national consensus on the propriety of such legislation; slave states insisted that it was essential to the preservation of their institutions, some free states insisted that it was unconstitutional, and other free states adopted such legislation themselves.[164] Historians have reasonably suggested that a primary cause of the federal government's failure to adopt qualitative restrictions on immigration before the Civil War was the slave states' jealous insistence on maintaining power over the movement of free blacks as a states' right.[165]

The legislation restricting free blacks was voluminous, and it has been intensively studied.[166] This chapter can therefore limit itself to some illustrative discussion and to placing these restrictions in the context of state regulation of immigration. It will also contrast them with the regulation of the international slave trade, the one form of immigration regulation in which the federal government was actively involved before the Civil War.

Prohibiting the Immigration of Free Blacks

The objections raised to the migration of free blacks were various. Many white inhabitants of the "free" states shared in racial prejudice against blacks and opposed what we would now call a multiracial society.[167] Many also professed fear that Southern slave owners would emancipate slaves who were no longer able to work and send them to burden the Northern states.[168] As a result, several free states erected barriers to the entry of blacks. Blacks seeking to reside in some Northern states were obliged to give surety not to become a public charge and for good behavior.[169] In other instances, blacks were forbidden to move into the state altogether, sometimes pursuant to the command of the state constitution.[170] There is reason to doubt how often these laws were actually enforced, but attempts were made, and as late as 1864 the Illinois Supreme Court upheld a conviction, fine, and forcible indenture for the crime of entry by a mulatto.[171]

In slave states, the mere visibility of black people living in freedom was regarded as a grave threat to the operation of the system of slavery.[172] Moreover, slaveholders feared that free blacks would foment or facilitate escape or conspire to bring about slave revolts.[173] Revolutionaries from the West Indies and, later, black citizens of states where abolitionism flourished were particularly feared.[174] As the nineteenth century progressed, the ideological struggle between abolitionists and the defenders of slavery as a virtuous institution founded on the alleged biological inferiority of blacks accentuated the anomalous position of free blacks in slave states. Attitudes toward free blacks hardened, and Southern legislation became even more hostile.[175] True, public opinion was divided throughout the antebellum period, and many whites recognized the important economic and social roles that free blacks played.[176] But even where this recognition suspended the enforcement of restrictive laws, their threat remained.[177]

Slave state legislation usually barred the entry of free blacks who were not already residents of the state.[178] Penalties were often imposed on persons bringing in free blacks.[179] Over time, some states extended these prohibitions to their own free black residents who sought to return after traveling outside the state, either to a disapproved location or to any destination at all.[180] Slave states often required emancipated slaves to leave the state forever, on pain of reenslavement.[181] Shortly before the Civil War, several slave states considered forcing their free black populations to choose between enslavement and expulsion,[182] and Arkansas actually passed such legislation.[183]

To the extent that these laws were directed at immigration from abroad, they had some congressional support. Several of the state prohibitions on the entry of free blacks had been enacted in the wake of the successful slave revolt in Saint Domingue, which ultimately produced the nation of Haiti.[184]

These states did not welcome French slave owners bringing with them slaves who might have been infected with the dangerous idea of a universal right to liberty, or free people of color fleeing the factional violence in Saint Domingue. Nor did they welcome free blacks expelled from other French colonies that feared a replication of the revolt.[185] In 1803 the Southern states succeeded in obtaining the enactment of a federal statute prohibiting the importation of foreign blacks into states whose laws forbade their entry.[186] Thus, as in the case of quarantine, the states secured federal cooperation in the enforcement of their immigration laws. John C. Calhoun later invoked this "precedent" as recognizing

> the very important right, that the States have the authority to exclude the introduction of such persons as may be dangerous to their institutions—a principle of great extent and importance, and applicable to other States as well as slaveholding, and to other persons as well as blacks, and which may hereafter occupy a prominent place in the history of our legislation.[187]

Laws prohibiting the free black citizens of one state to enter another state arguably raised serious questions under the Privileges and Immunities Clause of the federal Constitution.[188] On the other hand, nineteenth-century courts did not recognize an unqualified right of interstate travel for all categories of citizens.[189] The exclusion of free blacks excited national controversy when Missouri attempted to enter the Union under a constitution that expressly required it.[190] An obfuscating compromise was reached under which Missouri agreed not to apply this provision inconsistently with the Privileges and Immunities Clause;[191] but even if strictly observed,[192] this concession would have left considerable scope for application, given that most Southern states did not regard their own free black residents as citizens.[193] Moreover, it was widely argued that free blacks were not "citizens" of the free states in the constitutional sense, a position ultimately adopted by the majority in the Dred Scott decision.[194]

Slave states also subjected their free black residents to more stringent regulations and criminal laws than whites.[195] In most states, free blacks were required to register to demonstrate their free status and their entitlement to reside and were subject to frequent demands to produce proof of their registered status.[196] Free blacks could be banished from the state or from the country for certain offenses, in addition to or instead of the punishment meted out to whites.[197] For a brief period, Virginia combined enslavement and banishment as punishment, by providing for free blacks to be sold into slavery and transported beyond the borders of the United States,[198] although I am not sure how this practice could have been legally reconciled with the federal prohibition on the export of slaves.[199]

Because all of this legislation was intimately tied to the racial character of American slavery, the reader may be tempted to dismiss it as part of an obsolete law of bondage rather than view it as significantly related to immigration law. But the parallels between this legislation and late-nineteenth-century immigration law are striking. The first major immigration policy the federal government added was the exclusion of Chinese laborers in 1882; this category too was racially defined.[200] The federal legislation was preceded by a series of state legislative efforts on the West Coast to restrict and exclude the Chinese.[201] These efforts began in the 1850s, and the local anti-Chinese policy was often explicitly linked with contemporaneous anti-black policies.[202] The movement against the Chinese was partly a campaign for a white racial identity for the United States and partly a struggle between differing regimes of labor. The expressions of fear that free American labor could not compete with "coolie" labor mirrored the traditional argument of the Free Soilers that coexistence with slavery—and sometimes even with free blacks—would degrade free white labor.[203] In later years, the federal Chinese exclusion laws also adopted some of the techniques by which the mobility of free blacks had been restricted: first a prohibition on new immigration, then a bar to the return of lawful residents who traveled abroad, and finally a requirement that those already resident register and present proof of their legal presence, with the expulsion of persons not registered.[204]

The Seamen's Acts

Later themes of immigration law emerge clearly in another category of legislation against free blacks that requires fuller discussion: the regulation of free black seamen arriving in Southern ports. This legislation sparked a constitutional dispute that was carefully smothered, and it produced a major diplomatic embarrassment for the United States in the antebellum era. This is a story that has been told often, but one that needs to be placed in relation to immigration law.[205]

Among the first wave of Southern laws against the entry of free blacks, some contained express provisos to accommodate vessels whose crews included black sailors, so long as the sailors were to depart with their ships.[206] But Southern fears of insurrection intensified after the Missouri Compromise debate polarized national opinion on slavery, and particularly after the discovery of the Denmark Vesey conspiracy in 1822 in Charleston.[207] South Carolina was no longer willing to permit black sailors to wander at liberty even temporarily. It enacted a requirement that any black seamen arriving on a vessel be held in jail at its master's expense until the vessel left.[208] Several other states followed South Carolina's lead or adopted "quarantine" regulations requiring black crew members to remain on the ship and forbidding local blacks to communicate with them.[209]

The enforcement of such laws was calculated to infuriate both Northern states and foreign nations whose ships included black crew members. Several incidents arose in South Carolina in 1823. In one, the captain of an

American ship unsuccessfully sought relief from the state courts, and in another, a British captain complained to his government, which in turn protested to Secretary of State John Quincy Adams. Adams's intervention with South Carolina leaders seems to have produced a lull in enforcement, but a vigilante association in Charleston exerted contrary pressure.[210]

The conflict revived with the imprisonment of Henry Elkison, a Jamaican sailor on a British ship, pending his ship's departure from Charleston harbor. The case was brought before Supreme Court Justice William Johnson on circuit; the British consul in Charleston participated in the litigation on Elkison's behalf, and the vigilante association conducted the defense. Johnson held in *Elkison v. Deliesseline* (1823) that the statute infringed the exclusive federal power over foreign commerce and also the treaty of commerce and navigation between the United States and Britain.[211] He rejected the state's claim of "necessity," which had been formulated with a vehemence that foreshadowed the nullification crisis.[212] Nonetheless, Johnson concluded that he lacked jurisdiction to issue a writ to the sheriff for Elkison's release.[213] Johnson's opinion was violently denounced in South Carolina, and neither Johnson nor the federal government was able to prevent enforcement of the statute; in the meantime, Elkison apparently was released to depart with his ship.[214] Johnson continued the controversy by responding to his critics in both signed and pseudonymous essays.[215] This dispute formed an essential part of the background of *Gibbons v. Ogden* (1824), in which the Supreme Court first expounded the exclusivity and supremacy of congressional power over navigation as a form of interstate commerce.[216]

The Elkison case was only the first of the confrontations between Britain and the Southern states over the issue of black seamen.[217] Adams sought to calm the British by assuring them that he would try to prevent enforcement of the statute, but that in a federal system he would need time to persuade South Carolina officials.[218] South Carolina, however, definitively rebuffed him. Incidents continued in that and other states, and so, intermittently, did British protests. The treaty issue was particularly difficult because of an ambiguous clause in the commercial treaty making reciprocal liberty of commerce "subject always to the laws and statutes of the two countries, respectively."[219] The U.S. diplomatic stance changed after Andrew Jackson's attorney general took a more expansive view of states' rights and affirmed the states' authority to enact such laws;[220] he also relied in part on the 1803 federal statute forbidding the bringing in of foreign blacks excluded by state laws.[221] The Northern states also continued to protest, but Congress would not act.[222] In 1844 Massachusetts sent agents to South Carolina and Louisiana to institute judicial proceedings to test the constitutionality of the laws, but they were forced to flee under threat of mob violence.[223] Later in that decade, Secretary of State Buchanan instructed the

U.S. consul in Jamaica to cooperate in securing compliance with these state laws, and he informed the British that if they insisted that enforcement of the state laws violated the commercial treaty between the two nations, it would become necessary to abrogate the treaty.[224]

Ultimately the British learned to bypass Washington and to undertake diplomacy directly with the Southern states.[225] The consuls achieved some success in Louisiana and Georgia,[226] but they reawakened controversy in South Carolina, which was always quick to resent outside interference.[227] The consul in Charleston was replaced in 1853, and finally in 1856 his successor gained the concession of an amendment permitting black sailors to remain on their ships so long as bond was posted that they would not come ashore.[228]

The controversy concerning the exclusion of free black sailors is particularly important as an instance in which state immigration law created a persistent diplomatic embarrassment for the United States that the federal government proved powerless to solve. In the West, a similar embarrassment was threatened when California attempted to exclude Chinese immigrants. Indeed, since the anti-Chinese movement stigmatized the entire population of a single foreign power, it created greater potential conflict with China than the seamen's laws did with England or France. (During the era of the seamen's laws, the United States was less concerned about its image in Africa and refused diplomatic recognition to Haiti.) As the anti-Chinese movement escalated, however, the balance of power between the states and the Union was shifting. Open efforts to prevent Chinese immigration were precluded by the most-favored-nation clause of the 1868 Burlingame Treaty and reinforced by an express provision of the 1870 Civil Rights Act.[229] The Supreme Court showed itself both motivated and able to intervene against more covert exclusion efforts.[230] The end result was part of the post–Civil War transfer of the power to regulate immigration from the states to the federal government.

The Migration of Slaves

Conceived broadly as the migration of individuals into a state, immigration encompasses both voluntary and involuntary movement. Regulation of the international and interstate slave trades warrants attention in this context. So does the regulation of fugitive laves.

One of the U.S. Constitution's infamous compromises with slavery was the Migration or Importation Clause, which until 1808 barred Congress from prohibiting the importation of slaves into any of the original states that were willing to receive them.[231] By the time that period had expired, nearly every state where slavery had not been abolished enacted its own prohibition against the importation of slaves from abroad.[232] Congress quickly acted to add a federal prohibition of the international slave trade, but it left the interstate trade largely unregulated.[233] In later years, Congress enacted statutes tightening the federal prohibition.[234]

Because Congress was initially legally disabled from regulating the importation of slaves from abroad and was at all times politically disabled from regulating the interstate slave trade, much was left to the states.[235] State regulation of the movement of slaves took a variety of forms. Slave states had acted to prohibit the international slave trade in the period before Congress was empowered to do so, although their commitment to enforcing these laws was weak, and a movement to repeal the prohibition developed as the ideological defense of slavery hardened.[236] In addition, some slave states sought at various times to exclude the interstate slave trade[237] or to keep out individual slaves whose characteristics were considered objectionable.[238] Because these states' objection was usually not to slavery per se, these regulations may be considered comparable to traditional immigration laws.

Conversely, some free states had no fundamental objection to the entry of slaves as persons but rather condemned the institution of slavery; accordingly, instead of forbidding the entry of slaves into the state, they provided that slaves entering the state would be free.[239] When the slaves fled into the state against the will of a slave owner who then sought their return, the free state's policy could be overridden by the Fugitive Slave Clause of the Constitution and the federal legislation thereunder, although some states struggled to circumvent these limitations.[240]

Legislation in other free states more closely resembled traditional immigration regulation, for these states objected to the entry of blacks, whether slave or free. Illinois, as we have seen, banned all black immigration and sought to expel fugitive slaves rather than to protect them.[241]

IDEOLOGICAL RESTRICTION AND ALIEN REGISTRATION

Although this chapter does not attempt comprehensive coverage, some notice should be given to two further immigration policies that the federal government adopted for a short time: ideological restriction and alien registration. As even immigration lawyers vaguely remember, the federal government briefly entered the alien regulation business in 1798. The package of legislation known to history as the Alien and Sedition Acts included three statutes directed specifically at aliens, the Naturalization Act of 1798, the Alien Enemies Act, and the Alien (or Alien Friends) Act.[242]

The last-named was the notorious provision that gave the president unfettered discretion to arrest and deport any alien he regarded as dangerous; it will be discussed more fully in Chapter Four. It was aimed at aliens with radical (that is, pro-French) ideas. Its constitutionality was disputed, and it expired by its own terms in 1800, never to be renewed. The Alien Enemies Act, in contrast, which applied only during war, was uncontroversial at the time and is still on the books.[243]

The Alien Act was not the only instance of ideological restriction in the new nation. The Revolutionary period had witnessed ideological restriction at the state level in the form of prohibitions of the return of loyalists, and Virginia adopted a state precursor of the Alien Act in 1792.[244] Thereafter, ideological restriction expressed itself in the Southern efforts to "quarantine" free blacks and to exclude slaves who had been near the scene of conspiracies or insurrections.

Mandatory federal registration of aliens was attempted, but it was soon abandoned. The Naturalization Act of 1798 is commonly remembered for stretching out the residence period required before naturalization from five to fourteen years, an inhospitable policy that led to its repeal in 1802.[245] More interesting for present purposes, however, was the alien registration system imposed by section 4 of the act. It required all white aliens arriving in the United States to report themselves to a designated officer within forty-eight hours of arrival and to receive a certificate of registry; aliens already residing in the United States were required to register within six months. Not only was the certificate of registry mandatory evidence in a later naturalization proceeding, but aliens failing to register were subject to a fine and could be compelled to give security for their future behavior.[246]

This registration requirement may have had little effect; a few years after its passage, a newspaper described it as having "been disregarded both by aliens themselves and by the magistrates of places in which they resided."[247] In 1803 Congress was told that the threat of deportation under the Alien Act had deterred immigrants from calling themselves to the government's attention even by filing declarations of intent to become citizens.[248] The repeal of the Naturalization Act in 1802 eliminated the legal requirement that aliens register. At the same time, the 1802 Naturalization Act attempted to make registration at the time of arrival a documentary prerequisite to later naturalization (as required evidence of the period of residence).[249] This conditional requirement, however, did not produce compliance either. As James Buchanan reported to the House of Representatives in 1828, the registration provision of the 1802 act met with "almost universal" neglect, and it was accordingly repealed.[250] The comprehensive federal registration of aliens did not return until 1940.[251]

A COMMENT ON EFFECTIVENESS

Thus, state immigration law in the century preceding 1875 included five major categories: regulation of the migration of convicts; regulation of persons likely to become or actually becoming a public charge; prevention of the spread of contagious diseases, including maritime quarantine and suspension of communication by land; regionally varying policies relating to slavery, including the prohibition of the slave trade; and bans on the migration of free blacks, including the seamen's acts. Federal statutes backed up the state quarantine laws and state laws barring the importation of slaves or free black aliens. Federal diplomatic efforts gave some support to state policies against the "dumping" of convicts and paupers.

The legislation employed three principal methods for dealing with undesired immigration: return of the immigrant, punishment of the immigrant, and punishment of third parties responsible for the immigrant's arrival.[252] Some state laws provided for the return of immigrants in each of the five major categories. No laws threatened the punishment of convicts or paupers for immigrating, unless they had previously been removed; direct punishment was more frequently threatened against travelers evading quarantine restrictions and free blacks entering a state unlawfully.

The punishment of responsible third parties was employed in each of the five major categories. The prevalence of this strategy deserves some comment. Carrier sanctions have the advantage of being directed at the more deterrable participant in the forbidden transaction.[253] Carriers are repeat players with more to lose and less to gain from illegal immigration.[254] Moreover, the historically formative experiences of convict and pauper immigration included emigration induced by foreign public officials, with the full knowledge of the carriers. These factors, plus the transoceanic character of most nineteenth-century immigration, probably explain the long tradition of carrier sanctions in United States immigration law.

The resulting patchwork of immigration regulations was not very rigorously enforced. The most dramatic modes of immigration enforcement are the exclusion and return of immigrants and their deportation after entry. It appears that the number of such events was fairly small. One might be tempted to conclude that the state laws existed only on the books and had no practical effect.[c]

Considering only the exclusion and deportation rates, however, underestimates the impact of state immigration law. Quarantine laws, for example, operated by delay and not by permanent exclusion. In times of perceived peril, quarantine was more likely to be strictly enforced. Maritime quarantine might lead to the death of the would-be immigrant who was stopped at the port, rather than deportation to another country, or to admittance of the immigrant after she had survived the disease. But as a barrier to free migration it had serious practical significance.

---

[c] One might wish to go further and conclude that poor enforcement demonstrated that the true policy of the nation was to welcome all immigrants. But that would be reading too much into the failure of implementation. Poor enforcement characterized much state legislation of the nineteenth century. Poor enforcement has also characterized the federal immigration legislation of a later period.

Moreover, the legislation probably had some effect in deterring immigrants.[255] When enforced, for example, the bonding and commutation payment provisions of the passenger acts could increase the cost to the carrier. The size of the commutation payment for passengers identified as presenting a significant risk of future indigence could be quite substantial in relation to the price of the ticket.[256] The incidence of the cost increase is not certain, but to the extent that it was passed on to passengers it would increase the cost of the voyage, making it much harder for impoverished Europeans to emigrate or increasing the likelihood that they would emigrate to other states or other countries.[257] (However, the lack of control at the land borders made possible circuitous immigration to the regulating states.) Some of the handbooks for emigrants published in Europe advised emigrants where they faced exclusion.[258] Discriminating commutation systems may also have induced some screening of passengers by carriers.[259]

Perhaps more significantly, exclusionary legislation articulated local policy choices that signaled to carriers and European governments opposition to the "dumping" of paupers and convicts. Penalties may have decreased the willingness of carriers to contract with officials for the transportation of groups of poor or convicted persons. The federal diplomatic establishment sometimes expressly invoked state regulations in its protests against public facilitation of the emigration of undesired residents to the United States.[260] If the borders of the United States had been truly open to all comers, then European governments could have overtly pursued such policies and at certain periods would have.

Chapter Three

CONSTITUTIONAL LIMITS ON IMMIGRATION

REGULATION IN THE FIRST CENTURY:

FEDERALISM OBJECTIONS

STATE IMMIGRATION legislation might be less worthy of attention if such legislation had been clearly unconstitutional, and especially if it had been so regarded at the time. The usual narrative of immigration law history has emphasized a series of cases that, in retrospect, support the current doctrine that the regulation of immigration is an exclusive power of the federal government. Closer inspection reveals that these cases are more equivocal than the modern account admits and that other materials indicate greater acceptance of state power over immigration in the period before the Civil War. Moreover, some state regulation enjoyed the explicit endorsement of Congress. We cannot hope for a definitive answer to the question of the constitutionality of state immigration legislation before 1875, but we may attempt to gain a more accurate understanding of the range of contemporary opinion on the subject.

There are actually two issues of validity that should be considered separately. The sweeping objection to state immigration laws is that they infringe an exclusive federal power, usually identified in the nineteenth century as the foreign commerce power. (Later, in the *Chinese Exclusion Case* [1889],[1] the Court suggested that federal power to exclude aliens was inherent in the external sovereignty of the nation.) A more limited objection is that state regulation of immigration, as applied to an immigrant from a particular country, may violate an existing treaty between the United States and that country. This chapter will not consider individual-rights objections to state immigration laws, because the legislative power of the states was not limited by the Bill of Rights until the adoption of the Fourteenth Amendment in 1868.[2]

EXCLUSIVE FEDERAL POWER

The narrative familiar to immigration lawyers traces a progression through four phases of Supreme Court discussion. First, in *Gibbons v. Ogden* (1824),[3] in the course of invalidating the New York steamboat monopoly,

John Marshall clarified that the carriage of passengers was included within the meaning of "commerce," and he expounded in dictum the exclusivity of the federal commerce power. Second, the Taney Court retreated slightly in *Mayor of New York v. Miln* (1837),[4] upholding a state's power to demand that the master of a vessel provide data concerning the passengers being landed from the vessel after a transatlantic voyage; Joseph Story dissented on grounds of the exclusivity of the federal commerce power, claiming also that the lately deceased Marshall had agreed with him on the first hearing of the case.[5] On the third occasion, in the *Passenger Cases* (1849),[6] even the Taney Court invalidated state head taxes on passengers as an unconstitutional interference with foreign commerce, though by a bare majority. Finally, after the Civil War the Waite Court revisited the issue and unanimously declared the exclusive character of federal power over immigration in the companion cases *Henderson v. New York* (1876)[7] and *Chy Lung v. Freeman* (1876).[8] By that time, the federal government was more actively regulating immigration,[9] and the affirmation of exclusive federal power led to a rapid growth of federal immigration regulation over the next twenty years.

Even within this standard line of cases, there is a counterstory to be read that favors state authority. In *Gibbons v. Ogden*, Marshall had observed that some actions that might be regulated by Congress under its power over interstate or foreign commerce could also be regulated by a state under its power of police, so long as no actual conflict with federal legislation occurred.[10] Among the examples Marshall gave were the quarantine and health laws of the states. He interpreted the congressional statutes directing federal officers to assist in the execution of state quarantine laws as predicated on the constitutionality of those state laws.[11]

The majority in *Mayor of New York v. Miln* expanded this understanding of the police power to encompass the exclusion of other dangerous passengers. Although the Court limited its holding to the reporting provisions of the New York passenger act, which were directly before it, the opinion expressed approval of the general purpose of the state regulation.

> We think it as competent and as necessary for a state to provide precautionary measures against the moral pestilence of paupers, vagabonds, and possibly convicts; as it is to guard against the physical pestilence, which may arise from unsound and infectious articles imported, or from a ship, the crew of which may be laboring under an infectious disease.[12]

The concurring opinions were equally explicit, and less tentative about convicts.[13]

The *Passenger Cases* did not repudiate this understanding of the police power. The seriatim opinions addressed two slightly different cases. The New York case, *Smith v. Turner*, involved a statute levying head taxes on arriving crew members and passengers, for the support of a marine hospital and other purposes.[14] The other case, *Norris v. City of Boston*, involved the provisions of the Massachusetts poor law that levied a head tax on those alien passengers who were *not* considered likely to become a public charge (alien passengers who *were* considered likely to become a public charge could not be landed unless sufficient security was posted).[15] A bare majority of the Court agreed to invalidate the head taxes, but at least four of those justices indicated their approval of the pauper exclusions sanctioned by the *Miln* dicta.[16]

The majority's efforts to describe the limits of the state police power over immigrants yielded diverse formulations. Robert Grier invoked "the sacred law of self-defence" as justifying the exclusion of "lunatics, idiots, criminals, or paupers" and also the exclusion of free blacks from the slave states.[17] In fact, Grier focused his condemnation on interference by the seaport states with passengers *in transit to other states*, not with those intending to settle instate.[18] John McLean agreed that the states had not parted with "that power of self-preservation which must be inherent in every organized community. They may guard against the introduction of any thing which may corrupt the morals, or endanger the health or lives of their citizens."[19] Only James Wayne expressly confronted and rejected the dissenters' argument that the states had retained full discretion to identify and remove any persons they considered dangerous to their welfare.[20] For Wayne, there existed a limited set of categories of persons whom the states could rightfully exclude regardless of the will of Congress; these categories defined the boundary between the federal commerce power and the state police power. Not surprisingly, his list included paupers, vagabonds, fugitives from justice, and free blacks seeking to enter slave states.

The four dissenters saw no inherent limit to the states' sovereign authority over the entrance of aliens. Levi Woodbury maintained that

> it is for the State where the power resides to decide on what is sufficient cause for it,—whether municipal or economical, sickness or crime; as, for example, danger of pauperism, danger to health, danger to morals, danger to property, danger to public principles by revolutions and change of government, or danger to religion.[21]

Peter Daniel invoked at length the Jeffersonian polemics against the Alien Act of 1798 to demonstrate that power over the entry of aliens was vested exclusively in the states.[22] Chief Justice Taney insisted on the state's right to expel "any person, or class of persons, whom it might deem dangerous to its peace, or likely to produce a physical or moral evil among its citizens," without interference by Congress.[23] Taney also sounded the alarm with regard to recognition of a power in Congress to force the admission of free blacks into the slave states, and Woodbury from a Northern perspective warned that the states' power over the entry of foreigners, whether black or white, was indivisible.[24]

As this summary indicates, a truly exclusive federal power over interstate and international migration would have been highly threatening under antebellum conditions. The federal government would have been forced to choose policies controlling the transborder movement of both free blacks and slaves. This undercurrent to the commerce debate had been obvious from the beginning. As previously explained, the question of state authority had arisen before Justice William Johnson on circuit shortly prior to *Gibbons v. Ogden*, in the highly charged context of the exclusion of free black seamen from Southern ports.[25] Johnson's willingness to declare the statute unconstitutional contrasts with the caution of Marshall, expressed in an oft-quoted letter to Story.

> Thus you see fuel is continually added to the fire at which *exaltées* are about to roast the Judicial Department. You have, it is said, some laws in Massachusetts, not very unlike in principles to that which our brother has declared unconstitutional. We have its twin brother in Virginia; a case has been brought before me in which I might have considered its constitutionality, had I chosen to do so; but it was not absolutely necessary, and as I am not fond of butting against a wall in sport, I escaped on the construction of the act.[26]

In fact, the Supreme Court avoided a confrontation on these issues during Marshall's lifetime.

The Taney Court's decisions regarding fugitive slaves produced further reasoning supportive of a state police power over migration. In *Prigg v. Pennsylvania* (1842),[27] while maintaining the exclusivity of the federal government's authority to return fugitive slaves to out-of-state claimants, Story distinguished the state's power to exclude them for its own benefit:

> We entertain no doubt whatsoever, that the states, in virtue of their general police power, possesses full jurisdiction to arrest and restrain runaway slaves, and remove them from their borders, and otherwise to secure themselves against their depredations and evil example, *as they certainly may do in cases of idlers, vagabonds and paupers.*[28]

This dictum became holding in *Moore v. Illinois* (1853), where the Court affirmed a state criminal conviction for secreting a runaway slave, on the grounds that the state could rightfully prevent the immigration of persons "unacceptable" to it. Robert Grier observed:

> In the exercise of this power, which has been denominated the police power, a State has a right to make it a penal offence to introduce paupers, criminals, or fugitive slaves, within their borders, and punish those who thwart this policy by harboring, concealing, or secreting such persons. Some of the States, cotermi-

nous with those who tolerate slavery, have found it necessary to protect themselves against the influx either of liberated or fugitive slaves, and to repel from their soil a population likely to become burdensome and injurious, either as paupers or criminals.[29]

The lower courts understood the Supreme Court as approving state police power over certain categories of migrants. In some instances these cases were invoked as suggesting a broad state power, and in others they were read as limiting state power to a short list of traditional categories. For example, Chief Justice Lemuel Shaw had relied on *Gibbons* and *Miln* to support a head tax in lieu of bond for the support of pauper immigrants in his opinion (reversed by the Supreme Court) in *Norris v. City of Boston* (1842).[30] The police power was also invoked to uphold bond-posting statutes in Louisiana and New York.[31] The California Supreme Court, in contrast, denied the state's authority to require bonds or payment for those passengers who showed no sign of being "more likely than the average of mankind to become paupers, vagabonds, or criminals."[32] It had previously concluded that the state's police power extended to the expulsion of slaves[33] but not to the exclusion of Chinese immigrants.[34] Justice Field similarly held on circuit that the state's power of exclusion in "self-defense" was limited to traditional categories of health, crime, and poverty.[35]

The notion of a limited set of permissible state law exclusions raises an interesting question regarding the characterization of immigration policy as state or federal. To the extent that nothing in federal law *required* the states to enact the traditional exclusions, the choice of policy remained with the states. But to the extent that a short list of exclusion policies had privileged status in federal constitutional law, the federal judiciary shared responsibility for these policies, and they represented something more than local choices. Similarly, Congress shared responsibility for those policies that it reinforced with federal legislation, like quarantine and the exclusion of free blacks, and other policies for which it provided diplomatic intervention, like pauper and convict exclusion.[36]

Even the *Henderson* and *Chy Lung* cases, normally cited as extinguishing state power over immigration, left open the question of police power to exclude dangerous immigrants. *Henderson* involved New York's efforts to deal with pauper immigration by imposing a variation on the head tax invalidated in the *Passenger Cases*; masters of vessels were facially required to post bond against their passengers' becoming public charges but were permitted to commute the bond by a payment of $1.50 per passenger. In *Chy Lung*, a California statute granted officials broad discretion to demand bonds or commutation payments from masters as a condition of landing alien passengers, including one deemed "a lewd or debauched woman."[37] The Court viewed both statutes as invalid efforts to raise money from foreign immigration,[38] but it took the opportunity for a broad reexamination and affirmation of congressional power over immigration.

Nonetheless, the Court avoided opening the nation's borders. The cases were decided in a transition period; Congress had just begun to regulate immigration from Europe, addressing some of its criminological aspects but not yet its poverty and public health aspects.[39] Accordingly, while striking down New York's imposition of commutation payments on all passengers as an unconstitutional interference with foreign commerce, the Court added: "Whether, in the absence of [action by Congress], the States can, or how far they can, by appropriate legislation, protect themselves against *actual* paupers, vagrants, criminals, and diseased persons, arriving in their territory from foreign countries, we do not decide."[40]

Although this language may suggest doubt regarding traditional categories of state immigration control, their continuing validity was assumed in other commerce cases decided shortly thereafter.[41] And in 1886 the Court went out of its way to uphold the traditional subjection of vessels in foreign commerce to state quarantine regulations as a matter of local concern for which uniform national legislation was not required.[42] The Court repeated this endorsement of state quarantine laws as late as 1902.[43]

IMMIGRATION UNDER TREATIES

One final objection to state immigration legislation should be considered here: its possible inconsistency with treaties. The federal government had enacted affirmative immigration law from the beginning of the republic by entering into treaties of friendship, commerce, and navigation with other nations. These treaties created reciprocal rights of entry for purposes of commerce, subject to certain conditions. The extent of those rights and conditions was subject to dispute, and they were probably consistent with most state immigration restrictions.

The state head taxes in the *Passenger Cases* (1849) conceivably burdened rights of free ingress granted under a commercial treaty with Great Britain.[44] Several justices in the *Passenger Cases* asserted this conflict as an additional reason for invalidating the head taxes but without offering a careful analysis of the treaty language and its implications for the powers of the state; relevant considerations are sprinkled among the majority and dissenting opinions.

An initial question to be resolved is whether ordinary immigrants, not carrying on commerce themselves, enjoyed rights of access under the treaty.[45] In fact, when the federal government finally adopted quantitative restrictions on immigration in the 1920s, it concluded that they did not—

preserving access as nonimmigrants for merchants and their families satisfied the United States' obligations under the typical commercial treaty.[46] If this answer is not a modern reinterpretation, then such treaties had only limited potential for conflict with state immigration laws.

Even without so limiting the scope of the treaties, one could ask whether the treaty language rendering the rights granted "subject always to the laws and statutes of the two countries, respectively," subordinated the right of access to nondiscriminatory state laws[47] and if so, whether the relevant standard of nondiscrimination requires equality with the state's own citizens, with citizens of sister states, or with nationals of the most favored nation.[48] A broad reading of the "subject always to the laws" proviso could leave states substantial discretion to adopt categorical exclusions of "undesirable" classes, applied uniformly to interstate and international migration (or perhaps just to international migration). Discrimination against a particular treaty partner would be invalid, as the courts told California.[49]

If the broad reading of the proviso is rejected, the possibility remains that a constitutional line between the federal commerce power and the state police power could be read into the treaty, preserving those prerogatives that the federal government could not invade; or more directly, that the federal government lacked the power to enter into a treaty overriding state immigration laws based on traditional police power concepts.[50] Under current constitutional understandings of the commerce clause and the treaty power, this strategy would fail, because the reach of Congress's immigration power is complete and because the treaty power is now viewed as extending beyond the content of Congress's other enumerated powers. But these understandings were not established in the mid-nineteenth century, and some majority justices in the *Passenger Cases* appeared to believe that the federal government could not deprive the states of core police powers over immigration.[51]

Alternatively, a treaty could be interpreted in accordance with Justice John Marshall Harlan's later dictum in *Yamataya v. Fisher* (1903), that even if it had not contained

> that specific exception, we should not be inclined to hold that the provision in the treaty with Japan, that the citizens or subjects of each of the two countries should have "full liberty to enter, travel, or reside in any part of the territories of the other contracting party," has any reference to that class, in either country, who from their habits or condition, are ordinarily or properly the object of police regulations designed to protect the general public against contact with dangerous or improper persons.[52]

Had the issue of state exclusion of paupers or criminals from a treaty nation been squarely presented before the Civil War, the Supreme Court would most likely have validated the traditional exclusions in this manner.

Thus, even those state immigration statutes that lacked the express consent of Congress cannot be dismissed in retrospect as clearly ultra vires. The nineteenth-century search for the mysterious line between the exercise of police power and the regulation of commerce left indeterminate room for state control of immigration. The uncoupling of migration from slavery as a result of the Civil War made federal regulation possible, and the coincidence that the first new pressure for immigration restriction involved discrimination against a particular country made federal regulation necessary. The advocates of Chinese exclusion called upon Congress to do what the states could not. The *Chy Lung* decision also introduced an emphasis on the foreign affairs implications of abusive immigration regulation. This shift in focus set the stage for the justification of federal immigration power as an aspect of the nation's external sovereignty a decade later in the *Chinese Exclusion Case* (1889).[53] Through a dialectical process, federal regulation steadily expanded, and the Supreme Court steadily contracted state powers. But it is anachronistic to project this modern constitutional understanding into the earlier period.

Chapter Four

THE RIGHTS OF ALIEN FRIENDS WITHIN

THE UNITED STATES

COUNSEL FOR THE CITY in *Mayor of New York v. Miln* (1837) began his rebuttal of the foreign shipmaster's argument with an expression of displeasure that, "although a stranger among us, he has undertaken to teach us constitutional law."[1] The view that aliens should not presume to make claims under the Constitution has been articulated not only with respect to violations of federalism, as in *Miln*, but also with respect to violations of rights.

The ambiguities of the social contract tradition regarding aliens' rights were not resolved in the drafting of the United States Constitution. Unlike their contemporaries in France, who produced a Declaration of the Rights of Man and of the Citizen, the drafters of the federal Bill of Rights did not take care to distinguish between the respective rights of citizens and persons. James Madison and his political allies were forced to address this postponed issue only a decade later, in response to the Alien and Sedition Acts of 1798.[2] The resulting debate over aliens' rights was the first of the major confrontations over the scope of American constitutionalism.

This chapter will begin with an examination of the debate itself, paying close attention to the political theory lying behind the claims of the debaters. Detailed examination here is necessitated by the fact that historians of the period have devoted primary attention to the Sedition Act. Then it will show how the Madisonian position on the rights-bearing capacity of aliens, which was the mainstream position of his time, was later confirmed in the judicial exposition of American constitutional law. This favorable attitude toward the rights of aliens is further evidenced by the extension of rights of political participation to aliens in numerous states and territories in the nineteenth century, which further complicated the relation of aliens to the social contract.

THE ALIEN ACT DEBATES

The notion of restricting the Constitution's reach to citizens was vigorously debated in the polemics over the constitutionality of the Alien and Sedition Acts. These statutes embodied the extreme Federalists' reaction to the im-

portation of dangerous revolutionary ideas from France, which they saw
being spread by French agents, Irish immigrants, and Jeffersonian Republicans. The Alien Act of 1798 posed in stark form the question whether
aliens had constitutional rights, because it subjected them to expulsion on
mere suspicion through orders issued ex parte by the president.[3] The importance of this controversy as a test of principle, however, was magnified by
its incorporation into Jefferson's political strategy and by the subsequent
prestige of the Jeffersonian defense of individual and states' rights.

The Jeffersonian Republicans viewed the Alien and Sedition Acts as an
effort to destroy their party. Nonetheless, the acts also offered an opportunity: although they would be used to punish criticism of the administration,
public revulsion against them could prove to be a springboard to electoral
victory. The Alien Act served as a useful exemplar of Federalist tyranny,
and it continued to play a substantial role in Republican publicity. It allegedly exceeded the delegated powers of Congress, violated the separation of
powers, and transgressed the explicit constitutional rights to trial by jury
and due process of law.

The rights-bearing capacity of aliens was not the sole or even the major
focus of the struggle—the Sedition Act and the developing concept of
states' rights took center stage. But in systematically attacking or defending all portions of the Alien-and-Sedition package, this contentious generation laid the foundation for future thought on the place of aliens in American constitutionalism. These arguments were refined at three stages: during
the original opposition to the bill, during the passage of the Virginia and
Kentucky Resolutions protesting against the acts, and in James Madison's
1800 report for the Virginia legislature in defense of the resolutions.

The Virginia and Kentucky Resolutions were Jefferson's great vehicles
for denouncing the Alien and Sedition Acts. Concealing their own participation, he and Madison enlisted the aid of local allies to shepherd resolutions through the state legislatures, asserting the unconstitutionality of the
statutes and the urgency of taking measures against them.[4] These resolutions expounded the Constitution as a compact among the states. The rights
of the states as parties included the right to identify violations of the compact by the federal government. Accordingly, the resolutions declared the
unconstitutionality of the Alien and Sedition Acts.

The Virginia and Kentucky Resolutions evoked critical counterresolu-
tions from a majority of the other states.[5] The Federalists had some success
in shifting the focus from the merits of the Alien and Sedition Acts to the
disunionist tendencies of the resolutions. They also continued to excite
public fears of sanguinary French agents.

The Virginia Republicans prevailed upon Madison to enter the Virginia
House of Delegates in order to lend his prestige openly to this struggle.[6]
Madison then drafted a report, which the legislature adopted in January

1800, restating the case for the Virginia Resolutions. In later years, this report was extravagantly praised as a summation of Jeffersonian doctrine and the "principles of '98."[7] Reprinted at various dates, and incorporated verbatim in Elliot's Debates, it kept accessible for further use (or distortion) a fuller account of those principles than the resolutions themselves.

Federalists and the Membership Approach

The existing reports of the debates in the House of Representatives on the passage of the Alien Act show that the major themes had already emerged.[8] Albert Gallatin, the foreign-born leader of the Jeffersonian forces in the House, argued that the generality of the Constitution's language, particularly in its references to "persons" rather than "citizens," made its protection available to aliens.[9] The Federalists not only countered these arguments clause by clause, but made a more fundamental response: aliens were not parties to the Constitution; it was not made for their benefit; and they had no rights under it. Harrison Gray Otis, for example, sneeringly noted "that 'we, the people of the United States,' were the only parties concerned in making that instrument. [I find] nothing in it which [binds] us to fraternize with the whole world."[10]

The Federalists thus gave a nativist twist to the social contract background of American constitutionalism. Citizens, as parties to the compact, could assert constitutional rights. But aliens were not parties and had to look elsewhere for their rights—for example, to the law of nations, which recognized the power of a nation to expel aliens at will.

In the debates on the Virginia Resolutions, the Federalists in the House of Delegates made these fundamental arguments as well as clause-specific ones. They reiterated that aliens were not "parties" to the Constitution and therefore had no rights under it. The rights of citizens were determined by the Constitution, but the rights of aliens by the law of nations. References to Vattel showed that aliens could be expelled at will under the law of nations, which afforded no trial by jury.[11]

The argument of George Keith Taylor, who led the Federalist attack on the resolutions, shifted repeatedly between two versions of this argument. One form, which today we would say was based on the right/privilege distinction, started with the proposition that under the law of nations (as also under American law) the alien has no right to remain. Expulsion therefore does not deprive the alien of liberty or any other right, and procedural rights do not attach. The second version of the argument went further and insisted that "aliens[,] not being a party to the compact, were not bound by it to the performance of any particular duty, nor did it confer upon them any rights."[12]

After the Republicans supplemented the Virginia Resolutions with an

Address of the General Assembly to the People, the Federalists issued an *Address of the Minority*.[13] The evidence indicates that George Keith Taylor's brother-in-law John Marshall took a hand in writing this address, along with General Henry Lee.[14] For whatever reason, the claim that aliens had no rights disappeared from the minority's argument—they defended the constitutionality of the Alien Act on narrower grounds, including the right/privilege argument: "Certainly a vested right is to be taken from no individual without a solemn trial, but the right of remaining in our country is vested in no alien; he enters and remains by the courtesy of the sovereign power, and that courtesy may at pleasure be withdrawn."[15]

Lee also omitted the nativist claim from his succeeding series of essays, *Plain Truth*, although he vigorously maintained that only the people of the United States, and not the states, formed the Constitution.[16]

More extreme Federalists, however, continued to employ the membership argument. A House select committee repeated it in the report to the House of Representatives on the inexpediency of repealing the Alien and Sedition Acts:

> It is answered in the first place, that the Constitution was made for citizens, not for aliens, who of consequence have no rights under it, but remain in the country and enjoy the benefit of the laws, not as matter of right, but merely as matter of favor and permission, which favor and permission may be withdrawn whenever the Government charged with the general welfare shall judge their further continuance dangerous.[17]

The legislatures of Massachusetts and Vermont incorporated it in their official replies to the Virginia and Kentucky Resolutions, respectively.[18]

In Pennsylvania, an aggressive state court judge named Alexander Addison, who had already played a role in putting down the Whiskey Rebellion, also devoted his energies to these polemics.[19] He included *A Defence of the Alien Act* among his published grand jury charges.[20] He maintained that "aliens are not parties to [the Constitution], and therefore can claim no benefit under it, unless they are expressly named."[21] Addison further elaborated his argument in a pamphlet attacking Madison's 1800 report for the Virginia Assembly.[22] He emphasized that the people of the United States were one people, raised to nationhood by the Declaration of Independence.[23] The foreign affairs powers, including power over aliens, were extraconstitutional.

> The restrictions of the constitution are not restrictions of external and national right, but of internal and municipal right. And power over aliens is to be measured, not by internal and municipal law, but by external and national law. It affects not the people of the United States, parties and subjects to the constitution; but foreign governments, whose subjects the aliens are.[24]

Naturalization changed an alien's status by conferring a vested right, but admission of an alien to reside in the United States did not.[25] "As aliens are not entitled to the privileges of citizens, any farther than the constitution and laws direct, and as the constitution says nothing of them, the legislature has a right to prescribe in what manner they shall be dealt with."[26]

Thus, the repertoire of Federalist defenses of the Alien Act included one that portrayed the Constitution as a contract among the American people, for their sole benefit. Even resident aliens had no rights against Congress under such a Constitution but rather were remitted to a background source of law, the law of nations, for whatever protection it afforded them.

The Federalists' social contract argument against aliens' rights may be most strongly articulated through a combination of solidaristic republicanism and textual interpretation. The republican argument for withholding constitutional rights from aliens rests on behavioral assumptions differing from those of both Vattel and Hobbes. In a republic,

> [E]ach man must somehow be persuaded to submerge his personal wants into the greater good of the whole. This willingness of the individual to sacrifice his private interests for the good of the community—such patriotism or love of country—the eighteenth century termed "public virtue." A republic was such a delicate polity precisely because it demanded an extraordinary moral character in the people.[27]

A constitutional structure designed in the hope of maintaining this delicate polity might confer rights that could not be safely entrusted to outsiders. When defining qualifications for citizenship, political rights, and officeholding, many in the new nation expressed concern that foreign immigrants were insufficiently attached to the good of the country or to republican principles.[28] Nonimmigrant visitors could pose an even greater threat, especially if they were loyal citizens of another republic. As the French Revolution turned radical, some Federalists feared that its propagandists would also corrupt the American people.[29] "Aliens having the least interest in the prosperity of this country," charged Judge Addison, "and owing the least duty (only a temporary duty) to it, were the most likely to yield themselves the readiest agents of France."[30]

Presuming that the limited electorate, a majority of which ratified the Constitution, had authority, the Preamble to the Constitution indicates that this electorate represented, and acted on behalf of, the entire people. Recalling that the Constitution sets forth the mutual agreements of the people might give reason for interpreting its provisions as relating only to citizens, except where the context obviously dictates otherwise.[31] Thus, the solidaristic strain in republicanism could exert its exclusionary force on the entire Constitution through a membership-oriented interpretation of the social contract.

Jeffersonians and the Mutuality of Legal Obligation Approach

The opposition party, in the course of refuting the Federalists' membership argument, developed a different statement of the Constitution's character. When the membership argument surfaced in the House debates on the Alien bill, Edward Livingston made a twofold response. Like Gallatin, he emphasized that the relevant clauses used general language and that an alien was surely a "person."[32] But he also invoked the traditional doctrine linking allegiance to protection.

> It is an acknowledged principle of the common law, the authority of which is established here, that alien friends . . . residing among us, are entitled to the protection of our laws, and that during their residence they owe a temporary allegiance to our Government. If they are accused of violating this allegiance, the same laws which interpose in the case of a citizen must determine the truth of the accusation, and if found guilty they are liable to the same punishment.[33]

With further development, this argument eventually provided a normative basis for freeing constitutional guarantees from the restrictive implications of the Preamble.

In presenting the resolutions to the Virginia House of Delegates, John Taylor of Caroline distinguished between the Alien Act's violation of the Constitution and its denial of human or natural rights.[34] The constitutional defects he identified were deprivation of common law rights without due process, denial of trial by jury, and exercise of judicial power by the president. The natural rights were "freedom of speech, freedom of person, a right to justice, and to a fair trial."[35]

Taylor supported aliens' entitlement to constitutional rights with three arguments. First, he relied on the generality of the text: the due process clause "literally reached aliens, by using in all places the term 'persons,' not 'natives'"; Article III extended the judicial power to "all cases" and required the trial of "all crimes" by jury.[36] Second, he gave a strong republican argument that favored the literal interpretation. The Alien Act transgressed fundamental republican principles by creating a class of persons wholly dependent on the president. Grave dangers to the liberty of citizens would result from "making a President in fact a king of the aliens."[37] Moreover, accepting this distortion would serve as a precedent for future usurpations in the construction of the Constitution.[38] Third, even under the law of nations aliens "were entitled and subjected to the sanctions of municipal law," and "the Constitution was a sacred portion of municipal law."[39] In rejecting the claim that aliens' rights were defined by international law rather than by the Constitution, Taylor invoked the orthodox Jeffersonian principle of construction: the federal government had only enumerated powers and could not "at pleasure dip their hands into the inexhaustible treasuries of the common law and law of nations."[40]

Madison incorporated similar arguments in his 1800 Report. In defending the Virginia Resolutions he could not deny that the Constitution was a compact; nor did he claim that aliens were parties to it. But he pointed out that the parties, for reasons of their own, might have limited the federal government's power over aliens:

> [I]t is said, that aliens not being parties to the Constitution, the rights and privileges which it secures cannot be at all claimed by them.
>
> To this reasoning, also, it might be answered, that although aliens are not parties to the Constitution, it does not follow that the Constitution has vested in Congress an absolute power over them. The parties to the Constitution may have granted, or retained, or modified, the power over aliens, without regard to that particular consideration.[41]

He emphasized the extreme to which the Federalists had taken the argument: "If aliens had no rights under the Constitution, they might not only be banished, but even capitally punished, without a jury or the other incidents to a fair trial."[42] He did not spell out in the Report why the parties to the Constitution would have taken the trouble to erect so high a barrier against such a result, although he did observe that the practices of "barbarous countries, under undefined prerogatives, or amid revolutionary dangers, . . . will not be deemed fit precedents for the government of the United States."[43]

The Report continued:

> But a more direct reply is, that it does not follow, because aliens are not parties to the Constitution, as citizens are parties to it, that whilst they actually conform to it, they have no right to its protection. Aliens are not more parties to the laws, than they are parties to the Constitution; yet, it will not be disputed, that as they owe, on one hand, a temporary obedience, they are entitled, in return, to their protection and advantage.[44]

Madison viewed as fundamental the distinction between alien enemies and alien friends.[a] As to alien enemies, the Constitution's grant of the war power gave Congress the usual authority under the law of nations.[45] The legal relations of alien friends, however, are not so defined.

> Alien friends, except in the single case of public ministers, are under the municipal law, and must be tried and punished according to that law only.
>
> . . . the offence being committed by the individual, not by his nation, and

---

[a] Alien enemies are the subjects of an enemy nation in time of war; all others are alien friends. See, e.g., 1 William Blackstone, Commentaries on the Laws of England *360–61 (1979 reprint).

against the municipal law, not against the law of nations,—the individual only, and not the nation, is punishable; and the punishment must be conducted according to the municipal law, not according to the law of nations.[46]

For all the usual reasons, the Alien Act was "repugnant to the constitutional principles of municipal law."[47]

Thus, even while reserving to the states the rights of a compact, Madison asserted the character of the Constitution as *law*. Aliens, by exposing themselves to the burdens of the United States' legal system, were entitled to insist on the observance of the whole of that legal system, including the "particular organization and positive provision of the Federal Constitution."[48]

The reconciliation of social contract theory with the actual, known constitutional history of the young nation presented difficulties that would become more urgent as sectionalism evolved toward disunion. The origins of most societies were veiled by the mists of antiquity, but the history of the English in America was documented, and the federal Constitution had recently been established in the name of the people to form a more perfect union. That Constitution was clearly not a contract between the people and the new government, an artificial entity that did not yet exist.[49] "Only a social agreement among the people, only such a Lockean contract, seemed to make sense of their rapidly developing idea of a constitution as a fundamental law designed by the people to be separate from and controlling of all the institutions of government."[50] As Hamilton wrote in *The Federalist No. 78*, "A constitution is, in fact, and must be regarded by the judges, as a fundamental law."

Because Vattel had explicitly prefigured this conception of a constitution as a fundamental law decreed by the people after their act of union, one may regret his failure to address whether fundamental laws were included among those to which aliens were entitled. But the Madisonian defense treated an affirmative answer as following a fortiori. It may be restated as follows: Aliens, being people, have the same natural rights as others. A constitution is a positive fundamental law, whose purpose is to structure the institutions of the state in ways that facilitate government while safeguarding natural rights (though whose may be debated). Even from the citizens' point of view, protecting the rights of aliens made sense. The rights (natural or otherwise) of aliens and of citizens are intertwined, and oppression of aliens could indirectly harm citizens. Arbitrary government power over aliens would disrupt and discourage desired relations between aliens and citizens, whether marriage, friendship, commerce, or education.[51] Moreover, as the Jeffersonian federalism–based argument illustrates, elimination of aliens' negative liberty vis-à-vis the federal government decreases the positive liberty of citizens acting within their states, because a state power to admit aliens and an unbridled federal power to expel them cannot coexist. And, in the paranoid vein beloved by republican thinkers, aliens rendered dependent by unchecked government power would become tools for subversion of the liberty of citizens.

More fundamental, however, was the argument grounded in the mutuality of obligation. By entering the country, aliens subject themselves to the power of the government and the requirements of local law in almost every respect just as citizens do.[52] Their consent is no more tacit than that of most citizens, and their natural rights share the risk of government abuses.[53] To the extent that the Constitution's language does not exclude aliens from its coverage, therefore, its positive provisions should be applied so as to ensure respect for natural obligation.

THE DOMINANCE OF THE MUTUALITY OF OBLIGATION APPROACH

The debates on the Alien Act produced no obvious immediate winner. In retrospect, the outcome seems personified in the rise of John Marshall, one of the moderate Federalists who defended the act without denying the constitutional rights of aliens.[54] John Adams never directly employed the powers granted to him under the Alien Act. He did sign warrants for the arrest of several outspoken foreigners, at the urging of his extremist secretary of state Timothy Pickering, but they either left voluntarily or evaded capture.[55] By the time the act expired in June 1800, Adams had dismissed Pickering and replaced him with Marshall. At the end of Adams's term, Marshall became chief justice.

In his three and a half decades as chief justice, John Marshall's court rendered decisions on numerous points that had figured in the debates on the Alien and Sedition Acts and the Virginia and Kentucky Resolutions. The character of the Constitution as law or compact figured prominently in Marshall's struggle with the emerging Southern states' rights school. In a further metamorphosis of the Virginia Resolutions and Report, the states' rights movement insisted that the states were the focus of the social contract(s), and that as separate sovereignties rather than as a united people they had then become parties to the Constitution as a compact. The law of nations provided models for the remedial rights of confederated sovereigns, including self-help and dissolution. This dispute also became significant in controversies over the geographical scope of the Constitution, to which we will turn in Chapter Five. But as regards the rights of aliens, it should be emphasized that the polemics of Spencer Roane, John Taylor,[56] and later the South Carolina nullifiers created pressure for the Supreme Court and its supporters to emphasize the character of the Constitution as what Marshall had called it in *Marbury v. Madison* (1803)—"a fundamental and paramount *law*."[57] This emphasis on the Constitution as law supported Madison's argument that aliens could claim its benefits.

The Marshall Court repeatedly protected aliens against the states by vindicating the authority of federal treaties, which the Constitution made "the supreme Law of the Land."[58] Marshall had a direct stake in this process—on the assumption that treaty rights would be respected, he had embarked upon "the one important financial adventure of his life," the purchase of the Fairfax estate.[59] The Taney Court continued the federal supremacy approach, scrutinizing state measures against aliens for inconsistency with treaties, the federal commerce power, and federal control of foreign affairs.[60] Nonetheless, despite a variety of dicta in the Supreme Court and on circuit,[61] no case before the Civil War gave the Court occasion to hold that aliens were possessors of constitutional rights. One major factor contributing to this silence was the fact that the Bill of Rights applied only to the federal government, and the regulation of aliens was carried out largely by the states. As we have seen in Chapter Three, the antebellum cases testing state power over immigration were decided on federal supremacy grounds rather than individual rights grounds.

The notion that rights might be limited to parties to the social contract did not disappear altogether. Although Taney did not address the rights of white aliens in the Dred Scott decision (1857), he did combine elements of social contract reading of the Constitution with a pseudohistorical positivistic analysis in order to conclude that blacks, whether slave or free, were permanently excluded from the people of the United States, for whose sole benefit and protection the Constitution was formed.[62] Even as to white aliens, the nativist Samuel F. B. Morse argued in an anti-Catholic tract that the Preamble demonstrated the Framers' intent to limit the blessings of liberty to "ourselves and our posterity."[63]

The decisive testing ground for the question of aliens' rights emerged with the anti-Chinese movement on the West Coast.[64] Before 1868, the California Supreme Court invalidated discriminatory state legislation on supremacy clause and commerce clause grounds.[65] But the peculiar circumstances that had paralyzed the federal government in matters of race were transformed by the Civil War. The legislative history of the 1866 Civil Rights Act and the Fourteenth Amendment demonstrates an awareness of the mistreatment of the Chinese on the Pacific coast.[66] Both the wording of the Fourteenth Amendment and the debates call attention to the rights of aliens as "persons" within the due process and equal protection clauses.[67] The 1870 Civil Rights Act supplemented these clauses with a fuller listing of some relevant protections.[68] Thus reinforced, the federal courts entered into a lengthy struggle with California.[69]

The occasion thereby arose for the Supreme Court to declare unequivocally that aliens were persons entitled to rights afforded in general terms by the Constitution. Invalidating yet another persecution of the Chinese in California, the Court provided a unanimous statement in *Yick Wo v. Hopkins* (1886).

> The Fourteenth Amendment to the Constitution is not confined to the protection of citizens. It says: "Nor shall any State deprive any person of life, liberty or property without due process of law; nor deny to any person within its jurisdiction the equal protection of the laws." These provisions are universal in their application, to all persons within the territorial jurisdiction, without regard to any differences of race, of color, or of nationality; and the equal protection of the laws is a pledge of the protection of equal laws.[70]

This interpretation was not controversial; indeed Hopkins's attorneys had not denied the principle.[71] But abolition had removed the legal commitment to slavery that had inhibited judicial affirmation of the Constitution's "universal" protection of persons within the United States.

With this principle settled, other major issues of the Alien Act debate—the substance and procedural scope of the federal deportation power—were refought over the next decade in the Supreme Court, in the context of the new federal immigration laws. In *Fong Yue Ting v. United States* (1893), the Court upheld the power of deportation without the protections of the criminal process.[72] Field's dissent quoted at length from Madison's Report[73] and maintained that

> [a]liens from countries at peace with us, domiciled within our country by its consent, are entitled to all the guaranties for the protection of their persons and property which are secured to native-born citizens. The moment any human being from a country at peace with us comes within the jurisdiction of the United States, with their consent . . . he becomes subject to all their laws, is amenable to their punishment and entitled to their protection.[74]

The majority, in turn, invoked Vattel and later writers to show that every nation had the power to expel aliens.[75] Nonetheless, the majority agreed that aliens within the territory were subject to the laws and insisted that it was expounding, not denying, the constitutional rights of aliens.[76] Thus, the right/privilege argument of the moderate Federalists like John Marshall and Henry Lee became part of the American constitutional law concerning immigration. It has persisted to this day, making deportation an anomalous qualification to the general recognition of aliens' constitutional rights within United States territory.

The Court kept its promise three years later by unanimously striking down a congressional act that subjected Chinese unlawfully within the country to one year's imprisonment at hard labor before their deportation, without indictment or trial by jury.

Applying this reasoning to the Fifth and Sixth Amendments, it must be concluded that all persons within the territory of the United States are entitled to the protection guaranteed by those amendments, and that even aliens shall not be held to answer for a capital or other infamous crime, unless on a presentment or indictment of a grand jury, nor be deprived of life, liberty or property without due process of law.[77]

Thus the Court held even Congress to the approach based on the mutuality of legal obligation, and confirmed that nonmembership in the social compact does not deprive individuals present within the United States and subject to its laws of the concomitant right to the protection of the fundamental law of the land.

THE EXTENSION OF POLITICAL RIGHTS TO ALIEN RESIDENTS

The relation of aliens to the social contract and constitutional rights becomes further complicated when one recalls the tradition of alien suffrage in the United States. The inclusion of some alien residents with other residents in the electorate became a widespread practice over the course of the nineteenth century. For some proponents of this practice, alien suffrage was a necessary consequence of democratic theory, because alien residents were as much a part of the community of the governed as citizen residents and thus deserved a voice in the government. Federal constitutional law, however, never adopted such a mandatory account of alien suffrage; rather, the federal Constitution has always been interpreted as permitting the citizenry to reserve voting rights to themselves, and has generally been interpreted as permitting individual states to enfranchise aliens if they pleased. Alien suffrage declined in the early twentieth century as the states' desire for immigrants decreased, and many Americans are unaware that it ever existed.[78]

The Progress of Alien Suffrage

The history of alien suffrage must be sought at the state as well as the federal level, because the federal Constitution originally left voting rights, even in federal elections, in the hands of the states. The federal constitutional convention had decided not to supplant varying state voter qualifications with a uniform federal rule; instead it had specified that the members of the House of Representatives should be chosen "by the People of the several States," and that "the Electors in each State shall have the Qualifications requisite for Electors of the most numerous Branch of the State Legislature."[79] Until 1913, the senators were selected by the state legislatures and therefore indirectly by the state electors; Article II leaves it to the states to decide how presidential electors will be chosen.[80] Because Congress was empowered to propose constitutional amendments to be ratified by the state legislatures, state electoral laws also conferred an indirect voice in the amending process.[81]

The reference to "the People" as the electors could have been read as precluding alien suffrage in national elections if that term designated a uniquely defined political community of citizens. But the complex federal and territorial structure of the United States has fostered greater pluralism in the definition of political community and consequently a more flexible notion of popular sovereignty. Federal constitutional interpretation has thus steered a middle course between membership and mutuality.

Some early examples of alien suffrage were linked with the confused relationship between state and federal citizenship, which has its own difficult history. In the immediate post-Revolutionary period, citizenship in an individual state was the dominant concept.[82] The 1787 Constitution added a concept of national citizenship, reinforced by a congressional power over naturalization, but did not specify the intended relationship between citizenship in a state and in the nation.[83] It took three decades to settle the exclusivity of the federal power to naturalize to national citizenship, and even thereafter the possibility of state conferral of state citizenship seemingly remained.[84] The relationship of national citizenship to state citizenship was only partly clarified by the adoption of the Fourteenth Amendment, which limited the power of the states to withhold state citizenship from national citizens.[85] The Fourteenth Amendment also continued the tradition of denying national citizenship to many Native Americans, who were clearly United States nationals in the international sense and who were eligible voters in some states.[86]

The case of Vermont illustrates how the uncertain structure of citizenship law could affect alien suffrage. Vermont had included in its constitution of 1777 a provision admitting foreigners to the rights of natural-born subjects after one year's residence and an oath of allegiance.[87] After its admission to the Union, Vermont retained that provision with only slight modification.[88] Aliens appear to have voted freely in some parts of Vermont, eventually raising the concern that local practice conflicted with the federal naturalization power.[89] The state constitution was amended in 1828 to redress this perceived conflict, although aliens who were already freemen were not deprived of their status (such transition rules grandfathering in existing alien voters proved to be a frequent feature in the evolution of alien suffrage rules).[90] A similar process occurred in Virginia, which naturalized and enfranchised aliens well into the 1840s, and ceased only after Congress had debated the practice in a contested election case.[91]

The tradition of alien suffrage in territories, however, resulted from federal initiative. The Northwest Ordinance of 1787 provided for elected representatives in the territory once there were five thousand "free male inhabitants," and it contemplated voting by both former citizens of the states and other such "inhabitants."[92] Although the ordinance was originally enacted by the Congress of the Confederation, it was immediately reaffirmed by the first Congress under the Constitution, without relevant change, and its suffrage provisions were incorporated into the organic acts of several later territories.[93] This experience had further influence when two of the first states admitted from the Northwest Territory, Ohio and Illinois, conferred the franchise on "white male inhabitants" rather than "citizens."[94]

With increasing levels of immigration from a variety of source countries, the political rights of "foreigners" became more controversial. The antebellum nativist movements favored restrictive immigration and naturalization policies and sometimes even the denial of political rights to naturalized citizens.[95] During the first wave of nativist agitation in the 1830s, objections were raised in Congress against the admission of Michigan as a state under a constitution that enfranchised alien inhabitants.[96] Actually, the enfranchisement of aliens by the original Michigan constitution was rather modest, including only white male inhabitants who were resident in the state at its effective date.[97] Although Michigan did gain admission, during the succeeding decade the organic act of every new territory, and the constitution of every new state formed from the territories, limited the franchise to citizens of the United States.[98]

An innovation in Wisconsin opened new ground for compromise between the proponents and opponents of alien suffrage. In the Wisconsin Territory of the 1840s, the Democratic Party sought the support of the large immigrant population by emphasizing the links between the Whigs and the nativist movement.[99] This polarization strategy resulted in an effort to revive alien suffrage. The statehood constitution ultimately adopted the compromise formula of permitting white male aliens to vote if they had made a declaration of intent to be naturalized under the federal naturalization laws.[100] Since 1795, federal naturalization procedure had provided that aliens must first declare under oath to a competent court their intention to apply subsequently for citizenship (known colloquially as "taking out first papers") and had postponed eligibility for actual naturalization ("second" or "final papers") until three years after the declaration.[101] The declaration could be made at any time after arrival, did not divest aliens of their prior nationality, and did not legally oblige them to complete the naturalization process.[102] In fact, the declaration did not even include an oath of present allegiance to the United States. Nonetheless, the declaration could be portrayed as some evidence of attachment to the country, in order to broaden the base of support for enfranchising noncitizens.[103]

The declarant alien qualification for suffrage became increasingly common in the nineteenth century. Shortly after the admission of Wisconsin, Congress adopted it in the organic act for the Oregon Territory, and the next year for the Minnesota Territory.[104] Alien suffrage was not initially afforded, however, in the new lands acquired in the Mexican War.[105] Thereafter, Congress enfranchised declarant aliens in the Washington, Kansas, Nebraska, Nevada, Dakota, Wyoming, and Oklahoma Territories.[106] In all nine of these territories, Congress imposed the additional requirement of an oath to support the United States Constitution.

Some, though not all, of the territories that permitted alien suffrage retained it when they achieved statehood.[107] Older states also joined the trend.[108] When Indiana and Michigan adopted new constitutions in the early 1850s, they enfranchised declarant aliens.[109] Reportedly, this change reflected competition for immigrants among the Midwestern states.[110] Numerous former Confederate states adopted the same tactic, at least temporarily, after the Civil War.[111]

The Theoretical Significance of Alien Suffrage

It is difficult to determine the significance of the practice of alien suffrage for an understanding of aliens' rights in the United States, because history does not indicate a uniform theoretical basis for the practice, even where it existed. For some, the inclusion of alien residents in the electorate reflected American ideals of universal suffrage and mutuality between the government and the governed; for others, suffrage policies were matters of political choice driven by instrumental concerns. Some perceived a contradiction between alien voting and self-government by the citizenry, others saw no such contradiction, and a third viewpoint reconciled alien suffrage with popular sovereignty by recharacterizing enfranchised aliens as members of the sovereign people.

The early nineteenth century witnessed a strong movement toward the abolition of property qualifications for the franchise in the name of "universal manhood suffrage," and the supporters of alien suffrage sometimes invoked this ideal.[112] The Illinois Supreme Court concluded that its constitution extended "the right of suffrage to those who, having by habitation and residence identified their interests and feelings with the citizen, are upon the just principles of reciprocity between the governed and governing, entitled to a voice in the choice of the officers of the government, although they may be neither native nor adopted citizens."[113]

Under this view, residence rather than nationality determined membership in "the governed," and a government deriving its powers from the consent of the governed should enfranchise alien residents. Some members of the Democratic Party, which traditionally relied on the immigrant vote, emphasized their party's name and ideals, seeking to strengthen the immigrants' partisan identification in the face of the threatening countertrend of nativism.[114] The limits of this "universality," however, may be seen in the Democratic Party's simultaneous opposition to voting rights for black citizens and in the fact that women's suffrage enjoyed little support in any party.[115]

Alien suffrage was also urged for instrumental reasons. It could serve as an encouragement to immigration.[116] The argument was sometimes made in competitive terms—that immigrants' choices of destination could be influenced by the early grant of political rights and that states that insisted on naturalization as a prerequisite for voting were saddling themselves with a competitive disadvantage.[117] After the abolition of alien suffrage at the statewide level in Vermont, the state supreme court described the continuing existence of alien suffrage at the local level as "a wise policy . . . in some degree a preparatory fitting and training for the exercise of the more important and extensive rights and duties of citizens."[118] Debates over alien suffrage could also be influenced by calculations over aliens' likely voting patterns, as became particularly clear in the congressional debates over the Kansas-Nebraska Act, where immigrants' expected opposition to slavery determined the sectional alignment.[119]

To some opponents of alien suffrage, the practice ruptured the fundamental connection between citizenship and voting and threatened the ideal of popular sovereignty.[120] An early statement of this view appeared in an 1811 opinion of the Supreme Judicial Court of Massachusetts, analyzing the principles of apportionment for the state house of representatives.[121] The court began with the "unquestioned principle" that

> as the supreme power rests wholly in the citizens, so the exercise of it, or any branch of it, ought not to be delegated by any but citizens, and only to citizens. . . . And if the people intended to impart a portion of their political rights to aliens, this intention ought not to be collected from general words, which do not necessarily imply it, but from clear and manifest expressions, which are not to be misunderstood.[122]

The court therefore concluded that the provisions authorizing "inhabitants" or "residents" to vote must be construed as referring solely to citizens. But so long as aliens gained no political rights thereby, poll taxes paid by aliens could be taken into account in apportioning representatives to the towns.[123]

The states that gave aliens full voting rights were not necessarily indifferent to the concept of popular sovereignty. Most of their constitutions included express popular sovereignty clauses, typically stating that all political power was "inherent in the people."[124] Some states merely accepted the fact that aliens as well as citizens could vote. But others sought to reconcile popular sovereignty with alien suffrage by concluding that alien voters were citizens of the state, though not of the United States. The Wisconsin Supreme Court confronted this problem in a series of cases in the 1860s.[125] The court explained at length in *In re Wehlitz* (1863) that, as far as state law was concerned, declarant aliens were citizens of Wisconsin.

> [A]lthough it may be possible for the state to confer the right of voting on certain persons without making them citizens, yet I should think it would require very strong evidence of a contrary intention to overcome the inference of an intention to create a citizenship when the right of suffrage is conferred. . . . [T]he rights of voting and holding office are always given as the most complete and perfect attributes of citizenship.[126]

The court described the independence of state citizenship from United States citizenship as an acceptable consequence of the dual-sovereign system of federalism.[127] A few other state courts similarly construed declarant alien voters as citizens of the state,[128] and Alabama expressly declared their citizenship in its reconstructed constitution.[129]

Whatever Alabama may have thought, the Supreme Court was certain that aliens were not citizens of the state within the meaning of the federal Constitution. As part of its argument rejecting a constitutional claim for women's suffrage in *Minor v. Happersett* (1874), the Court denied that there was any necessary connection between state citizenship and the right to vote and observed that

> citizenship has not in all cases been made a condition precedent to the enjoyment of the right of suffrage. Thus, in Missouri, persons of foreign birth, who have declared their intention to become citizens of the United States, may under certain circumstances vote. The same provision is to be found in the constitutions of Alabama, Arkansas, Florida, Georgia, Indiana, Kansas, Minnesota, and Texas.[130]

The federal courts were equally sure that unnaturalized alien voters were not "citizens of a State" within the meaning of the provisions authorizing federal jurisdiction over suits between citizens of different states.[131]

Even the federal courts, however, relied on an intuitive connection between voting and citizenship in developing a doctrine of collective naturalization upon the admission of a territory to statehood. The issue appears to have arisen first in Louisiana, where both the state and federal courts held that the congressional enabling act, by authorizing the noncitizen inhabitants to participate in the formation of a state constitution, had recognized them as citizens of the future state.[132] The Supreme Court eventually confirmed a version of this doctrine in *Boyd v. Nebraska ex rel. Thayer* (1892), maintaining that the admission of a state naturalizes "those whom Congress makes members of the political community, and who are recognized as such in the formation of the new State with the consent of Congress."[133] Thus alien residents could be authorized to vote as aliens in the territory and would then become citizens when the territory achieved admission as a state. Because Congress had permitted only citizens and declarant aliens to vote on the Nebraska constitution, the Court concluded that only declarant aliens and their families were naturalized by the admission of Nebraska.[134]

Where voting was restricted to declarant aliens, it could be argued that the modification of citizen sovereignty was modest. The federal government treated declarant aliens in some respects as inchoate citizens.[135] At various periods, the federal government issued passports to declarant aliens, and it intermittently asserted the authority to protect domiciled declarant aliens when they traveled outside the United States.[136] The federal government has also viewed declarant aliens as particularly fair game for military conscription. The history and theory of drafting aliens in the United States have been quite complex.[137] The inclusion of declarant aliens in the first federal draft, during the Civil War, appears to have reflected both the large pool of available immigrants and an insistence that prospective citizens who were already voting should share the burden of military service.[138] This conscription provoked a flurry of diplomatic correspondence, which was resolved by permitting a declarant alien to avoid the draft if he abandoned his intention to naturalize and left the country, but only if he had not yet voted.[139] It deserves to be emphasized that alien soldiers fought for the North in the Civil War and that alien voters were among the People who adopted the Civil War Amendments. Declarant aliens were also designated for conscription in the Spanish-American War and the First World War.[140]

Thus, the ideology of declarant alien suffrage in particular may have reflected a broad concept of democracy, but it also rested on an empirical view of European immigrants as future United States citizens. The latter aspect becomes especially salient when one recalls the racial implications of declarant alien suffrage. Prior to 1870, only "free white persons" could be naturalized under the general naturalization laws, and so only whites could participate in the declaration of intent process.[141] In 1870 "aliens of African nativity and persons of African descent" were made eligible for naturalization, but the ineligibility of other immigrants, most prominently the Chinese, was deliberately maintained.[142] The Fifteenth Amendment addresses the question of racial discrimination in voting and prohibits disenfranchisement only of citizens of the United States. Far from implying the impropriety of alien suffrage, this limitation resulted from a clear recognition that aliens did vote and a fear that a broadly written amendment would force Pacific coast states to permit Chinese immigrants to vote.[143] The practical operation of declarant alien suffrage after the Civil War involved the exclusion of Chinese and other Asian immigrants from the franchise. Chinese immigrants finally became eligible for naturalization in 1943, but by then the period of declarant alien suffrage was over.[144]

Later voting-rights amendments similarly limited their scope to the rights of citizens, protecting them against discrimination on such grounds as sex, age, and failure to pay a poll tax.[145] The Seventeenth Amendment, in contrast, which instituted the direct election of senators by the people of the states, relied on the same state qualifications as used for the House of Representatives and thus increased the scope of alien suffrage as it existed at the time.[146]

The Decline of Alien Suffrage

The exclusion of aliens from the protection of the Fifteenth Amendment illustrates the effective operation of the assumption that the franchise could be, but need not be, shared with aliens. Once the desire for new immigrants faded, so did the popularity of alien suffrage. In the 1890s, the closing of the frontier and increases in immigration from eastern and southern Europe gave rise to a movement for the restriction of European immigration. This movement ultimately led to the enactment of a literacy requirement for immigrants in 1917 and the imposition of immigration quotas based on national origin in the 1920s. Meanwhile, the changing attitude toward immigration also caused the repeal of alien suffrage provisions.[147] The First World War unleashed pervasive hostility against Germans and German culture in the United States. That hostility, along with shock at the idea of voting by enemy aliens, prompted several more states to abolish alien suffrage at that time.[148] By 1928, no state afforded alien suffrage in statewide or federal elections.[149] This situation persists in the United States today.

It is more difficult to assess the current status of alien suffrage at the local level. Alien residents are eligible to vote in municipal elections in several Maryland towns.[150] Aliens also qualify as electors and candidates in the decentralized school board elections of New York City and Chicago.[151] A referendum in November 1991 in Takoma Park, Maryland, attracted media attention when voters narrowly approved enfranchising alien residents.[152] The victory inspired the discussion of undertaking similar efforts elsewhere, and it appeared that a new cycle of controversy over alien suffrage in the United States might be beginning.[153] Proposals that would increase the power of Latino communities through alien voting, however, have met with resistance from African American as well as Anglo citizens.[154] The demand to reserve suffrage for citizens escalated when opponents of liberalized registration procedures for citizens in federal elections (the "motor voter" bill) excited popular indignation against the possibility that loose administration would lead to voting by undocumented aliens.[155] The current backlash against immigration in the wake of the 1990 Immigration Act and the weakened economy makes a widespread revival of alien suffrage improbable in the near future.

The idea of at least limited alien suffrage is unlikely to go away, however, because of a different precedent—the extension of alien suffrage in local elections in Europe under the auspices of the European Communities. The Maastricht Treaty on European Union, which entered into force in 1993, commits member states to afford nationals of other member states residing in their territory the right to vote and run for office in municipal (not national) elections.[156] The treaty accompanies this reciprocal privileging of member state nationals with the grandiose title "Citizenship in the European Union," but proposals to mandate similar rights for the pragmatic purpose of facilitating the mobility of workers and professionals predated the treaty, and some member states had already amended their electoral laws.[157] If the North American Free Trade Agreement represents the United States' first step along the regional trail blazed by Europe, then other pressures for alien suffrage—including pressure from U.S. citizens who would benefit from reciprocity—may bring the idea back onto the political agenda.

Chapter Five

THE GEOGRAPHICAL SCOPE OF

THE CONSTITUTION

T HE CONTRAST between membership and mutuality of obligation approaches resulting from the ambiguities of the social contract tradition has not been limited to the constitutional rights of aliens within American territory. Instead, it has been mirrored by opposing approaches to identifying the territory where constitutional rights apply. The question of the Constitution's geographical scope has involved two aspects: the applicability of constitutional limitations to government action within the territory of a foreign sovereign or on the high seas and their applicability to government action within territory of the United States that has not been admitted to statehood. In a debate that still continues, United States territories have been assimilated to both extremes—as firmly within the Constitution's reach as any state, or as far beyond it as England or Japan.[1]

Throughout most of American history, these issues arose primarily within the context of expansion of the national territory. As the United States grew beyond the original thirteen states, and turned from the framework of self-government to a framework for governing others, the implications of distributing rights became more complex. Aside from the original sin against Native Americans, the United States did not generally rely on permanent caste distinctions to prevent linking the constitutional rights of citizens of the states who traveled or migrated to the territories and those of the preexisting population they encountered there. The "extension" or "nonextension" of constitutional rights to new territory affected both state citizens and indigenous residents. Doubts about the "fitness" of newly acquired French, Spanish, Mexican, Hawaiian, Puerto Rican, and Filipino subjects therefore conflicted with self-interest in a debate over localizing the Constitution.

As in the case of aliens, the two most common approaches to the Constitution's coverage rested on an expansive use of the mutuality of obligation approach and a restrictive approach relying on a heightened form of membership requirement. The mutuality analysis stressed the character of the Constitution as a fundamental law and concluded that acquisition of sovereignty over a territory was sufficient to extend the fundamental law there. In the turn-of-the-century phrase, constitutional rights "followed the flag." The nineteenth-century version of mutuality, however, was strictly territorial, and it went no further than the flag. The membership approach to geographical scope personified sectors of the globe and extended constitutional rights to new sectors only with the consent of certain of the prior sectors. Citizens who moved to the wrong sector would find that they had alienated their rights. One extreme form of this approach conceived of the Constitution as created by the states and for the states. This version preserved the symmetrical character of consent, because admission to statehood occurred at the request of a new state with the consent of the old. In contrast, less extreme versions of the membership approach affording some territories the benefits of membership made the consent one-sided, because the consent of the territories was not sought.

The approach based on mutuality of legal obligation dominated in the courts in the nineteenth century but faced a resurgence of its membership rival in the wake of overseas expansionism at the turn of the century. Membership theories facilitated colonialism. Developments since then have produced a mosaic of inconsistent rules and rationales rather than a true synthesis, and both membership and mutuality remain available resources of constitutional argument.

The Constitution and the Territories in the Era of Continental Expansion

The seeds of continuing disagreement were sown in 1787, when the political leaders of the new nation took two steps visibly in tension with their republican principles. First, in drafting the Constitution, they granted Congress full legislative power over the District of Columbia, which would not be within a state and which would therefore have no voice in choosing the legislators exercising that ultimate power.[2] Second, in July 1787, the Congress of the Confederation adopted the Northwest Ordinance, a framework for governing the territory north of the Ohio River ceded to Congress by the states. The ordinance contemplated an initial stage of territorial existence in which the population would have no power of self-government.[3] Repeatedly during the next century, advocates would draw paradoxical conclusions from these denials of representation: they would reverse the logic of republicanism in order to claim that regions excluded from political participation were necessarily excluded from the scope of the Constitution altogether.

These themes may already be detected in the surviving documentation of the controversy resulting from the first great territorial expansion—the acquisition of Louisiana.[4] This "magnificent purchase"[5] redefined the United States and compromised many of the principles that Jefferson thought he had vindicated in the election of 1800. Jefferson and his advisers stifled their doubts about the constitutional authority of the national government to acquire foreign territory, and to admit new states into the Union from later-acquired territory, as the treaty with France seemed to require.[6] The latter problem especially provoked the Federalist opposition, which insisted that the states' ratification of the Constitution authorized Congress to admit new state parties to the constitutional compact only from the territory then existing.[7] Some invoked the Preamble as evidence that the Constitution was designed only for the territory held or claimed by the original thirteen states.[8]

From their assumption regarding the social contract, most of these Federalists argued toward a restrictive conclusion concerning the rights of the inhabitants.[9] The Constitution did not contemplate the incorporation of the territory as a state, and therefore Congress was entitled to govern it as a colonial dependency.[10] Some Republicans adopted the Federalist conclusion that, as a ceded country, Louisiana was subject only to the discretion of Congress;[11] a majority of the Republicans compromised their principles sufficiently to assure Jefferson the broad powers he desired for himself and his territorial governor.[12] A few of the dissenting Republicans expressly founded their constitutional objections on a mutuality of obligation approach, insisting that Congress could not acquire legislative power over the territory without being bound there by constitutional prohibitions.[13]

The Louisiana debates seem to have resolved nothing, although they set a precedent for the triumph of expediency over principle in the initial stages of territorial governance. These issues not only recurred in the course of routine administration of justice, but became questions of great political moment when the constitutional status of the territories seemed likely to determine the fate of slavery and therefore of the nation.

Marshall and Calhoun: Mutuality in the American Empire

We have already seen how Chief Justice John Marshall's nationalist vision of the Constitution as judicially enforceable law strengthened the approach based on mutuality of legal obligation and benefited the position of aliens. His stance similarly favored the District of Columbia and the territories. Unexpectedly, Marshall's nationalist approach aligned with the differently motivated arguments of John C. Calhoun and Roger Taney, leading to a dominance of the mutuality approach in the nineteenth century.

Although Marshall gladly passed up the Court's first opportunity to decide whether constitutional limitations constrained Congress in the District of Columbia,[a] he returned to the issue in *Loughborough v. Blake* (1820),[14] a case challenging Congress's power to impose a direct tax on the District of Columbia. Marshall found the requisite power in the first clause of Article I, section 8, which authorizes Congress to collect "Taxes, Duties, Imposts and Excises" but requires the last three to be "uniform throughout the United States."[15] He then asked:

> Does this term designate the whole, or any particular portion of the American empire? Certainly, this question can admit of but one answer. It is the name given to our great republic, which is composed of states and territories. The district of Columbia, or the territory west of the Missouri, is not less within the United States, than Maryland or Pennsylvania; and it is not less necessary, on the principles of our constitution, that uniformity in the imposition of imposts, duties and excises should be observed in the one, than in the other.[16]

Somewhat overconfidently, this passage expresses Marshall's theme of national unification and echoes a sentence in *McCulloch v. Maryland* (1819).[17] In that opinion, Marshall had insisted on considering the Constitution as "emanating from the people, [and not] as the act of sovereign and independent states."[18] But by 1820, the rancor of sectional division had made itself manifest in the debates leading to the Missouri Compromise, and the limits of congressional power over the territories were becoming a hotly disputed issue.[19]

Marshall directly addressed the Constitution's force in a territory in the well-known but perplexing case of *American Insurance Co. v. Canter* (1828).[20] The insurance company attacked a judgment of a court created by the territorial legislature of Florida, which purported to exercise admiralty jurisdiction. The company argued that the territory of Florida lacked the power to vest such jurisdiction in its court, because admiralty jurisdiction was reserved to federal courts under Article III. On circuit, Justice William Johnson rejected this claim, finding that the specification of jurisdiction under Article III was inapplicable because Florida was an after-acquired

---

[a] United States v. More, 7 U.S. (3 Cranch) 159 (1805). In this odd sequel to Marbury v. Madison, 5 U.S. (1 Cranch) 137 (1803), the circuit court dismissed an indictment against a Federalist justice of the peace for the District of Columbia for levying fees that had been abolished by the new Republican Congress. The circuit court held that the diminution of the judge's revenues violated Article III. The prosecution claimed that the Constitution was inapplicable in the District: "The constitution is a compact between the people of the United States in their individual capacity, and the states in their political capacity. Unfortunately for the citizens of Columbia, they are not in either of these capacities." 7 U.S. (3 Cranch) at 167. The case was argued in the Supreme Court in February 1805, in the midst of the impeachment trial of Justice Samuel Chase. As in *Marbury*, however, Chief Justice Marshall managed to avoid resolving the consitutionality of Jefferson's judiciary policy by finding a jurisdictional objection to hearing the case. See James M. O'Fallon, The Case of Benjamin More: A Lost Episode in the Struggle over Repeal of the 1801 Judiciary Act, 11 L. & Hist. Rev. 43 (1993).

territory: the Constitution did not apply there, and Congress was bound only by the law of nations in governing it.[21] In the Supreme Court, Canter's attorneys reiterated this membership approach, insisting on the phrasing of the Preamble: "The constitution was established by the people of the United States, for the United States." Florida was not one of those states. "If the constitution is in force in Florida, why is [Florida] not represented in Congress?"[22]

These arguments led Marshall to address questions of acquisition and government of territory. In reply, Marshall asserted that in accordance with the usage of nations, once a territory is ceded to another nation, the political laws that govern the relationship between the inhabitants and their sovereign necessarily change.[23] The treaty of cession covering Florida stipulated that its inhabitants be "admitted to the enjoyment of the privileges, rights and immunities of the citizens of the United States." Therefore, "It is unnecessary to inquire, whether this is not their condition, independent of stipulation. They do not, however, participate in political power; they do not share in government, till Florida shall become a state."[24] Thus, Marshall rejected once more the fallacy that constitutional limitations can attach only upon admission to the Union as a self-governing state, although he left ambiguous what would have happened absent the treaty.

Turning to the particular constitutional issue at hand, Marshall held that the power to govern the territories, whether implied from the war power or the treaty power or expressly granted by Article IV, gave Congress the authority to establish courts in addition to those contemplated by Article III of the Constitution and to vest them with admiralty jurisdiction. "In legislating for [the territories], congress exercises the combined powers of the general, and of a state government."[b] Canter therefore prevailed, though not on the broadest grounds that his counsel advanced.[25] The Constitution *was* in force in Florida.

By the late 1820s, John C. Calhoun's conception of the nature of the Union was diametrically opposed to Marshall's, and yet he reached similar

---

[b] 26 U.S. (1 Pet.) at 546. The phrasing of Congress's power as combining those of general and state governments, which was later also used to describe Congress's power in the District of Columbia, contained an ambiguity that has since caused confusion. It refers to the absence of a division of powers on the model of federalism. See Benner v. Porter, 50 U.S. (9 How.) 235, 242 (1850). But like other assertions of "plenary" grants of power, it is susceptible to misreading as a power free of all constitutional limitations. The proposition that Congress can enact any legislation in the territories that a state can enact within its borders may be misinterpreted as freeing Congress from those constitutional limits that do not apply to state governments. Under the present regime of "selective incorporation" of the Bill of Rights in the Fourteenth Amendment, this error would still have significant consequences; under the antebellum system whereby the Bill of Rights did not apply to the states at all, it would have enabled Congress to do practically anything except pass bills of attainder and ex post facto laws, or grant titles of nobility.

conclusions regarding the extension of the Constitution to the district and the territories, conclusions that were ultimately affirmed by the Taney Court in the 1850s.[26] In the wake of the so-called Tariff of Abominations of 1828, Calhoun was asked to draft an essay to guide the deliberations of the South Carolina legislature on measures in response to the tariff.[27] After study of the prior states' rights literature, including the Virginia and Kentucky Resolutions and Madison's Report, he produced the South Carolina Exposition and Protest on nullification.[28] Once the nullification crisis had passed, Calhoun developed his theories further, for the purpose of denying congressional power over slavery in the District of Columbia and the territories. He developed two arguments that enabled him to reach this conclusion. One subjected the federal government to implied constitutional obligations as agent or trustee for the sovereign states. The other treated express provisions of the Constitution as directly applicable in the District of Columbia and the territories.

Calhoun rejected the natural rights tradition from which the abolitionists drew their arguments, as well as the idea of a state of nature or an original social contract subjecting a people to government.[29] According to Calhoun, government was a social institution that arose naturally. Constitutions were artificial contrivances adopted by a people for the purpose of governing their government.[30] This was true of both the state and federal constitutions. He viewed the United States Constitution in particular as a "written, positive compact,"[31] embodying a contract or treaty among previously existing sovereign states; that is, among the people of the several states as distinct political bodies, not merely among their respective governments.[32] This agreement formed them into a "federal" union, a hybrid form that was neither a nation nor a mere confederacy or league of separate states.[33] Calhoun purported to rely on positive historical evidence, including the published journals of the Philadelphia Convention and the ratification proceedings, to reconstruct the actual bargain that underlay the Constitution.[34] Not surprisingly, he found both explicit and structurally implied protections for Southern slavery, which he regarded as essential to the preservation of Southern institutions.

Unlike the Louisiana Territory, which included a port city with a substantial non-English colonial population, later territorial acquisitions involved underpopulated tracts considered ripe for settlement by citizens of existing states. This made it easy for both sides to view conditions in the territories as implicating the rights of citizens of the states.[35] It may also have made it easy for Calhoun to accept the extension of positive constitutional protections, the traditional rights of Englishmen, to the future territorial population. And Calhoun argued that such extension was expressly required by the supremacy clause.[36] Vis-à-vis the several states, the Constitution was a compact, but vis-à-vis the federal government it was a governing law. The supremacy clause made it clear that the Constitution was "the law of the land," including "the territorial possessions of the United States; or, as far as their authority might otherwise extend."[37] Thus, beginning with a contractual theory of the Constitution as an agreement among the states for their own benefit, Calhoun deduced that constitutional prohibitions were positive legal norms geographically coextensive with the legislative powers of Congress.

Webster and the State Membership Countertradition

The tradition restricting constitutional limitations to the states as members of the Union was most influentially articulated by Calhoun's great antagonist, Daniel Webster. Unlike Calhoun, Webster was not a systematic thinker—he was a lawyer, an orator, and a politician. Nonetheless, he was viewed as the principal constitutional advocate of his day, and he often took up the gauntlet as Calhoun's antagonist on behalf of New England and the Union. He agreed with Calhoun in viewing the Constitution in positivist terms and in reading it as a compromise with slavery. Political exigencies therefore pushed him to insist on a position he had developed in the course of his legal practice, that the Constitution was legally binding only within the boundaries of the states.

Webster's celebrity as a defender of the Union arose from two Senate speeches refuting Calhoun and the nullifiers: his famous Reply to Hayne in 1830 and his response to Calhoun on the Force Bill in 1833.[38] He rejected the nullifiers' view of the Constitution as an agreement among sovereign states, insisting that the national government was the creation of a single supreme power, the people of the United States.[39]

> [T]he Constitution of the United States, founded in or on the consent of the people, may be said to rest on compact or consent; but it is not itself the compact, but its result.[40]

> This consent of the people has been called, by European writers, the social compact; and, in conformity to this common mode of expression, these conventions speak of that assent, on which the new Constitution was to rest, as an explicit and solemn compact, not which the States had entered into with each other, but which the people of the United States had entered into.[41]

The Constitution was "not a league, compact, or confederacy, but a fundamental law."[42] The people had made the Constitution a supreme law and had created a national judiciary to resolve disputes about its meaning.[43] Webster thus reformulated the nature of the Union in terms derived from Marshall Court decisions, some of which he had argued himself.[44]

Despite his nationalism and his insistence on the Constitution as a fundamental law, Webster viewed its geographical scope as narrower than the

American nation. He had become involved in territorial questions back in 1819, joining the public debate on the Missouri Compromise.[45] As co-counsel on the prevailing side in *American Insurance Co. v. Canter* (1828),[46] Webster argued that the Constitution had no application to an acquired territory. Like Justice Johnson on circuit, Webster derived the status of the American territories from general principles of public law and not from American political theory. He also employed the usual reverse-republican fallacy, arguing that because a territory lacked political rights, it must have no rights at all.[47] Although Webster won the case, he lost this part of the argument. Chief Justice Marshall held that the Constitution did extend to Florida, leaving open the question of what triggered this extension.

Oddly, Webster seems never to have recognized that Marshall rejected his approach. He repeated the same arguments in his 1849 debate with Calhoun over territorial government in the region newly acquired from Mexico. Senator Isaac Walker of Wisconsin had offered an amendment that purported to "extend" the Constitution over the territory.[48] From the Calhounite perspective, this amendment would declare that the constitutional protection of slaveholders' "property" extended to the territories.[49] Webster denied not only that the Constitution applied to the territories of its own force, but even that it was possible to extend it to them.[50]

Webster's rhetorical position was quite peculiar. Other senators insisted that the Constitution, as "a compact and agreement between sovereign States," could not be "extended" except by admitting further states.[51] Webster's formulation was very close to this: though he insisted that the Constitution was not a compact but the *product* of a compact, he limited the protection of individual rights to those regions that exercised the sovereign political power of the national government. Surely this is a variant of the membership interpretation. But Webster, having famously combated the notion of the Constitution as a compact, avoided this terminology.

Despite its logical weaknesses, Webster's membership-in-the-Union approach was popular with those who opposed the spread of slavery but recognized the Constitution's accommodations to it.[52] Although the mutuality of obligation approach gained a wider currency in the courts and the Calhounites won a Pyrrhic victory in the Dred Scott decision, the association of the opposite view with the prestigious Webster helped lay the foundation for a partial retreat in the Insular Cases.

A Continental Equilibrium

The Taney Court finally attempted to eliminate uncertainty about the status of the territories. The territorial courts had dealt as best they could with these issues for the first half of the nineteenth century.[53] They received more explicit guidance from a series of Supreme Court cases reflecting the mutuality approach in the 1850s, establishing an equilibrium that held for as long as the United States' manifest destiny was limited to the North American continent.

Some of these decisions directly involved the fatal issue of slavery, and others implicated it only indirectly.[54] For example, in *Webster v. Reid* (1851), the Court relied evenhandedly on the Seventh Amendment and the Iowa Territory organic statute to vindicate the right to civil jury trial against a special act of the territorial legislature.[55] In *United States v. Dawson* (1854), the Court held that Article III, Section 2, rather than the Sixth Amendment, dictated the constitutional venue requirements for crimes committed in the "Indian country."[56]

If any doubts remained about whether the Court would apply the Constitution to the territories, Chief Justice Roger Taney sought to dispel them in *Scott v. Sandford* (1857).[57] He argued that Congress was subject to both implied and express constitutional limitations in legislating for the territories.[58] Taney insisted that property rights in slaves were protected in the territories by the due process clause of the Fifth Amendment. He disposed of contrary arguments from natural or international law by insisting on the terms of the Constitution as he understood them, "positive and practical regulations plainly written down." Taney's logic followed Calhoun's:

> [The protection of persons and property under the Constitution] is not confined to the States, but the words are general, and extend to the whole territory over which the Constitution gives it power to legislate, including those portions of it remaining under Territorial Government, as well as that covered by the States. It is a total absence of power everywhere within the dominion of the United States, and places the citizens of a Territory, so far as these rights are concerned, on the same footing with the citizens of the States, and guards them as firmly and plainly against any inroads which the General Government might attempt, under the plea of implied or incidental powers.[59]

None of the justices indicated any disagreement with Taney's statement that the Constitution in general, and the Bill of Rights in particular, bound Congress in the territories. The dissenters agreed expressly. Justice John McLean, who was himself holding in reserve an implied limitation *against* the expansion of slavery,[60] asserted that "the Constitution was formed for our whole country. An expansion or contraction of our territory required no change in the fundamental law."[61] Justice Benjamin Curtis's celebrated dissent defined the limits of congressional power over the territories as follows: "[I]n common with all the other legislative powers of Congress, it finds limits in the express prohibitions on Congress not to do certain things; that, in the exercise of the legislative power, Congress cannot pass an ex post facto law or bill of attainder; and so in respect to each of the other prohibitions contained in the Constitution."[62] Curtis met Taney on the merits of the due process argument, concluding that due process could not be understood as requiring the maintenance of slavery.[63]

The taint of the Dred Scott decision did not cause judicial reaction against the mutuality of obligation approach.[64] In the midst of the Civil War, the Supreme Court of Washington Territory proudly declared: "The Constitution of the United States is co-extensive with the vast empire that has grown up under it, and its provisions securing certain rights to the accused in criminal cases, are as living and potent on the shores of the Pacific as in the city of its birth."[65] During that same period, the Supreme Court was unanimous in assuming that an act of Congress retracting a vested right to tracts of land in a territory would be void.[66] Referring to both the Constitution and the laws extending it, the post–Civil War Court also scrutinized a variety of claims under the Bill of Rights, including cruel and unusual punishment and right to jury trial.[67] In an odd pair of cases in 1897, the Court expressed uncertainty as to whether the Seventh Amendment applied of its own force in a territory, and then two weeks later it rejected the doubt.[68]

The strength of the late-nineteenth-century settlement of the geographical issue may be seen in the Court's observance of it through most of the next great political controversy over the territories, the battle against polygamists in the Church of Jesus Christ of Latter-day Saints in Utah.[69] The federal polygamy statutes applied only in the territories and other places over which the federal government had exclusive jurisdiction.[70] This limitation resulted not from the inapplicability of the Constitution to such places, but from the belief that states had exclusive control over their domestic-relations laws.[71]

Through most of this struggle, Congress conceded that it was bound by the Constitution generally, and the First Amendment in particular, in legislating for the Utah Territory.[72] There were lapses, however, as in 1882, when a senator from Florida invoked Webster's argument that "the Congress of the United States in legislating for the Territories is not hampered by constitutional restrictions or limitations; that the Preamble of the Constitution tells us it was made for States and not for Territories."[73]

The Supreme Court's seminal decision in *Reynolds v. United States* (1879) involved the Sixth Amendment rights to an impartial jury and to confrontation, in addition to its crucial First Amendment holding refusing to protect polygamy as an exercise of religion.[74] The importance of *Reynolds* in constitutional history lies precisely in its acceptance as precedent in free exercise cases generally, rather than as a special rule for territories. A later case, *Hans Nielsen, Petitioner* (1889), upheld a constitutional objection, this time to violation of the double jeopardy guarantee.[75]

Some ambiguity returned, however, in Justice Joseph Bradley's opinion for the majority in the climactic 1890 decision upholding Congress's dissolution of the church corporation and forfeiture of its assets.[76] By that point it was hopeless to defend the church on the basis of religious freedom, but its lawyers invoked the sacred rights of property and the nascent concept of economic due process.[77] After a series of quotations of orthodox case law on the status of the territories, Bradley wrote:

> Doubtless Congress, in legislating for the Territories would be subject to those fundamental limitations of personal rights which are formulated in the Constitution and its amendments; but these limitations would exist rather by inference and the general spirit of the Constitution from which Congress derives all its powers, than by any express and direct application of its provisions.[78]

This dictum would support much mischief in later years.

A year later, Justice Stephen Field emphasized the strictly territorial consequences of the mutuality approach in *In re Ross* (1891).[79] The case involved an American seaman tried before an American consul for murder committed aboard an American ship in a Japanese harbor, pursuant to Japan's grant of extraterritoriality to American nationals. Ross claimed that trial in the consular court denied him his constitutional rights to grand jury indictment and trial by jury. A unanimous Court relied on both practical and theoretical reasons in rejecting this claim.[80] Field, who believed strongly in the territorial character of law,[81] characterized the Constitution's scope as follows:

> By the Constitution a government is ordained and established "for the United States of America," and not for countries outside of their limits. The guarantees it affords against accusation of capital or infamous crimes, except by indictment or presentment by a grand jury, and for an impartial trial by a jury when thus accused, apply only to citizens and others within the United States, or who are brought there for trial for alleged offences committed elsewhere, and not to residents or temporary sojourners abroad. The Constitution can have no operation in another country. When, therefore, the representatives or officers of our government are permitted to exercise authority of any kind in another country, it must be on such conditions as the two countries may agree, the laws of neither one being obligatory upon the other.[82]

The language of the argument came from the conflict of laws and emphasized the primacy of territorial sovereignty as the basis of legal obligation. Japan as a sovereign nation had the ultimate right to forbid the consul to conduct a jury trial within its territory; therefore the Constitution was not legally binding on the consul.

Field's logic was slippery: our Constitution had no binding force on the government of Japan, but that does not mean that the United States government, in negotiating an extraterritoriality treaty with Japan, was free to negotiate for a system of trial that violated our Constitution. That the Constitution does not bind their government does not mean that it *cannot* bind ours, perhaps to inaction. Indeed, Field's opinion devoted more space to demonstrating that United States jurisdiction extended over Ross than to demonstrating that the United States Constitution did not extend over the consul.[83] Nonetheless, Field treated the Constitution as extending only as far as the nation's power of legislation was plenary, to cases where it could govern by right, not by consent or comity.

WE THE PEOPLE, INCORPORATED

A second legacy of the Dred Scott decision ultimately produced a transformation in the terms of the debate over American constitutionalism. After the Civil War Amendments, the Constitution was no longer committed to a conflict with natural law. Over the next few decades, "due process of law" became a rubric under which conservative economic interests persuaded the justices to confer on themselves the power of enforcing natural law as positive law.[84] The resulting expansion of judicial discretion opened new ground for compromise between full equality of constitutional rights and relegation to extralegal status—territories could be judicially shielded from absolute despotism without receiving all the rights of the metropolis.

At the same time, the United States' manifest destiny was shifting from the filling out of an underpopulated continent to imperialist competition with other great powers. This meant acquiring more distant territory, some of it densely populated by peoples whom the expansionists were not prepared to regard as equals. As a result, the Supreme Court, though at first by a bare majority, chose to occupy this intermediate ground, reincarnating the geographically restrictive social compact approach in the doctrine of "incorporated territories" in the Insular Cases.[c] The underlying theories were most cogently expressed in the opinions of Justices Edward Douglass White and John Marshall Harlan, respectively concurring and dissenting in *Downes v. Bidwell* (1901).[85] White's innovation maintained the Constitution as the measure of federal power over territories supposedly designated

[c] This imprecise term refers both to the nine cases relating to the constitutional and legal status of Puerto Rico and the Philippines argued in 1901, and to the entire series of cases from DeLima v. Bidwell, 182 U.S. 1 (1901), to Balzac v. Puerto Rico, 258 U.S. 298 (1922), that established the framework of second-class status for overseas territories.

For readers new to this material, it may be unfortunate that tradition has associated the word *incorporate* with both the applicability of the Bill of Rights to federal action in the territories and the applicability of the Bill of Rights to actions of the states. In the first case, the reference is to incorporating the territory into the United States, and in the second, to incorporating the Bill of Rights into the Fourteenth Amendment.

by Congress as welcome to full status but limited protection in other territories to a minimal set of background rights described as fundamental. Harlan, in contrast, continued the traditional insistence that wherever Congress acquired sovereignty, the rights of the written Constitution followed as part of the fundamental law.

Historians have explained the expansionist impulse of the 1890s as a product of numerous converging factors.[86] Having put both the Civil War and Reconstruction behind it, the nation confidently sought recognition as one of the great Western powers and was willing to join in the scramble to colonize weaker peoples to achieve that goal. Social Darwinism abetted religious zeal in a resurgence of the rhetoric of manifest destiny and the historic mission of the Anglo-Saxon race. It also influenced the cult of naval power, which required a network of bases. Colonialism was also one way, although not the only way, of ensuring foreign markets for increased American productive capacity.

Calls for the subjection of foreign peoples provoked an equally complex anti-imperialist movement, including such diverse elements as Samuel Gompers, Charles Francis Adams, Jr., Andrew Carnegie, and the powerful Speaker of the House, Thomas Reed.[87] Some anti-imperialists were blatant racists and opposed any form of union with the substantial nonwhite populations of potential acquisitions. Labor feared their competition. Others argued that white Americans had already demonstrated their unfitness as trustees for non-European peoples and that the conduct of empire would destroy American republican institutions.

Like slavery, expansionism intertwined moral, political, and constitutional issues. It was surely too late to argue (though some did) that as a matter of constitutional law territories of the United States had the right to govern themselves rather than be governed by Congress. Taney's opinion in *Scott v. Sandford* (1857) would, however, support a somewhat narrower objection to colonialism, that territory could be acquired only for the purpose of making future states of the Union; "no power is given to acquire a Territory to be held and governed permanently in that character."[88] Moreover, when the Fourteenth Amendment overruled Taney's view on citizenship, it added for the first time a constitutional guarantee of American citizenship, which could be read as conferring that exalted status on everyone born in a territory after its acquisition, regardless of race or culture.[89] Citizenship would confer a variety of particular rights not available to aliens, including the right to relocate to the mainland. Finally, there remained the express constitutional rights and limitations applicable generally to persons; precedent suggested that residents of the territories would be entitled to them. One highly practical set of questions involved Congress's power to maintain tariffs on goods imported from overseas possessions and whether those possessions must be subjected to the same tariffs on foreign goods as the mainland.

The turn-of-the-century debate on the Constitution and distant island territories began with the proposed annexation of Hawaii in 1893.[90] It accelerated through the Spanish-American War and its aftermath, the appropriation of significant portions of Spain's overseas colonial empire.

Many of the authors combed history, including the antebellum debates on the Constitution in the territories, for support. Some took the traditional view that the Constitution constrains government action wherever the United States is sovereign,[91] and others invoked its ancient rival, the claim that the Constitution was made only for the states.[92] Besides judicial and legislative precedents, some of the traditionalists supported their arguments with natural rights rhetoric[93] and the danger that American republicanism would be destroyed by imperial habits.[94] In response, several of their opponents invoked the wording of the Preamble,[95] the authority of Daniel Webster,[96] the practices of other nations,[97] the odiousness of the Dred Scott decision,[98] and the alleged inferiority of various non-Anglo-Saxon races.[99] Some anti-imperialists argued the applicability of the Constitution in order to prove that the United States must divest itself of such ungovernable territory.[100]

The most significant novelty was presented by Abbott Lawrence Lowell, political science professor and later president of Harvard University.[101] After exploring the terms of acquisition of prior territories, he concluded that the lawmakers and the treaty makers had the freedom to choose whether to designate an acquired territory as part of the United States. If they did not so designate it, then

> constitutional limitations, such as those requiring uniformity of taxation and trial by jury, do not apply. It may well be that some provisions have a universal bearing because they are in form restrictions upon the power of Congress rather than reservations of rights. Such are the provisions that no bill of attainder or ex post facto law shall be passed, that no title of nobility shall be granted, and that a regular statement and account of all public moneys shall be published from time to time. These rules stand upon a different footing from the rights guaranteed to the citizens, many of which are inapplicable except among a people whose social and political evolution has been consonant with our own.[102]

Lowell's distinction between applicable and inapplicable provisions, based on verbal form rather than substance, had no future. His distinction between two kinds of acquired territories, however, based on a political decision to make them part of the United States, would eventually persuade a majority of the Supreme Court.

The first Insular Cases, of which the central and most famous was

Downes v. Bidwell (1901), produced a splintered Court.[103] *Downes* held Congress free of the constitutional requirement of uniformity in taxing Puerto Rico. Henry Billings Brown, the only common member of the majority in all the cases, wrote the lead opinion, speaking only for himself. He relied for the most part on the state membership approach: "The Constitution was created by the people of the United States, as a union of States, to be governed solely by representatives of the States. . . . In short, the Constitution deals with States, their people, and their representatives."[104] Brown dismissed much of the prior judicial discussion as dictum and rejected the *Scott v. Sandford* holding, preferring the contrary authority of Webster, Thomas Hart Benton, and the Civil War. Nonetheless, Congress could by positive enactment extend the Constitution to particular territories; once done, this process could not be reversed. He then undermined his own argument by suggesting that there might be certain "prohibitions [that] go to the very root of the power of Congress to act at all, irrespective of time or place," or "certain natural rights, enforced in the Constitution," that might automatically be binding in all territories.[105] Yet, as we are a nation, presumptively "our power with respect to [acquired] territories is the same power which other nations have been accustomed to exercise with respect to territories acquired by them."[106] Brown's peroration made explicit his desire not to create obstacles to Congress's pursuit of an imperial destiny.[107]

The more important contribution came from Justice Edward Douglass White. He offered a new constitutional synthesis for the new age, winning the concurrence of Justices George Shiras and Joseph McKenna and eventually capturing a majority.[108] White firmly rejected Brown's notion that Congress had discretion whether or not to extend the Constitution.[109] He observed that the Constitution was applicable everywhere and at all times—but that did not mean that its limitations on power were applicable everywhere. The issue was not whether the Constitution itself was operative in Puerto Rico, but whether the particular constitutional provision invoked should be interpreted as applying to Puerto Rico; and White believed he had a systematic approach to this problem of interpretation. The applicability of constitutional limitations depended not on the whim of Congress, but on an objective inquiry "into the situation of the territory and its relations to the United States."[110]

Under White's scheme, the federal government had the power to choose among four courses with respect to foreign territory: to admit it as a state; to incorporate it into the United States as a territory and make it an integral part of the United States; to acquire it but leave it as merely a territory appurtenant to the United States; or to leave it foreign by not acquiring it. Congress could not "extend" the Constitution, but it could extend the United States. Full constitutional protection was reserved for territories that Congress had incorporated into the United States, as opposed to those merely acquired.[111] White did not explore the relationship between incorporated territories and states, relying largely on precedent for his notion that becoming "part of" the United States resulted in further geographical extension of full constitutional protection. He focused instead on the distinction between incorporated and unincorporated territories.

White insisted that his forefathers must have intended their country to have the same sovereign right to determine the status of newly acquired territories that other sovereigns enjoyed under the law of nations. He quoted a description of that right from Halleck's *International Law*, embodying the view of Vattel, Grotius, Pufendorf, and others that a conquering state may hold new territory under that territory's old constitution, extend to it the state's own constitution, or pursue such third alternative as seems appropriate.[112] He reinforced the need for this discretion by invoking the nation's right to protect the birthright of its own citizens by withholding citizenship from acquired populations that might belong to "an uncivilized race" and be "absolutely unfit to receive it."[113]

White did not explore the moral question of where the United States got the right to "liberate" Spanish colonies whose populations had done it no wrong and then to hold them as conquered territories appurtenant without their consent. The international law of his day had left behind Enlightenment idealism in such matters. But White did not wholly relegate unincorporated territories to the ruthless positivism of late-nineteenth-century international law. He maintained that even unincorporated territories benefit from "inherent, although unexpressed, principles which are the basis of all free government . . . restrictions of so fundamental a nature that they cannot be transgressed."[114]

White did not make clear how to identify those fundamental prohibitions that extend to unincorporated territories. But one might suspect that he had updated the membership approach by making the background natural law rights legally enforceable. And indeed a few years later, in a case refusing grand and petit jury rights to inhabitants of Hawaii, White simply cited decisions holding those rights inapplicable to action of the *states* and denied that they were "fundamental provisions of the Constitution, which were by their own force applicable to the territory."[115] In other words, he employed the same kind of natural law methodology then being used to decide Fourteenth Amendment due process cases.

The most fully articulated dissent came from the elder Justice John Marshall Harlan.[116] Harlan unambiguously expounded a conception of the Constitution based on the mutuality of legal obligation. Against Brown, he asserted, "The Constitution speaks not simply to the States in their organized capacities, but to all peoples, whether of States or territories, who are subject to the authority of the United States."[117] He tied this argument in with the wording of the supremacy clause; that this speaks of the Constitution as " 'the supreme law of the land,' is a fact of no little significance. The 'land' referred to manifestly embraced all the peoples and all the territory, whether within or without the States, over which the United States could exercise jurisdiction or authority."[118]

Against White, he insisted that the proper understanding of when a territory was "a part of, and incorporated into, the United States" was whether it was "for all purposes of government by the Nation, under the complete jurisdiction of the United States . . . subject to all the authority which the National Government may exert over any territory or people."[119]

Harlan distinguished vehemently, if not wholly convincingly, his prior decision in *Neely v. Henkel* (1901), which arose out of the American occupation of Cuba in the wake of the Spanish-American War.[120] "Temporary" military occupation of foreign territory, without the intention of acquiring sovereignty, did not bring it under the Constitution.[121]

Harlan exhibited not only the territorialist disposition of the nineteenth-century mutuality approach, but also its characteristic insistence on compliance with positive constitutional provisions, regardless of whether they had any basis in natural law: "If the Constitution is in force in any territory, it is in force there for every purpose embraced by the objects for which the Government was ordained."[122] Harlan's literal demands continued his ongoing dispute with his colleagues over the applicability of the Bill of Rights to the state governments through the Fourteenth Amendment.[123] Harlan stubbornly insisted that the Bill of Rights identified "certain guarantees of the rights of life and liberty, and property, which had long been deemed fundamental in Anglo-Saxon institutions," with which the states were not free to experiment.[124]

Over the next decade, White solidified the Court behind his brainchild.[125] In *Balzac v. Porto Rico* (1922), Chief Justice William Howard Taft, the former governor of the Philippines, explained that even the conferral of United States citizenship on the residents of Puerto Rico in its 1917 organic act did not suffice to incorporate it in the United States.[126] Taft added:

> We need not dwell on another consideration which requires us not lightly to infer, from acts thus easily explained on other grounds, an intention to incorporate in the Union these distant ocean communities of a different origin and language from those of our continental people. Incorporation has always been a step, and an important one, leading to statehood.[127]

As a result, the defendant newspaper editor had no right to jury trial in his misdemeanor prosecution for libeling the island's governor.

There is no justification for sentimentality about the Insular Cases. It was noted earlier that writers in the natural law school approved of conquerors who permitted a new territory to keep its old constitution. The Insular Cases did not represent such an accommodation to the conquered; rather they were designed for the convenience of the conqueror. Nonetheless, they claimed to offer unincorporated territories a skeletal constitution that protected natural/fundamental rights and that therefore might be minimally worthy of the imputed consent of those present in the territory. Over the years, the list of rights has grown in parallel with (but has not kept up with) the expansion of Fourteenth Amendment due process rights against state governments.[128] Thus, in one sense, *Downes* and *Balzac* bring us back to the Alien Act debate: the Constitution as written for "We the People" in the States and in those territories admitted onto the path to statehood, natural and statutory rights in those territories that are not. But those natural rights that the Court chooses to recognize become part of the fundamental law in the territory and, unlike eighteenth-century natural law, override positive statutes in the manner of due process.

Modernism and Extraterritoriality

The preceding history makes possible a deeper understanding of the Supreme Court's watershed decision in *Reid v. Covert* (1957),[129] which ended the regime of strict territoriality, and the subsequent controversies over the extraterritorial extension of modern American constitutionalism with its emphasis on individual rights. Justice Hugo Black's plurality opinion in *Reid v. Covert*, a classic of Warren Court reform,[130] reinvigorated the mutuality of legal obligation approach and even contained some passages that were susceptible of a universalist interpretation. Since that time courts and commentators have struggled—mostly on a case-by-case basis—with the international ramifications of an expanding constitutionalism.

The groundwork for the modernist breakthrough in *Reid v. Covert* lies in the variety of constitutional changes intervening between the 1920s and the 1950s. By the 1950s, military and economic crises had vastly increased the power of the executive branch. The United States had consolidated its great-power status and had gone on to become a superpower. American soldiers and American corporations had spread pervasively across the globe, and the exercise of prescriptive jurisdiction on the nationality principle had become more common. Freewheeling judicial review had struggled against the New Deal and lost, and substantive due process was reputedly dead and buried. In *Brown v. Board of Education* (1954),[131] the Warren Court had reestablished the commitment to racial equality that its predecessors had compromised after Reconstruction—the Court would no longer be able to call upon the frank racism that informed the rationale of the Insular Cases.

The Second World War and the following occupation had brought pressures for the wider application of constitutional rights. The Supreme Court rejected, sometimes over dissents, challenges brought by American soldiers, civilians, and former enemies to actions of military authorities abroad.[132] The best-known of these cases is *Johnson v. Eisentrager* (1950), denying the availability of habeas corpus to German soldiers convicted as war criminals overseas for assisting the Japanese army in China after Germany's surrender.[d] Justice Jackson objected to the anomaly of extending the protection of the Bill of Rights to "irreconcilable enemy elements, guerrilla fighters and 'werewolves'" in occupied territory.[133] The Court of Claims twice held the government liable under the takings clause to citizens for actions of the army abroad.[134]

The challenges finally succeeded on rehearing in *Reid v. Covert* (1957). The companion cases involved criminal prosecutions in England and Japan—by courts-martial and therefore without independent Article III judges, indictment, or jury trial—of widows of servicemen charged with

---

[d] 339 U.S. 763 (1950) (Jackson, J.). Most of the opinion in *Eisentrager* limits attention to the status of enemy aliens and emphasizes that the "disabilities this country lays upon the alien who becomes also an enemy are imposed temporarily as an incident of war and not as an incident of alienage." Id. at 772. Nonetheless, the opinion also contains a few dicta concerning aliens in general. The most important one reads as follows:

> The alien, to whom the United States has been traditionally hospitable, has been accorded a generous and ascending scale of rights as he increases his identity with our society. Mere lawful presence in the country creates an implied assurance of safe conduct and gives him certain rights; they become more extensive and secure when he makes preliminary declaration of intention to become a citizen, and they expand to those of full citizenship upon naturalization. During his probationary residence, this Court has steadily enlarged his right against Executive deportation except upon full and fair hearing. And, at least since 1886, we have extended to the person and property of resident aliens important constitutional guaranties—such as the due process of law of the Fourteenth Amendment.
>
> But, in extending constitutional protections beyond the citizenry, the Court has been at pains to point out that it was the alien's presence within its territorial jurisdiction that gave the Judiciary power to act.

Id. at 770–71 (citations omitted). This passage, which some have taken to suggest a sliding scale of constitutional protection for concentric categories of persons, is confusing upon closer examination, since there were no additional constitutional rights accorded to declarant aliens; Jackson may have been discussing constitutional and statutory "rights" together. Moreover, although his final assertion is roughly consistent with the territorial approach of the period, it overlooks the fact that the presence of an absent alien's property within the United States also justified judicial protection. See Russian Volunteer Fleet v. United States, 282 U.S. 481 (1931); cf. Sardino v. Federal Reserve Bank of New York, 361 F.2d 106, 111 (2d Cir. 1966) (Friendly, J.). Thus, the discussion of nonenemy aliens' rights in the majority opinion involves some of the usual failings of generalities addressed to issues not actually before the Court.

Justice Black's dissent expressed willingness to extend at least some constitutional protections to former enemy aliens in occupied territory. See 339 U.S. at 791 (Black, Douglas, and Burton, JJ., dissenting).

murdering their husbands. On first hearing, a majority treated the cases as routine applications of the Insular Cases and *In re Ross* (1891).[135] Amid unusual assertions that time constraints had prevented the Court from considering the case fully,[136] rehearing was granted, and on the second round the Bill of Rights burst the bounds of territoriality. But the new majority of six split between two opposing rationales.

Black's opinion for the plurality of four (with Chief Justice Earl Warren, Justice William O. Douglas, and Justice William Brennan) began its constitutional discussion with a heavy emphasis on citizenship.

> At the beginning we reject the idea that when the United States acts against citizens abroad it can do so free of the Bill of Rights. The United States is entirely a creature of the Constitution. Its power and authority have no other source. It can only act in accordance with all the limitations imposed by the Constitution. When the Government reaches out to punish a citizen who is abroad, the shield which the Bill of Rights and other parts of the Constitution provide to protect his life and liberty should not be stripped away just because he happens to be in another land.[137]

In confronting the precedent of *In re Ross*, Black emphasized the tension between its holding that American criminal laws can have extraterritorial applicability and its holding that the American Constitution cannot; here he cited modern cases sustaining the exercise of jurisdiction on the nationality principle, beginning with *United States v. Bowman* (1922).[138]

Black also permitted himself to conflate the application of constitutional limitations in foreign countries with the application of constitutional limitations in unincorporated territories.[139] He suggested that the Insular Cases might be distinguished "in that they involved the power of Congress to provide rules and regulations to govern temporarily territories with wholly dissimilar traditions and institutions whereas here the basis for governmental power is American citizenship."[140] But he made clear his dissatisfaction with those cases and their tendency to "destroy the benefit of a written Constitution and undermine the basis of our Government."[141] Black rejected judicial discretion to identify "fundamental" rights applicable outside the continental United States.[142] This was hardly surprising, given Black's ongoing campaign to incorporate the Bill of Rights in the Fourteenth Amendment, both to protect individual liberties prized by the framers and to diminish reliance on the subjective opinions of judges.[143]

Some have interpreted Black's opinion as adopting an organic law view of the Constitution, dictating a universalist interpretation of constitutional rights. Until this point, universalism had played almost no role in American constitutionalism because the overwhelming acceptance of strict territoriality, even for citizens, had focused attention on the question of how closely the Constitution followed the flag. The second, third, and fourth sentences in the paragraph quoted earlier might lend some support to a universalist reading, but in other respects Black's opinion reveals a pronounced emphasis on the citizenship of the defendants. The paragraph continues by citing as illustrations of its principle Saint Paul's assertion of the rights of Roman citizenship,[144] and the British constitutional principle that Englishmen carry with them "the duty of obedience to the lawful commands of the Sovereign, and . . . all the rights and liberties of British Subjects."[145]

Black's plurality opinion in *Reid v. Covert* thus represents a modern realignment of the mutuality of obligation approach, taking into fuller account the exercise of prescriptive jurisdiction over American citizens worldwide under the nationality principle. The Bill of Rights not only follows the flag, but also follows every United States citizen, just as the legislative power of Congress does. Black's attitude of rigorous positivism resonates more with the views expressed in Justice Curtis's dissent in *Scott v. Sandford* (1857) than with those of the elder Harlan. But all of Black's predecessors in the mutuality approach would agree with him that "[t]he rights and liberties which citizens of our country enjoy . . . have been jealously preserved from the encroachments of Government by express provisions of our written Constitution."[146]

Justice Felix Frankfurter and the second Justice Harlan filed separate concurring opinions in *Reid v. Covert*.[147] These justices were defenders of a restrained residuum of the substantive due process doctrine and staunch opponents of Black's incorporation theory of the Fourteenth Amendment.[148] Frankfurter accordingly wrote with approval of White's methodology in the Insular Cases. He agreed that the Constitution itself was everywhere applicable, though some of its provisions might not be.[149] Frankfurter observed that

> [t]he "fundamental right" test is the one which the Court has consistently enunciated in the long series of cases . . . dealing with claims of constitutional restrictions on the power of Congress to "make all needful Rules and Regulations" for governing the unincorporated territories. The process of decision appropriate to the problem led to a detailed examination of the relation of the specific "Territory" to the United States. This examination, in its similarity to analysis in terms of "due process," is essentially the same as that to be made in the present cases in weighing congressional power to make "Rules for the Government and Regulation of the land and naval forces" against the safeguards of Article III and the Fifth and Sixth Amendments.[150]

Harlan agreed that

> the question is *which* guarantees of the Constitution *should* apply in view of the particular circumstances, the practical necessities, and the possible alternatives which Congress had before it. The question is one of judgment, not of compulsion. And so I agree with my brother Frankfurter that, in view of *Ross* and the *Insular Cases*, we have before us a question analogous, ultimately to issues of

due process; one can say, in fact, that the question of which specific safeguards of the Constitution are appropriately to be applied in a particular context overseas can be reduced to the issue of what process is "due" a defendant in the particular circumstances of a particular case.[151]

Frankfurter and Harlan explicitly limited their discussions to concluding that the procedure at issue—the military trial of civilian dependents, without indictment, without jury, and in a capital case—failed this flexible test. Frankfurter ostentatiously refused to state whether any lesser combination of these elements would violate the Constitution.[152] Harlan expressly stated that he remained persuaded that affording jury trial to civilian dependents prosecuted for "run-of-the-mill offenses" would be impractical for the very reasons of cost and difficulty of administration that the dissenters considered sufficient to justify denial of jury trial in capital cases.[153]

For the most part, Frankfurter and Harlan reasoned *from* the Insular Cases and not about them. They treated those cases as precedent for the proposition that some degree of constitutional protection extended "overseas" and explained the exceptions as resting on practical, not theoretical, distinctions. They did not ask what made federal jury trials more "impractical and anomalous" or "uncongenial" in the territory of Puerto Rico in 1922 than in the state of Louisiana in 1813.[154]

Frankfurter and Harlan held out the possibility of more widespread constitutional protection than had previously been afforded but at the cost of diluting its content. Their approach might support the constitutional enforcement of bedrock human rights, even those of aliens, against United States action in foreign countries without "anomalous" extension of domestic institutions. At the same time, the "due process" inquiry freed itself of both constitutional text and natural law as either benchmarks or justifications.[155] The availability of a particular right would vary from context to context in accord with judicial evaluations of practicality. This balancing approach contemplated an extraordinary degree of both judicial discretion and deference to the choices of the political branches.

These characteristics were confirmed three years later in *Kinsella v. United States ex rel. Singleton* (1960) and its companion cases, where Frankfurter and Harlan were willing to extend the benefit of *Reid v. Covert* to civilian employees of the armed services accused of capital crimes but dissented from its extension to noncapital crimes.[156] In those cases, Justice Tom Clark bowed to precedent but rejected the discretionary due-process-balancing approach of the Frankfurter-Harlan concurrences, converting the *Reid v. Covert* plurality into a majority.[157]

Thus, *Reid v. Covert* expressly ended the period during which the application of constitutional rights outside the borders of the United States could be avoided by the claim that the Constitution applied only within the United

States' own territory. But justices who played intellectual leadership roles within the Court remained divided on the proper explanation for this result. The plurality sought to repudiate the geographic membership approach of the Insular Cases, and the concurrences sought to extend it. The rhetoric of some opinions included a particular emphasis on United States citizens as the individuals whose rights ought not to disappear outside U.S. territory. Further elaboration and the establishment of a consensus on the Constitution's operation abroad was left to the future. Today, almost forty years later, that future consensus has not yet appeared.

PART TWO

THE PRESENT AND THE FUTURE

Chapter Six

RIGHTS BEYOND OUR BORDERS

HISTORY CAN SHOW us how earlier generations defined the personal and geographical scope of constitutional rights. It can also illuminate the sometimes conflicting normative visions underlying the rules they adopted and the political factors that assisted or impaired their fidelity to those visions. Sorting out this legacy facilitates deliberation about what the Constitution should mean for the generations alive today.

To resolve the question of the proper scope of the individual-rights provisions of the United States Constitution, it is useful to ask what rights in a constitution are *for*, and in particular what United States constitutional rights are for. The general question may receive different answers in different constitutional traditions, and consequently the scope of rights under different constitutions may vary. In this chapter, I will argue that a modern reworking of the mutuality of obligation approach, extending the full protection of the written Constitution to United States citizens wherever they may be, and to aliens outside the United States in those instances where the U.S. government seeks to subject them to its laws, best reflects the function of individual rights in American constitutionalism.

As an interpretive enterprise, this inquiry has interrelated normative and descriptive aspects. The scope of constitutional rights under a given constitution cannot be determined in isolation from the constitutional text and an awareness of the range of rights protected under that constitution.[a] An interpretive inquiry must also pay close attention to the constitutional tradition's own understanding of the function of constitutional rights, to the extent that this can be ascertained. Determinations regarding the scope of rights should preferably be coherent with other constitutional practices regarding the place of the constituted government in the world at large.

In the case of American constitutionalism, conflicting conceptions of geographical scope have led to serious indeterminacy in the modern period. Descriptive inquiries can go only so far; sparse case results can be reported,

---

[a] The latter constraint is familiar from other contexts—for example, accounts of the function of the Fourteenth Amendment, focusing on whether it makes the Bill of Rights applicable against the states, must grapple with the presence of the Second and Seventh Amendments in the Bill of Rights, and accounts of the procedural or substantive function of the Fifth Amendment's due process clause must grapple with the absence of any express equality guarantee applicable to the federal government.

but in some respects the status quo cannot be described with sufficient certainty even to be critiqued. The question of scope must be resolved primarily by deliberative choice among alternative approaches on the basis of their normative characteristics and their coherence with less unsettled constitutional practices.

The United States Constitution has long been understood as a fundamental law within the meaning of the social contract tradition—a design for government and limitations on government that protect the interests of the governed sufficiently to form part of a justification of their obligation of obedience to it. Establishing a legitimate government empowers that government to generate obligations that would not exist in anarchy or in a state of nature. Government interference with individuals' freedom or property can then be justified as a means of enforcing these obligations or preexisting natural obligations.

Under the Constitution, the legitimation of the government's authority to impose and enforce obligations rests on several elements. First, the Constitution creates a republic, in particular a representative democracy in which the actions of the federal government are subject to the check of periodic elections. The Constitution sets up a framework within which the government is to be structured, distributing powers to institutions both for reasons of efficacy and to create the well-known checks and balances. Both the original Constitution and the subsequent amendments also contain guarantees of particular rights, limitations on the content of government activity and the modes of its exercise, without which the people were reluctant to confer authority upon the government. From the perspective of the 1790s and perhaps the 1890s, some of the individual-rights provisions of the Constitution represented direct protections of natural rights, and others were more indirectly justified; in the 1990s there is less widespread agreement on the existence of "natural" or suprapositive rights.

Although American constitutionalism attributes part of the legitimacy of the government's authority to the consent derived from periodic elections, political rights have always been limited to an electorate narrower than the full class of persons within the nation's territory subject to that authority. Originally, the electorate was quite narrow; even today there are groups, such as children, felons, and aliens, who may be excluded. The nonpolitical, individual rights (the older terminological distinction between political and civil rights has lost its currency) have always been more widely distributed.

The rationale of the mutuality approach has been the presumption that American constitutional rights and the obligation of obedience to American law go together; particular provisions may be more narrowly interpreted because of textual or structural arguments, but in the absence of contrary indications the rights and the obligations are coextensive. Law here includes not only legislation, but also judicial or executive acts that impose obligation. The constitutional rights of aliens present within the territory (whether resident or just passing through) correlate with their pervasive subjection to the law (the "local allegiance" of English common law).

The nineteenth-century idea that constitutional rights follow the flag but go no further reflected a conviction as to the incomplete nature of legal obligation outside the sovereign's territory. The United States generates obligations only in some of the contexts in which it acts; in other contexts the United States is merely one participant (though in recent years a major participant) in an international order whose rules it cannot dictate. The notion that particular states are endowed with particular territories over which they exercise sovereignty derives from that order and was assumed as a background rule by the authors of the Constitution.

In fact, however, United States law has never been completely restricted to United States territory.[1] As the exercise of extraterritorial legislative power has become more frequent, the normative purpose of the mutuality of obligation approach requires broader application. The *Reid v. Covert* plurality recognized that need with regard to citizens abroad, who are subject to national legislative power absent exceptional circumstances. Since that time, courts have struggled with the availability of constitutional rights to aliens abroad, whose subjection to United States law is the exception rather than the rule, depending on particular circumstances linking their conduct to the United States. Under the mutuality approach, when the United States asserts an alien's obligation to comply with American law as a justification for interfering with the alien's freedom or property, the alien is presumptively entitled to the protection of all constitutional rights in the interaction. (Again, specific textual or other arguments may exceptionally demonstrate that a particular right is either reserved to citizens or geographically limited.)

Unlike citizens, aliens abroad could not claim the protection of constitutional rights under this version of the mutuality of obligation approach every time the United States acted to their disadvantage. For example, the United States government sometimes acts in foreign countries in circumstances in which it is claiming no authority over the foreign nationals with whom it interacts. The action may be consensual—the United States may offer financial assistance to a foreign political party whose ideology it favors or contract for the purchase of supplies needed at an overseas office— or nonconsensual—an American intelligence agent may engage in surveillance that violates the privacy rights of a foreign national under local law, but the foreign national is under no obligation to cooperate.

The modern form of the mutuality approach that I will defend extends constitutional rights to aliens abroad only in those situations in which the

United States claims an individual's obedience to its commands on the basis of its legitimate authority. The mutuality approach would not afford domestic constitutional rights to the residents of an adversary nation during armed hostilities; nor would it restrict an ideologically based policy of aid to foreign political parties.

The virtues of the mutuality-of-legal-obligation approach may be exhibited in a progression of contexts. This chapter will begin with the rights of U.S. citizens outside the states and then continue to the more controversial subject of the rights of aliens abroad.

CONSTITUTIONAL GEOGRAPHY AND THE RIGHTS OF CITIZENS

The Insular Cases

Before turning to truly extraterritorial contexts, we should devote a moment's attention to the Insular Cases, in which the turn-of-the-century Supreme Court diverged from the mutuality of obligation approach. From the normative perspective of the naturalist social contract tradition that underlay the U.S. Constitution, the Insular Cases were grievously wrong. For the federal government to acquire total governing power over new territories—more complete, in fact, than in the states—without the consent of the local population and without according them (or according transplanted citizens of the states) the rights reserved under the Constitution raises starkly the question of how the exercise of such governing power can be legitimated.

The Insular Cases did meet the naturalist tradition partway by recognizing and making judicially enforceable certain "fundamental" guarantees, seemingly the minimum core of natural rights. But, as the elder Harlan so patriotically protested, this constitutionalism was not *our* constitutionalism. Although the fundamental-rights approach of the Insular Cases bore some formal resemblance to the Fourteenth Amendment due process doctrine of its day, under which only fundamental provisions of the Bill of Rights applied to the states, this parallel does not excuse the Insular Cases. The populations of the states were already protected against the *federal* government by the entire Bill of Rights, and in theory they had full power to design state constitutional protections against their own state governments. The Insular Cases did not afford any vehicle for constitutional self-determination by the subject peoples.[b] And when one recognizes that the

---

[b] In one sense, the Insular Cases provided a vacuum in which Congress could, if it wished, allow subject peoples to design their own local institutions. But even where indigenous practices have been accommodated, the Insular Cases doctrine leaves them vulnerable to displacement at the will of Congress and gives local populations no vehicle for protecting themselves against federal power.

ultimate justification for this reversal of constitutional practice was to facilitate the emulation of European colonial powers and rule over peoples "unfit" for American citizenship, the lowering of normative standards seems all the more a betrayal.

Another reason why the Fourteenth Amendment analogy cannot excuse the Insular Cases doctrine is that the identification of constitutional provisions applicable in overseas territories has not kept pace with the identification of provisions applicable to the state governments. Courts do not employ an impartial concept of fundamentality to choose the rights most deserving of protection in both contexts. Fifth Amendment due process affords individuals in the less privileged territories fewer rights than Fourteenth Amendment due process.

It might be argued today that however wrong they were at the beginning of the century, the passage of time has woven the Insular Cases into the fabric of American constitutionalism. But from a contemporary perspective that claim also fails. No persuasive normative basis for the Insular Cases has been put forward, and the result in *Reid v. Covert*, not just Black's plurality opinion, severely undermined their foundation. It is hard to see the coherence of an approach that leads to the conclusion that American citizens cannot be tried by the federal government for capital offenses without jury trial in Japan but can be so tried in Puerto Rico.

Territoriality and the Rights of Citizens Abroad

The long survival of strict territoriality, however, had a severe logic of its own. The distinction between being inside and being outside the borders of the United States is not a constitutional irrelevancy. The Constitution is an artifact of an era of territorial nation-states, and that era is not yet over. The Constitution obviously intends that the United States will have a territory and that the federal government will place a high priority on maintaining its dominance vis-à-vis other nation-states in that territory. Text and legislative history confirm that the Fourteenth Amendment guarantees citizenship at birth only to persons born within United States territory, precisely because they are subject to the fullest measure of United States sovereignty.[2] The legal obligation of even citizens in foreign countries to comply with United States law, especially outside relatively tight-knit enclaves such as ships and military bases, is extremely difficult to administer and enforce. The difficulties may be especially severe when the citizen is a dual national residing in her other country of nationality. Thus, the conceptual dodge that was used to justify strict territoriality—that United States law was not binding of its own force, and so neither was the Constitution—did not wholly lack a basis in reality.

Nonetheless, relying on this difference of degree to make constitutional rights unavailable to citizens on the high seas or in foreign countries creates serious anomalies that become increasingly visible as the exercise of government power abroad becomes more frequent. First, deciding whether government action against an individual has occurred inside or outside the United States involves familiar difficulties of situs. For example, if the State Department declares that an individual is no longer a United States citizen, that action could be viewed as taking place at the location where the decision was made, at the location where the individual was at the time, or at the location where the decision first had practical consequences for the individual (for example, she was refused permission to board a flight from Paris to New York). Second, to the extent that the government is constitutionally bound within but not beyond its borders, it possesses substantial power to subvert constitutional limitations by choosing where and when to act against citizens who make the error of traveling or acquiring property abroad or of submitting to military service.

Given that the drafting of the Bill of Rights reflected inattention to the problematics of government activity abroad rather than a conscious effort to design entitlements solely for application within the territory, the overthrow of strict territoriality represents an appropriate evolutionary response to changes in the technology of transportation and communication, background international practices, and American self-assertion. The question then arises which constitutional rights are extraterritorially applicable. The mutuality of obligation approach respects the written Constitution by making all the rights it contains presumptively applicable; as an approach to interpretation it leaves room for textual references or other inputs to rebut the presumption.[c]

Although the mutuality approach combines the greatest degree of historical fidelity and contemporary normative appeal, even the antiquated strict territoriality rule had greater interpretive plausibility than the boundlessly flexible approach of Frankfurter and the younger Harlan. Frankfurter and Harlan's touchstone in applying the Constitution to federal action abroad was a "due process" approach equating with "fundamental fairness" in light of practicality, parallel to their approach to the incorporation of provisions of the Bill of Rights into the Fourteenth Amendment for application to the states. But their Fourteenth Amendment methodology had at least a tenuous textual grounding in the language of the Fourteenth Amendment, which explicitly commits the states to due process of law. The only provision of the Bill of Rights with a geographic referent is the

---

[c] For example, the requirement in Article I, Section 8 that "[e]xcises shall be uniform throughout the United States" need not apply to excises on extraterritorial transactions; the requirement in the Sixth Amendment that a jury be drawn from "the State and district wherein the crime shall have been committed" need not apply to crimes committed abroad.

venue clause of the Sixth Amendment; otherwise, the language of the Bill of Rights provides no reason for believing that the due process clause is any more applicable abroad than any other clause.

The global due process approach relies at most on a historical and structural argument: the development of an incorporation doctrine for the Fourteenth Amendment has created a hierarchy of fundamentality within the Bill of Rights. The existence of the hierarchy justifies the courts in turning back to disincorporate less fundamental rights vis-à-vis federal action abroad. But, like the Insular Cases doctrine, the global due process approach does not actually mirror the division into fundamental and nonfundamental rights employed under the Fourteenth Amendment.

The touchstone of global due process is government flexibility, not natural rights. The approach presumes that the language of the Constitution will not control federal action abroad, and it sets a low threshold of "impracticability." One can certainly sympathize in the abstract with the government's need not to be bound by impracticable constraints. Concretely, however, the doctrinal structure of most constitutional rights already includes accommodations to the government's legitimate interests. The practical consequences of extraterritorial location may be taken into account in determining the effect of a constitutional right, without ousting that right altogether at an initial stage.

By jettisoning claims of a substituted normative foundation in natural law, Frankfurter and Harlan further compounded the error of the Insular Cases. If justices no longer believe in objective natural rights, then they have even less justification for adopting an approach that tends, in Black's apt words, to "destroy the benefit of a written Constitution and undermine the basis of our Government."[3]

ALIENS ABROAD AFTER THE FALL OF TERRITORIALITY

Once the taboo against treating constitutional rights as effective beyond the nation's boundaries has been overcome, the question arises whether this development should be restricted to citizens. The legacy of the Alien Act debates includes the fundamental rejection of the claim that citizenship is the key to rights-bearing capacity under the Constitution. Moreover, not even the Insular Cases relied on a distinction between the rights of American citizens and the rights of subject peoples in the territories. Are the rights of aliens nonetheless wholly dependent on presence within the United States?

The Supreme Court finally gave a partial answer to this question in *United States v. Verdugo-Urquidez* (1990).[4] The majority denied that nonresident aliens have rights under the Fourth Amendment with regard to a

U.S. government search of their property abroad. Once more the justices were fragmented among different approaches. I will describe this contemporary debate and place it in context for the light it sheds on the analysis that follows.

Recent History

As the Bill of Rights expanded under the Warren Court and the early Burger Court, lower courts read *Reid v. Covert* broadly as confirming citizens' rights against federal action on the high seas and in foreign countries. A substantial body of criminal procedure cases resulted, as well as occasional noncriminal cases.[5] Some courts were hesitant to deny similar protection to aliens abroad,[6] and one well-known holding boldly provided such protection.[7] There were also a series of lower-court decisions, more difficult to characterize, affording the protection of constitutional rights to aliens in unusual territories that were subject to the governing power of the United States but where the United States was not sovereign. Such territories included the Panama Canal Zone, United Nations Trust Territories in the South Pacific, and the American Sector of West Berlin.[8]

By 1987, the American Law Institute was prepared to restate as to citizens: "The provisions of the United States Constitution safeguarding individual rights . . . generally limit governmental authority whether it is exercised in the United States or abroad." But it still regarded the rights of aliens as less certain.[9] At the same time, over the 1970s and 1980s, American self-confidence in global affairs was shrinking, and this era of limits prompted arguments that the United States could ill afford constitutional constraints not binding on its partners and rivals.[10]

Modern international law permits nations to apply their laws in certain circumstances to actions taken by noncitizens outside the nation's territory, because of the effects of those actions on the government, its territory, or sometimes even its citizens outside the territory. Since the Second World War, the United States has greatly increased its exercise of jurisdiction on these bases, often to the alarm of our European allies.[11] More recently, the United States has intensified its effort to combat the narcotics trade by prosecuting aliens for acts committed far outside the United States. Once these defendants have been brought to the United States for prosecution, courts have afforded them full substantive and procedural rights at trial under the Constitution, as even the strict territoriality rule would require.[12]

Courts were more divided, however, in responding to Fourth Amendment objections to search and seizure incidents occurring on the high seas or in foreign countries.[13] Such an incident finally gave the Supreme Court the occasion to address the extraterritorial rights of aliens in the post–*Reid v. Covert* world, in the 1990 case of *United States v. Verdugo-Urquidez.*[14] Verdugo-Urquidez was a Mexican drug lord being prosecuted for narcotics trafficking activities. By the time the case came to the Supreme Court, he had been convicted in a separate prosecution for involvement in the notorious torture-murder of DEA agent Enrique Camarena Salazar. Verdugo-Urquidez was seized by Mexican police and delivered into American custody at a California border station. The next day, while he was incarcerated in San Diego, DEA agents, in concert with Mexican police, searched his home in Mexicali, Mexico, and found business records of his narcotics-smuggling enterprise. A divided Ninth Circuit panel suppressed this evidence as having been seized in violation of the warrant clause of the Fourth Amendment. The Supreme Court reversed, with six justices (in three different opinions) agreeing that the search should be upheld because the warrant clause of the Fourth Amendment had no application to the search of a nonresident alien's property in a foreign country. Three justices dissented.

Chief Justice William Rehnquist's opinion was denominated the Opinion of the Court, and Justice Anthony Kennedy purported to concur in it, but Kennedy's concurring opinion diverged so greatly from Rehnquist's analysis and conclusions that Rehnquist seemed really to be speaking for a plurality of four.[15] Rehnquist marshaled a series of arguments in the membership tradition, which individually pointed toward different but overlapping conclusions: (1) that Verdugo-Urquidez had no Fourth Amendment rights at all, (2) that aliens have no Fourth Amendment rights with regard to United States government action abroad, and (3) that aliens have no constitutional rights whatsoever with regard to United States government action abroad.

Verdugo-Urquidez was unquestionably within the United States at the time the search in Mexico occurred. To say that he had no Fourth Amendment rights at all, therefore, would involve a retreat from the traditional mutuality of obligation approach to aliens' rights *within* the United States. Only four justices, however, lent credence to this argument; Kennedy expressly rejected it. Rehnquist engaged in a tentative "textual exegesis" of the Fourth Amendment's opening words: "The right of the people to be secure." He suggested that the phrase "the people" was used as a "term of art" in the Constitution and "refers to a class of persons who are part of a national community or who have otherwise developed sufficient connection with this country to be considered part of that community."[16] Verdugo-Urquidez, having been involuntarily brought into the United States shortly before the search, was not within this class.[d]

---

[d] The argument that a defendant has *no* Fourth Amendment rights because he is in the country involuntarily is shocking and unacceptable. To argue that searches of the body cavities of a prisoner in a San Diego jail who has recently been brought into the United States by force are unlimited by the Fourth Amendment would be a perversion of the notion of the moral relevance of consent. In one sense, this argument is deeply faithful to American tradition: slaves were involuntarily in the country, and they had no constitutional rights either.

Rehnquist next turned to the argument for the narrower proposition that nonresident aliens have no Fourth Amendment right against searches and seizures of their property abroad, which was what the opinion actually described itself as holding. He cited historical data including the Framers' primary concern with searches within the United States and their probable assumption that the Fourth Amendment did not limit searches and seizures on the high seas during the quasi-war with France in the 1790s. His opinion mentioned only seizures of foreign vessels, but the statutes and the cases of the period also involve seizures of American vessels trading with France.[17] If these data suggest anything, however, it is that *no one* has Fourth Amendment rights outside the nation's borders, which was the prevailing view under both the mutuality and the membership approach until *Reid v. Covert.*

The opinion reached stronger ground with a formalist argument from precedent: no prior case holds that aliens have constitutional rights against United States action abroad; some cases have denied that they have such rights; and the Insular Cases hold that even American citizens have less than the full set of constitutional rights in "unincorporated territories."[18] This is perfectly true. To find that aliens have extraterritorial constitutional rights would be an extension of prior law. *Reid v. Covert* does not *require* such an extension as a matter of precedent, because *Reid v. Covert* involved citizens. But that does not suffice to explain why the recognition of extraterritorial constitutional rights in *Reid v. Covert* does not destroy the persuasive power of the earlier precedents.

Finally, at the end of his opinion, Rehnquist gave two linked reasons why aliens should not have extraterritorial Fourth Amendment rights. First, grave uncertainties would be created for the United States' employment of armed force abroad in non-law-enforcement situations.[19] Second, conditions abroad often differ from local conditions in ways that would make the observance of constitutional requirements an inappropriate hindrance to law enforcement activities. "For better or worse, we live in a world of nation-states in which our Government must be able to 'functio[n] effectively in the company of sovereign nations.'"[20] At least as regards the Fourth Amendment, this is an unabashedly Hobbesian membership approach.

The diversity of arguments Rehnquist employed left the scope he intended for the Fourth Amendment very unclear. At times, especially in his textual argument, he appeared to assert that there was a single standard for determining who was included in the phrase "the people." At other times, he appeared to subscribe to a model of concentric circles, in which aliens progressed by degrees toward effective membership in the national community. He quoted Justice Robert Jackson's observation in *Johnson v. Eisentrager* that "[t]he alien . . . has been accorded a generous and ascending scale of rights as he increases his identity with our society."[21] The opinion's reasoning is self-contradictory concerning whether *resident* aliens are protected against unreasonable searches when they travel abroad.

Justice Kennedy purported to concur in the majority opinion but formulated his reasons quite differently. He denied that the reference to "the people" in the Fourth Amendment had any limiting significance. Kennedy maintained that "the Constitution does not create, nor do general principles of law create, any juridical relation between our country and some undefined, limitless class of noncitizens who are beyond our territory."[22] Things might be different extraterritorially with regard to citizens, "as to whom the United States has continuing obligations."[23] Kennedy explicitly positioned himself in the line of Harlan's concurrence in *Reid v. Covert*, tracking its reasoning and quoting it at length. He adopted the view that the question of what the Constitution requires abroad "can be reduced to the issue of what process is 'due' a defendant in the particular circumstances of a particular case."[24] Extending the Fourth Amendment's warrant requirement to extraterritorial searches of aliens' property would be "impracticable and anomalous." Kennedy apparently believed that this was always true as regards nonresident aliens, but he expressly left open the issue of extraterritorial searches of citizens' property.[25] In other respects, Kennedy wrote narrowly à la Harlan, agreeing to uphold the present search without stating categorically that nonresident aliens always lacked extraterritorial rights under the Fourth Amendment's "unreasonable searches" clause.

By limiting his conclusion to searches of nonresident aliens' property, Kennedy implicitly left open the applicability of the Warrant Clause to resident aliens traveling abroad. The context-specific character of the "due process"–type analysis could be compatible with a concentric circles model, in which the "limitless class of noncitizens who are beyond our territory" stood outside constitutional protection but aliens with closer relations to the United States received a progressively greater degree of constitutional protection.

The dissenters responded with mutuality of obligation arguments, although Justice William Brennan's opinion sometimes went further. A member of the *Reid v. Covert* plurality, Brennan placed his argument in that tradition, expressly referring to the requirements of "mutuality."

> Respondent is entitled to the protections of the Fourth Amendment because our Government, by investigating him and attempting to hold him accountable under United States criminal laws, has treated him as a member of our community for purposes of enforcing our laws. He has become, quite literally, one of the governed.[26]

Other portions of his opinion, however, suggested that security against unreasonable searches was a natural right incorporated by the Framers in the

Constitution, and that it might also restrict non-law-enforcement actions in pursuit of national security in peacetime.

Justice Harry Blackmun's brief dissent aligned itself with Brennan's mutuality of obligation argument but dissociated itself from any suggestion of broader applicability to circumstances in which the government did not "purport to exercise *sovereign* authority over the foreign national."[27] Blackmun, moreover, would limit the content of extraterritorial Fourth Amendment protection, at least as regards nonresident aliens, to the "unreasonable searches and seizures" clause; he expressed agreement with the government's argument that "an American magistrate's lack of power to authorize a search abroad renders the Warrant Clause inapplicable to the search of a noncitizen's residence outside this country."[28] A conclusion of this kind remains possible under the mutuality approach as an interpretation of a particular clause.[29]

Thus, *Verdugo-Urquidez* reflects the same lack of consensus about the proper scope of American constitutionalism as did *Reid v. Covert* and the first Insular Cases: substantial blocs of justices subscribed to opposing theories, and no single approach attracted a majority. The history of these disputes has revealed the political and jurisprudential assumptions underlying these varying approaches and demonstrates that the distance between Rehnquist's opinion and Kennedy's concurrence is wider than a superficial reading might suggest. All three of the dissenters have since left the Court, and for the present American law may face a choice between the Kennedy-Frankfurter-Harlan global due process approach and Rehnquist's Hobbesian membership approach. I will proceed to argue, however, that the area of agreement between the Brennan and Blackmun dissents—a form of the approach based on the mutuality of legal obligation—represents the best account of American constitutionalism.

Mutuality and Extraterritorial Obligation

Let us proceed directly to the hardest case: aliens outside the United States who have never been inside the United States. The United States has increasingly asserted the right to subject such persons to American law when their actions outside the country have effects within the country or on American citizens. If we ask how a constitution could legitimate the exercise of such power over aliens abroad, the social contract tradition provides three relevant alternatives.[30]

First, the mutuality of obligation approach affords the express protections of fundamental law, to the extent that their terms permit, as a condition for subjecting a person to the nation's law. Government's interference with the freedom or property of any human being must be justified, and when the justification relies on the individual's obligation to obey U.S.

law, the criteria for justification include government's respect for constitutional rights. Second, the minimum that a naturalist approach would tolerate would be extending to aliens abroad a supplementary fundamental law including only those protections directly required by natural law. Finally, a Hobbesian approach disdains the legitimation of the exercise of power outside the commonwealth, because "the Infliction of what evill soever, on an Innocent man, that is not a Subject, if it be for the benefit of the Commonwealth, and without violation of any former Covenant, is no breach of the Law of Nature."[31]

These options lead to a series of challenges that must be overcome by a defender of the mutuality approach as the best account of U.S. constitutionalism. First, some would claim that the question has already been framed too narrowly: constitutional rights constrain all government interaction with aliens, wherever it occurs, and regardless of whether the government justifies its interference with the alien on grounds of legal obligation. Second, some would claim that resort to the Constitution in this context is erroneous, because the United States Constitution does not contemplate any binding rights for aliens abroad. Third, some would claim that the mutuality approach aims in the right direction, but too generously. Express constitutional rights should not be presumptively applicable; instead, aliens abroad should be content with a much narrower set of constitutional rights selected by noninterpretive means.

In other words, mutuality of obligation must be compared with three rival theories of U.S. constitutionalism: universalism, Hobbism, and global due process. I will take them up in that order.

MUTUALITY OF OBLIGATION VERSUS UNIVERSALISM

One may think of the mutuality of obligation approach as identifying a sphere in which a nation's law operates, which was once defined in geographical terms but now is viewed more broadly. The modern version of the mutuality approach proposed here defines that sphere differently for citizens and for aliens; citizens are always subject to the nation's law, and so always protected by constitutional rights, whereas aliens are within the sphere either when they are within the nation's territory or on specific occasions when the nation attempts to exact obedience to its laws.

A universalist seeking support in social contract theory might offer a more expansive view of the mutuality approach. The universalist would argue that the relevant sphere is now the entire planet. There are federal statutes to which the United States demands universal obedience—foreign nationals abroad are legally forbidden to arrange for the smuggling of drugs into the United States, to counterfeit the coinage of the United States, and so forth—and the universalist would conclude that all the human beings on earth have become subjects of the American social contract. Accordingly, the United States would be required to recognize and respect their constitutional rights in all the contexts in which it interacts with them; not just when it seeks to apply its law, but also when it exercises military force against them or interacts consensually in a commercial or foreign aid context.

The rejection of universalism, in this guise or any other, as a methodology for interpreting the Constitution rests on both historical and normative grounds. The universalist's interpretation would transcend the concerns of a single social contract and bind the government to the rules of a just world order, regulating the international use of armed force and injustices arising from the global distribution of wealth. A constitution could serve that function, but nothing in the text or history of the United States Constitution suggests that it offers itself as a solution to this broader problem.

The Constitution confers war-making powers but contains no specification of the permissible occasions for their use. As Madison wrote in *The Federalist*, defending Congress's authority to raise armies in time of peace, "If a federal Constitution could chain the ambition or set bounds to the exertion of all other nations, then indeed might it prudently chain the discretion of its own government, and set bounds to the exertions for its own safety."[32] Similarly, the Constitution restricts the ability of United States officials to accept gifts from foreign nations but does not correspondingly limit United States efforts to purchase influence abroad.[33] The Constitution authorizes Congress to collect taxes to provide for the general welfare of the United States, without expressly binding the government to humanitarian foreign aid policies.[34] Although the United States has gained in strength and security since the eighteenth century, American constitutional tradition has persistently left open the substance of the United States' international relations, a fact reflected in the refusal to make international law as such constitutionally binding on Congress and the president.[35]

One may concede that a human being has moral rights against coercion or manipulation by other persons or groups that are not asserting sovereignty over her and still decline to adopt a universalist approach to the interpretation of constitutional rights. The individual-rights provisions of the Constitution do not purport to state moral duties that are owed by all persons and groups; rather they state more exacting requirements that American citizens considered necessary constraints on the government's exercise of sovereignty. Some of these requirements may also be universal obligations, but the Constitution includes too full a list to read as if they all were. For example, jury trial is not a universally necessary method of resolving disputes, and the requirements of religious and ideological neutrality read out of the speech and religion clauses of the First Amendment cannot be applied to all contexts of human interaction. It might make sense to design a two-track constitution that makes separately enforceable both the government's universal obligations and the broader set of obligations it incurs as sovereign. But the United States Constitution is not written that way. Universalism would overburden the government by attempting to enforce in the broader context constraints chosen for the narrower one.

Conversely, universalism could also pose dangers to constitutional rights at home. As has been recognized in other contexts, constitutional protections may suffer dilution when they are extended into areas previously thought outside their coverage. Arguments for limiting the rights in their new application have a way of filtering back to undermine the original core.[36]

Thus, constitutional rights should not be interpreted as restricting all government action against all persons in all places, even when the government does not assert its sovereignty over the individual. This does not mean that such uses of force or wealth are immune from demands for justification; it simply means that the standards of justification are not to be sought in the United States Constitution.

MUTUALITY OF OBLIGATION VERSUS HOBBISM

A Hobbesian would take Madison's caution against rigid constitutional restrictions on the raising of armies much further and deny constitutional rights in all circumstances to aliens abroad. This Hobbesian strain is easily identified in Chief Justice Rehnquist's *Verdugo-Urquidez* opinion: no minimum of personal or domestic privacy remains enforceable through the core of the Fourth Amendment, and the alien's rightlessness results from his nonmembership in the community.[e] In characterizing this position as Hobbesian, I am not placing exaggerated emphasis either on the location of rights in a constitution or on judicial review. Rehnquist did not argue that the contours of Fourth Amendment rights abroad were nonjusticiable or that aliens' privacy rights were adequately protected by nonconstitutional law. He specifically encouraged the executive and legislative branches to feel that they were not constitutionally constrained in searching aliens' property abroad and that there were no limits on their power unless they chose to create some.

The standard defense of a Hobbesian approach to extraterritorial action rests on national insecurity. The Commonwealth is in a state of nature, that is, war, with the rest of the world, and its only external obligations are those resulting from explicit promises. Hobbesians fear being unilaterally

[e] Portions of Rehnquist's opinion contemplate that some aliens—for example, lawful permanent residents—would be members of the community, but the entire opinion takes a Hobbesian attitude to those who are not members.

disarmed.[37] But Hobbes understood well the consequences of this theory for legal obligation: a Commonwealth may exercise force against outsiders, but persons within the territory of Commonwealth B generally have no obligation to obey the laws of Commonwealth A.[38] Thus the Hobbesian argument would enable the government to withhold constitutional rights, but only at the price of delegitimating its claim to obedience.

The Hobbesian also faces another obstacle. He must explain how one could justify grafting a Hobbesian approach to the rights of aliens abroad onto an otherwise anti-Hobbesian constitutional tradition.

The Hobbesian might argue that interactions between a government and aliens outside its territory, unlike interactions between the government and its citizens or aliens within its territory, lie outside the sphere of social contract analysis because of the absence of consent. Claims about the actual or tacit consent of citizens and of aliens within the territory to government authority may be predicated on retention of citizenship or entering or failing to leave the territory, but when a nation extends its laws to aliens abroad, there is no action by which these aliens can withdraw themselves from the class of the governed and conversely no act that can be interpreted as expressing actual or tacit consent.

Given the impossibility of finding consent, the Hobbesian would assert that contractarian arguments could not justify legislative power over aliens abroad and that the Constitution should not be extended in an attempt at justification that is doomed to failure. Many would respond, however, that this argument rests on a distinction without a difference; authors since Hume have emphasized the strained character of claims of actual or tacit consent, as opposed to hypothetical consent, even of later generations of citizens.[39]

The Hobbesian cannot shrug off these criticisms by asserting that regardless of what more careful thinkers have concluded, American constitutional tradition has incorporated this flawed dependence on actual or tacit consent. Such an assertion would be belied by juxtaposing the Hobbesian approach to the rights of nonresident aliens abroad with the treatment of the same individuals as criminal defendants or civil litigants in the courts of the United States. If we take seriously the Hobbesian claim that these aliens have no constitutional rights abroad at all, then it would seem to follow that there are no constitutional limits on the content of the laws to which they may be subjected,[40] at least so long as the imposition of sanctions does not take place within the United States.[41] For example, the United States could make it a crime for a foreign national abroad to publish a defense of the moral propriety of international terrorism, to terminate her pregnancy by an American male without his consent, to refuse the CIA permission to install listening devices in her home, or to preach so-called fundamentalist Islam. Congress could set up tribunals on military bases or naval vessels, where the procedure at trial would be free of constitutional constraints. Executing the sentence abroad might provide the greatest flexibility, but so long as the punishment were not cruel and unusual, it might even be possible to execute it in the United States.[42]

In contrast, American courts have not treated foreign defendants brought involuntarily into United States territory for trial virtually as enemies to be dealt with at will. Courts have generally assumed that their authority over such defendants must be exercised within the bounds of constitutional constraint, including the constitutional rights that govern trial procedure, and that the substance of the criminal statutes said to have been violated abroad is subject to judicial review.

Why should the nonresident alien defendant become protected by the Bill of Rights when brought into the United States for trial? As Chief Justice Rehnquist accurately observed in *Verdugo-Urquidez*, the fact of being extradited or kidnapped into the United States does not itself signify the alien's undertaking of any voluntary, consensual relation with the United States. Conceivably the more effective subjection of the defendant to obligations of compliance with United States law after arrival in the United States favors the extension of constitutional rights to the defendant. But civil defendants, whose presence in the United States is not required for the litigation to proceed at all, are also entitled to constitutional protections at trial. And in the civil context, the Supreme Court has held that the very absence of minimum contacts between an alien defendant and the jurisdiction creates a due process right to have the court dismiss the lawsuit.[43]

Thus the character of the defendant as a nonresident alien, or even as an alien who has *never* entered the United States, does not determine the applicability of a wide range of constitutional provisions when the courts of the United States are proceeding to judgment. Before *Reid v. Covert*, this phenomenon could be rationalized by treating the situs of the litigation as determinative under a theory of the territoriality of constitutional obligation, but that argument can no longer be sincerely employed.

Instead, as I have argued, the observance of constitutional limitations in a trial in federal district court against a nonresident alien defendant rests on the role that the system of constitutional rights plays in legitimating the United States' assertion of legal obligation as a basis for exercising coercion against the alien. That same consideration would also require its application in an extraterritorial tribunal of the United States.

MUTUALITY OF OBLIGATION VERSUS GLOBAL DUE PROCESS

Unlike the Hobbesian approach, which subjects aliens to sovereign command without corresponding rights against the sovereign, the global due process approach originated by Frankfurter and Harlan, and further applied by Justice Kennedy, envisions some judicially enforceable constitutional limitations on government action abroad. Not only is it, generally speaking, a form of constitutionalism, but it also has an obvious pedigree in the Insular Cases, which imposed on the unincorporated territories a fundamental law including minimal protections of natural rights. Global due process may now be the dominant U.S. approach to aliens' rights abroad.

Nonetheless, global due process as currently practiced is merely analogous to, rather than equal to, an approach based on a core of natural rights or international human rights. The global due process approach embodies judicial discretion to reject, after deferential inquiry, the applicability of constitutional rights to government action abroad in situations where they would appear "impracticable and anomalous."[44] The precise content of this standard cannot presently be specified, but its permissiveness may best be illustrated by Frankfurter and Harlan's conclusion that military trials are permissible for noncapital cases involving civilians abroad and by their view that it justifies the departures from constitutional practice approved in the Insular Cases.[45]

The argument against global due process as regards aliens is largely an overlay of two arguments already made: the argument against Hobbesian rightlessness and the criticisms of the Frankfurter-Harlan positivization of the Insular Cases approach for citizens in their concurrences in *Reid v. Covert*. Admittedly, if global due process is all that is required for citizens abroad, neither the text of the Constitution nor the tradition of its interpretation provides support for a claim that aliens abroad are entitled to *more*.[46]

If, however, broad considerations of practicality do not suffice to oust the written Constitution for aliens within the United States or for American citizens (including dual nationals) residing abroad, then why should they have that effect for aliens abroad? An additional relevant factor might be that international law, albeit not constitutionally binding on Congress, places somewhat stricter limits on the circumstances in which the United States may apply its laws extraterritorially to aliens residing in foreign territory than to American citizens residing abroad. Although these limits do not eliminate the need for legitimating United States authority over aliens abroad, it might be argued that this lesser authority can be legitimated with a lesser set of rights.

Yet these factors have not prompted courts to depart from the Constitution once an alien defendant is brought within the United States for trial. Compliance with constitutional rights as written, despite the locus of the offense charged, does complicate the task of making American law enforceable against persons outside the nation's borders. For example, when the government attempts to prove the commission of a crime abroad, its reduced capacity for collecting evidence abroad creates substantial difficulties, and moving the trial to the United States may increase rather than decrease the difficulty of proof. Allowing the defendant to refuse to testify against herself eliminates one of the best sources of evidence likely to be found in the United States and often gives the defendant a right she would not have had under her own legal system. Nonetheless, alien defendants extradited or kidnapped into the United States enjoy the Fifth Amendment privilege against self-incrimination. They have no more been relegated to a flexible due process approach to their rights at trial than to a state of Hobbesian rightlessness. Within the United States, via unthinking application of the old territoriality rule, the written Constitution governs at trial.

If alien defendants have constitutional rights, then those rights should not be subject to diminution by the government's manipulation of situs. The narrow holding in *Verdugo-Urquidez* would not create incentives for manipulative behavior because it involved a search of immovable property, whose situs is fixed. But a global due process approach could create incentives for the government to interrogate arrested aliens or search their persons before bringing them to the United States or possibly even to try them outside the United States in order to avoid triggering constitutional limitations that would otherwise apply. Proponents of global due process would perhaps respond that concerns about manipulation are less compelling in the case of nonresident aliens, who might be considered as "normally" located abroad, than in the case of citizens, whose "normal" presence inside the United States might indicate a different baseline.

Criticism of the global due process approach should not be seen as a dismissal of the concern that the government not be bound by truly impracticable restraints. This concern can be accommodated in extraterritorial situations, as it already is in domestic situations, by a contextual assessment of the factors impairing the government's achievement of its interests. Constitutional rights are rarely absolute but usually yield to pressing government needs upon showings of necessity, reasonableness, or exigent circumstances. Both the Fourth Amendment prohibition of unreasonable searches and the Fourth Amendment's Warrant Clause invite such analysis. Particular problems arising from the location or the allegiances of individuals may properly influence evaluations of reasonableness or exigency. Thus, a constitutional right may sometimes have disparate consequences as applied to aliens and citizens abroad, even though the right is not declared unavailable to aliens.

More fundamentally, it is not clear how any branch of government, and in particular a positivist Supreme Court, can make the trade-offs necessary for designing a separate extraterritorial constitution for aliens or a progression of separate constitutions for different categories of aliens based on their proximity to full membership. Frankfurter's confidence that he could carry out a due process project for the rights of citizens against the federal government in the international context obviously mirrored his similar attitude toward the rights of persons against the states under the due process clause of the Fourteenth Amendment. In the latter context, history did not vindicate Frankfurter's confidence—ultimately, he was unable to communicate any objective basis for his choices, and his rival Hugo Black had increasing success in incorporating provisions of the Bill of Rights into the Fourteenth Amendment. The relatively greater degree of objectivity, as well as the greater degree of textual support, argues in favor of applying the Constitution as written under the mutuality of obligation approach.

Thus global due process presents more a political compromise than an elaboration of principle or an act of constitutional interpretation. It may develop a pedigree in constitutional case law through the passage of time, particularly now that Chief Justice Rehnquist has shifted emphasis to the concurrences in *Reid v. Covert*. Advocates who consider half a loaf better than none may accept it, although the Constitution and its history afford more support to the full loaf of the mutuality approach.

Before leaving the subject of global due process, a defense of the mutuality of obligation approach should also address the normatively sounder model from which global due process derives: the model that extends a minimal constitutional protection of natural rights to aliens abroad. In comparison with this latter model, the global due process approach is asking the wrong question: the Court should not be inquiring as to which constraints present problems of practicality, but rather as to which rights a government must respect in order to justify its claim to obedience.

Admittedly, no modern justice has argued for this approach, a fact attributable in part to positivistic jurisprudential assumptions.[47] The difficulty of its judicial implementation would also be daunting. One possibility might be to adopt as aliens' extraterritorial constitutional rights the minimum standards of international human rights law. (I mean this description literally: to adopt international human rights norms as constitutionally binding, beyond the power of any branch of government to infringe.)[48] Those standards, however, develop over time, and direct incorporation of international law into the Constitution would stand in tension with the United States' long-standing version of a dualist tradition: unlike the constitutions of certain other nations, the United States Constitution does not bind the national legislature to comply with its obligations under international law.[49] Moreover, Supreme Court majorities have denied the constitutional status of certain internationally protected rights, including civil and political rights, and especially economic and social human rights, even for citizens.[50]

The other alternative is for the Court itself to determine aliens' natural rights and the minimum government machinery necessary to protect them. This task may be more complicated than simply weeding through the Bill of Rights. Eliminating an individual right also increases the reach of the authority that the remaining rights must justify, and by definition aliens abroad enjoy no compensating political rights.

The product would be an unwritten constitution with a vengeance. It is hard to see why the justices would think that this task had been assigned to them or that they could perform it well.

Chapter Seven

CROSSING THE BORDER

T HE MODERN recognition that aliens both inside and outside the borders of the United States enjoy the protection of certain constitutional rights should also inform the analysis of their rights in crossing those borders. In other words, the anomalous position of immigration law in American constitutional law must be reevaluated.

The need for reevaluation does not depend on the acceptance of the mutuality of obligation approach to constitutional rights proposed in this book; rather, it follows from any approach to constitutional interpretation that recognizes *some* constitutional rights for aliens outside the borders, including the global due process approach of Justice Kennedy. The particular substantive constraints on immigration law may vary depending on which approach governs the inquiry, although the ultimate answers given will also be influenced by other interpretive factors and value judgments.

Current constitutional doctrine is unclear about whether the constitutional rights of aliens impose constraints on the substantive criteria adopted by Congress for the admission, exclusion, and deportation of aliens. In fact, current doctrine is ambiguous in two different respects: it is unclear whether the rights of aliens impose judicially enforceable constraints on immigration policy, and, if not, it is unclear whether such constraints do not exist or are merely outside the realm of judicial enforcement. It is therefore necessary to separate the question of the legal existence of constitutional constraints from the question of their judicial enforceability.

The nature of the ambiguity has changed over the years. From the late nineteenth century until the early 1970s, the Supreme Court declined to engage in judicial review of immigration policy. In two leading cases of the 1970s, however, the Court allowed the rights of citizens affected by the exclusion of an alien to justify a narrowly limited form of judicial review of the criteria for exclusion.[1] Lower courts have sometimes assumed that the rights of the aliens themselves could also justify this limited form of judicial review, but the Supreme Court has not spoken clearly to the issue.

The ambiguity concerning judicial enforceability is not new but dates from the seminal *Chinese Exclusion Case* (1889). When the Supreme Court has declined to review immigration legislation, it has been unclear whether the refusal resulted from Congress's absolute freedom to choose or from a determination that the Constitution assigned to Congress itself the power to judge the constitutional objection as a "political question."

This chapter will explore whether aliens' rights can give rise to valid constitutional questions about immigration policy before discussing which branch of government has the authority to answer such questions. For the most part, I will limit the inquiry here to *substantive* immigration law—grounds of admission, exclusion, and deportation—and not immigration *procedure*, which raises problems of its own.[2]

Do Constitutional Rights of Aliens Constrain Immigration Policy?

The Unconvincing Arguments for Absolute Discretion

A variety of reasons have been offered in support of the conclusion that substantive criteria for admission or deportation are not constrained by constitutional limitations. These include the nature of national sovereignty and independence, the character of alien visitors as guests of the nation, preservation of national identity, and the rightlessness of aliens outside the national territory. At the same time, these arguments have sometimes been presented in a manner that suggests a limitation on the power of judicial review rather than a denial of constitutional constraint.

The starting point remains Justice Stephen Field's opinion for a unanimous Supreme Court in *Chae Chan Ping v. United States* (1889), also known as the *Chinese Exclusion Case*.[3] The decision upheld the constitutionality of Congress's absolute ban on the admission of Chinese laborers, even as applied to a long-time resident who had temporarily returned to China in reliance on a government certificate guaranteeing his entitlement to reenter the United States.[4] Historically, the decision was influenced by the same racist assumptions as the Insular Cases (1901),[5] but it set forth more general reasoning in support of congressional power. Field explained:

> That the government of the United States, through the action of the legislative department, can exclude aliens from its territory is a proposition which we do not think open to controversy. Jurisdiction over its own territory is to that extent an incident of every independent nation. It is a part of its independence. If it could not exclude aliens it would be to that extent subject to the control of another power.[6]

He added:

> To preserve its independence, and give security against foreign aggression and encroachment, is the highest duty of every nation, and to attain these ends nearly all other considerations are to be subordinated. It matters not in what form such aggression and encroachment come, whether from the foreign nation acting in its

national character or from vast hordes of its people crowding in upon us. The government, possessing the powers which are to be exercised for protection and security, is clothed with authority to determine the occasion on which the powers shall be called forth; and its determination, so far as the subjects affected are concerned, are necessarily conclusive upon all its departments and officers.[7]

It is worthwhile to disentangle four propositions from this argument: (1) The independence and sovereignty of the nation entail its absolute control over the entry of aliens into its territory. (2) The migration of persons from one nation to another may be treated as if it were a transaction between the two governments, governed by extraconstitutional rules. (3) The independence and identity of the nation must not be adulterated or overwhelmed by the addition of uninvited aliens. (4) The degree of threat is for the political branches, not the judiciary, to evaluate.

The Supreme Court extended Field's reasoning to support a judicially unreviewable power to deport aliens already residing in the United States in *Fong Yue Ting v. United States* (1893).[8] Field dissented from that extension and added a fifth proposition to distinguish between the exclusion power and the deportation power: (5) Excluded aliens have not yet come within the national territory, and constitutional rights have no extraterritorial application.[9] The majority, however, maintained that "[t]he right of a nation to expel or deport foreigners, who have not been naturalized or taken any steps toward becoming citizens of the country, rests upon the same grounds, and is as absolute and unqualified as the right to prohibit and prevent their entrance into the country."[10]

Of these five propositions, the fourth concerns the assignment of decisional authority to Congress or the courts; it will be discussed in the next section. If we examine the other propositions in order, it appears than none of them justifies unlimited power to exclude or expel aliens.[11]

The independence and sovereignty of the nation entail its absolute control over the entry of aliens into its territory.   Field's conception of national sovereignty reflected the worldview of late-nineteenth-century international law, which was characterized by unflinching positivism, expansive notions of sovereignty, and the denial that individuals could be "subjects" (or rights holders) in international law.[12] The natural law presuppositions of Enlightenment writers on international law were in eclipse, and they remained so until the revival of human rights law in the wake of the Second World War.[13]

One can readily agree that the sovereignty and independence of the United States would be impaired if other nations could unilaterally force it to accept or retain their citizens without its consent. But the consent expressed through the making of international law and treaties in the community of nations is also a form of national consent. In the postwar era, international human rights norms may impose limits on a nation's discretion to expel or exclude aliens.[14] Sovereignty is a more relativized concept today, and absolute control over the movement of persons in its territory is no longer regarded as a necessary ingredient of sovereignty.

Furthermore, Field's argument in the *Chinese Exclusion Case* conflated the sovereignty of the nation with the power of the federal government. In the United States, the people are sovereign, not the government, and the Constitution embodies limits that the people have placed on the power of government. Our national sovereignty does not entail the absolute right of the federal government to exclude *citizens* from the national territory. The independence and sovereignty of the nation are also consistent with the existence of constitutional limits on the federal government's power to exclude aliens, designed to respect the rights of those aliens or of citizens wishing to interact with them. Other Western democracies, such as France and Germany, recognize constitutional limits on their governments' power to control immigration.[15]

Field's argument assumes national solidarity in rejecting the alien and overlooks the existence of individual citizens. It treats an alien as an invader if she is not invited by the nation, although citizens may have invited her, and it has led to the assumption that an admitted alien is a guest of the nation rather than of an individual host. This "guest theory"[16] has been used to characterize the government's admission of the alien as a retractable privilege, comparable to a private landowner's invitation, instead of characterizing the exclusion of the alien as an interference with the personal liberty of the alien or of the relatives, friends, or business associates whom the alien has really come to visit. With proper attribution, the landowner analogy could become more illuminating. The federal government does not own all the land in the United States either; it merely has some powers of regulation over most of it. Similarly, the federal government is most often not the alien's host, but rather a gatekeeper. The government's power to exclude or expel the alien should therefore be qualified to the extent that the alien's freedom of movement and the host's freedom of association are included in constitutionally protected liberty. Field recognized this point only a few years later in *Fong Yue Ting*, arguing in dissent that Congress did not have absolute power to deport aliens once they had entered the territory where their constitutional rights attached.

Thus, the external sovereignty argument for unlimited power over immigration was flawed to begin with and carries even less persuasive force today. Sovereignty over territory may give the government power to regulate entry in order to prevent harms that would result from the arrival in the territory of particular aliens, such as crime or the spread of disease, or from the arrival of too many aliens, such as overloading the economy or government services. But an absolute right to exclude each alien for good reasons, bad reasons, or no reasons is not inherent in sovereignty.

The migration of persons from one nation to another may be treated as if it were a transaction between the two governments, governed by extra-constitutional rules.   The assimilation of immigration to foreign aggression in the *Chinese Exclusion Case* employs the common metaphor of an "alien invasion" and treats a foreign national as if she were an agent of her government regardless of the actual relations between them. This approach comports less with reality than with the forms of nineteenth-century international law, which perceived only nations, not individuals, as subjects.

As the Supreme Court elevated immigration control from a form of domestic regulation to a form of international interaction, it appeared to change the governing standards from domestic law to international law. The Court sought the extent of the federal government's power in the "accepted maxim[s] of international law" or the "general principles of public law" rather than in the U.S. Constitution.[17] Although earlier cases of the 1870s and 1880s categorized immigration control as a regulation of foreign commerce within the enumerated powers of Congress,[18] the *Chinese Exclusion Case* has come to stand for the idea of immigration control as an unenumerated, or even extraconstitutional, power inherent in nationhood.

In essence, this approach echoes the extreme Federalists' argument in favor of the Alien Act of 1798. As Judge Alexander Addison had contended, "[P]ower over aliens is to be measured, not by internal and municipal law, but by external and national law [that is, the law of nations]. It affects not the people of the United States, parties and subjects to the constitution; but foreign governments, whose subjects the aliens are."[19] The Federalists had applied this argument to aliens *within* United States territory, denying that they had any constitutional rights whatever; as we saw in Chapter Four, the Supreme Court firmly rejected that interpretation of the Constitution in the nineteenth century, even in the context of immigration procedure. Justices Field and Brewer attempted to reconcile the existence of aliens' rights within the territory with an absolute power of exclusion by insisting on the extraterritorial character of exclusion. Their brethren in the majority, however, who inferred an absolute power to deport as well as to exclude, had no such avenue for reconciling these fundamentally inconsistent approaches.

The notion of extraconstitutional foreign relations powers resurfaced occasionally in later years, as in Justice Oliver Wendell Holmes's suggestion in *Missouri v. Holland* (1920) that the treaty power might not be bound by the Constitution,[20] and in Justice George Sutherland's theory of preconstitutional sovereignty vested in the president in *United States v. Curtiss-Wright Export Corp.* (1936).[21] Today, however, the Supreme Court more frequently insists that "[t]he United States is entirely a creature of the Constitution. Its power and authority have no other source. It can only act in accordance with all the limitations imposed by the Constitution."[22]

Thus, the claim that immigration regulation rests on an extraconstitutional power conflicts with fundamental assumptions of constitutionalism in the United States. The claim that constitutional rights are irrelevant to immigration regulation because migration concerns the relations between governments and not the government's relations with individuals is both obviously false and inconsistent with other aspects of the legal treatment of immigration.

The independence and identity of the nation must not be adulterated or overwhelmed by the addition of uninvited aliens. Field justified Chinese exclusion in part by invoking fantasies of an American civilization overwhelmed by the immigration of more numerous Chinese who refused "to assimilate with our people or to make any change in their habits or mode of living."[23] In practical terms, the threat did not exist and in any event would not have justified the exclusion or expulsion of the modest number of Chinese already residing in the United States.[24] But in the abstract, the concern is a legitimate one, as the European appropriation of North America may demonstrate.

In a democracy, unlike an absolute monarchy, the populace constitutes a self-governing political community. The distribution of membership in the community determines the electoral inputs that influence the government's policy choices. Moreover, if the community does not perceive itself as artificially constructed or accidental, it may generate a distinctive national identity through a combination of political and broader social processes. The distribution of membership in the community provides some of the boundaries for this process of forming national identity and is itself one of the ingredients of national identity.

At the same time, political communities are not hermetically sealed from outside influences. Their domestic politics may be affected by occurrences and intellectual developments beyond their borders. National identities are dynamic, not static, and are similarly subject to external contributions. Still, at the extremes it would seem possible to distinguish the slow drift of national identity from the sharp discontinuity of a conquest.

The question then is whether the preservation of the relative autonomy of domestic politics and national identity requires an absolute government power to exclude and expel aliens. *Some* power to control access to membership would appear necessary if a democratic community wishes to maintain its independence and continuity. *Some* power to control the long-term settlement of aliens would also appear necessary, because a minority citizenry is unlikely to remain dominant over a majority of disenfranchised residents indefinitely—even if this could be considered democracy.

These considerations do not yet justify an absolute power over exclusion and expulsion. One might continue to investigate whether a national identity could be so fragile, or whether its symbolic boundaries could be so essential, that every uninvited alien would threaten the national identity in the tautological way in which the obligation to admit an uninvited alien contradicts absolute sovereignty.

It is more important, however, to focus specifically on the United States' national identity and the United States' independence. The claim that the independence and identity of the United States require a power to exclude and expel aliens that is immune from constitutional limitation overlooks the central place of the United States Constitution itself in defining the national identity.[25] Whatever may be true of other countries, the reconciliation of majority desires with individual rights is part of the American national identity and the American conception of self-government.[26] Self-preservation does not require that our government be free to ignore those principles whenever it regulates immigration.

Thus, the preservation of independence and identity does not justify an unlimited power over immigration, particularly in the United States.

Excluded aliens have not yet come within the national territory, and constitutional rights have no extraterritorial application. The outdated character of the territoriality argument has been a major theme of this book. The seminal immigration cases were decided at the turn of the last century, when the dogma of a territorially limited Constitution prevailed.

In fact, the territoriality argument always involved a slight fudge, resting on unstated policy grounds. The exclusion cases were habeas corpus cases, brought by aliens inspected at ports of entry but already within U.S. territory. Deeming those aliens extraterritorial served the practical goal of giving the government an opportunity to apply laws that would have been subject to no constitutional constraint if the government had been able to inspect passengers in midocean. Holmes summarized this legal fiction in *United States v. Ju Toy* (1905), explaining how an entering passenger could have no due process right to fair procedures in the adjudication of his claim of U.S. citizenship.

> In view of the cases which we have cited it seems no longer open to discuss the question propounded as a new one. Therefore we do not analyze the nature of the right of a person presenting himself at the frontier for admission. *In re Ross*, 140 U.S. 453, 464. But it is not improper to add a few words. The petitioner, although

physically within our boundaries, is to be regarded as if he had been stopped at the limit of our jurisdiction and kept there while his right to enter was under debate.[27]

Holmes's invocation of the territoriality argument in *Ju Toy* illustrates that it remained relevant to the constitutional analysis of immigration law at the turn of the century, even though the majority in *Fong Yue Ting* had rejected Field's argument that considerations of territoriality favored constitutional limitations on the power to deport aliens who were already present.

The territoriality argument should have collapsed once the proposition of *In re Ross* (1891), that "[t]he Constitution can have no operation in another country," was rejected. The claim that aliens outside the United States have no right to enter the United States may or may not be correct, but it can no longer be based on the proposition that while they are outside the United States they have no constitutional rights at all. Instead, it is necessary to focus on the question what rights aliens have outside the United States, and how these relate to their ability to cross the border.

Freedom to Enter, Side Constraints, and Freedom to Remain

Three separate inquiries should be distinguished here: whether aliens in general possess a constitutional right to enter the United States, whether there are special circumstances in which exclusion or expulsion would infringe some other constitutional right of particular aliens, and whether aliens already present possess a constitutional right to remain. The first inquiry concerns the scope of the right to liberty in the sense of freedom of movement. The second inquiry concerns the side constraints on the regulation of migration. The third inquiry combines features of both. I will undertake these inquiries in turn and discuss the interaction of each with both the mutuality of obligation approach and the global due process approach.

FREEDOM TO ENTER

Immigration case law is rife with assertions that admission to the United States is a privilege and never a right. That characterization would follow as a corollary from the assumption that the government possessed an absolute and unqualified power over immigration. If one concludes instead that the arguments for government power over immigration support only a qualified power, then the question recurs whether admission may be a right—not necessarily an absolute right prevailing over all contrary considerations, but a prima facie right that cannot be infringed without adequate justification.

The substance of the proposed right involves a special case of the generally recognized right of freedom of movement. In nonconstitutional terms, freedom of movement includes freedom from physical restraint and freedom to go where one pleases, subject to respect for the rights of others. These are classic examples of natural liberty.

Freedom of movement is also one of the central historical meanings of the liberty protected by the due process clauses of the Fifth and Fourteenth Amendments. Freedom from physical restraint has been shielded by the writ of habeas corpus. Indeed, the Supreme Court has always recognized that an alien denied entry is sufficiently restrained of liberty to support the issuance of a writ of habeas corpus to inquire into the lawfulness of the restraint.[28] The modern Supreme Court has recognized freedom of interstate travel as a fundamental constitutional right, and freedom of international travel as an aspect of liberty under the due process clause.[29] Congress has declared the right of expatriation to be "a natural and inherent right of all people."[30] Aliens, like citizens, possess the right of freedom of movement within the United States,[31] and outside the United States they should possess the right not to be physically restrained by the United States and not to have their liberty of movement within other countries restricted by the United States.[32] These analogies may suggest that a qualified right to enter the United States should also exist.

The right to freedom of movement is not, however, a uniform concept in American constitutional law. Different forms of freedom of movement vary in the intensity of their protection. The Supreme Court has strictly protected the right to interstate travel, partly because it expresses the unity of the national territory and the equality of status among the citizens of the several states in addition to a human right of locomotion.[33] Physical restraint, though the severest restriction of freedom of movement, is less rigorously protected; in fact, Supreme Court case law does not reveal a consistent approach to the methodology of review.[34] The citizen's right to international travel may amount to only a liberty interest, "subject to reasonable government regulation."[35] The Supreme Court has not had occasion to spell out the standards governing interference with a citizen's right to permanent expatriation.

Whether these parallels can support the existence of a freedom of entry may depend on the resolution of a different disputed issue of due process methodology. Justice Antonin Scalia has contended that in interpreting the due process clause, the Court must "refer to the most specific level at which a relevant tradition protecting, or denying protection to, the asserted right can be identified."[36] On this view, freedom of movement could be dissolved into a series of more specific constituent instances, or a right of entry could be excluded from the general freedom of movement as a historical exception. More often, however, justices do not regard history as determinative of the scope of a right; instead they demand a contemporary normative justification for its contours.[37]

The reliability of history as a guide to the interpretation of the due process clause in this connection is also questionable because the Supreme Court has already rejected the eighteenth- and nineteenth-century understandings of liberty of movement in the case of citizens. As we saw in Chapter Three, antebellum constitutional thinking tended to attribute to each state similar authority over migration across its borders from abroad and from sister states. Freedom of movement was denied to the poor, whether aliens or citizens. Even the banishment of citizens for crime was permitted. After all these practices have yielded to freedom of movement, the accompanying restrictions on aliens should also be subject to question.

A general right to freedom of entry would presumably amount to no more than a liberty interest subject to reasonable, or even rational, limitations. If the right of citizens to travel outside the borders of the United States receives only that level of constitutional protection, then the right of aliens to travel into the United States would be no stronger. The exercise of a general liberty to enter the United States for purposes of business or pleasure would seem to be no more fundamental than the activities of business or pleasure in which the traveler intends to engage; ordinarily, such activities are subject to rational regulation.

An interpretation of the Constitution based upon the mutuality of obligation approach might or might not recognize a liberty interest in freedom of entry. That approach would disqualify some but not all of the arguments against freedom of entry. The simple territoriality argument would fail, and a friendly visitor would not be equated with an invading agent of a hostile government. Although the mutuality approach asserts fidelity to the written Constitution, that document is so laconic regarding freedom of movement that textual methods of interpretation yield little guidance about its scope.

Under the mutuality approach, the government's attempt to restrict an alien's entry would be viewed as an interference with natural liberty grounded in an assertion of legal obligation, and would therefore activate constitutional limitations on behalf of the alien. The early case law itself emphasizes that the exclusion of aliens is an exercise of control over them, grounded in sovereignty over territory. The alien should therefore be able to assert whatever constitutional rights she has, including a liberty interest in freedom of entry if one exists. Because location by itself is not determinative, that liberty interest should be available regardless of whether the alien was being deported or excluded. If the alien is merely being denied a visa at a foreign consulate, then the government has not yet exercised physical force against the alien. Nonetheless, the visa application is part of a unified process for determining which aliens will be detained at the border or prevented from boarding an airplane or other vehicle. It is therefore appropriate to view the denial of a visa as functionally similar to the denial of entry that it foreshadows.

Under a global due process approach, an alien abroad could claim only those rights that are fundamental, or only those rights whose extension to aliens abroad would not be "impracticable and anomalous." A global due process analyst could well conclude that a liberty for all persons to enter the United States was not fundamental, or that recognizing that liberty as a constitutionally protected right would be "impracticable and anomalous." The enormous numbers of potentially immigrating aliens and the wide range of political, military, environmental, medical, and economic factors that could generate efforts to enter the United States might lead the analyst to conclude that recognizing the right would be impracticable, particularly if the standard of review would have been reasonableness rather than rationality. (It is difficult to see how a requirement of mere rationality could ever be impracticable.) The global due process analyst might use traditional assumptions concerning the relationships among individuals, their states of nationality, and foreign states to characterize a right of entry as anomalous.

Given the flexibility and context-specific nature of global due process analysis, however, there might be particular categories of aliens for whom liberty of entry would not be considered impracticable and anomalous, such as returning residents, relatives of United States citizens, or (less likely in the current climate) refugees. If global due process analysts imagine concentric circles of progressively more protected aliens based on their relationships to the United States, then liberty of entry might become available in some inner circles. Probably a global due process analysis would continue the legal fiction of treating aliens in exclusion as functionally outside the borders; if not, the analysis would apply primarily to aliens denied visas abroad.

SIDE CONSTRAINTS

Regardless of whether a liberty interest in entry exists, the Constitution may still impose significant limitations on federal immigration power if other rights of aliens place side constraints on the denial of entry. In some instances, interference with a right is the express purpose of immigration policy, as when the government excludes or expels aliens on grounds of race, religion, or political belief. In other instances, interference with a right is the foreseeable consequence of a policy designed for other purposes, as when exclusion on grounds of poverty or disease, or deportation for crime, separates families.

Traditionally, the notion of an absolute right to exclude or expel has encompassed the rejection of such side constraints. Racial discrimination was central to U.S. immigration policy from 1882 through the first half of the twentieth century. Exclusion and deportation for revolutionary advocacy began somewhat later but continued until 1990. The Supreme Court has upheld these policies in the past and has denied the existence of constitutional limitations on the exclusion of family members.[38]

The early reasoning in favor of this result may be found in *United States ex rel. Turner v. Williams* (1904).[39] John Turner was an anarchist lecturer, who was deported after he entered the United States despite his excludability as an anarchist. When Clarence Darrow invoked the First Amendment in Turner's defense, Chief Justice Fuller replied:

> We are at a loss to understand in what way the act is obnoxious to this objection. . . . It is, of course, true that if an alien is not permitted to enter this country, or, having entered contrary to law, is expelled, he is in fact cut off from worshipping or speaking or publishing or petitioning in the country, but that is merely because of his exclusion therefrom. He does not become one of the people to whom these things are secured by our Constitution by an attempt to enter forbidden by law. To appeal to the Constitution is to concede that this is a land governed by that supreme law, and as under it the power to exclude has been determined to exist, those who are excluded cannot assert the rights in general obtaining in a land to which they do not belong as citizens or otherwise.[40]

The simplest interpretation of this passage is that, on grounds of territoriality, aliens outside the United States have no First Amendment rights; therefore the First Amendment does not constrain exclusion policy; therefore an excludable alien who is deported after entry cannot raise First Amendment objections to his excludability, because this would negate the power of exclusion.[41]

An alternative reading, less dependent on territoriality, would construe "these things" as meaning the right to engage in First Amendment activities *in this country*. The absolute power of exclusion makes entry a privilege rather than a right, and freedom of speech does not entail a right to enter the United States in order to speak there. The passage would then be the immigration law equivalent of the famous epigram by which Holmes justified the government's firing of a policeman for his political speech: "The petitioner may have a constitutional right to talk politics but he has no constitutional right to be a policeman."[42] The greater power includes the lesser, and a privilege may be withheld from those who exercise a constitutional right.

In the intervening years, both the territoriality explanation and the right/ privilege explanation for denying First Amendment constraints on the exclusion power have lost their force. Aliens abroad may indeed have First Amendment rights. The distinction between rights and privileges is no longer determinative but has yielded to a more complex analysis of unconstitutional conditions on the distribution of benefits.[43] Similarly, equal protection requirements apply even to the distribution of "privileges." Thus, other constitutional rights of aliens can place side constraints on the regulation of entry, regardless of whether there exists a constitutional liberty interest in freedom of entry itself.

Nonetheless, a core of the reasoning in *Turner* remains significant. A right to engage in constitutionally protected activity does not necessarily imply a right to come to the United States to engage in that activity. If the incidental restriction on freedom of speech resulting from an immigration rule unrelated to speech (such as exclusion for poverty, disease, or crime) were subjected to the usual First Amendment analysis for incidental restrictions, the rule would be upheld so long as it furthered a substantial government interest.[44] Avoiding financial burdens and preventing disease and crime would count as substantial government interests. The tautological government interest in controlling which aliens enter the country should not be counted as substantial, but if it were, incidental burdens would be automatically self-justifying. When the exclusion ground does not restrict freedom of speech incidentally but is aimed directly at the alien's past or anticipated speech, as in *Turner* itself, more difficult questions arise, which I will discuss in the next chapter.

The Supreme Court finally recognized the incidental burdens of exclusion on the First Amendment rights of *citizens* to communicate with excluded aliens as placing some constitutional limit on immigration policy, in *Kleindienst v. Mandel* (1972).[45] Although the Court denied that any rights of the excluded alien limited the government's power, it did weakly scrutinize the executive decision to exclude him. This slight but highly significant departure from the legacy of the *Chinese Exclusion Case* has begun the long-delayed process of reconciling immigration policy with constitutionalism.

The "incidental" effect of general exclusion grounds on familial rights of both citizens and aliens deserves particular attention.[46] In *Moore v. City of East Cleveland* (1977), the Supreme Court invalidated on substantive due process grounds a zoning ordinance that made it impossible for a grandmother and two of her grandchildren to live together in that city.[47] Immigration barriers that do not respect family unity may make it impossible for some families to find *any* country where they can live together, thus destroying a central feature of family life. Moreover, where the family includes both aliens and citizens, the federal government should not lightly force an American citizen to choose between family life and remaining in the United States. Exclusion can thus be more devastating to familial rights than to speech rights, where the alien retains the opportunity to speak abroad and to reach an American audience through media that do not require physical presence. The Supreme Court's decision in *Fiallo v. Bell*

(1977) understandably extended its weak scrutiny to immigration legislation that discriminated against certain categories of family members already in the United States.[48]

Under the mutuality of obligation approach, whether or not a constitutional liberty interest in freedom of entry were recognized, government restrictions should still be subject to side constraints based on fundamental constitutional rights, such as freedom of speech, freedom of religion, familial rights, and equal protection. Denial of entry represents an assertion of governing authority over the alien and, as I will illustrate in Chapter Eight, may place significant pressure on the alien's exercise of liberty abroad. These constraints would require some substantial justification for incidental burdens on fundamental rights and could require greater justification for more deliberate restriction of those rights through regulation of entry. Because location is not determinative, these side constraints would be applicable in the context of deportation, exclusion, and visa denial.

Under a global due process approach, only those rights whose application would not be impracticable and anomalous would impose side constraints on denial of entry. Presumably such fundamental individual rights as freedom of speech, free exercise of religion, familial rights, and equal protection are not themselves too impracticable and anomalous to extend abroad. A global due process analyst would probably focus the inquiry more narrowly on the context of entry and might conclude that requiring respect for an otherwise practicable right like family unity in that context would be impracticable, with regard to some or all aliens. Reasoning of this kind might permit a global due process analyst to eliminate some of the side constraints on exclusion or denial of visas.

Global due process analysis would not, however, undercut the availability of constitutional rights as constraints on grounds of deportation. Deportation occurs from within the United States, as a matter of both fact and law.

FREEDOM TO REMAIN

If it were true that sovereignty over territory implied an absolute power to control the presence of aliens, then it would make sense to treat the exclusion of initial entrants, the exclusion of returning residents, and the deportation of residents as equally within the government's limitless discretion. Once the assumption of absolute sovereign control is rejected, however, the constitutional rights of aliens and citizens should become available as side constraints on the power of deportation.

There also remains the question whether, without focusing on the violation of a specific side constraint like familial rights, freedom of speech, or equal protection, a substantive due process liberty of alien residents to remain in the United States should be recognized. Because deportation involves deprivation of the physical liberty of a person within the territory, at a minimum a rational justification should be required.[49] Logically, for any given alien, liberty to remain should be at least as protected as liberty to enter, because otherwise considerations that would justify removing the alien would not justify keeping her out. Moreover, an alien's liberty to remain might be more strongly protected than the general freedom of aliens to enter the country.

Several factors combine in support of a substantial liberty of lawful resident aliens to remain.[50] Freedom to remain is a particular form of the broader freedom of movement. There is a significant constitutional difference between preventing someone from acquiring a benefit and depriving her of what she has already lawfully acquired. The daunting multitude of potential entrants in the world contrasts with the more manageable number of aliens already residing lawfully in the United States.

As an alien resides in the United States for a longer period of time, it is foreseeable and highly probable that she will develop a network of personal associations, integrating into some segment of American society and adapting to its way of life. Recognizing these consequences does not require an exaggerated view of the efficacy of the American melting pot or a rigid vision of assimilation to a single American norm. To lead more fulfilling lives, immigrants develop knowledge, skills, and relationships—they "invest in human capital"—that would be wasted if they had to return to their country of origin. They may adopt ideals or life goals that could not be realized in their native countries. Some of these attachments to the United States may implicate particular constitutional rights that serve as side constraints on deportation, but many do not, and their cumulative effect is greater than the sum of the parts. Lawful residents incur this reliance with the government's consent, and the government should owe some respect to this reliance.

The typical legal response to this argument is a countervailing assertion of voluntarism: if alien residents have so much at stake, then they should naturalize.[51] That option was not open to the Chinese immigrants in the seminal cases, who were barred from naturalization on racial grounds, but today naturalization criteria are more equitable and more generously applied. Aliens become eligible for naturalization after five years' permanent residence (three years if married to a citizen).[52] So long as the United States makes naturalization a genuine option within a relatively short period, it might be argued that the side constraints of independent constitutional rights and a ban on arbitrariness provide sufficient protection against deportation, without a stronger due process liberty to remain.

The Supreme Court has also considered failure to naturalize a justification for resident aliens' vulnerability to deportation because aliens remain subject to their allegiance to a foreign state.[53] This fact may account for the disabilities of enemy aliens in wartime and for certain country-specific measures in other times of international tension,[54] but it has no visible relevance to the question whether long-time residents should be subject to deportation for minor criminal offenses.

If a liberty to remain were recognized, then defining its scope would require attention to the relationship between form and substance in immigration law. Current U.S. immigration law depends heavily on a distinction between permanent resident aliens and nonimmigrant aliens, who are regarded as temporarily admitted but in many cases may remain indefinitely. In practical terms, some nonimmigrants may be more thoroughly linked to their local communities than some permanent residents. Nonetheless, the clarity of a constitutional rule that turns on ascertainable factors might justify reserving heightened constitutional limits on deportation for permanent residents. However, the adoption of such formal distinctions into constitutional doctrine should not operate to place constitutional protection within the free disposition of Congress. A constitutional norm should accomplish more than simply giving Congress an incentive to abolish the status of permanent resident and admit genuine immigrants for renewable terms of years.

Neither the mutuality of obligation approach nor the global due process approach tells us very much about whether an alien's liberty to remain should be more protected than her freedom of entry. They do refute some of the traditional arguments against constitutional limits on the deportation power and explain why it would be inaccurate to criticize liberty to remain as converting a rightless guest into a protected tenant. The emphasis on fully enforcing the written Constitution under the mutuality of obligation approach would not require that the citizen's absolute right to remain be extended to aliens, because the citizen's right is not merely an implication from the constitutional protection of liberty of persons, but rather derives from the structure of the Constitution and the relations it creates between the nation and its citizens. The flexibility and context-specific character of the global due process approach might lead to the conclusion that restrictions on the deportation power were more practicable than restrictions on the exclusion power, and these features would facilitate judicial discretion in identifying the category of aliens whose liberty to remain was more strongly protected.

AN ASIDE, TO HOBBESIANS AS WELL

If one somehow concluded from the foregoing that aliens had no rights with respect to their exclusion from the United States, and even if one adhered to a Hobbesian approach and denied that aliens outside the United

States *ever* had constitutional rights, it would still be necessary to reevaluate current law in light of the impact that immigration restrictions have on persons inside the United States, including citizens with alien relatives. If the reason why constitutional objections cannot be raised by would-be immigrants is that those immigrants are not rights holders under the Constitution, then their sponsoring relatives inside the United States should be empowered to object on the basis of their own rights. It is grotesque that current judicial doctrine affords no remedy when a consular visa denial prevents a citizen's spouse from entering the country, thus treating the event as of lesser significance than when a customs official prevents a citizen's suitcase or dog from entering the country.[55]

ARE THE CONSTITUTIONAL LIMITS JUDICIALLY ENFORCEABLE?

The more enduring legacy of the *Chinese Exclusion Case* in constitutional doctrine is not the claim that constitutional limits on the immigration power do not exist, but the claim that courts should be wary of enforcing them. Field's admonition that only the political branches were empowered to decide whether a flow of immigration had become a threat to national security initiated the tradition of treating the justifiability of substantive immigration rules as a "political question."[56] Since 1972, that tradition has motivated an exceptionally deferential standard of review rather than no review at all, but the standard is so weak that it renders the constitutional limits judicially unenforceable in practice.

A discussion of the relationship of immigration regulation to the political question doctrine must first confront the disputed character of the political question doctrine itself. The original meaning of the term "political question," as Chief Justice Marshall used it in *Marbury v. Madison* (1803), referred to the desirability of a measure that violated no legal right.[57] Such questions were left for the political branches (the legislature and the executive) to resolve. Later, however, the Court asserted that even the constitutionality of a measure could be a "political question," in the sense that the political branches rather than the courts were empowered to decide it. Justice Brennan has summarized:

> Prominent on the surface of any case held to involve a political question is found a textually demonstrable constitutional commitment of the issue to a coordinate political department; or a lack of judicially discoverable and manageable standards for resolving it; or the impossibility of deciding without an initial policy determination of a kind clearly for nonjudicial discretion; or the impossibility of a court's undertaking independent resolution without expressing lack of the respect due coordinate branches of government; or an unusual need for unquestion-

ing adherence to a political decision already made; or the potentiality of embarrassment from multifarious pronouncements by various departments on one question.[58]

These reasons are thought to require courts not to provide their own answers to some questions of constitutionality.

To give a concrete example, if Congress declared a war to liberate a holy land from infidels, and this crusade were challenged as lacking any secular justification and therefore a violation of the Establishment Clause of the First Amendment, judges might assert that the validity of the declaration of war was a political question. Under the first version, this assertion would really mean that the court had decided that there was no conflict between the Establishment Clause and a crusade, perhaps because that clause does not constrain Congress's power to declare war at all. Under the second version, the assertion would mean that the judges denied their power to decide the constitutional issue but that conscientious legislators were obliged to determine for themselves whether the motivation of the war was consistent with the Establishment Clause.

In a famous article, Louis Henkin questioned the need for a "political question doctrine," arguing that there are very few constitutional questions removed from the courts' power of decision in the second sense. Instead, most invocations of the political doctrine really express the first version or simply decline to provide a judicial remedy as a matter of equitable discretion.[59] He explained the Supreme Court's political question decisions involving foreign relations and immigration as concluding that the challenged measures were within the constitutional power of the political branches.[60]

I will assume, to the contrary, that a broader category of true political questions (in the second sense) may exist and that cases involving foreign relations may sometimes be among them. This chapter has already discussed the reasons for rejecting the first of the three interpretations of the political question doctrine as applied to immigration policy, the view that constitutional rights do not constrain immigration policy. Henkin's third option, equitable discretion, does not fit the immigration cases—exclusion cases are typically brought on habeas corpus, and the courts have freely granted the writ for statutory violations and have never suggested that they were refusing it on discretionary grounds where constitutional violations are alleged. We should therefore consider the remaining possibility, that immigration policy escapes judicial review (or, more recently, that normal standards of judicial review are suspended) because of its "political" character.

Although this form of the political question doctrine has been subjected to severe scholarly criticism, in the context of foreign relations as well as elsewhere, I will assume its validity for purposes of this discussion.[61]

Justice Brennan summarized the Court's reasons for characterizing some foreign relations questions as political:

> Not only does resolution of such issues frequently turn on standards that defy judicial application, or involve the exercise of a discretion demonstrably committed to the executive or legislature; but many such questions uniquely demand single-voiced statement of the Government's views. Yet it is error to suppose that every case or controversy which touches foreign relations lies beyond judicial cognizance. Our cases in this field seem invariably to show a discriminating analysis of the particular question posed, in terms of the history of its management by the political branches, of its susceptibility to judicial handling in the light of its nature and posture in the specific case, and of the possible consequences of judicial action.[62]

Those reasons have at most very limited applicability to the constitutional review of immigration policy.

No textually demonstrable commitment of all questions of immigration policy, including constitutionality, to the political branches exists. Indeed, the most obvious textual basis for the federal immigration power is the commerce clause, which speaks indistinguishably of foreign commerce, interstate commerce, and commerce with Indian tribes. The Supreme Court does not regard application of the commerce clause as an issue committed to the political branches.

Justice Field's analogy between immigration and invasion in the *Chinese Exclusion Case* attempted to place immigration in the context of war and foreign relations. Sometimes immigration policies are chosen because of their impact on foreign relations, as, for example, the president's suspension of the entry of certain Panamanian nationals associated with the Noriega regime in June 1988 or the retaliatory investigation of the visa status of Iranian students after the seizure of the American embassy in Tehran in 1979.[63] Whether the relations between the United States and these countries necessitated such a differentiated response, and how much influence these measures were likely to have on these countries' conduct, are questions that a court would have great difficulty resolving.[64] Even when immigration policies are not chosen for foreign relations impact, their justifiability may sometimes turn on factual circumstances in a foreign country that are difficult to ascertain or that are so politically sensitive in the international arena that the courts feel obliged not to contradict the government's official determination.

Such instances are, however, the exception rather than the rule. In the first century of U.S. immigration regulation, the standard immigration problems of poverty, disease, and crime were handled as matters of legitimate local concern. The Supreme Court's decisions regarding state immigration law betray no suggestion that its validity was nonjusticiable or that the necessity for excluding particular classes of aliens raised factual issues too difficult for a court to decide. To the contrary, the justices were prepared to debate the extent of the state's power of self-preservation; whether the state was entitled to identify novel categories of aliens that threatened its interests, or limited to a short list of traditional state concerns; and whether particular statutes were drafted narrowly enough to be justified by that power.

Today as well, the vast bulk of immigration enforcement involves such routine matters as poverty, crime, regulatory violations, and protection of the domestic labor market. These restrictions do not rely on sensitive foreign policy choices for their justification. They do not even depend on political or economic conditions in foreign states but focus on local conditions in the United States. These restrictions concern the relationship between our government and aliens as individuals, not the relations between governments, and have no incalculable diplomatic consequences that would create an exceptional need for the government to "speak with one voice."

The Supreme Court began exaggerating the foreign policy nexus of immigration regulation in 1876, as a justification for taking immigration powers away from California, which had abused them. The Court observed in *Chy Lung v. Freeman* that "a silly, an obstinate, or a wicked commissioner may bring disgrace upon the whole country, the enmity of a powerful nation, or the loss of an equally powerful friend."[65] But that argument proves vastly too much. Any power of regulation over aliens is susceptible to abuse. The Court has not gone on to deprive states of the power to punish aliens for local crimes or to tax foreign corporations.[66] Yet subjecting an alien to the death penalty is more likely to cause a diplomatic incident than deporting him.[67]

Nonetheless, this distorted characterization of immigration policy has continued to inform the modern Supreme Court's view that the constitutionality of immigration restrictions, although not strictly a political question, requires an extraordinarily deferential standard of review. The Court explained its deferential stance in *Fiallo v. Bell* (1977) as follows:

> "[s]ince decisions in these matters may implicate our relations with foreign powers, and since a wide variety of classifications must be defined in the light of changing political and economic circumstances, such decisions are frequently of a character more appropriate to either the Legislature or the Executive than to the Judiciary," and "[t]he reasons that preclude judicial review of political questions also dictate a narrow standard of review of decisions made by the Congress or the President in the area of immigration and naturalization."[68]

The Court refused to distinguish among immigration criteria that were more closely or less closely related to foreign policy concerns. Instead, the Court viewed all admission and exclusion grounds as subject to narrow review, including the banal example of discrimination against illegitimate children and their fathers, on which the case turned.

Given the hollowness of the foreign policy rationale, it might be argued more generally that immigration legislation cannot be evaluated by "judicially discoverable and manageable standards," but rather depends on "an initial policy determination of a kind clearly for nonjudicial discretion." The optimal level of permanent immigration and the optimal allocation of opportunities within that level among such categories of potential immigrants as scientists, investors, and domestic workers are unlikely subjects for judicial resolution. They involve value choices concerning national identity, population density, economic growth, and global distribution of resources that should be made democratically. As Michael Walzer has observed, "The distribution of membership is not pervasively subject to the constraints of justice."[69] But the emphasis here should be on "pervasively"—justice (and the United States Constitution) places some distinct constraints on the allocation of those opportunities. That allocation cannot be designed to create a restrictive racial identity for the United States. It cannot be designed to favor one religion over another. Standards of this kind are as discoverable and manageable in the immigration context as in most other fields of law.[70]

The indiscriminate suspension of normal standards of judicial review of immigration policy endangers not only the rights of aliens, but also the rights of citizens. Among the early-twentieth-century Supreme Court decisions denying that family unity limited the federal government's power to exclude or deport, some involved spouses and children of citizens.[71] In the very case where the Supreme Court moved from nonreview to extraordinarily deferential review, it emphasized that constitutional scrutiny was based solely on the First Amendment rights of citizens harmed by the alien's exclusion.[72]

Ultimately, however, the application of "political question" reasoning—either as a denial of justiciability or as an extraordinarily deferential standard of review—cannot eliminate constitutional rights as constraints on immigration law. It merely impairs their enforcement by the independent judiciary and shifts the forum for their resolution to the political branches. These branches do not always live up to their constitutional responsibilities, but legislators and executive officials are obliged to seek conscientious resolutions of political questions of constitutionality.[73]

Chapter Eight

LIMITS OF THE POLITY: POLITICAL RIGHTS OF

IMMIGRANTS IN THE UNITED STATES

THE PREVIOUS chapter discussed the availability of other constitutional rights as side constraints on the federal power to exclude or expel aliens, but it reserved for fuller analysis here the interaction between the First Amendment and federal powers when the government seeks to exclude or expel aliens because of the content of their speech. Some countries regard the participation of aliens in political life as inherently problematic,[1] but U.S. law has treated aliens as protected from criminal punishment for their speech under the same standards as citizens. Indeed, the history of alien suffrage in the United States demonstrates a more individualistic conception of democracy (in contrast to the collectivist conception of democracy in countries such as Germany) that cannot claim to be endangered by the inclusion of alien residents in public debate. Current constitutional law still supports this individualistic conception of democracy and, as the first part of this chapter will show, would surely permit the reestablishment of resident alien suffrage.

The chapter will then turn to First Amendment limitations on exclusion and deportation grounds. Ideological grounds have played an important role in twentieth-century immigration law and have been highly controversial. The topic deserves attention for its own sake, and it may further illustrate how the rights of citizens and aliens constrain immigration policy once the veils of the absolute power and political question doctrines are lifted.

THE CONSTITUTIONAL VIABILITY OF ALIEN SUFFRAGE TODAY

The conditions that made alien suffrage politically attractive in the United States have receded into history, and the very existence of the practice is widely forgotten. The voting rights amendments to the Constitution prohibit discriminations only when they are directed against citizens, and the Constitution speaks of the Senate and the House of Representatives as being elected by "the People." This raises the question whether the Constitution as a whole should now be interpreted as prohibiting the grant of voting rights in state and federal elections to anyone other than citizens.

Because alien suffrage has rarely been debated here in the modern period, it will be necessary to approach this question indirectly, by considering other constraints on the construction of the political community. Ultimately, this examination will suggest that in the United States, a liberal interpretation of democracy as facilitating individual self-determination supports the conclusion that enfranchisement of alien residents remains a permissible option.[a]

The Supreme Court itself has spelled out the rudiments of political theory in language that might support the view that only a predefined citizenry can be considered "the People." In one of a series of cases upholding state laws excluding alien residents from certain categories of public employment, the Court explained:

> The exclusion of aliens from basic governmental processes is not a deficiency in the democratic system but a necessary consequence of the community's process of political self-definition. Self-government, whether direct or through representatives, begins by defining the scope of the community of the governed and thus of the governors as well: Aliens are by definition those outside of this community. Judicial incursions in this area may interfere with those aspects of democratic self-government that are most essential to it.[2]

It may be easy to dismiss this and similar intimations as dicta, since the cases themselves clearly hold only that the various disqualifications of aliens are permissible, and most of their language stresses the state's discretion. One of the cases upheld a statute excluding voluntarily nondeclarant aliens from employment as public school teachers, while authorizing the employment of declarant aliens and even "excusable" nondeclarants.[3] Indeed, in that case the Court noticed without objection that in New York City alien parents are permitted both to vote for and to be elected to local school boards.[4]

The long history of alien suffrage in the United States provides one substantial reason for continuing to interpret the Constitution as allowing the

---

[a] I will not revisit here the argument that the U.S. Constitution itself *requires* alien suffrage, for which see Gerald M. Rosberg, Aliens and Equal Protection: Why Not the Right to Vote?, 75 Mich. L. Rev. 1092 (1977). As far as constitutional interpretation is concerned, the combination of textual references to citizenship as a qualification for federal elective office and as a condition for protection by the voting rights amendments, which political and intellectual history confirms is no coincidence, plus the distinction between core and optional electorates outlined in this chapter, appears to support the Supreme Court's rejection of the equal protection argument for mandatory alien suffrage. See Skafte v. Rorex, 430 U.S. 961 (1977), *dismissing appeal from* 533 P.2d 830 (Colo. 1976). Moreover, the inclusiveness of the current naturalization laws goes a long way to rebut the claim for alien suffrage as a requirement of political justice. But see Jamin B. Raskin, Legal Aliens, Local Citizens: The Historical, Constitutional and Theoretical Meanings of Alien Suffrage, 141 U. Pa. L. Rev. 1391, 1441–56 (1993) (arguing for alien suffrage, at least at the local level, on democratic grounds).

enfranchisement of alien residents. Nonetheless, one may wonder whether principle as well as history supports a power of community self-definition broad enough to include a state's discretion to enfranchise alien residents.

It is first necessary to clarify what "defining the political community" should mean. Unless the Court was referring solely to events in the distant past, it cannot mean constituting a new political community from a state of nature. Rather, the Court was invoking the ongoing process of community self-definition through the maintenance or restructuring of an already organized community or a portion thereof. The rules for the distribution of the electoral franchise represent one method for marking off the boundaries of the political community, though not the only one. The rules determining qualification for office often differ from the rules for voting, and persons who are not entitled to vote still have other opportunities to make persuasive contributions to the political process. There are "passive" members of the community whose interests are entitled to the special consideration owed to members but who receive only "virtual representation." For example, the children of "active" members, or formerly "active" members who have lost the competence to act for themselves,[5] are surely within "the community of the governed," unless that term is twisted into a synonym for the electorate. The common disenfranchisement of felons could also be viewed as reducing them to passive status.

The ideal type of the republic may be a small unitary state with no crime, no physical or mental illness, and no children. The United States, however, is a large federal state, with crime, illness, children—and resident aliens. The political communities actually engaged in "basic governmental processes" in such states are narrower than the entirety of the community.

Core Electorates and Optional Electorates

The move toward universal citizen suffrage, in the sense of overturning restrictions of class, property, race, religion, and gender, has been a great achievement. It could, however, mislead us into concluding that questions of electoral qualification always have unique right answers. Modern legal doctrine on voting rights could have a similar tendency. In the United States, restrictive voting qualifications, with a few traditional exceptions, are now subject to "strict scrutiny" under the Equal Protection Clause. When the permissible qualifications are cumulated, they define a constitutionally privileged category of citizens (nonfelonious residents over the age of eighteen, and so on), which I will call the core electorate. The breadth of this core electorate is a measure of the success of the egalitarian reforms. Members of the core electorate have not infrequently succumbed to the temptation to identify the core electorate with the political community and to regard any enfranchisement of others as a dilution of their votes and a violation of their rights.

For example, in *Katzenbach v. Morgan* (1966), New York City voters sought an injunction against the enforcement of the Voting Rights Act of 1965, to the extent that it exempted persons who had been educated in Spanish in Puerto Rico from New York State's English literacy qualification.[6] The Supreme Court had upheld literacy requirements only seven years earlier, and it avoided overruling that decision.[7] Instead, it responded that the extension of voting rights could be upheld as within Congress's power on either of two grounds: because Congress had concluded that the English literacy test itself operated as an invidious discrimination against Puerto Rican residents,[8] or "as a measure to secure for the Puerto Rican community residing in New York nondiscriminatory treatment by government . . . [in] the provision or administration of governmental services, such as public schools, public housing and law enforcement."[9] In other words, even if persons literate only in Spanish were not within the core electorate, Congress could extend the franchise to them as a means of protecting their rights.

The expansion of a political community beyond its core electorate also occurs in connection with residence requirements. The contours of the law are less settled here, but several examples are available. The text of the federal Constitution repeatedly expresses an assumption that residence or inhabitancy indicates political membership in a state, but it never specifies that it is necessary for membership.[10] (The constitutional text is silent on the subject of membership in a political subdivision, as on all other matters of local government.)

Congress has twice overridden requirements of residence within a state for federal election purposes. In 1970 the Supreme Court validated a federal voting rights statute that gave *former* residents of a state the right to cast their votes in the state in presidential elections if they made an interstate move too close to the date of the election to vote in their state of actual residence.[11] Six justices upheld this grant as part of an amelioration of the conflict between durational residence requirements and the right to interstate travel;[12] they thus permitted the facilitation of other constitutional rights to prevail over a residential definition of the constituencies for the electoral college. Building on this decision, Congress has granted United States citizens who reside abroad and have no intention of returning the right to vote in their states of most recent former domicile in both presidential and congressional elections.[13] The legislative history includes findings that this grant was necessary to protect the interests of citizens who had exercised the right of international travel.[14] The constitutionality of this statute has not been resolved, but it seems only incrementally more dubious than the provision the Court upheld.

The requirement of residence for inclusion in the political community has also been relaxed in the context of local government. The lower federal courts have usually been quite accepting of the enfranchisement of non-residents who have identifiable interests to defend.[15] In 1962 the Supreme Court itself summarily upheld a voting scheme for a seaside resort town that extended the franchise to residents of the surrounding county who owned property in the town, and it would probably adhere to that decision today.[16]

These examples suggest that the Constitution does not provide a single "conception of a political community" that uniquely determines the electorate of each governmental unit, resulting in a neatly nested hierarchy of political communities, towns within counties within states within a nation. Rather, it affords government some discretion to supplement the core electorate with a variety of optional electorates, consisting of categories of persons who have interests implicated in the community's political process. This discretion is, however, still subject to the constitutional rules that govern the distribution of nonfundamental goods.[17] Some of these examples involve extensions of the franchise expressly justified by the optional voters' need to protect their interests; in others the courts have more ambiguously asserted that the interests provide a sufficient justification for enfranchising the optional voters.

The resulting variation in electorates necessitates a fragmented and fluid account of the People as a political agent. This should not be surprising, given the complex federal and territorial structure of the United States and its historical emphasis on individualism. Although the political activity of the core might be interpreted as the self-determination of a previously identified collectivity, the participation of optional electors appears to have a more individualist basis. Moreover, permitting peripheral groups to be provisionally enfranchised in order to protect identifiable interests suggests an instrumental valuation of their members' political participation.

Aliens as Optional Electors

We are now ready to inquire into the consistency of alien suffrage, apart from its historical pedigree, with generally operative principles of American constitutional law. The preceding discussion shows that the fact that resident aliens are not constitutionally guaranteed the right to vote does not in itself mean that enfranchising them would be constitutionally impermissible.[b] Resident aliens certainly have the types of interests that have justi-

---

[b] For the sake of simplicity, I will limit the discussion to aliens lawfully admitted for permanent residence, whose lawful domicile in the United States corresponds nicely to the tradition that citizens must reside in a community to be in its core electorate. Although there are exceptions, United States law generally admits aliens for permanent residence from the outset, rather than requiring aliens who intend to reside permanently to undergo repeated renewal of time-limited residence permits, as in some other countries.

fied the inclusion of other groups in optional electorates. An individual has a strong interest in having a say in the adoption of rules that will govern her conduct, regardless of whether she is a member in the fullest sense of the political community. If a property owner who resides in another state has an interest sufficient to support optional enfranchisement, then the same must be true of an alien who resides in the jurisdiction. More compellingly, the enfranchisement may be intended to protect alien residents from hostile government action; United States history offers ample reason for concern that their interests may be systematically disfavored in a political process that excludes them. The question, then, is whether something peculiar about their status disqualifies resident aliens from becoming an optional electorate.

Three interrelated concerns need to be addressed. First, the American conception of popular sovereignty may make citizenship in the nation an essential precondition for voting at all levels. Second, state enfranchisement of aliens may represent a trespass against federal powers. Third, some feature of alienage may unavoidably disqualify a person from participation in the political community. I will argue here that American constitutional tradition has drawn on more than one vision of democracy, and that it is not committed to a version that would forbid alien suffrage.

As far as the American conception of popular sovereignty is concerned, the historical discussion of the ideology of alien suffrage in Chapter Four has indicated a broad spectrum of opinions. It is useful here to distinguish between liberal interpretations of popular sovereignty as a vehicle for personal self-determination founded on the individual and communitarian interpretations of popular sovereignty as a vehicle for collective self-determination based on some theory that identifies the right collectivity. Although popular sovereignty is largely a theory of the ultimate source of political power, rather than a recipe for the structuring of individual government institutions, a communitarian interpretation of popular sovereignty could justify the conclusion that the people should never share their political power with nonnationals.

One communitarian alternative would support rather than undermine alien suffrage, namely an interpretation basing popular sovereignty in the population actually residing within the territory controlled by the state. This version could even imply that resident aliens must be enfranchised.[18] A second communitarian alternative, founded in ethnic nationalism, could identify the People with some preexisting portion of humanity sharing common ancestry and other cultural traits. A third communitarian alternative would formally identify the People as those persons holding national citizenship under positive law at any given time.

The liberal-individualist, the nationalist-communitarian, and the formal-communitarian perspectives have all been represented in the United States, outside the alien suffrage debate as well as inside it. The optional enfranchisement of citizens with interests to protect, in accordance with the characterization of the right to vote as "a fundamental political right, because preservative of all rights," illustrates the influence of the individualist interpretation of popular sovereignty.[19] So does the historic rallying cry against taxation without representation.

The United States did not escape the influence of the Romantic concept of ethnic nationalism that convulsed Europe in the nineteenth century. The Insular Cases (1901), with their emphasis on the nation's need to acquire overseas colonies without conferring the rights of citizenship on subjects who were racially unfit for it, implemented an Anglo-American nationalist vision of popular sovereignty. The Dred Scott decision (1857), declaring persons of African ancestry constitutionally ineligible for American citizenship, rested on a white nationalist vision of popular sovereignty, although its dicta simultaneously accept alien suffrage.[20] The rejection of these racial definitions of the nation, however, represents the fundamental achievement of twentieth-century constitutional law, resting on the Civil War Amendments. The United States is a nation of immigrants, and not just of white immigrants, which continually reshapes its identity through its immigration and naturalization practices. Its raison d'être is not to serve as the vehicle for the political self-determination of some preexisting bloodline.

The history of federalism supports the view that the Constitution does not make *national* citizenship a prerequisite for voting in the states. The doctrine that states may have "citizens" defined as such solely for internal purposes, employed in *Scott v. Sandford* to explain away voting by free blacks, has survived despite its association with that tainted decision. The citizenship clause of the Fourteenth Amendment does not even exhaustively specify the persons who may be considered citizens of the nation, let alone of a state. States employed this discretion not only with regard to alien voters, but also to enfranchise Native Americans who lacked national citizenship. In short, popular sovereignty in the United States has been a flexible notion, which has not restricted political power by a rigid definition of the People, and certainly not by the legal category of national citizenship. Nowadays, when the variations among electorates are minor and most exclusions from the franchise would be invalidated by the courts, there might be some instrumental advantages in the simplicity of a uniform definition of the electorate, but those instrumental advantages would have to be weighed against the advantages of permitting alien suffrage.

It also follows from this traditional flexibility that a state's enfranchisement of lawful resident aliens within its borders does not infringe the express federal power over naturalization or the implied federal power over immigration. National citizenship involves more than the right to vote in a state, and a state that enfranchises one of its alien residents has not purported to naturalize.

It is probably true, however, that modern constitutional law would permit Congress to enact a statute expressly prohibiting the states from enfranchising alien residents.[21] Although the infringement of state sovereignty would have troubled earlier generations, the states have shrunk sufficiently to enable the Supreme Court to view the prohibition as within the broad federal power to set the conditions on which aliens will be admitted to United States territory.[22] The entering wedge for the prohibition might be the need to restrict the political activities of enemy aliens in time of war, followed by a concern for less formal manifestations of international tension; alternatively, it could be within Congress's authority over naturalization to withhold voting rights from aliens until they are naturalized.

An examination of declarant alien suffrage illustrates the absence of an inherent barrier to an alien's participation in the political community. Regardless of whether the state adopted declarant aliens as local state citizens, full enfranchisement of declarant aliens represented an admission to the active political community of the state on the basis of mutual consent and residence. Declarant aliens had not yet been admitted to the overarching national political community, and therefore they lacked full rights of interstate mobility as well as rights of constitutional protection against deportation by the federal government. But declarant aliens were "on a citizenship track";[23] they had expressed their desire for national citizenship, and given the broad eligibility for naturalization as of right, it was largely a matter of time before they attained it.[24] As between the state and the voter, both a subjective and an objective political bond existed.

If we look beyond declarant aliens, we see that some resident aliens are ineligible or unwilling to naturalize. The moral status of naturalization criteria—whether a country should regard itself as free to adopt whatever naturalization policy it pleases, or whether a country that invites the long-term settlement of resident aliens may be morally obliged to offer them citizenship—could be debated, but for present purposes it may be better to assume arguendo that the United States' criteria are morally defensible. Although other categories could be considered, the most significant question would seem to be whether a state may extend voting rights to an alien who has freely rejected an opportunity to exchange a prior allegiance for exclusive allegiance to the United States. (As shorthand, I will call such persons nondeclarant aliens, though they are the polar extreme from, rather than the opposite of, declarant aliens.)

The political bond between a nondeclarant alien and the state is less strong than in the case of the declarant alien. The alien has voluntarily chosen to reside in the state and (under current law) has been admitted for the express purpose of living in the country indefinitely, after going through a complex administrative process. Opinions may differ as to whether the alien has "disappointed" the country by deciding not to naturalize; certainly nothing in the immigration laws makes desire for naturalization a criterion of admission or failure to naturalize a ground of deportation. The alien has voluntarily submitted to the state's governance for the duration of her residence in most respects as if she were a citizen.[25] Under American law, all aliens owe allegiance to the United States during their residence here.[26] United States law has always recognized resident aliens as at least passive members of the community to the extent of including them—in contrast to "Indians not taxed"—in the basis of apportionment.[27]

Both declarant and nondeclarant aliens are normally also members of a foreign political community—and not merely another political community, like a sister state. But even national political communities need not have mutually exclusive memberships. A state could confer its local citizenship on a declarant alien without demanding the immediate renunciation of her prior citizenship. United States nationality law is rather tolerant of multiple nationality. United States naturalization practice developed at a period when most of the relevant countries of emigration did not recognize a right of expatriation, and the constitutional principle of *jus soli* citizenship provides further opportunity for overlap.[28] Today, constitutional principles can even require the government to permit a United States citizen to acquire a foreign nationality by naturalization without relinquishing her United States citizenship.[29]

Nonetheless, a nondeclarant alien has decided not to undertake the full commitment entailed in a change of citizenship. Unwillingness to renounce a prior citizenship may reflect a wide variety of factors.[30] Sometimes unfavorable economic consequences under the former country's law, such as forfeiture of accrued pension rights or ineligibility to inherit from relatives, may be dominant. Political exiles may wish to preserve the option of return in case of an unlikely change in the character of the regime. Some business immigrants use the United States as a base for international activities while maintaining close ties with their homelands. Some binational couples maintain both nationalities in order to maximize mobility for both citizen and alien spouses. Some immigrants expect ultimately to retire to the land of their childhood. Others may have no intention to make practical use of their prior citizenship but view it as a part of their psychological identity which they are reluctant to renounce. Still others may find a United States identity repugnant and perhaps would not take it on even if they could maintain both nationalities.

Various communitarian theories may treat some or all of these reasons for failing to naturalize as fatal barriers to political participation. Communitarians may, however, be reluctant to require lifelong commitment to a community as a minimum condition for political participation. An immigrant's decision to maintain Italian nationality in order to preserve the right to live in Tuscany if she survives to retirement age may be no more disqualifying than a New Yorker's intention to retire someday to Arizona or to emigrate. American constitutional law does not treat the latter types of mobility as valid reasons for disenfranchising citizens. In the liberal tradition, participation and emigration are continuing choices.

From an individualist perspective, the nondeclarant alien's desire to maintain exclusive permanent allegiance to another nation is not inherently disqualifying but rather creates instrumental reasons for withholding the franchise. It may be more or less probable that the alien's political participation would be guided by an identification with the other nation's interests, rather than concern for the welfare of the community in which she resides. Undoubtedly this perception has formed an important part of the reason why states have chosen to deny aliens voting rights. This choice may reflect an understandable reliance on objective rather than subjective indicia: there are serious dangers in delegating to election officials the power to hold periodic individualized hearings on a voter's commitment to the welfare of the local community. Even if officials could be trusted not to make partisan or other invidious use of their authority, it would be difficult to specify what evidence of concern for another nation's interests could rebut a voter's profession of local commitment. Thus, broad classifications turning on status or oaths, which would be impermissible as applied to members of the core electorate, may be the state's only acceptable option. Still, as an empirical matter, it must be admitted that using nondeclarant alien status as a proxy for insufficient concern is extremely over- and underinclusive. American tradition does not demand of citizens a chauvinistic identification with the national interest to the exclusion of all other considerations; nor does the Constitution permit the disenfranchisement of dual nationals, citizens with strong ethnic identifications, or former Peace Corps workers.

Despite all this, a state may nonetheless conclude that under currently prevailing conditions, enfranchising both declarant and nondeclarant aliens would not create a risk of harm that outweighs the benefits to be achieved by including them in the state or local electorate. The state might base this judgment on a variety of factors, including what it knows regarding the commitment of its alien residents, their relative number, the disparateness of their national allegiances, and the relative absence of opportunities for a conflict of national interests.[31] Because the withholding of the franchise is instrumentally rather than intrinsically justified, nothing in the Constitution prevents the citizenry from deciding that its goals would be better met by the inclusion rather than exclusion of alien voters, just as nothing in the Constitution prevents them from deciding to accept the "risks" involved in enfranchising persons convicted of crime, nonresident property owners, and citizens not literate in English.

Thus a state's power to include declarant aliens within its political community is not simply an archaic survival. It is consistent with broad themes of American constitutional law, particularly the inclusive and rights-oriented themes of constitutional modernism. I have addressed this question primarily as it relates to full enfranchisement in the state electorate, which carries with it federal voting rights. A more restricted grant of voting rights at the municipal level or in special-purpose elections (where even corporations sometimes vote)[32] should be permissible *a fortiori*.

First Amendment Limits on Exclusion and Deportation

The exclusion or deportation of aliens because of their dangerous beliefs has a long history in the United States. The Alien Act of 1798 did not identify particular beliefs, but it authorized the president to deport aliens whom he believed to be "dangerous to the peace and safety of the United States" or "concerned in any treasonable or secret machinations against the government thereof."[33] At the same period, Southern states were adopting laws to prevent the arrival of slaves and free blacks from the West Indies, where the Haitian Revolution was in progress; these laws were backed up by a federal statute in 1803.[34] State attempts to insulate local slave populations from other slaves or free blacks who might be spreading ideas of freedom and insurrection continued throughout the antebellum period.[35] To place the state barriers in context, it should be remembered that many of them were not limited to aliens; that the Bill of Rights did not apply to the states prior to the adoption of the Fourteenth Amendment; and that even the First Amendment did not provide much protection for "dangerous" speech before the First World War.[36]

Once the federal government took over the regulation of immigration, its first effort at ideological exclusion focused on the Latter-day Saints. The statutory exclusion of polygamists in 1891, at the height of the struggle between Congress and the Mormon Church, followed a series of diplomatic interventions to reduce the flow of immigrant converts into the country.[37]

The modern tradition of ideological exclusion really began in 1903, once the assassination of President McKinley had overcome Congress's hesitancy to add anarchists to the list of excluded classes. The 1903 act excluded "anarchists, or persons who believe in or advocate the overthrow by force or violence of the Government of the United States or of all government or of all forms of law, or the assassination of public officials."[38]

Thereafter, the list of political doctrines with adverse immigration consequences expanded in accordance with America's fears of subversion, and so did the consequences. Advocating the unlawful destruction of property became a ground of exclusion in 1917, and advocacy of proscribed doctrines at any time after entry became a ground of deportation.[39] Exclusion and deportation were extended in 1918 to aliens affiliated with any organization that advocated or entertained a belief in proscribed doctrines.[40] Writing or circulating subversive literature, possession with intent to circulate, and contributing to organizations that advocated proscribed doctrines joined the statutory list in 1920.[41]

Since the Russian Revolution in 1917, Communists had become prominent targets of these provisions, and they were the major victims of the infamous Palmer Raids of 1919–20.[42] After the Supreme Court held in 1939 that deportation for membership required membership at the time when the deportation proceedings commenced, the Communist Party expelled all its alien members. Congress responded the next year by making former members of organizations that advocated proscribed doctrines permanently vulnerable to deportation.[43] The exclusion and deportation of Communists became the centerpiece of McCarthy-era immigration policy, and the Internal Security Act of 1950 wrote the Communist Party into the deportation grounds by name.[44] These provisions were recodified into the Immigration and Nationality Act of 1952, where they remained until 1990. The 1950 and 1952 acts also included broad discretionary grounds for the exclusion of aliens whose activities would be prejudicial to the public interest or endanger national security; President Truman cited these provisions as one of the reasons for his veto of both bills, but Congress overrode the vetoes.[45]

In the 1980s the positions of the president and Congress were reversed. Congress sought to limit the application of ideological exclusion grounds, and the Reagan administration sought to invoke them against critics of its foreign policy. The executive's reliance on the broader national security grounds led to a series of court challenges and congressional stopgaps.[46] Ultimately the end of the cold war permitted a revision of the statute.

The reform of the exclusion grounds in 1990 abolished most exclusion and deportation grounds based solely on an alien's beliefs, writings, or membership in organizations with designated beliefs.[c] Aliens who seek permanent residence in the United States, however, remain excludable if

---

[c] But see 8 U.S.C. §§ 212(a)(3)(B) (exclusion for association with broadly defined notion of terrorists), 241(a)(4)(B) (deportation for same), 212(a)(3)(C) (exclusion based on adverse foreign policy consequences of entry or activities), 241(a)(4)(C) (deportation for same). The latter provisions are narrower successors to the broad national security grounds of the 1950 and 1952 acts.

they have been members of "the Communist or any other totalitarian party" within recent years.[47] Aliens who actually engage in activities aimed at the overthrow of the United States government can also be excluded or deported.[48]

The Supreme Court had an opportunity to address the exclusion of aliens who advocated "the doctrines of world communism" in *Kleindienst v. Mandel* (1972).[49] The Nixon administration had refused to exercise its statutory authority to waive this exclusion ground for Ernest Mandel, a Belgian Marxist scholar, who had been invited to attend a conference at Stanford University. The Court began its analysis by asserting that Mandel was only a symbolic plaintiff, because "as an unadmitted and nonresident alien, [he] had no constitutional right of entry to this country."[50] The real plaintiffs were the U.S. citizen university professors whose First Amendment right to engage in dialogue with Mandel was curtailed by his exclusion. The Court construed their complaint, however, as directed against the executive waiver decision and as rightly conceding the constitutionality of the statute.[51] Ultimately, the majority found that the refusal of the waiver had been based on a "facially legitimate and bona fide" reason, Mandel's departure from his itinerary on a previous trip to the United States.[52] It concluded that no more than that was required to uphold an alien's exclusion against the First Amendment claims of his proposed audience.

Weak though the Court's scrutiny may have been, *Kleindienst v. Mandel* opened the door for judicial review of exclusion grounds for the first time since the *Chinese Exclusion Case* (1889) had shut it. Moreover, the Court's shift in focus from exclusion because of revolutionary advocacy to exclusion because of unauthorized detours raised the possibility that it would not accept the government's desire to deprive U.S. citizens of an alien's ideas as a "facially legitimate" reason under the First Amendment.[53] These developments may lead in the future to the freeing of judicial review of ideological exclusion and deportation from such encumbrances as the political question doctrine and indiscriminate deference. Even if they do not, the political branches must face their own responsibilities under the Constitution.

First Amendment side constraints on content-based exclusion and deportation would be fully operative under the mutuality of obligation approach. Both the rights of citizens and the rights of excluded and deported aliens would need to be considered. Under a global due process approach, the rights of citizens and the rights of aliens already within the United States should definitely operate as side constraints. A global due process approach might also recognize the First Amendment rights of excluded aliens as side constraints. After all, freedom of speech is as fundamental a right as exists in the American pantheon. Nonetheless, the current unpredictability of the global due process methodology makes it possible that the operation of overseas aliens' free speech rights as constraints on exclusion would be rejected as impracticable and anomalous.

I will consider separately how these side constraints would affect the exclusion of initial entrants (whether immigrant or nonimmigrant) and the deportation of resident aliens. These do not exhaust the configurations that arise, but they include the polar extremes.

The Exclusion of Initial Entrants for Speech and Association

Some critics of the United States' ideological exclusion policies contend that when the exclusion of an alien speaker results from the speaker's speech or associations, its constitutionality should be judged by the same standards as any other censorship of speech in the public forum, namely that the censorship must be narrowly tailored and strictly necessary to the achievement of a compelling government interest. Where the censored speech is the advocacy of revolutionary or other violence, the modern form of the clear and present danger test articulated in *Brandenburg v. Ohio* (1969) should be applied.[54] Only speech that is directed at producing imminent lawless action and that is in fact likely to produce imminent lawless action may be prohibited. The statutory exclusion of Mandel for advocating the "doctrines of world communism" was therefore unconstitutional, because his intellectual advocacy of revolution was neither directed at producing imminent lawless action nor likely to do so. It does not even matter whether Mandel has any constitutional rights, because his U.S. audience has a First Amendment right to listen to him. The First Amendment forbids the government to deny a U.S. audience access to ideas merely because the government considers them dangerous unless the *Brandenburg* test is met.

To avoid the force of this argument, the government would have to identify some legitimate basis for ideological exclusion, different from the desire to deprive the U.S. audience of access to dangerous ideas. The likely response would be that the government is not acting to prevent U.S. listeners from having access to the speaker's ideas but rather is allocating the gratuitous privilege of entry. Whether entry can be characterized as a gratuitous privilege depends on whether the due process clause affords aliens some liberty of entry, but in either case the withholding of the privilege, or the licensing of the right, would have to be evaluated under the modern unconstitutional conditions doctrine. Although neither case law nor scholarship provides clear guidance on how to identify unconstitutional conditions, the basic idea of the doctrine is to prevent the government from using its power to distribute benefits as a means of suppressing constitutional rights by buying them off or punishing their exercise.

Application of the unconstitutional conditions doctrine requires attention to the government's regulatory purposes. Identifying these purposes is sometimes difficult in immigration law because Congress has often assumed that it had unfettered discretion to reject aliens and has labeled them undesirable without further explanation. We may consider some of the major possibilities, without exhausting all aspects of ideological exclusion. For the sake of concreteness, I will concentrate on the example of exclusion because of Communist advocacy or affiliation.[55]

DENIAL OF A SUBSIDY

The government might argue that its purpose was not to suppress the speaker's ideas, but rather that its admissions policies facilitate the expression of alternative ideas. Admission to the United States operates as a form of subsidy of the activities in which the alien seeks to engage upon entry. The Supreme Court has repeatedly emphasized that the Constitution does not require the government to subsidize the exercise of First Amendment rights; when the government does subsidize the communication of ideas, it may often engage in viewpoint discrimination, subsidizing only views that serve its legitimate interests. In subsidizing other unrelated activities, however, the government may not penalize individuals for ideas they have expressed.

This line of reasoning might suggest that the viewpoint-based exclusion of Communist advocates like Mandel who seek to enter the United States for the very purpose of communicating ideas would be permissible. The prevention of revolutionary violence is undoubtedly a legitimate government interest. Even if the government is forbidden to achieve this interest by prematurely suppressing speech, it may decline to subsidize revolutionary advocacy. The viewpoint-based exclusion of Communist advocates who seek to enter the United States for other purposes, however, such as family reunification, might amount to a penalty on speech and thus an unconstitutional condition on the unrelated activity. That would depend on how free unconstitutional conditions analysis leaves the government to define narrowly the purpose of its subsidies. If the government could specify the scope of its immigration policy as the unification of families whose members do not advocate revolutionary violence, then the exclusion of Communist advocates might not amount to an unconstitutional condition on family unification (as so redefined).[56]

The argument as articulated relies too heavily, however, on the unanalyzed characterization of entry as a subsidy. Could denial of entry really be explained as a decision to reserve subsidies for alternative views? One relevant factor in identifying an unobjectionable government subsidy is whether the government is providing a narrowly targeted benefit for a specially qualified group or is excluding a disfavored group from a generally applicable benefit.[57] Immigrant and nonimmigrant admissions should be considered separately, because immigrant admissions are carefully limited in number and highly selective, and nonimmigrant admissions are numerically unlimited and far less selective.[58]

Nonimmigrants are admitted for varying lengths of time under a variety of categories, generally justified by the direct and indirect benefits of international travel and trade for the United States. The largest category of nonimmigrants includes temporary visitors for business or pleasure, travelers whose basic qualifications to enter the United States are that they are not coming to study or labor and do not appear likely to stay.[59] Perhaps most of the world's population would fail one or both of these tests, but the remaining pool of candidates for entry is quite large, and several millions are admitted each year.[60]

Current law selects most immigrants through three basic policies: family reunification, employment-based immigration, and diversification of the immigrant stream. Reunifying families serves humanitarian purposes and benefits the United States by improving the lives of the family members already present. Employment-based immigration involves the selection of immigrants whose skills and resources can benefit the national economy. In some instances, employment-based criteria may focus specifically on the quality of artistic or scientific work.[61] As regards diversification, it suffices for present purposes to notice that the diversification policy treats the immigrant's nationality as the source of benefit and is otherwise highly unselective.[62]

The ideological exclusion criteria cut across both the immigrant and the nonimmigrant categories, barring from entry persons whose initial eligibility did not depend on the government's desire to promote their speech. Even among the category of "aliens entering the United States to give speeches," only a narrow spectrum of views is barred; yet it appears far more accurate to subsume that category in the broader statutory category of aliens entering the United States temporarily on business. Thus the charge of violating the audience's rights cannot be refuted by comparing immigration control with a selective subsidy that merely facilitates the speech of some aliens while declining to facilitate the speech of others.

PREDICTION OF OTHER HARM

The government might argue that it is not using ideological exclusion grounds in order to deprive American audiences of constitutionally protected speech, but rather that it is using them predictively to protect American residents from constitutionally unprotected misconduct. In the past, the exclusion from public employment of members of organizations that advocated the violent overthrow of government was defended on the basis of their "potential for sabotage, espionage, or other activities directly injurious to national security" and the likelihood that they would "be either incompetent or untrustworthy in the performance of their duties."[63] Predictive judgments of harm from past conduct are common bases for excluding aliens.[64]

The First Amendment severely limits the government's power to punish people solely for their political statements or associations. To protect freedom of association from inhibiting burdens, the Court has also placed some limits on the government's power to act on an inference of likely behavior from an individual's political associations.[65] In evaluating exclusions from public employment and professional licensing, the Court has condemned schemes that swept too broadly by failing to distinguish between "sensitive" and "nonsensitive" positions and by failing to distinguish between active membership with knowledge of and commitment to an organization's unlawful goals and passive, unknowing, or uncommitted membership. Nonetheless, statements and associations are not absolutely protected. The Court has suggested that there are "sensitive" positions for which the mere fact of membership in a "subversive" organization may be disqualifying;[66] it has accepted the validity of partisan staffing of policy-making positions to ensure loyal program implementation;[67] and it has explicitly adopted a balancing test to reconcile public employees' freedom of political speech with their employers' interest in the effective functioning of the workplace.[68]

The old statutory exclusions for anarchist and Communist aliens, and the current statutory exclusions for members of Communist and other totalitarian parties, sweep quite broadly in a manner that the Supreme Court has often condemned. They do not track the distinctions among kinds of membership that the Court has favored in the domestic context, and they do not limit their exclusions to some "sensitive" area or position, aside from the entire United States. These exclusions could be justified as protections against harm under normal First Amendment principles only if the burden on the aliens' freedom of speech and association were less substantial than the burdens involved in the public employment and licensing cases,[d] or if other factors increased the government's need to employ such broad classifications.

The burden that exclusion places on the freedom of speech and association of a nonimmigrant like Mandel may indeed be lighter than the burdens that the Supreme Court has identified in domestic cases. The McCarthy-era loyalty inquisitions created the danger that individuals

---

[d] I assume here that the alien is protected by the First Amendment, as the mutuality of obligation approach entails, and as the global due process approach might or might not entail.

would avoid alliances with hard-line Communists to achieve lawful common goals and would avoid joining any dissident group for fear that they would unwittingly incur the legal consequences of membership in a Communist front organization. State and federal governments threatened sanctions in the spheres of public employment, bar admissions, labor union office, availability of passports, and even taxation. It would seem more likely that an individual would be deterred from political activity by the knowledge that it might someday bar her from employment by her own government than that she would be deterred by the knowledge that it might someday preclude her from visiting a particular foreign country. Moreover, U.S. law is likely to have a nontrivial effect on nonimmigrants only in those countries where the Communist (or other totalitarian) Party is lawful but not dominant; in countries that already prohibit such parties, and in countries governed by such parties, local incentives would probably overwhelm any U.S. deterrents.[e]

Once an alien has recognized herself as a potential immigrant to the United States, however, the burden on her freedom of political choice may be quite substantial. Immigrants for family reunification have heavy personal stakes in successful entry. Other immigrants may also derive great benefit from entry and have strong incentives to tailor their conduct over a period of years to comply with statutory criteria. Indeed, the current provisions on members of Communist and other totalitarian parties, which apply only to immigrants and which forgive prior membership after a few years have passed, operate almost as a bribe for formal resignation.

The government might also defend the breadth of the exclusion grounds by relying on the difficulty of making individualized determinations about the harm posed by incoming aliens. Immigrants, tourists, and business travelers have no special functions as such to perform for the United States, for which ideological traits would disable them, so the harm to be feared is the threat of deliberate subversion. While the alien is in a foreign country, and especially when the alien is a member of the governing party of a totalitarian country, the U.S. government has limited capacity to investigate the degree of the alien's commitment to its subversion. Once the alien has

---

[e] The minimal character of the burden on many nonimmigrants might even lead a critic to deny that their First Amendment rights should entail a side constraint on their exclusion. If one believed that there was no constitutional liberty interest in entry, and that denying entry was unlikely to inhibit a nonimmigrant's speech outside the United States, then perhaps one could conclude that the impact of U.S. law on the alien's liberty would be too limited to justify the invocation of the unconstitutional conditions doctrine. Because the burdens on nonimmigrants—for example, scholars and journalists—are not always insignificant, balancing in individual cases appears preferable to wholesale rejection of the applicability of the doctrine. In either case, the rights of the alien's domestic audience would still require consideration.

entered the United States, the government's capacity may increase, but the alien has the opportunity to cause trouble.[f]

If these considerations are not persuasive—and they may not be—then broad ideological exclusions could not be justified as means of preventing harm consistent with the First Amendment rights of entering aliens (assuming such rights exist). Perhaps these considerations lead to stricter First Amendment limits on the exclusion of immigrants, for whom the burden on speech is greater, than for nonimmigrants. Or if the further refinement of categories were appropriate, perhaps they would lead to different answers across a variety of immigrant and nonimmigrant categories.

NATIONAL SELF-DEFINITION

Finally, it has been suggested that exercises of the immigration power express the nation's process of self-definition. The provisions of current law excluding members of Communist and other totalitarian parties from permanent immigration to the United States and from naturalization might be viewed as attempts not to prevent the establishment of a dictatorship in the United States, but to express the nation's commitment to democratic government, by withholding membership from aliens who do not share "our" democratic ideals.[69] The rhetoric surrounding ideological exclusion from the United States has amply demonstrated its proponents' conviction that dissident ideas are "alien" and un-American.[70]

This interpretation applies most traditionally to naturalization, which directly defines the national community of citizens, and somewhat more expansively to the admission of permanent resident aliens, who form part of the national community of residents.[71] If the power of national self-definition also encompasses the exclusion of nonimmigrants, many of whom are only fleetingly present in the United States, then it must be broad enough to protect U.S. soil from any contact with heterodox ideas. Yet the Supreme Court has already rejected so sweeping a notion of the government's power to exclude "alien" ideas—the government cannot substantially burden, let alone prohibit, a citizen's willing receipt of Communist propaganda from abroad.[72]

The question then remains whether the First Amendment permits the government to designate certain ideas as un-American, and the alien hold-

---

[f] Tourists are often authorized to remain in the United States for six months; students and nonimmigrant workers may be admitted for several years. These are already substantial periods in which the alien has the chance to perform nefarious acts and the government has the chance to observe the alien. Therefore the government's argument of necessity may not be much greater in the case of immigrants than in the case of nonimmigrants.

ers of those ideas as properly excluded from membership in the form of permanent residence, purely in the name of national self-definition.[g]

The process of national self-definition may be carried on through purely majoritarian processes, or it may be subject to direct and indirect constitutional constraint. Constitutional provisions may themselves specify elements of the national self-definition, elevating them beyond the power of government and ordinary political processes to alter, or they may prohibit particular forms of national self-definition. Such constraints may or may not succeed; rather than preventing the pursuit of prohibited definitions, they may impair the acceptance of the Constitution itself. But within a functioning system of constitutional law, such constraints are legally binding.

The religion clauses of the First Amendment enshrined a regime of religious toleration at the national level and prohibited a sectarian definition of the national identity.[73] The Supreme Court majority in the Dred Scott case interpreted the Constitution as barring the government from admitting people of African descent to the national community of citizens; the Fourteenth Amendment reversed that decision and barred the government from excluding persons born in the United States and subject to its jurisdiction from the national community of citizens. Although that reversal did not suffice to prevent the practical continuation of a racially restrictive national identity for almost a century, that identity has been repudiated as a result of the revitalization of the Fourteenth Amendment.[74] In this century, the Supreme Court has also interpreted the Fourteenth Amendment as denying Congress the power to expel citizens from the national community by denationalization.[75]

These constraints on national self-definition should also operate to forbid certain justifications for immigration policies. It would contradict the religion clauses for Congress to exclude Catholics from immigrating on the ground that the United States is a Protestant country. It would contradict the Fourteenth Amendment for Congress to exclude nonwhite immigrants on the ground that the United States is "a white man's country."

Constitutional law thus operates as one means of national self-definition, legally as well as sociologically. The dominant conception of American nationhood in modern constitutional law includes not only the territory and its population, but a commitment to certain fundamental constitutional

---

[g] This book has not prepared the ground sufficiently for a discussion of naturalization, a field where ideological criteria have historically played an even larger role than in exclusion and deportation. Some aspects of this problem are treated in Gerald L. Neuman, Justifying U.S. Naturalization Policies, 35 Va. J. Int'l L. 237 (1994). It is important for critics of ideological exclusion not to play a shell game with national identity, rejecting ideological admissions criteria on the theory that residence is not full membership, and then rejecting ideological naturalization criteria on the theory that the resident alien is already a member.

principles limiting government power. Freedom of speech is one of those principles. In rejecting the automatic exclusion of members of Communist action organizations from employment in defense facilities, Chief Justice Earl Warren wrote:

> Implicit in the term "national defense" is the notion of defending those values and ideals which set this Nation apart. For almost two centuries, our country has taken singular pride in the democratic ideals enshrined in its Constitution, and the most cherished of those ideals have found expression in the First Amendment. It would indeed be ironic if, in the name of national defense, we would sanction the subversion of one of those liberties—the freedom of association—which makes the defense of the Nation worthwhile.[76]

This conception also informed the Supreme Court's analysis of the constitutionality of punishing flag burning. The majority insisted that "[p]unishing desecration of the flag dilutes the very freedom that makes this emblem so revered, and worth revering."[77] It also described as "one of our society's defining principles" Justice Robert Jackson's much-quoted statement in the flag salute case denying the power of government to "prescribe what shall be orthodox in politics, nationalism, religion, or other matters of opinion."[78] Even Justice John Paul Stevens in dissent, while arguing that respect for freedom of speech was consistent with disallowing flag burning as a means of expression, agreed that "the flag uniquely symbolizes the ideas of liberty, equality, and tolerance [and] embodies the spirit of our national commitment to those ideals."[79] Chief Justice William Rehnquist, in contrast, contended that the flag symbolizes the historical "Nation," that it "does not represent any particular political philosophy."[80]

The strength of freedom of speech in American constitutional law makes it implausible that Congress has the power to designate whatever ideas it chooses as un-American and impose burdens on persons who espouse those ideas, not to avoid any concrete harm, but solely to produce cultural homogeneity. For example, Congress can make Columbus Day a national holiday, but it cannot penalize citizens who use that day to mourn rather than celebrate the European conquest of America, and it could not bar them from all public employment in order to foster a pro-Columbian national identity.

If Congress cannot use its leverage as employer to manipulate the mix of public opinion in the United States, then it should also not be free to use the demographic weapon of immigration control for the purpose of isolating the holders of a particular political idea from their intellectual allies and reinforcing the ranks of their opponents. As we have seen, ideological exclusion is not merely a noncoercive attempt to facilitate an alternative persuasion. Thus, a broad power of ideological exclusion to shape national identity would appear to contradict the national commitment to freedom of speech and belief.

A more difficult question is whether constitutional law itself identifies a narrower range of ideas to which private individuals cannot adhere without forfeiting their claim to participate in the national identity, so that Congress could exclude the adherents without usurping a power to "prescribe what shall be orthodox." Justice Jackson once wrote about belief in the overthrow of the government, "If Congress has power to condition any right or privilege of an American citizen upon disclosure and disavowal of belief on any subject, it is obviously this one."[h] Others might choose a belief in racial equality, in freedom of speech, in religious freedom, or in popular sovereignty as an irreducible principle of American society whose rejection disqualifies an alien for permanent residence.[81]

Although the Constitution may commit the government to these ideals and may authorize it to encourage private allegiance to these ideals by noncoercive means, modern U.S. notions of freedom of speech and belief leave individual Americans free to dissent from them. In other contexts, the First Amendment has been understood as requiring U.S. society to accept much of the risk inherent in the paradox of liberal toleration of illiberal ideas. As the Court observed in one of the flag-burning cases, the Constitution "does not guarantee that other concepts virtually sacred to our Nation as a whole—such as the principle that discrimination on the basis of race is odious and destructive—will go unquestioned in the marketplace of ideas."[82]

In fact, the Constitution does not guarantee that even the government will remain forever committed to these ideals. U.S. constitutional law operates without a set of privileged irreducible principles. Unlike the constitutions of some other countries, the U.S. Constitution does not place its fundamental principles beyond the reach of the amending power[83] or authorize the government to ban political movements directed at the radical transformation of democratic institutions.[84] As Justice Oliver Wendell Holmes contended in one of his most celebrated dissents, "If, in the long run, the beliefs expressed in proletarian dictatorship are destined to be accepted by the dominant forces of the community, the only meaning of free speech is that they should be given their chance and have their way."[85] Whether that is the only meaning of free speech may be debated, but it is the modern U.S. approach.

[h] American Communications Ass'n v. Douds, 339 U.S. 382, 436 (1950) (Jackson, J., dissenting) (footnote omitted). He went on to conclude that Congress did not have that power over citizens. But he specifically observed (in the omitted footnote) that there was "no analogy between what Congress may require of aliens as a condition of admission or of citizenship and what it may require of a citizen." Id. n. 9. He also observed that the right of revolution against tyrannical governments was the foundation of the nation. Id. at 439–42.

Thus, the Constitution does not prescribe a political orthodoxy to which American citizens must adhere, and the First Amendment denies Congress the power to prescribe and enforce such an orthodoxy. It would appear, then, that characterizing immigration control as an exercise in national self-definition would not imply the power to exclude aliens with Communist or totalitarian beliefs from permanent residence purely because their beliefs are "un-American." The free speech rights of the excluded aliens, and the associational rights of citizens who share such beliefs, would prohibit such interference. Exclusion might be necessary to prevent more concrete harms, such as action by the aliens to create conditions incompatible with our chosen national identity, but that is another matter, to be judged by other standards.

If there were nonetheless some set of principles essential to national identity, on whose rejection Congress could legitimately impose coercive consequences, the question would remain whether the exclusion of immigrants with contrary views is an unduly burdensome means of protecting the national identity. The admission of individual aliens with undesirable beliefs would be unlikely to transform the national identity, given that some citizens may already hold those beliefs and that all citizens are guaranteed access to them. Moreover, content-neutral means of fostering continuity of national identity, such as limiting the numbers of immigrants overall or favoring immigrants with prior links to the United States like family members, are also available. Thus ideological exclusion may be both unduly burdensome and ineffective as a safeguard of national identity.

The Deportation of Resident Aliens for Speech and Association

However the question of ideological exclusion is resolved, the deportation of resident aliens on ideological grounds threatens serious damage to the American constitutional system. The history of alien suffrage in the United States underscores the anomalous character of a doctrine that attributed to Congress a power of deportation unfettered by constitutional limitations. Aliens in several states were simultaneously invited to share in the fullest exercise of political rights and threatened with expulsion based on disagreement with their political choices. This contradiction may not have been perceived as clearly at the time because modern First Amendment doctrine was still evolving during the period when the states phased out alien suffrage.[86]

Even without voting rights, the participation of resident aliens in the domestic political system through speech and association is essential for its proper functioning. As human beings, resident aliens have the same intrinsic interest in self-expression as citizens, but as members of the resident population subject to our federal, state, and local governments, aliens have a strong instrumental interest in communicating their needs and values to their neighbors. The fact that they cannot vote makes their interest in other channels of communication all the stronger. Conversely, the government and its electorate require the information that resident aliens communicate in order to design appropriate regulations. Moreover, being immigrants makes alien residents likely to have knowledge that most citizens lack concerning conditions in foreign countries, which may be relevant to debates concerning foreign policy or trade, or to the emulation of domestic policies that have succeeded or failed elsewhere. Indeed, some aliens are eligible to immigrate precisely because of their expertise.

The Supreme Court has long confirmed that aliens within the United States *have* First Amendment rights, as the opponents of the Alien and Sedition Acts contended.[87] This conclusion follows regardless of what approach is taken to aliens' extraterritorial rights. Like citizens, aliens in the United States cannot be punished for their speech without a strong showing of necessity. Nonetheless, the Court has refused to characterize deportation as punishment, viewing it instead as a civil regulatory method that Congress uses to bring about a preferred state of affairs (the absence of the deportee).[88] Thus aliens have been deported for speech for which they could not have been "punished."

As in the case of exclusion, depriving the U.S. audience of the alien's knowledge and ideas remains an illegitimate government purpose absent the imminence of harm required by the *Brandenburg* standard. One cannot soberly presume that aliens as a class have more seductive rhetorical gifts than citizens, and when particular aliens do, the facts may be evaluated accordingly under *Brandenburg*. If aliens are presumed to be so unfamiliar with American institutions that they are unduly susceptible to incitement, then they can be punished for any unlawful acts they commit, and the speakers who incite them—who might as easily be citizens as aliens—may find themselves punishable under *Brandenburg*.

The argument for the constitutional invalidity of ideological deportation has considerable force beyond that of the argument for the constitutional invalidity of ideological exclusion. Deportation has a far harsher impact on most resident aliens than many conceded "punishments," and the threat of deportation creates a greater chilling effect than many nonpunitive civil sanctions that courts have invalidated. Uprooting the alien from home, friends, family, and work would be severe regardless of the country to which the alien was being returned; breaking these attachments inflicts more pain than preventing them from being made. In addition, conditions in the particular country may confront the alien with poverty, disorder, general political repression, or targeted persecution on grounds of ethnicity, religion, politics, or gender.[89]

Aliens know that by entering the United States they become subject to U.S. law, and that the United States is the sovereign with whom they need to reckon in all phases of their lives for the duration of their residency. Thus the chilling effect of the threat to deport residents, unlike the threat to exclude nonresidents, is pervasive.

Conceptualizing deportation as the refusal to renew an invitation to be present might provide a verbal formula for glossing over all these consequences, but it does not realistically suffice to equate deportation with exclusion. Moreover, ideological deportation does not operate as the withdrawal of a subsidy any more than ideological exclusion does: it represents an exceptional sanction against people who were admitted for reasons other than their ideological qualifications.

Nor is censoring the alien's speech and associations after entry a reasonable condition designed to prevent concrete harm. Once the alien has become a resident, the government has the same opportunities and means for evaluating the risk of concrete harms, and the same opportunities and means for preventing them, that it has in the case of a citizen. The government also has the additional option of deporting the alien, on proof less than the reasonable doubt standard, if the alien conspires or attempts to commit genuine acts of terrorism, espionage, or revolutionary violence.[90]

Finally, even if there were some room for ideological exclusion in the name of national self-definition, deporting existing residents for their speech or associations would appear to be an inappropriate and disproportionate means of accomplishing that goal. The means are inappropriate because they come too late—the alien has already expressed "un-American" ideas on American soil, and no one, citizen or alien, can be punished for repeating them. Indeed, when an alien was not excludable, but becomes deportable, on ideological grounds, the probable explanation is that the alien learned his "un-American" ideas *here*, as many deported Communists did.[91] Repudiating the ideas by deporting the alien achieves very little self-definition at very great cost to the individual. If incremental gains in national self-definition by the repudiation of certain ideas are so important, it is difficult to understand why the First Amendment has been interpreted as protecting the citizens who express them. Moreover, ideological deportation grounds whose invocation the alien could not predict would cast their chilling effect over speech and association that the nation does prize more highly, thus impairing both First Amendment values and the United States' own self-definition.

Thus, the notion that resident aliens can be deported for constitutionally protected speech is an atavism in American law. Only the perception of deportation as the withdrawal of a privilege isolated from constitutional values has enabled this practice to continue. Regardless of whether a due process liberty to remain is recognized, the proper perception of deportation as subject to First Amendment side constraints requires that deportation grounds be evaluated by the normal constitutional standards, which will not permit deportation for speech for which the alien could not have been punished. Even if some impediment to the judicial enforcement of these constraints exists, the political branches are obliged to observe them in drafting and applying the laws.

The ideological exclusion of initial entrants presents some closer questions. Exclusion for the purpose of depriving citizens of the alien's speech is illegitimate unless the usual strict constitutional standards are met. Whether initial entrants have free speech rights that constrain immigration policy may depend on whether a mutuality of obligation or a global due process analysis controls. Exclusion statutes that rely categorically on speech or associations as a basis for predicting future misconduct may be invalid, but a contextual comparison of the government's need to rely and the burden placed on the alien's speech rights may be necessary. In such cases, it may be easier to justify the exclusion of nonimmigrants than the exclusion of immigrants.

The inclusion of alien residents in the political communities that make up the United States emphasizes the intertwining of aliens' First Amendment interests with those of citizens. Alien suffrage could be revived, but in its absence there is all the more reason to protect resident aliens' speech.

Chapter Nine

LIMITS OF THE NATION: BIRTHRIGHT CITIZENSHIP AND UNDOCUMENTED CHILDREN

THE UNITED STATES has long regarded American citizenship as "a most precious right."[1] Over the years, diverse conclusions have been drawn from this characterization—sometimes it is too precious to be denied without the highest justification; sometimes it is too precious to be bestowed on the unpopular.[2] In the infamous Dred Scott decision, Chief Justice Taney read the Constitution as making citizenship too precious to be shared with Americans of African descent.[3] After a bloody war between the friends and foes of that decision, Congress drafted a constitutional provision to mandate forever a contrary rule. The first sentence of the Fourteenth Amendment reads: "All persons born or naturalized in the United States, and subject to the jurisdiction thereof, are citizens of the United States and of the State wherein they reside."

The traditional interpretation of this citizenship clause guarantees American citizenship to all children born to aliens within U.S. territory, with a few minor exceptions.[a] The status of the alien parents is irrelevant; they may be permanent residents, lawful nonimmigrants, or unlawfully present. The United States thus follows a version of the *jus soli* rule of citizenship, citizenship by right of the soil, which it inherited from the common law of England. That principle contrasts with the *jus sanguinis* rule, citizenship by right of the blood, under which only the children of citizens inherit citizenship.[4]

Given the outcry against illegal aliens in recent years, it would be surprising if someone had not proposed denying citizenship to their children. Critics of the jus soli rule perceive it as awarding undeserved benefits to the children and their parents, as imposing excessive costs on other citizens, and as an undue encouragement to illegal immigration. California governor Pete Wilson has called for a constitutional amendment to exclude children of illegal aliens from the citizenship clause, and California representatives have introduced suggested amendments in Congress.

---

[a] The exceptions include children born to foreign diplomats, children born on foreign public vessels in U.S. waters, and children born to women accompanying an invading army. A more important exclusion, involving nonalien parents—Native Americans who are members of a tribe—will be discussed later in this chapter.

Two East Coast academics have contended that a constitutional amendment may not be necessary. In a 1985 book, they offered a revisionist interpretation of the citizenship clause, based on a new kind of membership analysis that would restrict the constitutional right of citizenship to children of citizens and permanent residents.[5] An examination of their argument, however, reveals that their interpretation goes beyond any meaning reasonably attributable to the constitutional text and that their effort to find a basis for this idiosyncratic reading in the legislative history of the Fourteenth Amendment is mistaken. Moreover, the authors have fallen prey to the open borders myth, arguing that the citizenship clause did not contemplate undocumented children because immigration was unrestricted before 1875.

Putting aside the interpretive question, the attack on American citizenship practice should be resisted. The jus soli rule entails disadvantages, but it is instrumentally justified as serving a very important principle. The original purpose of the citizenship clause remains valid today: children who are born and grow up in the United States should be full citizens, and no hereditary caste of exploitable denizens should be created.

THE REVISIONIST INTERPRETATION OF THE FOURTEENTH AMENDMENT

The revisionist constitutional argument was elaborated by Peter H. Schuck and Rogers M. Smith in their book *Citizenship without Consent: Illegal Aliens in the American Polity*. The book included a rich historical and political discussion of two opposed conceptions of the criteria for citizenship: citizenship by ascription, in which objective characteristics of individuals result in their assignment to a polity, without regard to the consent of the individual or of the polity, and citizenship by consent, a mutual, voluntary relationship depending on the consent of both the individual and the polity. The authors maintained that this dichotomy of theories was more fundamental than the contrast between two commonly employed rules, the Anglo-American jus soli (citizenship defied by birth within the territory of the state) and the continental jus sanguinis (citizenship defined by descent from a citizen father or possibly mother), both of which they characterized as ascriptive.[6]

As the authors recounted, Sir Edward Coke gave the classic exposition of the English law of ascriptive citizenship in *Calvin's Case* (1608),[7] which clarified the status of persons born in Scotland after the accession of James I to the Crown of England. The common law recognized as subjects of the king all those born within his realm and subject to his laws, even the children of aliens. Coke justified this as the result of a personal relationship of allegiance owed to the sovereign under natural law because of his protection of an infant at its birth. This natural debt bound the subject for life. The correlation between natural allegiance and jus soli was not perfect, however. If alien armies should occupy English soil, their children would not be under the protection of the king and would not be subjects. Also, the king's protection extended to children born to his ambassadors abroad.

The authors then described the emergence of a contrary, consensual theory of citizenship in Anglo-American thought. They emphasized Locke as an exponent of the view that citizenship depended on the explicit or tacit consent of the adult individual, who remained free to withdraw that consent and take on another allegiance.[8] Continental writers in the social contract tradition, like Rousseau, Vattel, and Burlamaqui, also linked citizenship to consent, but they emphasized more than Locke had that the consent must be mutual—the existing body of citizens had a right to decide whom they would welcome into the polity. Even children born within the state to citizen parents were citizens only because of the state's presumed consent.[9] Schuck and Smith noted that this made consent a double-edged sword, because the state's power to withhold or withdraw consent might be abused.[10]

The existence of both these traditions created an inherent tension in the notion of American citizenship. As a nation that had thrown off its former sovereign and also purported to claim the undivided allegiance of naturalized immigrants, the United States had need for consensual theories. The law of naturalization operated consensually, but American law regarding citizenship at birth largely followed the ascriptive common law tradition. The situation was further complicated by uncertainty concerning the degree to which American citizenship was defined by federal, as opposed to state, law.[11] The consensual strand realized its dangerous potential in the Dred Scott decision, in which Chief Justice Taney expounded American citizenship as a club open only to whites. "By making Dred Scott's citizenship turn upon the putative will and intention of the Framers to exclude all blacks from the American political community, Taney seemed to embrace the consensual conception of citizenship, subordinating the conventional ascriptive view."[12]

The citizenship clause of the Fourteenth Amendment, like its verbally different but functionally equivalent predecessor in the 1866 Civil Rights Act, was adopted to overturn the Dred Scott decision by reaffirming the citizenship of native-born blacks.[13] Schuck and Smith argued, however, that the legislative history of these enactments demonstrated an acceptance of both the ascriptive and consensual traditions. They focused especially on the denial of citizenship to Native Americans living under tribal authority. This exclusion was made express in the 1866 Civil Rights Act but appears in the citizenship clause only as a consequence of the limitation of citizenship to those born "subject to the jurisdiction" of the United States. The authors concluded that this phrase added "a transforming consensual conception of the necessary connection between an individual and his government,"[14] one that permitted Congress to withhold American citizenship from certain groups to whose membership the nation does not wish to consent. In their view, this interpretation was more consistent with our nation's liberal ideals.

The authors recognized that the Fourteenth Amendment mandated citizenship for children born within United States territory to parents who were citizens or permanent resident aliens. The logic they reconstructed for this mandate was that admitting the parents as lifelong members entailed the nation's tacit consent to citizenship for their future offspring.[15] No such guarantee was made to children of aliens admitted temporarily, or of undocumented aliens, to whose presence the nation has never consented.[16] The authors proposed that the Supreme Court revise its interpretation of the Fourteenth Amendment, so that Congress would have the power to decide whether or not it wished to deny American citizenship to these groups in the future. They insisted that such a change, if made, should be prospective only, and that Congress should not (even if it could) strip American citizenship from children already born on our soil.[17] They contended, however, that mandating citizenship for undocumented children impaired the nation's right of political self-definition.[18] Further, they argued that the contemporary welfare state made the rewards of unconsented membership too alluring to aliens and too costly to the nation.[19] They suggested that withholding citizenship could contribute to restored control over our borders, because ascriptive citizenship "can only operate, at the margin, as one more incentive to illegal migration."[20]

The authors' theoretical treatment of this subject is admirable in many respects, although their analysis has drawn criticism.[21] This chapter will discuss the *desirability* of denying citizenship to undocumented children later, in the context of proposals to amend the Constitution for that purpose. The distinctive feature of Schuck and Smith's book is the argument that this goal could be accomplished without a constitutional amendment. There are deep flaws, both logical and historical, in the effort to read their theoretical conclusions into the Fourteenth Amendment.

The authors observed that in the course of the Senate debates, the amendment's framers sought to exclude from its scope a few groups whom they did not regard as part of their society, and that the exclusion was accomplished by excepting infants "not subject to the jurisdiction" of the United States at birth from the guarantee of citizenship. Schuck and Smith contended that the language "not subject to the jurisdiction" embodied the consensual approach, and that jurisdiction for citizenship clause purposes could be equated with "a more or less complete, direct power by government over the individual, and a reciprocal relationship between them at the time of birth, in which the government consented to the individual's presence and status and offered him complete protection."[22] They concluded that if Congress withholds its consent to the "presence and status" of an infant, then the infant does not become a U.S. citizen. Thus, Congress has substantial power to determine the scope of birthright citizenship. They "claim that this interpretation best fits the language of the clause and the ways in which American lawmakers have defined the statuses of Native Americans and permanent resident aliens."[23]

This argument suffers from two distinct problems. The first problem arises at the theoretical level: a consensual approach to citizenship need not imply anything about the powers of Congress. The second problem arises in the details. Their "consensual" interpretation yields a less plausible account of the term "subject to the jurisdiction" and is less compatible with the results that the drafters of the citizenship clause intended than the traditional interpretation of the clause.

The Theoretical Problem: Constitution without Consent?

It is true that the politicians who drafted the citizenship clause understood that they had the power to decide who would receive citizenship. It was, after all, a constitution they were amending. But even if the drafters' assumption of power indicated an underlying consensual theory of citizenship, it would not follow that the rule they adopted defined citizenship by "consensual" criteria.

Once one notices that rules of citizenship can be embodied in positive law,[24] one finds an inherent ambiguity in the notion of a consensual approach to citizenship. *Any* freely adopted rule of citizenship expresses the consent of the society that adopts it. That consent can be embodied in a constitution as well as in a statute, and it may define relevant classes by using traditional ascriptive categories as well as those that others would approve as consensual. Schuck and Smith do not deny this fact, but their argument depends on losing sight of it.

A constitution is a mechanism by which a polity, through an extraordinary political process, adopts rules that bind the ordinary legislative process. The Fourteenth Amendment does not set out a theory of citizenship, but rather sets out a rule for determining who is a citizen. Part of that rule, by referring to an ill-defined power of naturalization, does imply a delegation to Congress of discretion to admit or reject alien applicants for citizenship. (In that respect, American law and even English law had always been consensual.) It does not follow that the part of the rule addressing citizenship at birth also delegates discretion to Congress.

The failure of the original Constitution to specify any criteria for birth-right citizenship had opened the door to the Dred Scott decision, and the Reconstruction Congress sought to remedy that omission. Senator Howard, the author of the citizenship clause, introduced it with the following expla-nation: "It settles the great question of citizenship and removes all doubt as to what persons are or are not citizens of the United States. This has long been a great desideratum in the jurisprudence and legislation of this coun-try."[25] This language hardly suggests a delegation of discretion over birth-right citizenship to Congress.

The framers of the Fourteenth Amendment had strong reason for treating the qualifications for birthright citizenship as an issue of constitutional di-mension. They had just overthrown a system founded on the denial of po-litical membership to a race of outsiders. Furthermore, the citizenship clause was designed to forestall future controversies, not only to stabilize the resolution of the African slavery question. For example, Senator Cowan, a vehement opponent of both the Civil Rights Act and the Four-teenth Amendment, predicted increasing difficulty over the Chinese on the Pacific coast. His insinuations must be read to be believed.

> I do not know how my honorable friend from California looks upon Chinese, but I do know how some of his fellow-citizens regard them. I have no doubt that now they are useful, and I have no doubt that within proper restraints, allowing that State and the other Pacific States to manage them as they may see fit, they may be useful; but I would not tie their hands by the Constitution of the United States so as to prevent them hereafter from dealing with them as in their wisdom they see fit.[26]

In response, the supporters of the citizenship clause expressly confirmed their intent to recognize the American citizenship of children born here to Chinese parents.[27] They refused the invitation to create a hereditary caste of voteless denizens, vulnerable to expulsion and exploitation.

Schuck and Smith did consider protection against this danger as a pos-sible purpose of the citizenship clause, but they rejected the danger as exag-gerated, given the availability of other constitutional rights, including non-discrimination.[28] Perhaps in an ideal constitutional world, other rights would exist and be enforced sufficiently to provide compensating protec-tion. But the framers of the Fourteenth Amendment remembered a different world, and the current constitutional world is hardly ideal. Doctrines that the Supreme Court has not yet overruled permit the deportation of aliens, even lawful permanent residents, for constitutionally protected conduct. Nondiscrimination provides, under current doctrine, a particularly hollow protection for hereditary illegal aliens.[29] The rights of the poor often go unenforced. We will return to the problem of hereditary illegality later in the chapter; for now, the framers' decision to use ascriptive citizenship to fight caste was clearly defensible.

Fitting the Data: Jurisdiction, Tribes, and the Immigrant-Nonimmigrant Distinction

The word *jurisdiction* has various meanings in American law, but it has never been defined in terms remotely resembling the elaborate construct on which the revisionist argument depends. The authors' effort to justify their proposal as a permissible "judicial reinterpretation . . . of ambiguous language"[30] turns on their claim that in employing the terminology of jurisdiction, the framers of the citizenship clause nonetheless meant to achieve results that are better captured by their new consensual definition.

The legislative history and the received judicial construction of the citizenship clause confirm that the framers of the Fourteenth Amendment did deny constitutionally mandated citizenship to a few categories of children, whom they regarded as not "subject to the jurisdiction" of the United States. These were the common law exceptions for aliens closely associated with a foreign government, and an American addition—Native Americans living under tribal quasi-sovereignty.[31] Schuck and Smith argued that their consensual theory best explained how these categories could be excluded from the citizenship clause, while resident aliens were included.

One might wonder how, under the nineteenth-century regime of strict territoriality, anyone within the United States could be not subject to its jurisdiction. The common law exceptions involved aliens who did not enter the country as individuals and submit to the laws but entered under the auspices of their governments with legal or factual immunity from local law. Children born on foreign public vessels or to ambassadors of foreign nations were covered by comity principles of international law that restrain the state's exercise of lawmaking power. Children born to parents accompanying an invading army enter under extraordinary circumstances that temporarily oust the operation of local law.[32] Thus, the correlation of allegiance and protection, the mutuality of obligation between the governed and the government, was suspended in these exceptional cases.

The crucial American addition was denial of citizenship to Native Americans born within their own organized political communities. Native Americans were not barred per se from constitutional birthright citizenship, but only if they were born within the governance of their tribes. Without seeking to justify the exclusion, one can explain it as follows. The tribes were separate, self-governing political communities whose sovereignty predated the Constitution. At the time of the adoption of the Fourteenth Amendment, the federal government did not exercise legislative power directly over their members but negotiated treaties with the tribes as sovereign powers.[33] That is why both the original Constitution and the Fourteenth Amendment excluded "Indians not taxed"—that is, those living under tribal governance, over whom Congress did not exercise the taxing power—from the basis of apportionment.[34] Native Americans living in their tribal societies were governed by their own legal systems, like aliens who had remained under their own governments and diplomats, and unlike alien immigrants and visitors, who submitted to the laws of the state and federal governments upon entry.[35] In their day-to-day lives, they were under the protection of their tribes, not of the state or federal government. The point was not that Native Americans had *dual* allegiances, to the tribe and to the United States, but that their allegiance to the United States was mediated through the tribe. The effective legal and military independence of many tribes from state or federal governance made this notion of "domestic dependent nations" more realistic in 1866 than it subsequently became.[b]

Thus, the term *jurisdiction* can be given a natural reading as actual subjection to the lawmaking power of the state; this interpretation fulfills the framers' intentions and echoes the common law notion of the king's "protection," ascriptive though that may be.[36] This is how the Supreme Court has explained the meaning of the citizenship clause.

The revisionist argument seeks to draw wholly different conclusions from this legislative history. It interprets *jurisdiction* as requiring the existence of *consent to citizenship*, that is, "a reciprocal relationship between them at the time of birth, in which the government consented to the individual's presence and status and offered him complete protection."[37] The authors then deduced that Congress had power to deny citizenship on consensual grounds to classes distinguishable in terms of the authors' notions of consent, even if those classes were not distinguishable in terms of any previous conception of jurisdiction. In particular, they agreed that the Constitution mandates citizenship for all children born in the United States to lawfully admitted permanent resident aliens. Yet they maintained that constitutionally guaranteed citizenship should be denied to children born to aliens who have been lawfully admitted on a less permanent basis, because the United States has not tacitly consented to citizenship for such children.[38] They accomplished this result by making consent to citizenship for these children an element of jurisdiction and then asserting that the nation has implicitly given its consent to permanent, but not temporary, resident aliens: "[T]he government has declined to consent to their political membership or permanent presence in the society."[39]

Why should we think that the nation has given the necessary consent to the children of permanent resident aliens but not to the children of any

---

[b] The federal government ceased negotiating treaties with Native American tribes in 1871 and began an aggressive campaign of assimilation to dismantle tribes in 1887, which continued into the 1920s. See Felix S. Cohen, Handbook of Federal Indian Law 105–07, 127–43, 639–45 (1982 ed.). Whether tribal societies could still be considered not "subject to the jurisdiction" of the United States today is an interesting question but fortunately moot, because all Native Americans born in the United States have been citizens by statute, regardless of their tribal status, since 1924. See Act of June 2, 1924, ch. 233, 43 Stat. 253, 8 U.S.C. § 1401(b).

other aliens?ᶜ To fit the data, the authors needed to reconcile their consent theory with the treatment of Chinese children in the legislative history of the citizenship clause and *United States v. Wong Kim Ark* (1898), a pillar of American citizenship law.[40] In *Wong Kim Ark*, the Supreme Court held that a child born in San Francisco to Chinese parents legally residing there was an American citizen, notwithstanding the fact that Congress had always excluded the Chinese from eligibility for naturalization, and notwithstanding the subsequent impact of anti-Chinese feeling on federal immigration legislation. This does not look like a consensual holding, and in fact the *dissent* in that case closely parallels Schuck and Smith's political theory: citizenship determined by birthplace was a feudal anachronism inappropriate for a society that had thrown off the chains of monarchy; Vattel and other writers on international law had correctly explained citizenship as dependent on descent from citizens and tacit consent; this country had never sought the Chinese as citizens but had barred them from citizenship as effectively as it could by legislation and treaties. Accordingly, the dissent concluded, children born to Chinese parents, even in San Francisco, cannot be citizens of the United States.[41] The majority, however, rejected this logical consensual argument. The majority agreed that the Chinese were barred from naturalization but insisted that the Fourteenth Amendment had placed the citizenship of native-born children beyond the power of Congress.[42] The citizenship clause codified the common law rules of citizenship by birth within the territory, with the single additional exception of Native Americans in tribal status. Children born to foreigners outside the diplomatic or military context, whether temporarily or permanently sojourning, became citizens at common law. In fact, the legislative history of the Fourteenth Amendment demonstrated Congress's awareness that one effect of the rule would be to confer citizenship on children born to the Chinese in California.[43]

Schuck and Smith shrugged off *Wong Kim Ark* as an "[e]xpansive, but not universal" use of ascriptive citizenship in the Fourteenth Amendment and would limit it to children of lawfully admitted permanent resident aliens.[44] This compromise ignores the havoc that *Wong Kim Ark* wreaks upon their theory of citizenship.[45] The decision rests squarely on the wording of

---

ᶜ The argument is even more circular than readers unversed in the intricacies of twentieth-century immigration law may realize. Current doctrine guarantees no alien "permanent presence," but at most presence until Congress changes its mind. Some permanent residents have rendered themselves deportable by later conduct, and others were mistakenly admitted and so have been deportable from the outset. Some nonimmigrants are admitted for very brief stays, but others are admitted on an indefinitely renewable basis. Refugees may be permitted to remain in a variety of statuses pending the solution of crises that will never be solved. The discretionary enforcement of the immigration laws produces other classes of aliens whom the federal government has resolved not to deport and who may remain forever in a twilight status. It is difficult to see how tacit consent theory can maintain its bearings amid the bewildering array of categories, of which these are only a sample.

the citizenship clause and the common law jus soli tradition that it incorporated, not on any special privileges of permanent residents.[46] In what sense had the United States given more consent to "the political membership or permanent presence" of Wong Kim Ark's parents than to a nonimmigrant alien? First, Congress had obviously not consented to their active political membership: Chinese immigrants were racially ineligible for naturalization throughout the nineteenth century.[47] This barred them from voting not only as citizens, but even through the regime of declarant alien suffrage, and the Fifteenth Amendment was deliberately drafted to preserve this barrier.[48] Second, Congress had never expressly consented to the parents' *permanent* presence; it had just failed to exclude them. The distinction between temporary and permanent admission to the United States did not exist until the twentieth century. Correspondingly, the Court's phraseology in *Wong Kim Ark* wanders unpredictably, failing to maintain any consistent distinction between parents residing permanently and parents temporarily present.[49] Moreover, the Chinese were generally regarded as "sojourners," provisional labor migrants, rather than settlers in the nineteenth century.[50] Third, by the time *Wong Kim Ark* was decided, the Supreme Court had made clear its view that aliens were subject to exclusion and expulsion whenever Congress found it expedient, regardless of what promises Congress might have made them, precisely in cases involving Congress's discriminatory actions against the Chinese.[51] If the phrase "subject to the jurisdiction" left Congress any flexibility for consent-based restrictions at all, surely the Court could have read it as leaving aliens whose reception was so chilly still "subject to the jurisdiction" of their native land and not of the United States.

Schuck and Smith sought to provide a context that would make their interpretation more plausible by suggesting that the framers had borrowed a minority variant of the Continental public law position on birthright citizenship, under which citizenship was determined by descent, but in which consent extended to the children of domiciled aliens as well as citizens.[52] Unfortunately, their evidence for the existence of such a variant depended on a dubious interpretation of the following sentence from Jean Jacques Burlamaqui's *Principles of Natural and Politic Law*:

> Now if the children of members of the state, upon attaining to the years of discretion, are willing to live in the place of their parentage, or in their native country, they are by this very act supposed to submit themselves to the power that governs the state, and consequently they ought to enjoy, as members of that state, the advantages naturally arising from it.[53]

This sentence is preceded by Burlamaqui's explanation of how mutual consent arises from the sovereign's presumed promise to members of the state that their descendants will also be members, "provided nevertheless that these descendants, when they attain to the use of reason, be on their part willing to submit to the government."[54] Evidently the "state" in the key sentence is the same state of which the parents are members, and to whose power the children must agree to submit.[d] Burlamaqui is not discussing children of domiciled aliens, as is clear for two reasons: first, the original French text actually specifies children of citizens (*Citoyens*), and second, even the translation emphasizes only two paragraphs later that "members of the state" is a synonym for citizens:

> Subjects are sometimes called *cives*, or members of the civil state; some indeed make no distinction between these two terms, but I think it is better to distinguish them. The appellation of *civis* ought to be understood only of those who share in all the advantages and privileges of the association, and who are properly members of the state either by birth, or in some other manner. All the rest are rather inmates, strangers, or temporary inhabitants, than members.[55]

Thus, Burlamaqui provides no basis for reconciling the authors' theory with the Fourteenth Amendment.

In short, the revisionist interpretation of the phrase "subject to the jurisdiction thereof" lacks plausibility as an exercise in interpreting the constitutional text. Rather, it seeks to *replace* the constitutional language with a meaning that the authors discerned in the legislative history. According to Schuck and Smith, the framers freed themselves from the common law ascriptive approach and incorporated modern consensual principles into the formula for constitutional citizenship. But this is an impossible characterization of the legislative history. The debates make it very clear that the framers of the Fourteenth Amendment did not view themselves as adopting revolutionary new principles of citizenship by consent. Taney had done that in the Dred Scott decision, denying blacks citizenship on the ground that whites did not consider them appropriate partners in the political community. The framers sought to overturn Taney's innovation and to reaffirm on a racially neutral basis the same principles that had always governed

---

[d] Schuck and Smith appear to deny this in asserting that "Burlamaqui's contrast of 'place of parentage' and 'native country' suggests that he believed that the 'place of parentage' should and would extend the opportunity for membership to the children of resident aliens." This is highly improbable because of the context of the sentence. Moreover, even if Burlamaqui were suddenly addressing how the children of citizens of one state could assert a right to citizenship in another state (their "place of parentage," loosely translating "*le lieu de leur famille*"), then his discussion would contain no restriction to children born to domiciled aliens.

Instead, Burlamaqui presumably meant that children of citizens submit to their parents' sovereign either by continuing to live with or near their parents, or by living anywhere in the sovereign's territory. The first alternative is needed in those cases where citizen parents live outside the sovereign's territory while maintaining their allegiance to the sovereign (for example, merchants). The descent of citizenship to children outside the territory is an important feature of the continental rule of *jus sanguinis*.

American citizenship for persons of European descent. As Senator Howard observed, "This amendment which I have offered is simply declaratory of what I regard as the law of the land already, that every person born within the limits of the United States, and subject to their jurisdiction, is by virtue of natural law and national law a citizen of the United States."[56] The framers did not see their object as charting a new, modern course for citizenship law; nor did the language they chose inadvertently impose such a course.

Fitting the Data: Illegal Aliens

The foregoing analysis is probably sufficient to refute the revisionist interpretation of the Fourteenth Amendment. Nonetheless, the application of that interpretation to children of illegal aliens also deserves attention, both because it is the politically salient category and because it illustrates a form of argument used in other contexts as well.[e] Schuck and Smith claimed that the framers of the Fourteenth Amendment could not have contemplated conferring citizenship on children of illegal aliens "for the simple reason that no illegal aliens existed at that time, or indeed for some time thereafter."[57] They painted a picture of an era of wholly unrestricted immigration, with the attendant implication that the Fourteenth Amendment could have nothing relevant to say about aliens whose entry into the country was unlawful or their children.[58] This argument is doubly fallacious. First, immigration was not unrestricted prior to 1875. Second, the revisionist interpretation would have defeated part of the central purpose of the Fourteenth Amendment: to protect the citizenship of African Americans born in the United States.

The authors dismiss too quickly the antebellum regulation of immigration.[59] As Chapter Two demonstrated at length, considerable regulation of immigration existed at the state level; most of it enjoyed a degree of federal endorsement; and some of it was backed by federal sanctions. It was only

---

[e] For example, the counting of undocumented aliens for apportionment purposes has been challenged on the theory that undocumented aliens are not "persons" within the meaning of the apportionment clauses:

> Most important, on each occasion when the phrase "whole number of persons" was adopted as part of the Constitution, there was no person who could be an undocumented alien; prior to the enactment of the first immigration statute in 1875, all aliens were lawfully present in the United States. Therefore, in determining who must be counted for congressional apportionment purposes, the term "persons" need not be read as embracing those possessing a status that did not exist at the time of constitutional enactment and amendment.

Jim Slattery & Howard Bauleke, "The Right to Govern Is Reserved to Citizens": Counting Undocumented Aliens in the Federal Census for Reapportionment Purposes, 28 Washburn L.J. 227, 231 (1988).

in 1876, after Congress had begun to restrict European immigration, that the Supreme Court began invalidating state exclusions as an interference with foreign commerce.[60] What implication do the earlier laws have for the rights of undocumented aliens and their children?

In relative terms, Schuck and Smith rightly observed that there was less public concern about border control in the era before the quantitative restriction of immigration. I have seen no evidence that the term *illegal alien* was in general use before 1875.[61] That term is more a colloquial label than a legal phrase, however.[62] Its central connotation is an alien whose presence in this country involves a violation of the law that has not been cured. There are, however, different manners in which an alien's presence could be said to violate the law,[63] and there are different forms of curative government action that may impart degrees of legality to the alien's presence.[64] The legal consequences of immigration-law violations vary greatly with circumstances and are constantly changing.

From the point of view of an individual state, an alien whose entry involved a violation of state law would seem to be an illegal alien. The parallel holds most strongly in those instances where the state law addressed its prohibition to the alien, or where physical removal of the alien was a legal sanction.[65]

The parallel may seem weaker when the state law punished a carrier or other third party but not the immigrant. Still, concentration of sanctions on the third party does not indicate that the immigrant was authorized to enter the United States, any more than concentration of sanctions on the seller indicates that a consumer is authorized to purchase forbidden goods or services. Whether the exclusionary purpose justifies considering unlawfully landed passengers as the equivalent of modern illegal aliens depends on whether one considers the salient feature of illegal status to be the objective contradiction between the alien's presence and the will of the territorial sovereign or the subjective culpability of the individual alien in violating a legal norm directed specifically to her. Federal immigration law is usually regarded as a system of civil regulatory control of the objective state of affairs, as exemplified by Justice Holmes's definition of deportation as "simply a refusal by the Government to harbor persons whom it does not want."[66] This objective character also explains the application of the label "illegal alien" to children and others who are not responsible for their presence in the United States.[67] Thus, state laws with only third-party sanctions may have produced further categories of illegal aliens.

The objective contradiction of expressed sovereign will would appear to be the relevant feature in analyzing the consequences of illegal alien status under a consent-based theory that makes an obligation of the polity depend on its voluntary invitation of aliens into the community. It is true, however, that Schuck and Smith sometimes emphasized the personal culpability of undocumented parents as part of their argument for denying citizenship to those parents' children.[68] Yet it is difficult to see why the culpability of the parents should be the determining factor in deciding upon the status of their children, who are powerless to control the place of their birth.

A further level of analysis is needed to decide whether a state's illegal aliens were also illegal aliens vis-à-vis the United States. In most cases, that depends on how one aggregates varying local criteria. The one uniform federal exclusion policy was the ban on the importation of slaves from 1808 on. But immigration law need not be territorially uniform. An excludable alien in New York is no less excludable because the same ground of exclusion is inapplicable in Guam.[69] The varying state laws in the nineteenth century were enacted by different governments, but some of those laws were backed up by federal statutes, and others enjoyed federal approval. If the policy of the United States was to leave certain categories of immigration regulation to the states, then constitutionally valid state immigration laws embodied the immigration policy of the United States. An illegal immigrant to Massachusetts who remained in Massachusetts would then be an illegal immigrant to the United States, even if that immigrant would have faced no barrier in entering Michigan. If we wish to frame this in terms of a theory of political consent, then the federal constitutional validity of state immigration laws would suggest that the state is authorized to withhold the polity's consent to the entry of an alien across the state's borders.

Thus, it seems fair to say that illegal aliens, even vis-à-vis the nation, have always existed in the United States. They are not a new phenomenon that could not have been contemplated by the Framers of the Constitution or the framers of the Fourteenth Amendment. I am aware of no evidence that children born in the United States to European parents whose entry involved a violation of state poor laws, state exclusion of criminals, or state quarantine laws was for that reason viewed as not a citizen of the United States, before or after the adoption of the Fourteenth Amendment. Nor am I aware of any evidence that children born in the United States to aliens who had failed to register during the brief period of mandatory federal registration were ever denied citizenship.[70] Absent such evidence, historical considerations would appear to reinforce, not undermine, the conclusion that children of undocumented parents are "subject to the jurisdiction" of the United States and therefore citizens.

The second defect in the authors' treatment of immigration history is far more important, however: they overlooked the problem of the citizenship of children of illegally imported African slaves. The prohibition of all further importation of slaves was not merely a local policy endorsed by Congress, but a uniform national policy from 1808 until the abolition of slavery.[71] Yet despite Congress's prompt exercise of its constitutional power, the shameful traffic continued.[72] Congress was forced to legislate repeatedly for its suppression up through the time of the Civil War.[73] But the borders of the United States proved as hard to patrol then as they are today. Conservative estimates of the numbers of illegally imported slaves put them in the tens of thousands.[74] On a few occasions, the government successfully carried out the intent of the statute that slave ships be intercepted and their passengers returned to freedom in Africa.[75]

Here, then, was a notorious category of illegal aliens whose presence in the United States was without the federal government's consent. If, as the revisionist argument insists, consent does not extend to the children of parents not lawfully admitted to the United States, then the Fourteenth Amendment did not constitutionally mandate American citizenship for the children of illegally imported slaves.[76] Yet there can be no doubt how a court in 1868 should have resolved any attack on the citizenship of former slaves whose parents or grandparents had been illegally imported.[77] Illegally imported slaves are not mentioned in the debates, but the framers made it clear that guaranteeing citizenship to *all* native-born blacks was their central purpose. Senator Trumbull's first draft of a citizenship provision for the 1866 Civil Rights Act stated "[t]hat all persons of African descent born in the United States are hereby declared to be citizens of the United States,"[78] and no one, including Schuck and Smith, has ever suggested that the Fourteenth Amendment was intended to cover *fewer* of the former slaves.[f]

This necessary conclusion cannot be reconciled with the consensual reading of the citizenship clause. The problem cannot be avoided by translating the framers' apparent solicitude for the former slaves directly into citizenship. As drafters of legislation and of the Constitution, they chose a form of words, and the consent must be sought in some tenable interpretation of the words. In fact, the consent of the framers is irrelevant: the mechanism of birthright citizenship operates by making the child's citizenship depend upon facts existing at the time of the child's birth. The authors agreed with the courts that constitutional birthright citizenship extends only to those who were "subject to the jurisdiction" of the United States *at the time of birth*.[79] There is no consistent principle by which the citizenship clause can be interpreted as simultaneously including all native-born former slaves and excluding all children of parents to whose entry into the country the nation has not consented.

---

[f] Similarly, fully overturning the Dred Scott decision would require a guarantee of citizenship for children born to free black parents who had entered the United States in violation of one of the state bans on free black immigration backed up by the federal statute of 1803. I give this category less emphasis because I know of no estimate of the number of persons it contained.

It is thus not far-fetched to suggest that the framers of the Fourteenth Amendment would have approved constitutionally mandated citizenship for children whose parents had come to our shores without the nation's consent. To the contrary, the Civil Rights Act and the citizenship clause embraced the descendants of tens of thousands of such parents, under criteria based on the fact of presence and subjection to United States law at birth, not on the manner of the parents' arrival.

AMENDING THE FOURTEENTH AMENDMENT

The defense of the American jus soli rule need not rest on historical and interpretive considerations. Because a constitutional amendment has been proposed, the shape of U.S. citizenship law should also be approached as an open question.[80] The advantages and disadvantages of the proposed amendments should be considered.

Two of the recent proposals would amend the citizenship clause by inserting limiting language. Representative Beilenson's version would reserve birthright citizenship for "persons born in the United States, and subject to the jurisdiction thereof, of a mother or father who is a legal resident of the United States."[81] Representative Gallegly's version would reserve it for "persons born in the United States, and subject to the jurisdiction thereof, of mothers who are citizens or legal residents of the United States."[82] It appears that despite the political emphasis on undocumented alien parents, both of these proposals would deny birthright citizenship to children whose parents were lawfully present but not resident in the United States, that is, most nonimmigrant aliens. Thus, they followed the Schuck and Smith design, except for Gallegly's limitation to mothers.[g] Representative Taylor's version aimed only at undocumented parents, continuing to guarantee birthright citizenship to children if either parent "is lawfully in the United States, or has a lawful status."[83]

---

[g] The only kind thing that can be said about the gendered version of the proposal is that it counterbalances the former rule that American citizenship descended to a child born abroad only through the father. The provisions in section 2 of the Fourteenth Amendment reducing the representation of states that disenfranchised male voters once disrupted the gender neutrality of the Constitution, but the Nineteenth Amendment restored it. It would be highly offensive to write gender discrimination into section 1 of the Fourteenth Amendment.

The proposal exhibits a disturbing indifference to the realities of female immigration. A substantial number of undocumented women are deliberately kept undocumented by their citizen or lawful resident alien husbands as a means of control. See Janet M. Calvo, Spouse-Based Immigration Laws: The Legacies of Coverture, 28 San Diego L. Rev. 593 (1991). By specifically denying citizenship to children born in such marriages, this proposal would increase the opportunity for abuse.

None of these proposals made clear what the status of the children would be, and none of these proposals included any compensating improvements in their rights. Presumably Congress would have discretion to determine their status and would most likely leave them in the position of undocumented aliens.[84]

Disadvantages of the Jus Soli Rule

Schuck and Smith identified a number of linked disadvantages to birthright citizenship for the children of undocumented parents, and the proponents of constitutional amendments have picked up on their themes.[85] First, it represents an unconsented increase in the citizenry. This is offensive per se for reasons of political theory; it uses up immigration slots that could be better allocated; and it provokes public resentment against immigration. Second, these unwanted citizens impose financial costs on the nation, state, and locality in education, medical care, housing, and welfare. Whether these are net costs in the aggregate to the nation is a subject of continuing controversy,[86] but we may assume that they are.[h] Third, the birth of citizen children makes it easier for undocumented parents to remain in the United States, either by invoking hardship to the children as a basis for discretionary relief from deportation or by having the children petition for the lawful immigration of the parents once the children reach the age of twenty-one. Fourth, several of these disadvantages are advantages to the parents, and so they operate, at least at the margin, as further incentives to illegal immigration.

We can start by pruning the list of disadvantages. Some of them exist in the eye of the beholder. As previously explained, undocumented aliens' children are only unconsented additions to the polity if the polity rejects the jus soli rule, and they incite opposition to immigration only among people who reject the jus soli rule (most of whom already oppose immigration on other grounds). If reasons exist that justify the constitutional jus soli rule, and the public accepts the reasons, then the first objection evaporates, and the second becomes much less important.

---

[h] Schuck and Smith were unwilling in 1985 to rely on the outcome of this disputed empirical issue. They wrote:

> [T]he question of birthright citizenship for the children of illegal and nonimmigrant aliens probably should not turn on the conclusions that such revenue-cost analyses reach, important as those analyses may be for policy guidance. Instead, we believe, this question should be resolved in the light of broader ideals of constitutional meaning, social morality, and political community.

Peter H. Schuck & Roger M. Smith, Citizenship without Consent: Illegal Aliens in the American Polity 113 (1985).

Other disadvantages depend on curable forms of generosity in existing immigration practice. Having citizen children is no legal defense to deportation, and the government often accepts the de facto deportation of citizen children as a necessary cost of enforcing the immigration laws against their parents.[87] Nonetheless, current law does permit deportable aliens to point to the citizen children born to them during their periods of unlawful presence as a reason for the immigration authorities to exercise extraordinary discretion to allow them to remain.[88] Most such efforts fail. If the opportunity to request clemency on these particular grounds creates undue incentives for illegal immigration, it can be eliminated directly; it is surely overkill to eliminate it indirectly by stripping the children of citizenship. Similarly, if Congress is indignant about aliens who sneak into the United States to have children in the hope of immigrating legally twenty-one years later, then Congress can bar such aliens from eligibility to immigrate on that basis. Thus, the particular disadvantage that Schuck and Smith identify is illusory. The problem they address does, however, pose a real normative dilemma: a society that affords birthright citizenship to the children of undocumented parents and yet wishes to control immigration may not be able to give full respect to both family unity and the right of citizens to remain in the territory.

The following other genuine disadvantages must still be recognized: The children of self-selected illegal immigrants may be less valuable additions to the U.S. population than other potential immigrants whom Congress might choose to admit in their place. The children may impose costs for education and other public benefits and services that exceed the benefits that the public will ever derive from them. And birthright citizenship may operate as an additional incentive to illegal immigration, because parents may want to obtain it for their children, and because they may use it to obtain some public benefits for themselves.

Schuck and Smith's assertion that citizenship "operate[s], at the margin, as one more incentive to illegal migration," suggests a recognition that withdrawing birthright citizenship would have a minor impact on the rate of illegal immigration.[89] Pregnant women would no longer have the incentive to make brief trips for the purpose of conferring citizenship on their children. Aliens would lose whatever incentive exists to enter for the purpose of obtaining the limited benefits, such as Aid to Families with Dependent Children (AFDC) and food stamps, available through their citizen children. But aliens who come for the sake of employment or to flee violent conditions in their home countries—as most do—would still have strong incentives for entry. Representative Gallegly would be just as concerned to protect his constituents from aliens who came to this country to "steal their jobs."[90] As David Martin has observed, if immigration enforcement were effective enough to counter those other incentives, the question of undocumented infants would lose its practical significance. Withdrawing birth-right citizenship is either a superfluous or an insubstantial element of an immigration control strategy.[91]

The Reasons That Justify the Jus Soli Rule

Surely the soil of the United States does not possess some magic quality by which every infant born there is tied to the soil or absorbs from the soil the quality of Americanism at birth. Consider the anecdotes concerning Mexican women who struggle across the border in the last hours of their pregnancies in order to confer U.S. citizenship on their children and then return to Mexico.[92] Viewing the individual case in isolation, it is hard to see why an infant who has spent only her first few days in Texas must be given U.S. citizenship. Compared with other infants born in Texas, there may be some inequality in denying this infant citizenship due to her parentage, an accident of birth over which she has no control. But the location of her birth is equally an accident over which the infant has no control. Once we accept the fundamental inequality that children born in Mexico to Mexican parents can be excluded from the United States, nationality will always be a matter of good or bad fortune from the infant's perspective. If the laws had been obeyed, she would have been born in Mexico, and perhaps the law should pretend that she *was* born in Mexico.

As a thought experiment, let us hypothesize an immigration agency that operates humanely, with an imperfect exclusion apparatus but superb enforcement efficiency in deportation. It identifies every alien who enters the United States unlawfully and courteously deports each one within a week of entry. The agency never errs in its deportation functions, and deported aliens do not reenter unlawfully. Assume that medical complications making it unsafe to move mother or child never arise and that childbirth services are not affected by the immigration enforcement regime. In this world of superefficient enforcement, there would be no injustice in abolishing birthright citizenship for children born to unlawful entrants. The children would have no individual claim to citizenship, and denying them citizenship would have no predictable adverse consequences on the rights of others. The children should not have been born in the United States, and they would not have been if the exclusion apparatus were better. Their presence was fleeting; the law does not concern itself with trifles.

Of course, that world is a fantasy. The real immigration service has vastly less success in identifying unlawful entrants and in deporting them rapidly; often it does not trouble to deport them at all. The agency has similar problems with aliens who enter lawfully as nonimmigrants and then overstay their visas. One study estimated that there were 700,000 undocumented aliens and 250,000 citizen children with undocumented mothers in

Los Angeles County in 1992.[93] An earlier study had estimated that citizen children were being born to undocumented mothers at the rate of 75,000 per year nationwide in 1980–81.[94] A General Accounting Office investigation into nationwide AFDC costs for citizen children of undocumented parents estimated that 103,000 households with at least one undocument parent and 89,000 households with both parents undocumented were receiving AFDC benefits in 1992.[95] Under the 1986 legalization program, the INS granted legal status to more than 1.2 million aliens who had unlawfully entered the United States and then remained in unlawful status for five years, and more than 250,000 who had entered lawfully and then overstayed their visas by five years.[96] One statistical analysis of the 1980 census suggested that the census had counted more than 500,000 undocumented aliens who had been in the country more than ten years, and more than 500,000 who had been in the country between six and ten years.[97] Current estimates of undocumented aliens nationwide exceed 3 million.[98]

Against this background, we cannot assume that children born as undocumented aliens will be promptly deported. Vast numbers of them will remain in the United States, for substantial periods of time or forever. The federal government has neither the resources nor the will to deport all the harmless children whose parents have immigrated illegally. The crucial question is what happens to those children.

In *Plyler v. Doe*, the Supreme Court observed:

> Sheer incapability or lax enforcement of the laws barring entry into this country, coupled with failure to establish an effective bar to the employment of undocumented aliens, has resulted in the creation of a substantial "shadow population" of illegal migrants—numbering in the millions—within our borders. This situation raises the specter of a permanent caste of undocumented resident aliens, encouraged by some to remain here as a source of cheap labor, but nevertheless denied the benefits that our society makes available to citizens and lawful residents. The existence of such an underclass presents most difficult problems for a Nation that prides itself on adherence to principles of equality under law.[99]

With those circumstances in mind, a bare majority of the Court invalidated Texas's exclusion of undocumented alien children from its public schools. The Court found it "difficult to understand precisely what the State hopes to achieve by promoting the creation and perpetuation of a subclass of illiterates within our boundaries."[100] Nonetheless, four justices dissented, contending that the Court's decision represented good social policy but bad constitutional law; and the majority itself indicated that it might have deferred to an identical policy adopted by Congress.[101]

Withdrawal of birthright citizenship would aggravate the caste division highlighted in *Plyler* by making undocumented status hereditary. The United States has traditionally gained great assimilative advantages from bringing the disabilities of alienage to an end after one generation.[102] One need only compare the situation in a country like Germany, which adheres to the jus sanguinis rule despite substantial immigration, to gain insight into the tragedies we are avoiding. Having encouraged labor migration on a theoretically temporary basis, Germany has found itself since the late 1970s with a growing population of former "guestworkers" and their descendants, of which the largest group are Turkish nationals. Children born to the guestworkers in Germany and children born there to those children remain alien residents, culturally isolated and subject to the rigors of the Aliens Act. They were discouraged from naturalization in the land of their birth, which saw little benefit to itself from their inclusion. Meanwhile, they have been subjected to discriminations that are excused as being based on citizenship rather than ethnicity.[103] Ironically, naturalization policy for the guestworkers and their descendants was loosened in 1990, the year in which East and West Germany reunited.[104] Unification unleashed displays of nationalism that further rejected the Turks and cost some of them their lives.[105] Aliens newly eligible for naturalization have been understandably reluctant to accept it, particularly because they must give up their prior nationality to obtain it. Yet for many of these children, the German society that rejects them offers the only way of life they have ever known. Returning to Turkey would mean culture shock as well as poverty.

At least the guestworkers' descendants in Germany are lawful residents. Hereditary undocumented aliens in the United States would be vulnerable to an even broader range of public and private retaliation. The continuous threat of deportation inhibits undocumented aliens from seeking the protection of the law against violence or exploitation.[106] That is a major part of their attraction for unscrupulous employers. The constitutional division of authority between state and federal governments also puts aliens at risk of hostile behavior from states that are frustrated by their lack of control over immigration enforcement. In recent years, California has witnessed a movement to deprive undocumented aliens of access to numerous benefits, from education, welfare, and public housing to emergency medical care and workers' compensation.[107] In November 1994, this movement culminated in the adoption of the voter initiative Proposition 187, which aimed at a comprehensive exclusion of illegal aliens from state-funded social services, medical care, and education.[108] Its provisions would also deny prenatal care to undocumented women whose children would be born as U.S. citizens, and they would discourage citizen children of undocumented parents from attending school by requiring school officials to investigate the parents' immigration status. Some of these restrictions would violate current federal statutory law, and others might offend the Equal Protection Clause under the reasoning of *Plyler v. Doe*.[109] Unfortunately, the continued viability of that precedent, let alone its extension to closely related contexts, is uncertain. Indeed, Chief Justice Rehnquist has consistently dissented from decisions invalidating alienage discrimination, and he claimed in *United States v. Verdugo-Urquidez* that whether undocumented aliens had Fourth Amendment rights was an open question.[110]

The stark legal distinction between the first generation of native-born children protected by the citizenship clause and their slightly older brothers and sisters who share the parents' undocumented status reflects the tradition of determining nationality at birth and the need for administrable rules more than the children's subjective realities. The government could hardly measure each child's subjective attachment to the United States. Birth in the United States serves as a very determinate and documentable place to draw the line between foreign ancestors and American descendants. For the later generations of native-born children, the link to their supposed foreign country is likely to become highly attenuated.

The bright-line character of the jus soli rule also protects children of U.S. citizens. At present, proof of citizenship reduces to proof of place of birth.[111] Adults who were born in the United States do not find themselves called upon to demonstrate the immigration status of their parents at the time of their birth, or of their grandparents at the time of their parents' birth. Not only may documents be inaccessible, but deciding from a complex fact situation whether an alien was in lawful status on a given day can become an extraordinarily difficult undertaking. Conceivably these determinations will be eased by the establishment of a nationwide registry of personal status on the European model. The United States has traditionally avoided this system, associating it with a police state, but immigration enforcement strategies may nonetheless move the country in that direction.[112]

Thus, as Schuck and Smith recognized, the net costs imposed by the citizen children of undocumented aliens, including the opportunity costs of using up immigration slots, must be balanced against the costs of denying them citizenship status given that so many of them will remain. These costs include the blighting of the children's lives and the harm to U.S. society and values that would result from the creation of a hereditary undocumented caste. There may also be costs to citizens rendered less secure in their citizenship by the adoption of citizenship criteria that are harder to prove.

Yet it would be a serious error to focus only on the magnitude of the injustice that would result if birthright citizenship were eliminated for some category of aliens' children and the law otherwise stayed the same. Constitutional limitations are intended to anticipate future occasions when the electorate or the legislature may betray the principles that they consider fundamental on more deliberate reflection. The framers of the Fourteenth Amendment could have overturned the Dred Scott decision simply by conferring on Congress the power to define the criteria for national citizenship, but they did not trust later legislatures to respect the rights of African Americans or Asian Americans. History has amply vindicated that judgment.

Future developments might similarly increase native-born children's need for citizenship. Observers agree that the United States has currently handicapped immigration enforcement through underfunding and inadequate legal frameworks while directing rhetoric and harsh symbolic measures against undocumented aliens.[113] One may assume that a public choice analysis of legislative response to inconsistent pressures from employers, civil libertarians, and various ethnic groups explains how this could happen inadvertently. But such mixed strategies can be pursued calculatedly as well. Congress could deliberately maintain a two-track immigration regime, under which some immigrants would be admitted as lawful permanent residents on a naturalization track and others would be induced to reside unlawfully and threatened with a sufficient risk of deportation to render them docile and to avoid the applicability of the amended citizenship clause. That scheme could be motivated by a combination of greed and contempt for human rights.

Alternatively, a dual migration scheme could be motivated by ethnic strife. The effort to maintain the dominance of English over Spanish in the United States might someday lead Congress to reduce legal immigration severely while still affording employers de facto access to Latin American labor pools. In a global environment of overpopulation and Third World underdevelopment, that strategy could transform the United States into precisely the sort of society that the Fourteenth Amendment sought to prevent.

The campaign for the "control of our borders" is partly a struggle over the future racial, linguistic, and cultural development of American society. The nation has faced such a struggle before and has concluded that it should not be waged through the high-stakes weapon of manipulating the citizenship of the native-born. The question now is whether to throw off that restraint and sacrifice the children of undocumented parents in order to reduce spending on public services and to achieve symbolic gains in the control of immigration. It seems historically appropriate that the political pressure for this proposal comes from California, just like Chinese exclusion and Japanese internment. This time, the United States should resist more firmly.

Chapter Ten

CONCLUSION

> [I]n the beginning, all the World was *America.*
> *(John Locke)*

THE UNITED STATES was once a world to itself. Oceans, deserts, and forests insulated it from other nations. The rigors of transportation in the age of sail and wagon impeded migration. Andrew Jackson won the Battle of New Orleans after the Treaty of Ghent had been signed but before the news could reach the combatants.

Technology has transformed those conditions. Sri Lankan refugees now find their way to New York in hours. Chinese dissidents communicate troop movements reported on American television back to their colleagues in Beijing by electronic mail. The United States arrests foreign military leaders for their sophisticated drug-smuggling operations.

The United States has adapted the interpretation of its Constitution to other technological transformations. The integration of the national economy, made evident by the Great Depression, made older notions of a distinct boundary between interstate commerce and intrastate commerce obsolete.[1] The government's expanded capability for electronic surveillance made property lines an inadequate protection for personal privacy.[2]

The increasingly global reach of U.S. government operations after the Second World War also required an adaptation. The Supreme Court supplied that adaptation in *Reid v. Covert,*[3] discarding the one-sided practice of letting government power expand without a corresponding expansion of the limits on government power designed to protect citizens' rights. But that case did not resolve the question of aliens' rights when the United States reaches beyond its borders to control or to harm them.

If we "must never forget, that it is *a constitution* we are expounding,"[4] then we should bear in mind the purpose of a constitution, to protect the rights of the governed. When the United States seeks to extend legal obligations to aliens abroad, the Constitution should extend rights along with them. At the same time, the majority opinion in *United States v. Verdugo-Urquidez* illustrates the strongly felt need for a limiting principle, so that judicial review will not find its *reductio ad absurdum* in due process of war.[5] For most of American history, the mutuality of obligation approach has provided that principle. Its sense of jurisdictional limits has proven capable of evolution and has lessened the temptation to retreat to forms of constitutionalism-for-members-only that were wrong in 1798 and are wrong today. Nonetheless, the center of the Supreme Court may currently be drawn to a global due process methodology that affords it discretion to recognize and unrecognize constitutional rights for aliens abroad after pragmatic calculations. Although this methodology has serious defects, it is better than Hobbesian cynicism.

The collapse of the assumption that aliens entering the United States pass from a rightless void into a land of undeserved freedom necessitates a reevaluation of the constitutional constraints on immigration law. The effects of a liberty interest to enter or to remain would probably be modest, but the side constraints resulting from enumerated constitutional rights like freedom of speech could require some significant changes in current law. Whether or not the courts accept the task of judicial review, the political branches should not feel free to label aliens as undesirable on constitutionally suspect grounds. The option of deporting resident aliens in retaliation for protected speech should be eliminated.

While the analysis of constitutional constraints on immigration involves an extension of constitutional practice, other forces have pressed for a retreat from the Constitution. Current efforts to repeal the guarantee of citizenship to the native-born children of illegal aliens would throw away hard-won gains in political wisdom. The proper response to illegal immigration is conscientious enforcement, not increasing the vulnerability of migrants and their children to exploitation. The denial that children of the undocumented are "subject to the jurisdiction" of the United States resonates dangerously with other political efforts to disclaim responsibilities toward illegal aliens. No human being subject to the governance of the United States should be a stranger to the Constitution.

NOTES

CHAPTER ONE

1. Scott v. Sandford, 60 U.S. (19 How.) 393, 407 (1857).

2. Cherokee Nation v. Georgia, 30 U.S. (5 Pet.) 1, 17 (1831); Johnson v. M'Intosh, 21 U.S. (8 Wheat.) 543 (1823).

3. See, e.g., Jules Lobel, The Constitution Abroad, 83 Am. J. Int'l L. 871 (1989); C.M.A. McCauliff, The Reach of the Constitution: American Peace-time Court in West Berlin, 55 Notre Dame Law. 682 (1980); John H. Mansfield, The Religion Clauses of the First Amendment and Foreign Relations, 36 DePaul L. Rev. 1 (1986); Jordan Paust, Introduction to and Commentary on Terrorism and the Law, 19 Conn. L. Rev. 697, 721–35 (1987); John A. Ragosta, Aliens Abroad: Principles for the Application of Constitutional Limitations to Federal Action, 17 N.Y.U. J. Int'l L. & Pol. 287 (1985); Stephen Saltzburg, The Reach of the Bill of Rights Beyond the Terra Firma of the United States, 20 Va. J. Int'l L. 742 (1980); Note, The Extraterritorial Application of the Constitution—Unalienable Rights?, 72 Va. L. Rev. 649 (1986).

4. See, e.g., Charles Fairman, Some New Problems of the Constitution Following the Flag, 1 Stan. L. Rev. 587, 644–45 (1949); Andreas Lowenfeld, Book Review, Hijacking, Freedom, and the "American Way," 83 Mich. L. Rev. 1000, 1009–11 (1985) (review of H. Stern, Judgment in Berlin (1984)); Paul Stephan, Constitutional Limits on the Struggle against International Terrorism: Revisiting the Rights of Overseas Aliens, 19 Conn. L. Rev. 831 (1987).

5. See Greenham Women against Cruise Missiles v. Reagan, 755 F.2d 34 (2d Cir. 1985); Langenegger v. United States, 5 Ct. Cl. 229 (1984); Ramirez de Arellano v. Weinberger, 745 F.2d 1500 (D.C. Cir. 1984), vacated and remanded as moot, 471 U.S. 1113 (1985); DKT Memorial Fund v. Agency for Int'l Dev., 887 F.2d 275 (D.C. Cir. 1989); Planned Parenthood Fed'n of Am. v. Agency for Int'l Dev., 838 F.2d 649 (2d Cir. 1988); Haitian Centers Council, Inc. v. McNary, 969 F.2d 1326 (2d Cir. 1992), vacated as moot, 113 S. Ct. 3028 (1993).

6. See United States v. Noriega, 746 F. Supp. 1506, 1528–32 (S.D. Fla. 1990) (rejecting on the merits challenge to arrest by means of invasion as a violation of due process).

7. Yick Wo v. Hopkins, 118 U.S. 356 (1886); Wong Wing v. United States, 163 U.S. 228 (1896). The Court had never suggested a contrary holding before that time.

8. Compare United States v. Mendoza-Lopez, 481 U.S. 828 (1987); Plyler v. Doe, 457 U.S. 202 (1982); and Wong Wing v. United States, 163 U.S. 228 (1896), with United States v. Verdugo-Urquidez, 494 U.S. 259, 272–73 (1990) (characterizing the Fourth Amendment's protection of unlawfully present aliens as an open question).

9. See, e.g., Asahi Metal Indus. Co. v. Superior Court, 480 U.S. 102 (1987); Russian Volunteer Fleet v. United States, 282 U.S. 481 (1931); see also Sardino v. Federal Reserve Bank, 361 F.2d 106, 111 (2d Cir. 1966) (Friendly, J.).

10. The classic holding is United States v. Ross, 140 U.S. 453 (1891) (no constitutional rights in the trial of capital offense by the American consul in Japan).

11. See Downes v. Bidwell, 182 U.S. 244 (1901); Balzac v. Porto Rico, 258 U.S. 298 (1922); Torres v. Puerto Rico, 442 U.S. 465 (1979).

12. 354 U.S. 1 (1957).

13. United States v. Verdugo-Urquidez, 494 U.S. 259 (1990).

14. Cf. Perez v. Brownell, 356 U.S. 44 (1958) (upholding the involuntary expatriation of a Mexican-American dual national who voted in a Mexican election), overruled, Afroyim v. Rusk, 387 U.S. 253 (1967); Sanchez-Espinoza v. Reagan, 770 F.2d 202 (D.C. Cir. 1985) (dismissing, inter alia, constitutional claims brought by Nicaraguan citizens against the support of contras).

15. See United States v. Verdugo-Urquidez, 494 U.S. 259, 288 (1990) (Brennan, J., dissenting); see Chapter Six.

16. This sort of reasoning is evident in Chief Justice William Rehnquist's opinion in United States v. Verdugo-Urquidez, 494 U.S. 259 (1990). See Chapter Six.

17. This appears most clearly in In re Ross, 140 U.S. 453 (1891) (Field, J.), as discussed in Chapter Five.

18. Schooner Exchange v. McFadden, 11 U.S. (7 Cranch) 116, 136 (1812). Through the lens of conflict of laws, this way of thinking grew more rigid over the course of that century, from the comity approach of Joseph Story to the vested rights doctrine of Joseph Beale. See, e.g., Elliott Cheatham, American Theories of Conflict of Laws: Their Role and Utility, 58 Harv. L. Rev. 361 (1945); Joseph Story, Commentaries on the Conflict of Laws 19–38 (1834); 1 Joseph Beale, A Treatise on the Conflict of Laws § 73 (1916); Slater v. Mexican National R.R. Co., 194 U.S. 120 (1904) (Holmes, J.).

19. See, e.g., Fairman, note 4 supra; Stephan, note 4 supra.

20. 3 Emer de Vattel, The Law of Nations; or, Principles of Natural Law (1916) (Charles G. Fenwick trans. ed. 1758). On Vattel's prestige, see, e.g., J.L. Brierly, Law of Nations 37–40 (6th ed. 1963); 1 James Kent, Commentaries on American Law *18 (2d ed. 1832); Frank S. Ruddy, International Law in the Enlightenment 281–310 (1975); but see Brown v. United States, 12 U.S. (8 Cranch) 109, 140–41 (1814) (Story, J., dissenting).

Conversely, Rousseau, who stood outside the natural rights tradition, will receive less attention here than his place in the history of political philosophy might suggest, for three principal reasons. First, for a Swiss living in France, he had little to say on the subject of aliens and their rights. Second, the distinctive features of Rousseau's political thought appear not to have been influential in eighteenth-century America, and his reputation there suffered as a result of the French Revolution. See Paul M. Spurlin, Rousseau in America, 1760–1809, at 63–70, 101–13 (1969). Third, the crucial debate occurred in the United States at the time of the Alien and Sedition Acts, which embodied a reaction against the French Revolution, so that neither side had any incentive to invoke Rousseau.

21. J.W. Gough, The Social Contract 27–35 (2d ed. 1956).

22. See, e.g., 2 Jean Jacques Burlamaqui, The Principles of Natural and Politic Law 30–31 (Thomas Nugent trans. 1823); John Locke, The Second Treatise of Government, in Two Treatises of Government 390–94 (Peter Laslett ed. 1965); 3 Vattel, note 20 supra at 88–89. But see Thomas Hobbes, Leviathan 255 (C.B. MacPherson ed. 1985).

23. Hobbes, note 22 supra at 272, 375–76.

24. 2 Samuel Freiherr von Pufendorf, De Jure Naturae et Gentium Libri Octo 974–75 (1934) (Charles H. Oldfather & W.A. Oldfather trans. of 2d ed. 1688).

25. E.g., id. at 1068–72, 1077–78.

26. Locke, note 22 supra at 401–02.

27. Gough, note 21 supra at 143.

28. 3 Vattel, note 20 supra; see also 2 Burlamaqui, note 22 supra at 26–27, 45–46; Jean Jacques Rousseau, The Social Contract, reprinted in Political Writings 57, 108–09 (Roger D. & Judith R. Masters trans. ed. 1964). Thomas Rutherforth defined a "civil constitution" as a contract between the people and their government but noted that it could be called a law. Thomas Rutherforth, Institutes of Natural Law; Being the Substance of a Course of Lectures on Grotius De Jure Belli et Pacis, read in St. John's College, Cambridge 291–93 (1832 ed.) (first published 1754–56).

29. 3 Vattel, note 20 supra at 5, 114; see 2 Christian Freiherr von Wolff, Jus Gentium Methodo Scientifica Pertractatum 12–13 (Joseph H. Drake trans. 1934). On Vattel's relationship with Wolff, see, e.g., 3 Vattel at 6a–9a.

30. 3 Vattel, note 20 supra at 17.

31. See Gerald Stourzh, Constitution: Changing Meanings of the Term from the Early Seventeenth to the Late Eighteenth Century, in Conceptual Change and the Constitution 45–48 (Terence Ball & J.G.A. Pocock eds. 1988) (emphasizing Vattel's role in this process).

32. Hobbes, note 22 supra at 273. Becoming a subject in a Hobbesian commonwealth does not guarantee much in the way of rights.

33. Hobbes, note 22 supra at 360. We will find a brand of neo-Hobbism in Chief Justice Rehnquist's opinion in United States v. Verdugo-Urquidez, 494 U.S. 259 (1990). See Chapter Six.

34. Robert Nozick, Anarchy, State and Utopia 54–55 (1974); see also Lea Brilmayer, Consent, Contract and Territory, 74 Minn. L. Rev. 1, 10–17 (1989).

35. See, e.g., 2 Pufendorf, note 24 supra at 363–66; Rutherforth, note 29 supra at 489; 3 Vattel, note 20 supra at 92, 154; James A.R. Nafziger, The General Admission of Aliens under International Law, 77 Am. J. Int'l L. 804, 810–15 (1983).

36. 2 Pufendorf, note 24 supra at 354–44; 3 Vattel, note 20 supra at 144; 2 Wolff, note 29 supra at 150–51.

37. 2 Burlamaqui, note 22 supra at 31; 2 Pufendorf, note 24 supra at 994; Rutherforth, note 29 supra at 265; 3 Vattel, note 20 supra at 144; 2 Wolff, note 29 supra at 151–52; see also Locke, note 22 supra at 392.

38. See 2 Burlamaqui, note 22 supra at 31; Locke, note 22 supra at 394; 2 Pufendorf, note 24 supra at 995; 3 Vattel, note 20 supra at 87, 146; 2 Wolff, note 29 supra at 152–53. At common law, aliens within the realm were regarded as local, temporary subjects. See Calvin's Case, 7 Coke Rep. 1a, 6a (1608); 1 William Blackstone, Commentaries on the Laws of England *359 (1979 reprint). Blackstone even listed them as one of the divisions of the people. Id. at *354.

39. 3 Vattel, note 20 supra at 7; cf. 2 Wolff, note 29 supra at 10–11, 19, 84–86 (distinguishing between positive law of nations and natural law, which confers only imperfect rights). Contra, 2 Pufendorf, note 24 supra at 221–29 (fully equating the law of nations with theologically grounded natural law). Vattel also described an intermediate category of obligations that were external but imperfect; that is, they were created as positive international law, but they included an element of discre-

tion that made it inappropriate to compel compliance. 3 Vattel at 7. Purely internal obligations were always imperfect.

40. 3 Vattel, note 20 supra at 149–51; 2 Wolff, note 29 supra at 174.

41. E.g., 3 Vattel, note 20 supra at 92, 154; 2 Wolff, note 29 supra at 81; accord, Rutherforth, note 29 supra at 489. The distinction between the sovereign's external right to exclude and its unenforceable natural obligation to admit made Vattel ammunition for both sides in debates over immigration and its consequences. See Nafziger, note 35 supra at 812 (discussing this susceptibility of Vattel).

42. 3 Vattel, note 20 supra at 145.

43. Id. at 139.

44. Id. at 87.

45. 2 Wolff, note 29 supra at 152; see also id. at 153 ("[T]hey are bound only to do and not to do the things which must be done or not done by citizens at the time under the same circumstances, except in so far as particular laws introduce something else concerning foreigners").

46. 3 Vattel, note 20 supra at 144, 146.

47. Id. at 146–48; 2 Wolff, note 29 supra at 166–73. See also 2 Pufendorf, note 24 supra at 371–72 (on restriction of intermarriage).

48. This notion later developed into the contention for an "international minimum standard of justice," as opposed to merely requiring "national treatment." See, e.g., Restatement (Third) of Foreign Relations Law of the United States §§ 711, 712 (1987).

49. 2 Burlamaqui, note 22 supra at 50–51; 2 Pufendorf, note 24 supra at 1274–75; Rutherforth, note 29 supra at 569–72; 3 Vattel, note 20 supra at 33–34; cf. 2 Wolff, note 29 supra at 447–48 ("in a doubtful case it may not be assumed that the kingdom is patrimonial").

50. 2 Burlamaqui, note 22 supra at 152–54; 2 Pufendorf, note 24 supra at 1288–90; Rutherforth, note 29 supra at 569; 3 Vattel, note 20 supra at 14, 100–01; 2 Wolff, note 29 supra at 510–11.

51. 2 Burlamaqui, note 22 supra at 211–12; Rutherforth, note 29 supra at 594; 2 Wolff, note 29 supra at 444–46.

52. 2 Burlamaqui, note 22 supra at 214; 3 Vattel, note 20 supra at 309–12; cf. 2 Wolff, note 29 supra at 446–48 (victor acquires absolute sovereignty over vanquished, not limited by laws of either, unless surrender is conditional).

53. 2 Burlamaqui, note 22 supra at 70–71, 212–15; 3 Vattel, note 20 supra at 20–21, 80–81; 2 Wolff, note 29 supra at 47.

54. 3 Vattel, note 20 supra at 86, cited in Pollard's Lessee v. Hagan, 44 U.S. (3 How.) 212, 225 (1845).

55. Yick Wo v. Hopkins, 118 U.S. 356 (1886).

56. Yamataya v. Fisher, 189 U.S. 86 (1903).

57. Shaughnessy v. United States ex rel. Mezei, 345 U.S. 206 (1953).

58. Galvan v. Press, 347 U.S. 522, 530–31 (1954) (citation omitted). Frankfurter was quoting from Justice Oliver Wendell Holmes's famous aphorism that in law, a page of history may be worth a volume of logic. New York Trust Co. v. Eisner, 256 U.S. 345, 349 (1921).

59. Fiallo v. Bell, 430 U.S. 787, 793 n. 5 (1977); Kleindienst v. Mandel, 408 U.S. 753 (1972).

60. 430 U.S. at 794.

CHAPTER TWO

1. See John Higham, Send These to Me: Immigrants in Urban America 71–80 (rev. ed. 1984) (explaining the slow "transformation" of the Statue of Liberty into an immigration icon). Lazarus's poem "The New Colossus" was written in 1883 as part of a fund-raising drive for the erection of the statue, which finally occurred in 1886; a tablet containing the text of the poem was placed on the statue's pedestal in 1903. As David Martin has pointed out, the federal exclusion of immigrants on a variety of grounds, including the likelihood of their becoming a public charge, had already begun by the time Lazarus wrote. See David A. Martin, Major Issues in Immigration Law 1 (1987).

2. Indeed, much of the border was *physically* open, in the sense of not being controlled by any authority derived from the government of the United States. Instead, it was either unregulated wilderness or land controlled by unconquered indigenous peoples. See, e.g., Oscar J. Martínez, Troublesome Border 55–62 (1988). But that did not change in 1875.

3. Some authors, myself included, have been led astray by the compilation "State Immigration Legislation" in volume 39 of the 1911 Report of the Dillingham Commission. S. Doc. No. 758, 61st Cong., 3d Sess. (1911). Few of the statutes to be discussed in this chapter are included there.

4. Factors against include the following: the immigration was involuntary, the involuntary immigrants were not viewed legally as being fully persons, and calling the slave trade immigration seems offensively euphemistic. On the other hand, modern immigration laws do apply to involuntary as well as voluntary migration— see Plyler v. Doe, 457 U.S. 202, 219–20 (1982); D'Agostino v. Sahli, 230 F.2d 668 (5th Cir. 1956)—and subjection to the slave trade was the migratory experience of the ancestors of many Americans. Cf. Roger Daniels, Coming to America 54–55 (1990) (deploring the artificial cleavage between black history and immigration history reinforced by the failure to view the slave trade as a form of migration).

5. For some forms of normative analysis, it matters whether the state restrictions that existed were legally valid; for other historical purposes, it would not matter whether they were legally valid, so long as they were actually enforced or potential immigrants were deterred by the belief that they would be enforced.

6. This definition may seem broader than colloquial usage, but in fact it is consistent with the definition of "immigration" used in demography and is narrower than the definition of "immigration laws" in 8 U.S.C. § 1101(a)(17).

7. To the Printers of the Gazette (1751), in Benjamin Franklin, The Autobiography and Other Writings (Peter Snow ed. 1982).

8. See, e.g., Edith Abbott, Historical Aspects of the Immigration Problem 542–47 (1969 reprint) (reprinting provisions of three statutes of Virginia, Maryland, and Delaware); A.G.L. Shaw, Convicts and the Colonies 32–33 (1966). The 1718 act gave courts statutory authority to impose transportation to the colonies as punishment for certain felonies. Earlier, transportation had been accomplished through the grant of a conditional pardon by the Crown, which required the consent of the criminal. After 1718, transportation became a more common occurrence. See 11 William Holdsworth, A History of English Law 573–75 (1938).

9. See A. Roger Ekirch, Great Britain's Secret Convict Trade to America, 1783–1784, 89 Am. Hist. Rev. 1285 (1984).

10. See Mollie Gillen, The Botany Bay Decision, 1786: Convicts, Not Empire, 97 Eng. Hist. Rev. 740 (1982).

11. See Act of Feb. 10, 1787, 1787 Ga. Acts 40.

12. 13 J. of Cong. 105–06 (Sept. 16, 1788).

13. See Act of Oct. 1788, 1788 Conn. Acts & Laws 368.

14. See Act of Feb. 14, 1789, ch. 61, § 7, 1789 Mass. Acts 98, 100–01; Act of Mar. 27, 1789, ch. 463, 1788–89 Pa. Acts 692; Act of Nov. 4, 1788, No. 1542, 1788 S.C. Acts 5; Act of Nov. 13, 1788, ch. 12, 1788 Va. Acts 9.

15. See Pa. Act of Mar. 27, 1789, ch. 463. New Jersey later borrowed this provision from Pennsylvania. See Act of Jan. 28, 1797, ch. 611, § 3, 1797 N.J. Acts 131, 131.

16. Mass. Act of Feb. 14, 1789, ch. 61, §§ 6, 7. These provisions were later adopted by Rhode Island. See Act of 1798, § 17, 1798 R.I. Laws 348, 358.

17. For later enactments from the first group of states, see, e.g., Ga. Code, pt. 1, tit. 2, ch. 2, § 48 (1867); Act of Feb. 16, 1794, ch. 32, § 16, 1794 Mass. Acts & Laws 375, 384; Act of Apr. 15, 1851, No. 368, § 1, 1851 Pa. Laws 701; Va. Code tit. 54, ch. 198, § 39 (1849).

18. See, e.g., Act of Feb. 24, 1821, ch. 22, § 6, 1821 Me. Laws 90, 91–92; Act of Jan. 6, 1810, ch. 138, § 7(3), 1809–10 Md. Laws; N.J. Act of Jan. 28, 1797, ch. 611; Act of Apr. 25, 1833, ch. 230, 1833 N.Y. Laws 313; R.I. Act of 1798, § 16.

19. I have found no earlier New York statute excluding convicts, unless they were covered by the provision of the poor laws concerning a passenger who "cannot give a good account of himself." Act of Mar. 7, 1788, ch. 62, § 33, 1788 N.Y. Laws 133, 146. The 1833 statute appeared at the beginning of the first wave of nativist agitation. See David H. Bennett, The Party of Fear: From Nativist Movements to the New Right in American History 49–50 (1988). The statute also followed a widely publicized incident of the transportation of convicts from Hamburg in 1832. See S. Exec. Doc. No. 42, 28th Cong., 2d Sess. 2–4 (1845); Günter Moltmann, Die Transportation von Sträflingen im Rahmen der deutschen Amerikaauswanderung des 19. Jahrhunderts, in Deutsche Amerikaauswanderung im 19. Jahrhundert 147, 150–55 (Günter Moltmann ed. 1976).

20. See David W. Galenson, White Servitude in Colonial America: An Economic Analysis 179–80 (1981); Robert J. Steinfeld, The Invention of Free Labor: The Employment Relation in English and American Law and Culture, 1350–1870, at 163–72 (1991).

21. One early exception might be mentioned, involving the intervention of Rufus King in the fall of 1798, while ambassador to Great Britain, to prevent the release of Irish political prisoners on condition of their departure for the United States. King acted, however, in the spirit of the newly adopted Alien Act of 1798, rather than from concern about criminality per se. See 2 Charles R. King, The Life and Correspondence of Rufus King 635–49 (1895).

22. See, e.g., Sen. Res. of Feb. 2, 1847, Cong. Globe, 29th Cong., 2d Sess. 305 (1847); Sen. Res. of Dec. 23, 1844, Cong. Globe, 28th Cong., 2d Sess. 62.

23. See, e.g., S. Exec. Doc. No. 161, 29th Cong., 2d Sess. 2 (1847) (Switzerland and Baden); S. Rep. No. 173, 28th Cong., 2d Sess. 133–34 (1845) (reprinting the translation of a proclamation directing police to prevent the shipment of criminals through the port of Bremen); Moltmann, note 19 supra at 178–81 (attributing the

German states' halting of the practice to their desire for good commercial relations with the United States).

24. S.J. Res. 24, 39th Cong., 1st Sess., 14 Stat. 353 (1866). Examples of inquiries and protests by the Grant administration were collected and submitted to Congress in H.R. Exec. Doc. No. 253, 43d Cong., 1st Sess. (1874).

25. Act of Mar. 3, 1875, § 5, 18 Stat. 477 (excluding "persons who are undergoing a sentence for conviction in their own country of felonious crimes other than political or growing out of or the result of such political offenses, or whose sentence has been remitted on condition of their emigration").

26. See 8 U.S.C. § 212(a)(2).

27. See Act of Feb. 5, 1917, ch. 29, § 19, 39 Stat. 874, 889.

28. As I mention later, slaves and free blacks were especially vulnerable to banishment.

29. Perhaps it would be better to suppress this discussion, given Justice Antonin Scalia's application of the New Antiquarianism to the Eighth Amendment. See Harmelin v. Michigan, 501 U.S. 957 (1991) (opinion of Scalia, J., joined by Rehnquist, C.J.). The Supreme Court has not resolved whether banishment from the country is cruel and unusual punishment. But see Dear Wing Jung v. United States, 312 F.2d 73 (9th Cir. 1962); State v. Sanchez, 462 So.2d 1304 (La. App. 1985). An affirmative answer does not inexorably follow from Trop v. Dulles, 356 U.S. 86 (1958), which involved denationalization rather than banishment. Nor does a negative answer follow from the cases involving the deportation of aliens, which rest conspicuously on the ground (or fiction) that deportation is not punishment. See, e.g., Bugajewitz v. Adams, 228 U.S. 585, 591 (1913) (Holmes, J.); Fong Yue Ting v. United States, 149 U.S. 698, 709 (1893).

30. 4 U.S. (4 Dall.) 14, 19 (1800) (opinion of Paterson, J.); id. at 20 (opinion of Cushing, J.) ("The right to confiscate and banish, in the case of an offending citizen, must belong to every government"); cf. In re Look Tin Sing, 21 F. 905, 910–11 (C.C.D. Cal. 1884) (Field, J.) ("[N]o citizen can be excluded from this country except in punishment for crime. Exclusion for any other cause is unknown to our laws, and beyond the power of congress").

31. See Ala. Const. of 1819, art. I, § 27 (citizens only); Ark. Const. of 1874, art. II, § 21; Ill. Const. of 1818, art. VIII, § 17; Kan. Const. of 1859, Bill of Rights, § 12; Miss. Const. of 1817, art. I, § 27 (citizens only); Ohio Const. of 1802, art. VIII, § 17; W. Va. Const. of 1872, art. III, § 5.

Exile received a different kind of mention in provisions of other state constitutions that were modeled on the "law of the land" clause of Magna Carta. These provisions directed that no one should be, inter alia, outlawed or exiled, unless by the judgment of his peers or the law of the land. See, e.g., Ark. Const. of 1836, art. I, § 10; Md. Const. of 1776, Declaration of Rights, § 11; Mass. Const. of 1780, pt. I, art. XII. It does not seem appropriate, however, to view such clauses as giving express constitutional approval to the practice of exile, and indeed some constitutions included both provisions, e.g., Ill. Const. of 1818, art. VIII, §§ 8, 17.

32. See, e.g., 2 James Kent, Commentaries on American Law *33 (2d ed. 1832) (conditional pardon "equivalent, in its effect and operation, to a judicial sentence of exportation or banishment"); Gerald R. Miller, Note, Banishment—A Medieval Tactic in Modern Criminal Law, 5 Utah L. Rev. 365 (1957).

33. See, e.g., Act of Dec. 24, 1795, ch. 82, § 2, 1795 Md. Laws (authorizing commutation of sentence to banishment from state or country); Act of May 31, 1820, § 17, 1820 N.J. Pub. Acts 134, 137 (authorizing pardon conditioned on leaving state or country); Act of Mar. 8, 1780, ch. 154, § 5, 1780 Pa. Laws 319, 320 (authorizing pardon conditioned on leaving country); Ex parte Marks, 28 P. 109 (Cal. 1883) (leaving state); People v. James, 2 Cai. R. 57 (N.Y. Sup. Ct. 1804) (leaving country); Flavell's Case, 8 Watts & Serg. 197 (Pa. 1844) (same); State v. Fuller, 1 McCord 178 (S.C. 1821) (leaving state).

34. See, e.g., Lawrence M. Friedman, A History of American Law 280–84 (2d ed. 1985).

35. Courts in a few states have nonetheless held that because acceptance of a pardon is voluntary, pardons conditioned on banishment do not amount to exile or transportation within the meaning of a constitutional prohibition. See Ex parte Hawkins, 33 S.W. 106 (Ark. 1895); Ex parte Lockhart, 12 Ohio Dec. Reprint 515 (Super. Ct. 1855); Ex parte Snyder, 159 P.2d 752 (Okla. Crim. App. 1945); see also Carchedi v. Rhodes, 560 F. Supp. 1010 (S.D. Ohio 1982) (following Lockhart).

36. See People v. Potter, 1 Edm. Sel. Cas. 235, 1 Parker Crim. R. 47 (N.Y. Cir. Ct. 1846) (defendant pardoned in New York on condition of leaving the United States, and later arrested in Louisiana).

37. See, e.g., United States v. Jalilian, 896 F.2d 447 (10th Cir. 1990); Yadyaser v. State, 430 So.2d 888 (Ala. Crim. App. 1983); State v. Karan, 525 A.2d 933 (R.I. 1987).

38. See, e.g., David J. Rothman, The Discovery of the Asylum: Social Order and Disorder in the New Republic 20–25, 46–48 (1971); Stefan A. Riesenfeld, The Formative Era of American Public Assistance Law, 43 Calif. L. Rev. 175, 223–24 (1955); cf. James W. Ely, Jr., Poor Laws of the Post-Revolutionary South, 1776–1800, 21 Tulsa L.J. 1, 17–18 (1985) (settlement laws rarely enforced in South).

39. Article 4 began:

> The better to secure and perpetuate mutual friendship and intercourse among the people of the different States in this Union, the free inhabitants of each of these States, paupers, vagabonds and fugitives from justice excepted, shall be entitled to all privileges and immunities of free citizens in the several States; and the people of each State shall have free ingress and regress to and from any other State, and shall enjoy therein all the privileges of trade and commerce, subject to the same duties, impositions and restrictions as the inhabitants thereof respectively, provided that such restrictions shall not extend so far as to prevent the removal of property imported into any State, to any other State of which the owner is an inhabitant.

40. See Mayor of New York v. Miln, 36 U.S. (11 Pet.) 102, 142–43 (1837); Prigg v. Pennsylvania, 41 U.S. (16 Pet.) 539, 625 (1842). The right of the poor to travel was not vindicated until Edwards v. California, 314 U.S. 160 (1941); see also Shapiro v. Thompson, 394 U.S. 618 (1969) (invalidating residence requirements for welfare benefits). Persons who are fugitives in only a loose sense of the word still have a diminished right to travel. See Jones v. Helms, 452 U.S. 412 (1981).

41. See Rothman, note 38 supra at 290. For qualifications of Rothman's conclusions, see, e.g., Robert E. Cray, Jr., Paupers and Poor Relief in New York City and

Its Rural Environs, 1700–1830 (1988); James W. Ely, Jr., "There Are Few Subjects in Political Economy of Greater Difficulty": The Poor Laws of the Antebellum South, 1985 Am. Bar Found. J. 849; Steven J. Ross, "Objects of Charity": Poor Relief, Poverty, and the Rise of the Almshouse in Early Eighteenth-Century New York City, in Authority and Resistance in Early New York 138 (William Pencak & Conrad E. Wright eds. 1988).

42. See, e.g., Rothman, note 38 supra at 155–61.

43. Id. at 161–65; Michael B. Katz, The Undeserving Poor: From the War on Poverty to the War on Welfare 12–15 (1989).

44. See, e.g., Benjamin J. Klebaner, The Myth of Foreign Pauper Dumping in the United States, 35 Soc. Serv. Rev. 302 (1961) (finding claims inflated in quantitative terms).

45. Municipal ordinances as well as state statutes played a role in this system. See Benjamin J. Klebaner, State and Local Immigration Regulation in the United States Before 1882, 3 Int'l Rev. Soc. Hist. 269, 273–74, 281 (1958) (discussing ordinances of Newark, Perth Amboy, Charleston, and Norfolk). (Despite its title, this article deals almost exclusively with bonding and commutation provisions, a subcategory of laws dealing with the migration of the poor.)

46. See Henderson v. New York, 92 U.S. 259 (1876); Passenger Cases, 48 U.S. (7 How.) 283 (1849) (case involving Massachusetts law); Mayor of New York v. Miln, 36 U.S. (11 Pet.) 102 (1837). The fourth case is the Passenger Case involving the New York head tax for the support of the marine hospital, and the fifth case is Chy Lung v. Freeman, 92 U.S. 279 (1876), involving California.

47. See Act of Feb. 11, 1794, ch. 8, 1794 Mass. Acts & Laws 347. Although "warning out" took the form of an order to leave the town, its usual effect was only to prevent the newcomer from acquiring an entitlement to the support of the town in case of indigency. See, e.g., Robert W. Kelso, The History of Public Poor Relief in Massachusetts, 1620–1920, at 49–51 (1969) (reprinting 1922 ed.).

48. See Mass. Act of Feb. 11, 1794, ch. 8, § 2; Act of June 9, 1868, ch. 328, § 1, 1868 Mass. Acts & Resolves 247; Kelso, note 47 supra at 62.

49. Act of Feb. 26, 1794, ch. 32, §§ 9, 13, 1794 Mass. Acts & Laws 375, 379, 383. Litigation between towns over responsibility for particular indigent persons was very common in this period and represented a major inefficiency in the system.

50. Id. § 10, 13.

51. Id. § 15.

52. See Inhabitants of Deerfield v. Delano, 18 Mass. (1 Pick.) 465 (1823); Inhabitants of Greenfield v. Cushman, 16 Mass. 393 (1820); cf. Mass. Rev. Stat. ch. 46, § 24 (1836) (adding phrase "and with intent to charge such town with his support").

53. Mass. Act of Feb. 26, 1794, ch. 32, § 17.

54. See Emberson E. Proper, Colonial Immigration Laws 29–30 (1900).

55. See Act of Feb. 25, 1820, ch. 290, 1820 Mass. Laws 428. The amount and duration of the bond were repeatedly changed by later legislation; I will not burden the reader with all of these changes.

56. See Act of Mar. 19, 1831, ch. 150, § 1, 1831 Mass. Laws 719. The 1820 act had been titled "An Act to prevent the introduction of Paupers, from foreign ports or places," but its strictures had applied to all passengers lacking a settlement in the Commonwealth.

57. See Klebaner, note 45 supra at 277 (emphasizing difficulty of proving identity); see also Report of the Commissioners of Alien Passengers and Foreign Paupers: 1854, Mass. House Doc. No. 123, at 17 (1855) (hereinafter 1854 Commissioners' Report) (noting insolvency of a bonding company). In 1853 the commissioners of alien passengers were authorized to commute outstanding bonds for present payment "on such terms as in their judgment may promote the interest of the commonwealth." Act of May 23, 1853, ch. 366, § 1, 1853 Mass. Acts & Resolves 585.

58. Act of Apr. 20, 1837, ch. 238, § 2, 1837 Mass. Laws 270. The list of high-risk categories was modified over time. Compare id. § 2 ("lunatic, idiot, maimed, aged or infirm persons incompetent in the opinion of the officers so examining, to maintain themselves, or who have been paupers in any other country") with Act of Mar. 20, 1850, ch. 105, § 1, 1850 Mass. Acts & Resolves 338 ("a pauper, lunatic, or idiot, or maimed, aged, infirm, or destitute, or incompetent to take care of himself or herself without becoming a public charge as a pauper"); Act of May, 20, 1852, ch. 279, § 1, 1852 Mass. Acts & Resolves 195 ("any lunatic, idiotic, deaf and dumb, blind, or maimed person"); and Mass. Gen. Stat. ch. 71, § 15 (1859) ("insane, idiotic, deaf and dumb, blind, deformed or maimed person, among said passengers, or alien who has before been a public charge within this state"). The list was narrowed after the creation of an intermediate-risk category in 1852, which seems to have been a response to City of Boston v. Capen, 61 Mass. 116 (1851) (official cannot require bond for persons judged likely to become a public charge unless they are within listed categories).

59. Mass. Act of Apr. 20, 1837, ch. 238, § 3. Identification of high-risk passengers rested in the discretion of local officials, however, and was vulnerable to lax enforcement, particularly because financial responsibility for foreign paupers lay with the Commonwealth and not the town. See Mass. Sen. Doc. No. 109, at 8–9 (1847) (noting Boston official's unauthorized practice of accepting head tax in lieu of bond for high-risk passengers and proposing transfer of authority to state officials to ensure stricter enforcement); Act of May 10, 1848, ch. 313, 1848 Mass. Acts & Resolves 796 (implementing this transfer).

60. See Norris v. City of Boston, 45 Mass. 282, 287 (1842) (Shaw, C.J.), rev'd sub nom. Passenger Cases, 48 U.S. (7 How.) 283 (1849).

61. 48 U.S. (7 How.) 283 (1849).

62. See Act of Mar. 16, 1849, ch. 34, 1849 Mass. Acts & Resolves 20; Mass. Act of Mar. 20, 1850, ch. 105, § 1.

63. Mass. Act of May 20, 1852, ch. 279. In 1854, for example, payments varying between $5 and $25, and averaging $21, were received for 114 alien passengers in the intermediate-risk category. See 1854 Commissioners' Report, note 57 supra at 36. According to one author, the price of an adult's ticket from Liverpool to New York in 1850 averaged in the $17–$20 range. See Thomas W. Page, The Transportation of Immigrants and the Reception Arrangements in the Nineteenth Century, 19 J. Pol. Econ. 732, 738 (1911).

64. See Act of Apr. 2, 1872, ch. 169, § 1, 1872 Mass. Acts & Resolves 123. In the meantime, the state oscillated between the adoption and repeal of provisions affording a refund of the payment or a cancellation of the bond for low- and intermediate-risk alien passengers in transit through the state who left within forty-eight hours of arrival.

65. See Mass. Pub. Stat. ch. 86, §§ 5, 12 (1886). The labor importation provision, requiring bonds "conditioned that neither such person, nor any one legally dependent on him for support, shall within two years become a city, town, or state charge," originated in 1866. See Act of May 28, 1866, ch. 272, § 2, Mass. Acts & Resolves 253. By its wording, it appeared to cover any person lacking a settlement in the state, not just aliens.

66. See Act of May 24, 1851, ch. 342, §§ 3–5, 1851 Mass. Acts & Resolves 847.

67. See, e.g., 1854 Commissioners' Report, note 57 supra at 13–16.

68. Fitchburg v. Cheshire R.R., 110 Mass. 210 (1872).

69. Mass. Act of May 28, 1866, ch. 272, § 1.

70. Mass. Act of Feb. 26, 1794, § 13; see also Mass. Pub. Stat. ch. 86, § 38 (1886) (codified descendant of same provision). By 1859, the authority to remove paupers beyond the sea had been expressly limited to noncitizens. Mass. Gen. Stat. ch. 71, § 52 (1859).

71. See Kelso, note 47 supra at 122–23; see also 1854 Commissioners' Report, note 57 supra at 9 (criticizing failure of local officials to have carriers remove paupers).

72. See John R. Mulkern, The Know-Nothing Party in Massachusetts: The Rise and Fall of a People's Movement 39, 94–95 (1990). Mulkern points out that the implementation of this statute should be recognized as a major success for the nativists in the 1850s, though the statute itself was enacted before the election in which the Know-Nothing Party gained control of the state government. This interpretation contradicts the traditional assertion that the Massachusetts Know-Nothings did nothing to curb immigration. See id. at 103–04 & n.55.

73. Act of May 20, 1852, ch. 275, § 7, 1852 Mass. Acts & Resolves 190. In practice, some officials bypassed the statutory procedures and had paupers returned at public expense without seeking the approval of a justice of the peace. See 1854 Commissioners' Report, note 57 supra at 45 (objecting to this irregularity).

74. See, e.g., Report of the Commissioners of Alien Passengers and Foreign Paupers: 1855, Mass. House Doc. No. 41 (1856); Report of the Commissioners of Alien Passengers and Foreign Paupers: 1854, Mass. House Doc. No. 123 (1855); Mulkern, note 72 supra at 103, 138–39.

75. See Raymond A. Mohl, Poverty in New York: 1783–1825, at 55–59 (1971).

76. See Act of Mar. 7, 1788, ch. 62, §§ 5, 7, 1788 N.Y. Laws 133.

77. Compare id. § 10 with Act of Apr. 8, 1813, ch. 78, 1812–13 N.Y. Laws 279 (omitting this provision).

78. See N.Y. Act of Mar. 7, 1788, ch. 62, § 7; Mohl, note 75 supra at 58.

79. See N.Y. Act of Apr. 8, 1813, ch. 78, § 7.

80. See Act of Apr. 5, 1817, ch. 177, § 3, 1817 N.Y. Laws 176.

81. See Report of the Secretary of State in 1824 on the Relief and Settlement of the Poor (1824), reprinted in 1 New York State Bd. of Charities, Annual Report for the Year 1900, at 939 (1901) (hereinafter Yates Report); 1 David M. Schneider, The History of Public Welfare in New York State: 1609–1866, at 235–42 (1938).

82. See Act of Nov. 27, 1824, ch. 331, §§ 6, 8, 1824 N.Y. Laws 382.

83. See Yates Report, note 81 supra at 953.

84. See N.Y. Rev. Stat. pt. 1, ch. 20, tit. 1, § 64 (1829); N.Y. Rev. Stat. pt. 1, ch. 20, tit. 1, § 69 (1836); cf. Winfield v. Mapes, 4 Denio 371 (N.Y. Sup. Ct. 1847)

(affirming fine imposed on Pennsylvania officials for returning a pauper to New York State).

85. See N.Y. Act of Mar. 7, 1788, ch. 62, §§ 32, 33. Residents were also subject to fine for sheltering foreigners without notifying the city. The information required in the vessels' reports increased over the years. The reporting provision of the 1824 passenger act, upheld by the Supreme Court in Mayor of New York v. Miln, 36 U.S. (11 Pet.) 102 (1837), called for the name, place of birth, place of last legal settlement, age, and occupation of the passengers. See Act of Feb. 11, 1824, ch. 37, § 1, 1824 N.Y. Laws 27.

86. See Act of Apr. 3, 1797, c. 101, § 2, 1797 N.Y. Laws 134.

87. Under this regime, the vessel could avoid penalties by demonstrating that the alien passenger had been "taken or sent to some foreign country without having been suffered to land." Act of Apr. 1, 1799, ch. 80, § 5, 1799 N.Y. Laws 429. One author explains that "[t]he transoceanic removal policy for alien paupers quickly became unworkable" but does not indicate his basis for this explanation other than the laws themselves. Mohl, note 75 supra at 60. In contrast, city officials could directly order the removal to their home states of citizen passengers who were deemed likely to become chargeable. See N.Y. Act of Apr. 1, 1799, ch. 80, § 8; N.Y. Act of Feb. 11, 1824, ch. 37, § 3.

88. See N.Y. Act of Apr. 1, 1799, ch. 80, § 2.

89. See Klebaner, note 45 supra at 273 (citing figures of three and five dollars per passenger between 1817 and 1819).

90. See N.Y. Act of Apr. 1, 1799, ch. 80, § 3.

91. See Yates Report, note 81 supra at 1013 ("It is almost an every day occurrence for vessels from Halifax, St. Johns and other possessions of the British in North America, to land passengers at some of the eastern ports, generally at Fairfield in Connecticut, about 60 miles from this city, who proceed on foot to this place, and mix with the crowd unobserved"); Klebaner, note 45 supra at 273 (noting ease of violation in New Jersey); N.Y. Act of Feb. 11, 1824, ch. 37, §§ 1, 2; see also id. § 4 (requiring aliens entering city with intention of residing to report themselves within twenty-four hours and to specify the vessel in which they had arrived). In 1849, this loophole-closing feature was extended to passengers intending to proceed to any destination in New York State. Act of Apr. 11, 1849, ch. 350, § 1, 1849 N.Y. Laws 504.

92. See Friedrich Kapp, Immigration, and the Commissioners of Emigration of the State of New York 45–59 (1870); Schneider, note 81 supra at 304–05.

93. See Act of May 5, 1847, ch. 195, § 4, 1847 N.Y. Laws 182.

94. See id. § 3 ("any lunatic, idiot, deaf and dumb, blind or infirm persons, not members of emigrating families, and who from attending circumstances are likely to become permanently a public charge"); N.Y. Act of Apr. 11, 1849, ch. 350, § 3 ("any lunatic, idiot, deaf, dumb, blind or infirm persons not members of emigrating families or who from attending circumstances are likely to become permanently a public charge, or who have been paupers in any other country or who from sickness or disease, existing at the time of departing from the foreign port are or are likely soon to become a public charge"); Act of July 11, 1851, ch. 523, § 4, 1851 N.Y. Laws 969 (adding maimed persons, persons above the age of sixty years, widows with children, or any woman without a husband and with children).

95. N.Y. Act of May 5, 1847, ch. 195, § 2. A similar charge was soon imposed on alien passengers arriving in upstate ports, but the bonding system was not extended to those ports. See Act of Dec. 10, 1847, ch. 431, 1847 N.Y. Laws 557.

96. 48 U.S. (7 How.) 283 (1849). The New York passenger case, Smith v. Turner, involved not the New York passenger act, but rather the head tax for the support of the marine hospital. The companion case, Norris v. City of Boston, did involve the Massachusetts poor law.

97. See N.Y. Act of Apr. 11, 1849, ch. 350, § 1. The statute imposed more expensive bonding requirements for the higher-risk passengers. This statute also consolidated the commutation money with the head tax for the marine hospital that had been invalidated in the Passenger Cases. The head tax in the northern ports was similarly recast with a bonding option, but there was no inspection for higher-risk passengers in those ports. See Act of Apr. 11, 1849, ch. 405, 1849 N.Y. Laws 562.

98. 92 U.S. 259 (1876).

99. See N.Y. Act of May 5, 1847, ch. 195, § 3–5.

100. See, e.g., Annual Reports of the Commissioners of Emigration of the State of New York, 1847 to 1860, at 135 (1861) (1853 Report).

101. See, e.g., id. at 135, 177, 198, 215, 233, 255, 270 (271, 570, 54, 104, 170, 68 and 67 passengers "sent back to Europe at own request" in 1853, 1855, 1856, 1857, 1858, 1859, and 1860, respectively).

102. See, e.g., id. at 157 (1854 report) ("the Commissioners have not been negligent in applying the powers already given to them by the laws under which they act, in requiring the full bonds, and enforcing the penalties now provided in certain cases of this class, or of commuting them at a rate sufficient to provide for the probable expense of the support of such paupers, or on condition of returning such persons (especially if convicts) to their own country").

103. Id. at 213 (1857 report).

104. See Act of Mar. 21, 1821, ch. 122, § 18, 1821 Me. Laws 422, 433 (removal "by land or water to any other State or to any place beyond sea where he belongs"); Me. Rev. Stat. ch. 24, § 31 (1857); In re Knowles, 8 Me. 71 (1831).

105. See Act of June 27, 1820, ch. 26, 1820 Me. Laws 35; Act of Mar. 22, 1838, ch. 339, 1838 Me. Pub. Acts 497. Klebaner, note 45 supra, lists bonding and head tax provisions from Maine, New Hampshire, Massachusetts, Rhode Island, New York, New Jersey, Pennsylvania, Delaware, Maryland, South Carolina, Georgia, Alabama, Mississippi, Louisiana, Texas, and California.

106. See Margaret Creech, Three Centuries of Poor Law Administration: A Study of Legislation in Rhode Island 147 (1969). After 1838, the punishments included fine, confinement to the workhouse, or being bound to service for a year. See R.I. Rev. Stat. ch. 51, § 35 (1857).

107. See Act of June 1847, 1847 R.I. Acts 27; R.I. Rev. Stat. ch. 51, §§ 5–8 (1857); Creech, note 106 supra at 123–25. Creech noted that it was still a crime in 1936, when she wrote, to bring and leave in any town an unsettled poor person.

108. See Act of Mar. 29, 1803, §§ 21, 23, 1801–03 Pa. Laws 507, 525–26.

109. Id. § 23; see Klebaner, note 45 supra at 278 (giving examples of enforcement).

110. See Act of Mar. 5, 1828, No. 79, 1827–28 Pa. Laws 162; see also Priscilla

Ferguson Clement, Welfare and the Poor in the Nineteenth-Century City: Philadelphia, 1800–1854, at 55–57 (1985).

111. Klebaner, note 45 supra at 279.

112. See Act of Mar. 1833, ch. 303, § 2, 1832–33 Md. Laws; Act of Feb. 17, 1835, ch. 84, § 1, 1834–35 Md. Laws; Act of Jan. 30, 1850, ch. 46, 1849–50 Md. Laws; Klebaner, note 45 supra at 280.

113. Ely, note 41 supra at 859.

114. Id. at 874. Immigrants' preference for free states may have reflected antipathy to slavery or a sense of their greater opportunities in free society.

115. Id. at 861; Benjamin J. Klebaner, Public Poor Relief in Charleston, 1800–1860, 55 S. Car. Hist. Mag. 210, 218 (1954).

116. See S.C. Act of Mar. 25, 1738, No. 671, § 5; S.C. Rev. Stat. tit. 8, ch. 29, § 24 (1873). Klebaner records one effort by Charleston in 1832 to compel a captain to remove a pauper he had brought. Klebaner, note 115 supra at 218.

117. See Klebaner, note 115 supra at 218 (two dollars per steerage passenger, twenty-five cents per cabin passenger). Klebaner notes that commutation was made subject to the harbor master's consent in 1846.

118. See Joseph Logsdon, Immigration through the Port of New Orleans, in Forgotten Doors: The Other Ports of Entry to the United States 105 (M. Mark Stolarik ed. 1988).

119. Act of Mar. 16, 1818, § 2, 1818 La. Acts 110; La. Rev. Stat. § 15 (1852).

120. See Act of Mar. 26, 1842, ch. 158, 1841–42 La. Acts 454; Act of Mar. 21, 1850, ch. 295, 1850 La. Acts 225; Klebaner, note 45 supra at 280 ("Collections from this source reached a peak of more than $70,000 in 1854"); see also Commissioners of Immigration v. Brandt, 77 La. Ann. 29 (1874) (upholding bonding version of statute as consistent with Passenger Cases).

121. See S. Res. of Feb. 2, 1847, Cong. Globe, 29th Cong., 2d Sess. 305 (1847) (foreign criminals and paupers); S. Res. of Dec. 23, 1844, Cong. Globe, 28th Cong., 2d Sess. 62 (paupers and convicts); S. Res. of Mar. 19, 1838, Sen. J., 25th Cong., 2d Sess. 619 (foreign paupers); S. Res. of Jul. 4, 1836, Sen. J., 24th Cong., 1st Sess. 548 (paupers).

122. See E.P. Hutchinson, Legislative History of American Immigration Policy 1798–1965, at 40–41 (1981). Hutchinson asserts that the Senate passed the bill, but he cites only the House proceedings, and I have found nothing in the Senate debates or the *Senate Journal* that confirms his assertion. One might expect the states' rights obstacle to be more decisive in the Senate, because the South was more heavily represented there.

123. See, e.g., H.R. Rep. No. 1040, 25th Cong., 2d Sess. 47 (1838); Klebaner, note 44 supra at 304, 305.

124. See, e.g., H.R. Exec. Doc. No. 253, 43d Cong., 1st Sess. 1–6 (1874).

125. Act of Aug. 3, 1882, § 2, 22 Stat. 214. The statute also imposed a federal head tax, replacing the head taxes and surrogates invalidated by the Supreme Court in Henderson v. Mayor of New York, 92 U.S. 259 (1876).

126. See, e.g., Oleg P. Schepin & Waldemar V. Yermakov, International Quarantine (trans. Boris Meerovich & Vladimir Bobrov 1991); Wesley W. Spink, Infectious Diseases: Prevention and Treatment in the Nineteenth and Twentieth Centuries (1978); Hugh S. Cumming, The United States Quarantine System during the

Past Fifty Years, in A Half Century of Public Health 118 (Mazijck P. Ravenel ed. 1921).

127. See Compagnie Francaise de Navigation a Vapeur v. Louisiana State Bd. of Health, 186 U.S. 380, 396 (1902) ("[W]e think [the federal immigration laws] do not purport to abrogate the quarantine laws of the several States, and that the safeguards which they create and the regulations which they impose on the introduction of immigrants are ancillary, and subject to such quarantine laws").

128. See Jenna W. Joselit, The Perceptions and Reality of Immigrant Health Conditions, 1840–1920, in U.S. Immigration Policy and the National Interest: Staff Report to the Select Commission on Immigration and Refugee Policy app. A at 195, 209–30 (1981); Alan M. Kraut, Silent Travelers: Germs, Genes, and American Efficiency, 1890–1924, 12 Soc. Sci. Hist. 377, 378, 385 (1988).

129. See, e.g., Conn. Rev. Stat. tit. 91, § 6 (1821); Act of Dec. 17, 1793, § 3, 1793 Ga. Laws 25; Act of Mar. 10, 1821, ch. 127, § 13, 1823 Me. Laws 443; Act of June 20, 1799, ch. 9, § 14, 1799 Mass. Acts 308; Act of June 10, 1803, § 7, 1803 N.H. Laws 7; Act of Apr. 8, 1811, ch. 175, § 12, 1811 N.Y. Laws 246; Act of 1793, ch. 3, § 3, 1793 N.C. Acts 36; R.I. Pub. Laws, § 5 (1822); Va. Act of Dec. 26, 1792, ch. 129, § 8.

130. See, e.g., Conn. Rev. Stat. tit. 91, § 9 (1821) (interdiction of communication with town or place in adjoining state; willful violation subject to fine); Act of Jan. 1799, ch. 17, § 2, 1799 Del. Laws 4, 48 (may suspend altogether intercourse by land); Act of Apr. 17, 1795, ch. 327, § 4, 1794–95 Pa. Acts 734 (stoppage of intercourse with infected places within the United States; persons transgressing to be fined as well as quarantined).

131. Act of June 22, 1797, ch. 16, § 2, 1797 Mass. Acts & Laws 130. Maine also retained this provision after its separation from Massachusetts. See Act of Mar. 10, 1821, ch. 127, § 2, 1821 Me. Laws 443.

132. See Act of Mar. 27, 1794, ch. 53, § 2, 1794 N.Y. Laws 525.

133. For provisions regarding land quarantines, see, e.g., Ala. Code pt. 1, tit. 13, ch. 1, § 967 (1852); Conn. Rev. Stat. tit. 91, § 15 (1821); Ga. Code pt. 1, tit. 15, ch. 2, § 1402 (1867); Act of Apr. 1, 1803, ch. 178, § 16, 1803 Pa. Laws 593; Act of Dec. 5, 1793, ch. 19, § 2, 1794 Va. Acts 26. (Since the focus of this chapter is on the regulation of migration, I will not discuss the quarantine of nontravelers within their own houses or in hospitals.)

134. See, e.g., Ala. Code pt. 1, tit. 13, ch. 1, § 960 (1852); Act of Nov. 1793, ch. 34, § 2, 1793 Md. Laws; Act of June 20, 1799, ch. 9, §§ 8, 9, 1799 Mass. Acts 308; Va. Code tit. 25, ch. 86, § 13 (1849).

135. See, e.g., Act of Apr. 10, 1850, ch. 275, tit. 2, art. 1, 1850 N.Y. Laws 597, 599–600; Act of Apr. 11, 1799, §§ 4–7, 1799 Pa. Laws 489; Act of Sept. 26, 1868, No. 59, § 2, 1868 S.C. Acts Spec. Sess. 110, 111.

136. See, e.g., John Duffy, A History of Public Health in New York City 1625–1866, at 145 (1968); Charles E. Rosenberg, The Cholera Years 14 (1962). In retrospect, the yellow fever season reflected the life cycle at different latitudes of the mosquito that transmitted the disease.

137. See Schepin & Yermakov, note 125 supra at 25, 106–09, 208–09; Sidney Edelman, International Travel and Our National Quarantine System, 37 Temple L.Q. 28, 29 (1963); cf. Act of Mar. 18, 1858, No. 269, § 5, 1858 La. Acts 187 (more

favorable treatment of vessel presenting clean bill of health); Act of Apr. 4, 1798, § 5, 1798 Pa. Laws 289 (same).

138. See, e.g., Act of Feb. 3, 1812, § 1, 1812 N.J. Laws 19 (vessels from south of Georgia); Act of Apr. 4, 1820, ch. 229, § 4, 1820 N.Y. Laws 208 (vessels from the Mediterranean, Asia, America south of the equator, and Madeira, Canary, Cape Verde, Western, or Bahama Islands); id. § 5 (vessels passing south of Cape Henlopen, Del.); Pa. Act of Apr. 2, 1803, ch. 178, § 6 (vessels from the Mediterranean); Act of Apr. 2, 1821, ch. 126, § 1, 1821 Pa. Laws 210 (vessels from south of Cape Fear, N.C.). Conversely, a particular zone could be favored with less stringent quarantine regulation. See Act of Apr. 18, 1825, ch. 212, 1825 N.Y. Laws 322 (giving the ports of Canton and Calcutta more favorable treatment than other Asian ports). Duffy conjectured that this last New York statute resulted from lobbying by local merchants trading with those ports. Duffy, note 136 supra at 330.

139. See, e.g., Act of Mar. 15, 1855, No. 336, §3, 1855 La. Acts 471; Act of Apr. 9, 1856, ch. 147, § 24, 1856 N.Y. Laws 230; S.C. Act of Sept. 26, 1868, No. 59, § 23.

140. For a striking vignette of immigrants leaping from boats to break through quarantine lines, see Rosenberg, note 136 supra at 24.

141. See, e.g., Act of Nov. 19, 1799, ch. 836, 1799 N.J. Laws 654 ("Whereas it hath been represented to the legislature, that for want of due provision on the part of this state, the laws of the states of Pennsylvania and New-York, for preventing contagious diseases, have been repeatedly evaded"); Pa. Act of Apr. 11, 1799, ch. 228, § 7 (prohibiting entry of recently landed persons who would be subject to quarantine if they landed directly in Philadelphia); Duffy, note 136 supra at 165–66.

142. Duffy, note 136 supra at 330.

143. See, e.g., Conn. Rev. Stat. tit. 91, §§ 3, 6 (1821); Ga. Code pt. 1, tit. 15, §§ 1401, 1404 (1867); La. Act of Mar. 15, 1855, No. 336, §§ 13, 14; N.H. Act of June 10, 1803, §§ 1, 6; N.Y. Act of Apr. 10, 1850, ch. 375, tit. 2, art. 5, §§ 30, 31; N.C. Rev. Code ch. 94, §§ 1, 2, 5 (1855); Pa. Act of Apr. 1, 1803, ch. 178, §§ 4, 13; S.C Act of Sept. 26, 1868, No. 59, §§ 26–28.

144. Duffy, note 136 supra at 86.

145. See, e.g., id. at 124, 237–39; Rosenberg, note 136 supra at 72–81.

146. See Michael Les Benedict, Contagion and the Constitution: Quarantine Agitation from 1859 to 1866, 25 J. Hist. Med. 177, 183–84 (1970).

147. For the argument, see Erwin H. Ackerknecht, Anticontagionism between 1821 and 1867, 22 Bull. Hist. Med. 562 (1948). For local examples, see Duffy, note 136 supra at 134–35, 330–31, 353.

148. See Cumming, note 125 supra at 124–25.

149. See Duffy, note 136 supra at 349–50 (national); Schepin & Yermakov note 125 supra, passim (international); Les Benedict, note 146 supra at 178–81 (national).

150. See 5 Annals of Cong. 1227 (1796).

151. See id. at 1347–59 (remarks of Reps. S. Smith, W. Smith, Bourne, Sitgreaves, Hillhouse).

152. See, e.g., id. at 1348, 1358 (remarks of Reps. Giles, Holland) (self-defense); id. at 1350–51, 1358 (remarks of Reps. Milledge, Holland) (local conditions); id. at 1353, 1354 (remarks of Reps. Gallatin, W. Lyman) (internal police); id. at 1355 (remarks of Rep. Giles) (not object of commerce).

153. See id. at 1359 (46 to 23).

154. See Act of May 27, 1796, ch. 31, 1 Stat. 474.

155. See Act of Feb. 25, 1799, ch. 12, 1 Stat. 619.

156. 22 U.S. (9 Wheat.) 1, 203 (1824); see id. at 205–06.

157. Id. at 206.

158. See J. Res. of May 26, 1866, 14 Stat. 357; Cong. Globe, 39th Cong. 1st Sess. 2444–46, 2483–85, 2520–22, 2548–50, 2581–89 (1866); Les Benedict, note 146 supra at 184–93.

159. See Compagnie Francaise de Navigation a Vapeur v. Louisiana State Bd. of Health, 186 U.S. 380 (1902); Morgan's S.S. Co. v. Louisiana Bd. of Health, 118 U.S. 455 (1886); see also Louisiana v. Texas, 176 U.S. 1, 21 (1900); Patterson v. Kentucky, 97 U.S. 501, 505–06 (1879); Railroad Co. v. Husen, 95 U.S. 465, 472 (1878). For a different category of immigration-related health laws, see In re Wong Yung Quy, 2 F. 624 (C.C.D. Cal. 1880) (upholding state regulation and taxation of the disinterment and transportation of bodies of the deceased, despite interference with Chinese religious custom of returning migrants' bodies to China).

160. See Act of Apr. 29, 1878, ch. 66, 20 Stat. 37. Under this statute, consuls were to report the health conditions in foreign ports, and federal officials were authorized to impose quarantine if necessary in ports where no quarantine system existed, although they were not to interfere with existing state or municipal systems.

161. See Act of Feb. 15, 1893, ch. 114, 27 Stat. 449.

162. See Cumming, note 125 supra at 123; Edelman, note 137 supra at 33.

163. Terminology is a sensitive issue; I use the term "black" in the hope that it is currently the least offensive means of referring specifically to people who were either African or (partly or entirely) of African ancestry. It would be too misleading to use a term like "African American" in this context, because it is important to focus on the fact that the legislation discussed in this section applied, and in some instances was specifically designed to apply, to foreign nationals, e.g., British subjects.

164. Though categorizing states as slave or free may be a useful shorthand in this brief discussion, it should be remembered that there was considerable diversity within these categories, and that states' policies regarding both slavery and free blacks changed over time.

165. See Carl B. Swisher, The Taney Period 1836–64, at 393 (1974); see also In re Ah Fong, 1 F. Cas. 213, 216 (C.C.D. Cal. 1874) (No. 102) (Field, Circuit Justice) ("[W]e cannot shut our eyes to the fact that much which was formerly said upon the power of the state in this respect, grew out of the necessity which the southern states, in which the institution of slavery existed, felt of excluding free negroes from their limits").

166. See, e.g., Ira Berlin, Slaves without Masters: The Free Negro in the Antebellum South (1974); Barbara J. Fields, Slavery and Freedom on the Middle Ground: Maryland during the Nineteenth Century (1985); John Hope Franklin, The Free Negro in North Carolina 1790–1860 (1969 ed.); A. Leon Higginbotham, Jr., In the Matter of Color: Race & the American Legal Process: The Colonial Period (1978); Leon F. Litwack, North of Slavery: The Negro in the Free States 1790–1860 (1961); Paul Finkelman, Prelude to the Fourteenth Amendment: Black Legal Rights in the Antebellum North, 17 Rutgers L.J. 415, 430–43 (1986); A. Leon Higgin-

botham, Jr., & Greer C. Bosworth, "Rather Than Free": Free Blacks in Colonial and Antebellum Virginia, 26 Harv. C.R.-C.L. L. Rev. 17 (1991).

167. See George M. Frederickson, The Black Image in the White Mind 133–35 (1971) (1987 ed.); Litwack, note 166 supra at 66–67.

168. See Litwack, note 166 supra at 67–68.

169. See Act of Jan. 17, 1829, § 1, 1829 Ill. Rev. Code 109 (but excepting blacks who were citizens of one of the United States); Ind. Rev. Laws ch. 66, § 1 (1831); Act of Jan. 25, 1807, ch. 8, § 1, 1807 Ohio Acts 53; see also Act of Mar. 30, 1819, § 3, 1819 Ill. Laws 354 (requiring persons bringing slaves into the state for purpose of emancipation to post bond against the freedman's becoming a public charge).

170. See Act of Feb. 12, 1853, § 3, 1853 Ill. Gen. Laws 354; Act of June 18, 1852, ch. 74, § 1, 1852 Ind. Rev. Stat. 375; Act of Feb. 15, 1851, ch. 72, § 1, 1850–51 Iowa Acts 172; Ill. Const. of 1848, art. XIV ("The general assembly shall, at its first session under the amended constitution, pass such laws as will effectually prohibit free persons of color from immigrating to and settling in this State; and to effectually prevent the owners of slaves from bringing them into this State, for the purpose of setting them free"); Ind. Const. of 1851, art. XIII, § 1 ("No negro or mulatto shall come into, or settle in, the State, after the adoption of this Constitution"); Or. Const. of 1857, art. I, § 36 ("No free negro or mulatto, not residing in this State at the time of the adoption of this Constitution, shall ever come, reside, or be within this State . . . and the Legislative Assembly shall provide by penal laws for the removal by public officers of all such free negroes and mulattoes, and for their effectual exclusion from the State and for the punishment of persons who shall bring them into the State, or employ or harbor them").

Immigration lawyers will have noticed that the Oregon constitution expressly required employer sanctions. Indiana went further and wrote the employer sanctions right into the constitution. Ind. Const. of 1851, art. XIII, § 2 ("[A]ny person who shall employ such negro or mulatto, or otherwise encourage him to remain in the State, shall be fined in any sum not less than ten dollars, nor more than five hundred dollars").

171. See Nelson v. People, 33 Ill. 390 (1864) (The defendant in that case had probably been a slave, but the statute and most of the court's reasoning seem to apply equally to slaves and free persons); Paul Finkelman, An Imperfect Union: Slavery, Federalism, and Comity 88 n. 62, 95 n. 88, 154 (1981); Litwack, note 166 supra at 71–73; see also Finkelman, note 166 supra at 436–43 (on rarity of enforcement).

172. See, e.g., Berlin, note 166 supra at 88–89; Fields, note 166 supra at 39; Eugene D. Genovese, Roll, Jordan, Roll: The World the Slaves Made 411–12 (1974).

173. See, e.g., Berlin, note 166 supra at 95; Franklin, note 166 supra at 73.

174. See, e.g., Berlin, note 166 supra at 35–36, 114–15.

175. See, e.g., Berlin, note 166 supra at 364–70; Finkelman, note 166 supra at 234–35; Genovese, note 172 supra at 399.

176. See, e.g., Berlin, note 166 supra at 377–78; Fields, note 166 supra at 82–84; Franklin, note 166 supra at 140–41.

177. See, e.g., Berlin, note 166 supra at 331–35; Franklin, note 166 supra at 58.

178. See, e.g., Ala. Code pt. 1, tit. 13, ch. 4, art. 2, §§ 1033, 1034 (1852); Act of Jan. 20, 1843, § 2, 1843 Ark. Acts 61; Act of Jan. 28, 1811, ch. 146, § 1, 1811 Del. Laws 400; Act of Dec. 19, 1818, No. 512, § 3, 1818 Ga. Acts 126; Act of Mar. 16, 1830, § 3, 1830 La. Acts 90; Act of Jan. 3, 1807, ch. 56, § 1, 1806–07 Md. Laws; Miss. Code ch. 37, art. 2, § 80 (1848) (enacted June 18, 1822); Act of Feb. 12, 1827, ch. 21, 1826–27 N.C. Acts 13; Act of Dec. 20, 1820, § 2, 1820 S.C. Acts & Resolutions 22; Act of Dec. 12, 1793, ch. 23, § 1, 1793 Va. Acts 28; Berlin, note 166 supra at 92; Franklin, note 166 supra at 41–48; see also Ky. Const. of 1850, art. X, § 2 ("The general assembly shall pass laws providing that any free negro or mulatto hereafter immigrating to, and any slave hereafter emancipated in, and refusing to leave this State, or having left, shall return and settle within this State [*sic*], shall be deemed guilty of felony, and punished by confinement in the penitentiary thereof").

179. See, e.g., Miss. Code ch. 37, art. 17, § 4 (1848); N.C. Act of Feb. 12, 1827, ch. 21, § 4; S.C. Act of Dec. 20, 1820, § 3; Va. Act of Dec. 12, 1793, ch. 164 § 2. The North Carolina and Virginia statutes cited here made exceptions for free black crew members who departed with their vessels and free blacks who were servants of travelers passing through the state.

180. See, e.g., Del. Act of Jan. 28, 1811, ch. 146, § 4 (traveling outside state for six months); Act of Dec. 26, 1835, § 3, 1835 Ga. Acts 265 (unless traveling to "an adjoining State"); La. Act of Mar. 16, 1830, § 7 (traveling outside United States); N.C. Acts of 1830–31, ch. 14 (traveling outside state for ninety days); Act of Dec. 21, 1822, ch. 3, § 1, 1822–23 S.C. Acts & Resolutions 12 (leaving state for any length of time); Va. Code tit. 30, ch. 107, § 29 (1860) (leaving state for education, or traveling to free state for any reason); see also Act of Mar. 14, 1832, ch. 323, § 2, 1831–32 Md. Laws (traveling outside state for thirty days without first filing statement of intent to return; exception if visiting Liberia). Free black residents employed in certain occupations requiring travel were exempt from most of these prohibitions.

181. See, e.g., Ky. Const. of 1850, art. X, § 2; Va. Const. of 1850, art. IV, § 19 ("Slaves hereafter emancipated shall forfeit their freedom by remaining in the commonwealth more than twelve months after they become actually free, and shall be reduced to slavery under such regulation as may be prescribed by law"); Ala. Code pt. 2, tit. 5, ch. 4, § 2047 (1852); Act of Mar. 12, 1832, ch. 281, § 3, 1831–32 Md. Laws; N.C. Rev. Code ch. 107, § 50 (1855); Va. Act of Mar. 2, 1819, ch. 111, § 61; cf. La. Rev. Stat., Black Code §§ 78, 79 (1856) (jury to decide whether emancipated slave will be permitted to remain in state); Genovese, supra at 399.

182. See Berlin, note 166 supra at 370–80; Fields, note 166 supra at 80–82; Franklin, note 166 supra at 211–16; see also Va. Const. of 1850, art. IV, § 20 ("The general assembly . . . may pass laws for the relief of the commonwealth from the free negro population, by removal or otherwise").

183. See Act of Feb. 12, 1859, No. 151, 1858–59 Ark. Laws 175. The effective date of the legislation was ultimately postponed, but by then nearly all the free blacks had left the state. Berlin, note 166 supra at 372–74, 380.

184. See, e.g., Ga. Act of Dec. 19, 1793, 1793 Ga. Acts 24 (forbidding importation of slaves from West Indies and requiring free blacks entering state to give security for good behavior); Act of 1795, ch. 16, § 1, 1795 N.C. Acts 79 (emigrants

from West Indies forbidden to bring slaves or persons of color over the age of fifteen); Act of Dec. 20, 1794, 1794 S.C. Acts & Resolutions 34 (barring entry of slaves or free blacks from outside the U.S.); Act of Dec. 17, 1803, § 2, 1803 S.C. Acts & Resolutions 48 (barring entry of slaves or free blacks from the West Indies or South America or those who have ever been resident in the French West Indies).

185. The arrival of free blacks expelled from Guadeloupe provided the immediate impetus for the 1803 federal statute. See Petition to Prevent the Importation of Certain Persons Whose Admission Is Prohibited by Certain Laws of the State Governments (1803), reprinted in 1 The New American State Papers: Labor and Slavery 27 (1973); W.E.B. Du Bois, The Suppression of the African Slave Trade 84–85 (1969 reprint) (1896).

186. See Act of Feb. 28, 1803, ch. 10, 2 Stat. 205. The prohibition applied to importing or bringing in "any negro, mulatto, or other person of colour, not being a native, a citizen, or registered seaman, of the United States, or seamen, natives of countries beyond the Cape of Good Hope . . . provided always, that nothing contained in this act shall be construed to prohibit the admission of Indians." The exception for natives, citizens, and registered seamen of the United States was evidently added to accommodate the Northern view, expressed in the debates, that free African Americans had rights of interstate travel. See 12 Annals of Cong. 467–68 (1803) (remarks of Rep. Bacon). The statute also had the effect of making it a federal crime to import slaves into states where such importation was prohibited; the latter qualification was necessary because Congress lacked the power to outlaw importation until 1808.

187. John C. Calhoun, Speech in Reply to Criticisms of the Bill to Prohibit the Circulation of Incendiary Publications through the Mail (April 12, 1836), in 13 The Papers of John C. Calhoun 147, 156 (Clyde N. Wilson, ed. 1980) (arguing that Congress should also prohibit the mailing of abolitionist literature into the Southern states).

188. U.S. Const. art. IV, § 2, cl. 1 ("The Citizens of each State shall be entitled to all Privileges and Immunities of Citizens in the several States"); see, e.g., Scott v. Sandford, 60 U.S. (19 How.) 393, 425 (1857) (if a free black were a citizen, then "the State officers and tribunals would be compelled . . . to receive him . . . and allow him to enjoy all the rights and privileges of citizenship"); Smith v. Moody, 26 Ind. 299 (1866) (recognition of blacks as U.S. citizens invalidates state bar on entry).

189. But see Lemmon v. People, 20 N.Y. 562, 611 (1860) (Denio, J.) (dictum) ("[I]t does not seem to me clear that one who is truly a citizen of another State can be thus excluded, though he may be a pauper or a criminal, unless he be a fugitive from justice. The fourth article of confederation contained an exception to the provision for a common citizenship, excluding from its benefits paupers and vagabonds as well as fugitives from justice; but this exception was omitted in the corresponding provision of the Constitution").

190. See Mo. Const. of 1820, art. III, § 26 (duty of legislature "[t]o prevent free negroes and mulattoes from coming to and settling in this State, under any pretext whatsoever").

191. See J. Res. of Mar. 2, 1821, 3 Stat. 645 ("that no law shall be passed in conformity thereto, by which any citizen, of either of the states in this Union, shall

be excluded from the enjoyment of any of the privileges and immunities to which such citizen is entitled under the constitution of the United States"); Litwack, note 166 supra at 34–39.

192. A defense based on this compromise was successfully raised in the case of Andrew Hatfield, who was born in Pennsylvania and later moved to Saint Louis and was prosecuted there for residing without a license. See the brief summary under the title *Free Negroes in Missouri*, 3 Western L.J. 477 (1846). But a year later Missouri enacted a new statute expressing an absolute bar on the entry of free blacks, in the language of its 1820 constitution. Act of Feb. 16, 1847, § 4, 1847 Mo. Laws 103; Litwack, note 166 supra at 38.

193. See, e.g., Cooper v. Mayor of Savannah, 4 Ga. 68 (1848); State v. Newsom, 27 N.C. (5 Ired.) 250 (1844); State v. Claiborne, 19 Tenn. (Meigs) 331 (1838); but see State v. Manuel, 20 N.C. (4 Dev. & Bat.) 122 (1838).

194. See Scott v. Sandford, 60 U.S. (19 How.) 393 (1857). Pendleton v. State, 6 Ark. 509 (1846), and State v. Claiborne, 19 Tenn. (Meigs) 331 (1839), both reached this conclusion in the course of upholding state prohibitions on the entry of free blacks.

195. I discuss here only some aspects of this regulation that bear a particular relation to immigration regulation; I do not purport to be sketching a full picture of the subordinated position of free blacks or even to list the restrictions that would seem most significant to a general reader.

196. See, e.g., Ark. Act of Jan. 20, 1843, § 3; Act of Dec. 19, 1818, § 5, 1818 Ga. Acts 811; Miss. Code ch. 37, art. 2, § 81 (1848); Va. Act of Mar. 2, 1819, ch. 111, §§ 67–77; Berlin, note 166 supra at 93–94, 327–32.

197. See, e.g., Ala. Code pt. 1, tit. 13, ch. 4, art. 2, § 1040 (free persons of color imprisoned in penitentiary must leave state after discharge unless pardoned); La. Act of Mar. 16, 1830, § 9 (if convicted of writing or speaking against slavery or racial hierarchy, whites to be fined and imprisoned up to three years, and free persons of color to be fined and imprisoned at hard labor for up to five years and then banished from state for life); Act of Mar. 14, 1832, ch. 323, § 12, 1831–32 Md. Laws (free blacks may be banished to foreign country for noncapital offenses, at discretion of court); Md. Code art. 30, § 199 (1860) (any free black confined in penitentiary shall be banished from state after pardon or expiration of term); S.C. Act of Dec. 20, 1820, § 6 (if convicted of circulating antislavery writings, whites to be fined and imprisoned one year, and free persons of persons of color to be fined for first offense, and on second offense to be whipped and banished from state on pain of death).

198. See Va. Act of Feb. 21, 1823, ch. 32, 1823 Va. Acts 35 (imposing sale and transportation abroad as punishment for any free black or mulatto convicted of an offense previously punishable by two or more years in prison); Act of Feb. 18, 1825, ch. 45, 1824–25 Va. Acts 37 (same punishment for free black convicted of grand larceny). The Virginia provisions were repealed in 1828; see Act of Feb. 12, 1828, ch. 37, 1828 Va. Acts 29; Berlin, note 166 supra at 183. In the meantime, enslavement and transportation abroad as punishment for larceny had been upheld against constitutional challenge by the Virginia Supreme Court. Aldridge v. Commonwealth, 4 Va. 447 (1824) (ban on cruel and unusual punishment does not apply to free person of color).

States more frequently used sale and transportation abroad as a punishment for people who were already slaves. See, e.g., Act of Jan. 6, 1810, ch. 138, § 9, 1809–10 Md. Laws; N.C. Rev. Code ch. 107, § 39 (1855); Va. Code tit. 54, ch. 200, § 7 (1860); Philip J. Schwarz, The Transportation of Slaves from Virginia, 1801–1865, 7 Slavery and Abolition 215 (1986).

199. See Act of Mar. 22, 1794, ch. 11, § 1, 1 Stat. 347.

200. The first Chinese exclusion act, the Act of May 6, 1882, ch. 126, 22 Stat. 58, did not define "Chinese," and after the lower courts divided over whether it applied only to subjects of the Empire of China, Congress was careful to specify its broad scope. Compare United States v. Douglas, 17 F. 634 (C.C.D. Mass. 1883) (empire only), with In re Ah Lung, 18 F. 28 (C.C.D. Cal.) (Field, Circuit Justice) (entire race); see Act of July 5, 1884, ch. 220, § 15, 23 Stat. 115, 118 ("all subjects of China and Chinese, whether subjects of China or any other foreign power"); Act of Sept. 13, 1888, ch. 1015, § 3, 25 Stat. 476 ("all persons of the Chinese race").

201. See, e.g., Roger Daniels, Asian America: Chinese and Japanese in the United States since 1850, at 33–37 (1988); Charles J. McClain, Jr., The Chinese Struggle for Civil Rights in Nineteenth Century America: The First Phase, 1850–1870, 72 Cal. L. Rev. 529 (1984).

202. See Alexander Saxton, The Indispensable Enemy: Labor and the Anti-Chinese Movement in California 19–20 (1971); Ronald Takaki, Strangers from a Different Shore: A History of Asian Americans 100–03 (1990).

203. See Elmer C. Sandmeyer, The Anti-Chinese Movement in California 25–31 (1991 ed.); Saxton, note 202 supra at 33–37, 259–61; Takaki, note 202 supra at 101; cf. Eric Foner, Free Soil, Free Labor, Free Men 60–63, 266–67 (1970) (on arguments against slaves and free blacks); Litwack, note 166 supra at 158–61 (on arguments against free blacks).

204. See Act of May 6, 1882, ch. 126, 22 Stat. 58 (first exclusion act); Act of Oct. 1, 1888, ch. 1064, 25 Stat. 504 (forbidding return); Act of May 5, 1892, ch. 60, 27 Stat. 25 (registration and arrest and removal of unregistered); cf. Ark. Act of Jan. 20, 1843, §§ 6–8 (unregistered free blacks subject to fine and servitude to work off fine, repeatedly, until they depart state); Act of Dec. 26, 1835, § 2, 1835 Ga. Acts 265 (same). Not until 1986 did the federal government adopt the Midwestern technique of making the official certificate of lawful residence a key to sanctions against persons employing undocumented immigrants. Compare 8 U.S.C. § 1324a (making employment of unauthorized aliens unlawful and requiring employer to examine documentation of employment authorization) with Act of Jan. 17, 1829, § 1, 1829 Ill. Rev. Code 109 (imposing fines for hiring black who does not have certificate of compliance with procedure for gaining residence); Act of June 18, 1852, ch. 74, §§ 5, 7, 1852 Ind. Laws 375 (certificate of registration conclusive evidence in prosecutions against employers, unless notice to employer of fraud shown).

205. See, e.g., William W. Freehling, Prelude to Civil War: The Nullification Controversy in South Carolina, 1816–1836, at 109–17 (1968); Donald G. Morgan, Justice William Johnson: The First Dissenter 192–206 (1954); Swisher, note 165 supra at 378–82; William M. Wiecek, The Sources of Antislavery Constitutionalism in America, 1760–1848, at 132–40 (1977). Most accounts draw on a pair of articles, Philip M. Hamer, Great Britain, the United States, and the Negro Seamen Acts, 1822–1848, 1 J. So. Hist. 1 (1935) (hereinafter Hamer I), and Philip M.

Hamer, British Consuls and the Negro Seamen Acts, 1850–1860, 1 J. So. Hist. 138 (1935) (hereinafter Hamer II).

206. See, e.g., Act of Dec. 20, 1800, § 11, 1800 S.C. Acts & Resolutions 31; Act of Dec. 12, 1793, ch. 24, 1793 Va. Acts 28.

207. See, e.g., Freehling, note 205 supra at 53–61. Vesey was a carpenter in Charleston who had bought himself out of slavery and who preached freedom and equality. He allegedly planned an insurrection of slaves, slaughter of masters, and escape to Haiti, but the plot was discovered and repressed with numerous executions.

208. See Act of Dec. 21, 1822, ch. 3, § 3, 1822–23 S.C. Acts & Resolutions 12. In its original form, the statute provided that the seaman would be sold as a slave if the master failed to pay or left without him. This sanction was replaced a year later; see Act of Dec. 20, 1823, ch. 20, §§ 3, 12, 1823–24 S.C. Acts & Resolutions 60. The amendment also exempted crew members of U.S. and foreign naval vessels, so long as they did not come ashore after being warned to remain on board.

209. See, e.g., Act of Jan. 9, 1841, ch. 15, §§ 21–24, 1840–41 Ala. Acts 19 (black crew members to be confined in jail at vessel's expense until departure); Act of Dec. 26, 1826, § 5, 1826 Ga. Acts 161 (imposing curfew on black sailors and requiring vessels to post bond for compliance); Act of Dec. 22, 1829, 1829 Ga. Laws 168 (subjecting vessels with black crew members or passengers to "quarantine"); La. Act of Mar. 16, 1842, No. 123, § 1 (black crew members to be confined in jail at vessel's expense until departure); see also Act of Jan. 4, 1831, ch. 30, § 1, 1830–31 N.C. Acts 29 (subjecting vessels with black crew members or passengers to "quarantine"), repealed by Act of Jan. 14, 1832, ch. 19, 1831–32 N.C. Acts 14.

210. See Freehling, note 205 supra at 113; Hamer I, note 205 supra at 4–5.

211. 8 F. Cas. 493 (C.C.D.S.C. 1823) (No. 4,366).

212. See id. at 494 ("[T]hey have both strenuously contended, that ex necessitate it was a power which the state must and would exercise, and, indeed, Mr. Holmes concluded his argument with the declaration, that if a dissolution of the Union must be the alternative, he was ready to meet it"); Freehling, note 205 supra at 113–16.

213. See 8 Fed. Cas. at 497–98. Johnson held that the writ *de homine replegiando* would not lie against the sheriff but noted that it would lie against a private purchaser if the state really attempted to enslave and sell Elkison, as the South Carolina statute permitted. Federal habeas corpus jurisdiction had not yet been extended to persons held in state custody.

214. See Hamer I, note 205 supra at 7–9.

215. See Morgan, note 205 supra at 196–202.

216. 22 U.S. (9 Wheat.) 1 (1824); see also id. at 231 (Johnson, J., concurring).

217. Hamer also notes later protests from France. See Hamer II, note 205 supra at 144 n. 20.

218. See Hamer I, note 205 supra at 8–10. He also secured an opinion from the attorney general, agreeing with Johnson that the statute was invalid. 1 Op. Att'y Gen. 659 (1824) (Wirt).

219. See Convention of Commerce and Navigation, July 3, 1815, U.S.-U.K., 1815, art. 1. Hamer reports that the British themselves were uncertain that this treatment of British sailors violated the treaty, given that black sailors from Northern states were treated no better. See Hamer I, note 205 supra at 13–14.

220. 2 Op. Att'y Gen. 426 (1831) (Berrien); Hamer I, note 205 supra at 14–15. Berrien's successor as attorney general, Roger Taney, also drafted an opinion, which ultimately was not published, upholding the legislation; historians have noted how this draft prefigured Taney's arguments in the Dred Scott case two decades later. See Wiecek, note 205 supra at 139.

221. 2 Op. Atty. Gen. at 441–42. Chief Justice Marshall, in contrast, had construed this statute on circuit as not applying at all to foreign crew members who would be leaving with the vessel, on the somewhat ingenious ground that they brought the vessel in rather than vice versa. See Wilson v. United States, 30 F. Cas. 239, 244 (C.C.D. Va. 1820) (Case No. 17,846). For Marshall's oft-quoted comparison of the Wilson and Elkison cases, see Chapter Three.

222. See, e.g., Free Colored Seamen—Majority and Minority Reports, H.R. Rep. No. 80, 27th Cong., 2d Sess. (1843) (including attack on and defense of laws); Hamer I, note 205 supra at 22; Wiecek, note 205 supra at 139–40.

223. See Hamer I, note 205 supra at 22–23; Wiecek, note 205 supra at 140. That same year, a federal judge in Massachusetts declared Louisiana's statute unconstitutional on commerce clause grounds, while deciding a dispute over the wages due a black sailor who had been imprisoned under it. The Cynosure, 6 F. Cas. 1102 (D. Mass. 1844) (No. 3,529).

224. See Hamer I, note 205 supra at 25–27 & n. 94.

225. See Hamer II, note 205 supra (passim). When the news spread that the British were in direct diplomatic contact with South Carolina officials, this contact was criticized in other states as bolstering that state's secessionist notions of sovereignty.

226. See Hamer II, note 205 supra at 142–43; Act of Feb. 7, 1854, No. 94, 1853–54 Ga. Acts 106 (permitting black sailors to land subject to permission of local authorities); Act of Mar. 18, 1852, ch. 279, §§ 1, 2, 1852 La. Acts 193 (permitting black sailors to remain on vessel if bond was given for their removal, and to land where necesssary for their duties subject to the permission of local authorities). Louisiana backslid in 1859, necessitating further intervention. See Hamer II at 167–68; Act of March 15, 1859, No. 87, § 1, 1859 La. Acts 70.

227. See Hamer II, note 205 supra at 146–66; see also Roberts v. Yates, 20 F. Cas. 937 (C.C.D.S.C. 1853) (No. 11,919) (upholding constitutionality of the statute). The consul had initiated the Roberts litigation, and a state court case as well, on the dubious advice of Secretary of State Daniel Webster that South Carolina might respect a Supreme Court decision invalidating the statute. See Hamer II at 155–60.

228. See Hamer II, note 205 supra at 160–66; Act of December 20, 1856, No. 4311, 1856 S.C. Reports & Resolutions 573.

229. See Treaty of July 28, 1868, United States–China, art. 6, 16 Stat. 739 ("Chinese subjects . . . shall enjoy the same privileges, immunities and exemptions in respect to travel or residence, as may there be enjoyed by the citizens or subjects of the most favored nation"); Act of May 31, 1870, ch. 114, § 16, 16 Stat. 144 ("No tax or charge shall be imposed or enforced by any State upon any person immigrating thereto from a foreign country which is not equally imposed and enforced upon every person immigrating to such State from any other foreign country "); In re Parrott, 1 F. 481 (C.C.D. Cal 1880); In re Ah Fong, 1 F. Cas. 213, 217–18 (C.C.D.

Cal. 1874) (No. 102) (Field, Circuit Justice); McClain, note 201 supra at 561–67. Two earlier efforts to keep out the Chinese by discriminatory taxation had been invalidated by the state courts on commerce clause grounds, following the Passenger Cases. See Lin Sing v. Washburn, 20 Cal. 534 (1862); People v. Downer, 7 Cal. 170 (1857).

230. See Chy Lung v. Freeman, 92 U.S. 275 (1876).

231. U.S. Const. art. I, § 9, cl. 1 ("The Migration or Importation of such Persons as any of the States now existing shall think proper to admit, shall not be prohibited by the Congress prior to the Year one thousand eight hundred and eight"). Article V ruled out amendments of the Constitution that would lift this bar to congressional action.

232. See, e.g., Du Bois, note 185 supra at 71–74. South Carolina, however, first prohibited the trade and then repealed its prohibition. See Act of Dec. 17, 1803, § 1, 1803 S.C. Acts & Resolutions 48 (repealing former acts). Even this statute, however, prohibited the importation of slaves from the West Indies, since they might spread the spirit of revolt. See id. § 2; Du Bois at 72.

233. See Act of Mar. 2, 1807, ch. 22, 2 Stat. 426. The statute also imposed some regulation on the interstate coastwise trade, in order to increase the enforceability of the ban on the international trade. See 3 Op. Att'y Gen. 512 (1840) (Gilpin).

234. See, e.g., Act of Mar. 3, 1819, ch. 101, 3 Stat. 532; Act of Mar. 15, 1820, ch. 113, 3 Stat. 600; Act of June 16, 1860, ch. 136, 12 Stat. 40.

235. The constitutionality of federal regulation of interstate trade in slaves was also disputed. See Walter Berns, The Constitution and the Migration of Slaves, 78 Yale L.J. 198 (1968).

236. See Du Bois, note 185 supra at 71–73, 85–86, 168–83; Ronald T. Takaki, A Pro-Slavery Crusade: The Agitation to Reopen the African Slave Trade (1971).

237. See, e.g., Act of Dec. 31, 1796, ch. 67, 1796 Md. Laws (generally barring the importation of slaves into the state, with exceptions); Act of May 13, 1837, 1837 Miss. Laws 343 (prohibiting the introduction of slaves into the state for sale). Mississippi's power to prohibit the sale of slaves into the state was argued and then addressed in obiter dicta in Groves v. Slaughter, 40 U.S. (15 Pet.) 449 (1841), where six of seven justices affirmed the state's power to regulate. See id. at 507–08 (opinion of McLean, J.); id. at 508 (opinion of Taney, C.J.); id. at 510 (statement of Story, Thompson, Wayne, and McKinley, JJ.).

238. See, e.g., Act of Jan. 31, 1829, No. 23, § 13, 1828–29 La. Acts 38 (barring the introduction of slaves who had been accused of conspiracy or insurrection, or had even resided in any county while conspiracy or insurrection occurred there); Act of Jan. 29, 1817, § 1, 1816–17 La. Acts 44 (punishing the introduction of slaves previously convicted of certain crimes or insurrection); Va. Act of Mar. 2, 1819, ch. 111, § 3 (barring the introduction of slaves transported from other states for crime).

239. See generally Finkelman, note 166 supra. When a slave owner attempted to settle in a free state while bringing her slaves with her, the state's power to free them was largely uncontroversial, even in the South, at least until the 1850s. Emancipation was more controversial where the slave owner was only temporarily visiting the state or merely in transit through the state. See id. at 181–85.

240. See Fugitive Slave Act of 1850, ch. 60, 9 Stat. 462; Fugitive Slave Act of 1793, ch. 51, 1 Stat. 302; see also Robert M. Cover, Justice Accused: Antislavery

and the Judicial Process 159–91 (1975); Wiecek, note 205 supra at 155–59, 196–98, 286–87. See generally Thomas D. Morris, Free Men All: The Personal Liberty Laws of the North, 1780–1861 (1974).

241. See Act of Feb. 12, 1853, 1853 Ill. Laws 57.

242. These were the Act of June 18, 1798, ch. 54, 1 Stat. 566; Act of July 6, 1798, ch. 66, 1 Stat. 577; and Act of June 25, 1798, ch. 58, 1 Stat. 570, respectively. The Sedition Act, ch. 74, 1 Stat. 596, was a criminal statute equally regulating the speech of citizens and aliens, and not a regulation of migration.

243. See 50 U.S.C. §§ 21–23.

244. See Act of Nov. 16, 1792, ch. 62, § 2, 1792 Va. Acts 65 (declaring it "lawful for the governor . . . [to] compel [ ] to depart this Commonwealth, all suspicious persons" from foreign powers from whom the president "shall apprehend hostile designs" against the United States).

245. See Act of June 18, 1798, ch. 54, § 1, 1 Stat. 566, repealed by Act of Apr. 14, 1802, ch. 28, § 5, 2 Stat. 153.

246. Id. §§ 4–6. Justice Black, however, appears not to have had this statute in mind when he stated, "So violent was the reaction to the 1798 laws that almost a century elapsed before a second registration act was passed." Hines v. Davidowitz, 312 U.S. 52, 70–71 & n.28 (1941) (citing Alien Act and Alien Enemies Act).

247. See Frank G. Franklin, The Legislative History of Naturalization in the United States 107 (1906) (quoting from a January 1802 issue of the *Kentucky Palladium*).

248. See 12 Annals of Congress 569–77 (1803); Franklin, note 247 supra at 110–14. This and other arguments apparently resulted in the Act of Mar. 26, 1804, ch. 47, 2 Stat. 292, which waived the requirement of the filing of a declaration of intent before naturalization for all aliens who had been residing in the United States during the period when the 1798 Naturalization Act was in effect.

249. See Act of Apr. 14, 1802, ch. 28, § 2, 2 Stat. 153.

250. 4 Cong. Deb., pt. 2, at 2556 (1828) (remarks of Rep. Buchanan) ("The neglect is common, nay, almost universal, because aliens do not know the law, and would not, for sometime after their arrival, conform to it, even if they did. . . . [S]ome courts do, and others do not, carry this part of it into execution. . . . [I]t would be better at once to dispense with this registry"); see Act of May 24, 1828, ch. 116, § 1, 4 Stat. 310; Franklin, note 247 supra at 178–80.

251. See Alien Registration Act of 1940, ch. 439, 54 Stat. 670 (current version at 8 U.S.C. §§ 1301–1306). A special registration requirement had been imposed on Chinese immigrants in 1892. See Act of May 5, 1892, ch. 60, 27 Stat. 25.

252. The text applies here the convention that the involuntary physical return of an alien is distinguishable from punishment.

253. Cf. John Kaplan, Abortion as a Vice Crime: A "What If" Story, 51 Law & Contemp. Probs. 151, 164 (Winter 1988) (discussing deterrence of abortion by imposing criminal sanctions on physicians).

254. See Maryellen Fullerton, Restricting the Flow of Asylum-Seekers in Belgium, Denmark, the Federal Republic of Germany, and the Netherlands, 29 Va. J. Int'l L. 33, 93 (1988) (discussing asymmetric incentives under modern carrier sanctions provisions). The 1803 federal statute supporting the laws of the Southern states against the entry of free blacks imposed forfeiture of the vessel as one of the

penalties. Cf. 8 U.S.C. § 1324(b) (providing for forfeiture of vessels, vehicles, and aircraft for knowingly or recklessly bringing in an alien in violation of law).

255. I will not venture an estimate of the effectiveness of the laws against free black immigration. In the Southern states, the legal and social status of free blacks was so precarious that it would be difficult to separate their causal contributions from those of the ban on entry.

256. See note 63 supra (noting category where commutation payment under Massachusetts law slightly exceeded price of ticket for transatlantic crossing).

257. See Klebaner, note 45 supra at 284, 288–89.

258. See H.R. Rep. No. 359, 34th Cong., 1st Sess. 146 (1856) ("The circular[s] issued by the immigration agents in the interior of Germany, caution immigrants who are deformed, crippled, or maimed, &c., against taking passage to New York, and advise them to go by way of Baltimore, New Orleans, or Quebec, where the laws prohibiting the landing of immigrants of the above classes do not apply"); S.H. Collins, The Emigrant's Guide to and Description of the United States of America 67 (n.p., Joseph Noble 4th ed. n.d.) ("When paupers are sent by the parish, it is imperative that each family should have at least five pounds, and be able to produce it before they will be allowed by the American Government to set a foot in the United States: should this not be attended to, they will not be allowed to land"); Klebaner, note 45 supra at 288; Logsdon, note 116 supra at 109.

259. See Klebaner, note 45 supra at 288.

260. See H.R. Rep. No. 1040, 25th Cong., 2d Sess. 47 (1838) (re public charges); H.R. Exec. Doc. 253, 43d Cong., 1st Sess. 7–8 (same) (1874); see also id. at 10 ("[H]e is acting in opposition to the laws of the United States, by encouraging the shipment of criminals as emigrants to that country"); id. at 36 ("Against such an introduction of pauper population this Government must earnestly remonstrate as in violation of the laws of the United States and of international comity").

CHAPTER THREE

1. 130 U.S. 581 (1889).

2. Even before 1868, one could have argued that a particular state immigration law amounted to a bill of attainder or ex post facto law in violation of Article I, section 10 of the Constitution; the modern interpretation of those provisions, however, makes them inapplicable to exclusion and deportation grounds. See Galvan v. Press, 347 U.S. 522 (1954); Linnas v. INS, 790 F.2d 1024 (2d Cir. 1986).

3. 22 U.S. (9 Wheat.) 1 (1824).

4. 36 U.S. (11 Pet.) 102 (1837).

5. Id. at 160. The case had been reargued because of the initial disagreement among the justices.

6. 48 U.S. (7 How.) 283 (1849).

7. 92 U.S. 259 (1876).

8. 92 U.S. 275 (1876).

9. The Act of Mar. 3, 1875, ch. 141, 18 Stat. 477, excluding convicts and prostitutes, as well as increasing the stringency of the "coolie trade" statutes, is usually identified as the first federal immigration statute. See, e.g., 1 Charles Gordon & Stanley Mailman, Immigration Law and Procedure at 2–6 (rev. ed. 1991).

10. 22 U.S. (9 Wheat.) at 203–05.

11. Id. at 205–06.

12. 36 U.S. (11 Pet.) at 142–43.

13. See id. at 148 (opinion of Thompson, J.) ("Can anything fall more directly within the police power and internal regulation of a state, than that which concerns the care and management of paupers or convicts, or any other class or description of persons that may be thrown into the country, and likely to endanger its safety, or become chargeable for their maintenance?"); id. at 153b (opinion of Baldwin, J.) ("On the same principle by which a state may prevent the introduction of infected persons or goods, and articles dangerous to the persons or property of its citizens, it may exclude paupers who will add to the burdens of taxation, or convicts who will corrupt the morals of the people, threatening them with more evils than gunpowder or disease").

Story, in contrast, thought even the reporting provisions unconstitutional, because in excess of the reporting that Congress had required. See id. at 158–59 (Story, J., dissenting). He also addressed the broader issue and concluded à la Gibbons v. Ogden that the federal regulation of vessels carrying passengers affirmatively authorized the landing of all passengers in the states. Id. at 159.

14. See 48 U.S. (7 How.) at 283–84.

15. See id. at 285–86.

16. See id. at 410 (opinion of McLean, J.); id. at 426–27 (opinion of Wayne, J.); id. at 457 (opinion of Grier, J.). John Catron concurred in Grier's analysis of the police power question; see id. at 452 (opinion of Catron, J.). John McKinley's view is less clear; he purported to concur with the reasoning of McLean and Catron, but some passages in his brief opinion seem to imply a narrower view of state power. See id. at 452–55 (opinion of McKinley, J.).

17. Id. at 457.

18. See, e.g., id. at 457–58, 463–64 (opinion of Grier, J.).

19. Id. at 400 (opinion of McLean, J.); see also id. at 406, 410.

20. Id. at 426–29 (opinion of Wayne, J.).

21. Id. at 528 (Woodbury, J., dissenting).

22. Id. at 508–14 (Daniels, J., dissenting). The Alien Act is discussed at some length in Chapter Four.

23. 48 U.S. (7 How.) at 466 (Taney, C.J., dissenting). Samuel Nelson concurred in Taney's dissent. See id. at 518 (Nelson, J., dissenting).

24. See id. at 474 (Taney, C.J., dissenting); id. at 550 (Woodbury, J., dissenting).

25. See the discussion of the Elkison case in the previous chapter.

26. Letter from John Marshall to Joseph Story, Sept. 26, 1823, quoted in 1 Charles Warren, The Supreme Court in United States History 626 (1932).

27. 41 U.S. (16 Pet.) 539 (1842). In this much-studied case, the Supreme Court overturned a slave catcher's conviction under Pennsylvania law for removing an alleged fugitive slave from the state despite a state magistrate's refusal to issue a certificate of removal. Story interpreted the Fugitive Slave Clause of the Constitution as imposing a duty of affirmative implementation exclusively on the federal government; this contributed to his conclusion that the states could not impose procedural constraints on the master's right of recapture. See id. at 615–16.

28. 41 U.S. (16 Pet.) 539, 625 (1842) (emphasis added). The subject of state

power to prohibit the *sale* of slaves into the state had recently been addressed in dicta in Groves v. Slaughter, 40 U.S. (15 Pet.) 449 (1841), where six of seven justices affirmed the state's power. Id. at 507–08 (opinion of McLean, J.); id. at 508 (opinion of Taney, C.J.); id. at 510 (statement of Story, Thompson, Wayne, and McKinley, JJ.).

A similar distinction between expulsion for the state's internal benefit and delivery for the benefit of an outsider had appeared in the inconclusive case of Holmes v. Jennison, 39 U.S. (14 Pet.) 540 (1840). There the Court was evenly divided over the power of the state of Vermont to return a murder suspect to Canada for prosecution. Four justices concluded that Vermont's proposed surrender of Holmes to Canada for prosecution would have been tantamount to entering into an *agreement* for his extradition and would therefore trespass on the exclusive federal power to conduct intercourse with foreign governments. See id. at 573–74 (opinion of Taney, C.J., joined by Story, McLean, and Wayne, JJ.). The other four justices were more protective of the state's power to expel fugitives, at least in the absence of an actual agreement between Vermont and Canada. See id. at 584 (opinion of Thompson, J.); id. at 586–586h (opinion of Baldwin, J.); id. at 588 (opinion of Barbour, J.); id. at 596–97 (opinion of Catron, J.). Even those justices who took the narrower view of the state's authority, however, agreed that a state's police power included the power to exclude or expel an alien criminal for the protection of its own population. See id. at 568–69, 578 (opinion of Taney, C.J., joined by Story, McLean, and Wayne, JJ.); see also id. at 586–586h (opinion of Baldwin, J.).

29. 55 U.S. (14 How.) 13, 18 (1853) (Grier, J.).

30. 45 Mass. 282 (1842), rev'd, 48 U.S. (7 How.) 283 (1849).

31. Commissioners of Immigration v. Brandt, 77 La. Ann. 29 (1874) (citing *Miln* and *Passenger Cases*); Candler v. Mayor of New York, 1 Wend. 493 (N.Y. Sup. Ct. 1828) (citing *Gibbons*).

32. State v. S.S. Constitution, 42 Cal. 578, 586 (1872).

33. In re Perkins, 2 Cal. 424 (1852) (upholding the return of slaves who were in California at the time of statehood to out-of-state masters; citing *Prigg*). Cf. Nelson v. People, 33 Ill. 390 (1864) (upholding the exclusion of both slaves and free blacks from state).

34. Lin Sing v. Washburn, 20 Cal. 535, 578 (1862) (invalidating heavy residence tax on Chinese immigrants) ("We may dismiss from the case the question of the power of the States to exclude obnoxious persons, such as paupers and fugitives from justice, for it nowhere appears that the Chinese are a class of that description; nor does the act pretend to deal with them as such"). Stephen Field, at that time California's chief justice, dissented. Id. at 582 (Field, C.J., dissenting). Field's shifting positions on anti-Chinese legislation sometimes reflected his career interests.

35. In re Ah Fong, 1 F. Cas. 213, 216 (C.C.D. Cal. 1874) (No. 102) (Field, Circuit Justice) (listing convicts, lepers, persons afflicted with incurable disease, paupers, idiots, lunatics, and others likely to become a charge on the public). Field attributed broader views of the state's discretion to the distorting influence of the slave states' desire to exclude free blacks. Id. at 216–17.

36. Moreover, as previously mentioned, the Congress of the Confederation had urged the states to adopt convict exclusion legislation in 1788.

37. 92 U.S. at 277.

38. Although the Court stressed the danger to foreign relations posed by abusive state implementation, it also interpreted the California statute as having the "manifest purpose . . . not to obtain indemnity, but money." Moreover, "The amount to be taken is left in every case to the discretion of an officer, whose cupidity is stimulated by a reward of one-fifth of all he can obtain." Id. at 280.

39. The 1875 federal statute, in addition to increasing the barriers against the importation of unfree labor from Asia, generally prohibited the immigration of persons under sentence for nonpolitical crimes or whose sentence had been remitted on condition of emigration and of women imported for purposes of prostitution. Act of Mar. 3, 1875, ch. 141, § 5, 18 Stat. 477. In 1882 Congress further prohibited the landing of "any convict, lunatic, idiot, or any person unable to take care of himself or herself without becoming a public charge." Act of Aug. 3, 1882, ch. 376, § 2, 22 Stat. 214. Not until the 1890s did the federal government begin to take over state quarantine functions and to prohibit the admission of persons suffering from loathsome or dangerous contagious diseases. See Act of Mar. 3, 1891, ch. 551, § 1, 26 Stat. 1084.

40. Henderson, 92 U.S. at 275 (emphasis in original). Similarly, in Chy Lung, the Court noted:

> We are not called upon by this statute to decide for or against the right of a State, in the absence of legislation by Congress, to protect herself by necessary and proper laws against paupers and convicted criminals from abroad; nor to lay down the definite limit of such right, if it exist. Such a right can only arise from a vital necessity for its exercise, and cannot be carried beyond the scope of that necessity.

Chy Lung, 92 U.S. at 280.

41. See Patterson v. Kentucky, 97 U.S. 501, 506 (1879); Railroad Co. v. Husen, 95 U.S. 465, 471 (1878) (A state "may exclude from its limits convicts, paupers, idiots, and lunatics, and persons likely to become a public charge, as well as persons afflicted by contagious or infectious diseases; a right founded, as intimated in *The Passenger Cases* . . . by Mr. Justice Grier, in the sacred law of self-defence").

42. Morgan's S.S. Co. v. Louisiana Bd. of Health, 118 U.S. 455, 465–66 (1886); cf. Cooley v. Board of Wardens, 53 U.S. (12 How.) 299 (1851) (enunciating local concern doctrine). The Court had reaffirmed state power over quarantine as recently as 1874, in the course of invalidating a state tonnage tax intended to finance quarantine enforcement. Peete v. Morgan, 86 U.S. 581, 582 (1874) ("That the power to establish quarantine laws rests with the States, and has not been surrendered to the General government is settled in *Gibbons v. Ogden*").

43. Compagnie Francaise de Navigation a Vapeur v. Louisiana State Bd. of Health, 186 U.S. 380, 387 (1902).

44. The justices could not agree on which treaty was applicable, the 1815 Convention to Regulate Commerce and Navigation or the 1794 Jay Treaty. The same objection had been made in *Miln*, but the defendant did not make his nationality a matter of record, and the existence of a relevant treaty could not be determined. See Mayor of New York v. Miln, 36 U.S. (11 Pet.) 102, 143 (1837) (Barbour, J.). Both Philip Barbour and Smith Thompson further noted that such treaties subjected foreign citizens to the local laws governing local citizens. Id.; id. at 152 (Thompson, J.,

concurring). In fact, reporting obligations under the New York law did not depend on the nationality of the vessel or of its master.

45. See Passenger Cases, 48 U.S. (7 How.) 283, 411 (1849) (opinion of Wayne, J.) (yes); id. at 451 (opinion of Catron, J.) (yes); id. at 568 (Woodbury, J., dissenting) (no); id. at 506 (Daniel, J., dissenting) (no).

46. See Cheung Sum Shee v. Nagle, 268 U.S. 336 (1925); Robert R. Wilson, "Treaty-Merchant" Clauses in Commercial Treaties of the United States, 44 Am. J. Int'l L. 145 (1950).

47. See 48 U.S. (7 How.) at 408 (opinion of McLean, J.) (no, subject only to federal laws); id. at 426 (opinion of Wayne, J.) (no, subject only to subsequent regulation of conduct); id. at 451 (opinion of Catron, J.) (same); id. at 472 (Taney, C.J., dissenting) (yes). The language quoted is from Article 1 of the 1815 Convention; similar language appeared in Article 14 of the Jay Treaty ("but subject always as to what respects this article to the laws and statutes of the two countries respectively").

48. See 48 U.S. (7 How.) at 569 (Woodbury, J., dissenting) (same rights as "other foreigners"). If there is no limit on the substance of the "laws and statutes," then the access right is almost entirely nugatory.

49. See In re Ah Fong, 1 F. Cas. 213, 218 (C.C.D. Cal. 1874) (No. 102) (Field, Circuit Justice) (invoking most favored nation clause in 1868 Burlingame treaty with China); see also In re Quong Woo, 13 F. 229 (C.C.D. Cal. 1882) (same); In re Ah Chong, 2 F. 733 (C.C.D. Cal. 1880) (same); In re Parrott, 1 F. 481 (C.C.D. Cal. 1880) (same).

50. See 48 U.S. (7 How.) at 506 (Daniel, J., dissenting) (no such power conferred on federal government); cf. id. at 426 (opinion of Wayne, J.) (paupers, vagabonds, suspected persons, and fugitives from justice are not within the regulating power of the federal government).

51. See id. at 425–26 (opinion of Wayne, J.); id. at 457 (opinion of Grier, J.); id. at 400, 409 (opinion of McLean, J.).

52. 189 U.S. 86, 97 (1903) (deportation of recently arrived alien found likely to become a public charge consistent with treaty provision rendering liberty of entry subject to "the laws, ordinances, and regulations with regard to trade, the immigration of laborers, police and public security, which are in force or which may be enacted in either of the two countries").

53. 130 U.S 581 (1889).

CHAPTER FOUR

1. 36 U.S. (11 Pet.) 102, 121 (1837) (argument of Ogden). The insult is made more gratuitous by the fact that it depended on the usual convention of referring to arguments as those of the party rather than those of the attorney; obviously it was the alien's distinguished counsel, a citizen, who was expounding constitutional law.

2. See generally James Morton Smith, Freedom's Fetters: The Alien and Sedition Laws and American Civil Liberties (1956); John C. Miller, Crisis in Freedom: The Alien and Sedition Acts (1951); Dumas Malone, Jefferson and the Ordeal of Liberty 380–424 (1962). There were eventually four relevant statutes. The Alien Enemies Act, ch. 66, 1 Stat. 577 (1798), applies only in time of war; it is still in

force. 50 U.S.C. §§ 21–23. The Naturalization Act, ch. 54, 1 Stat. 566, extended the period of residence required before naturalization to fourteen years; it reflected the tendency of immigrants in the 1790s to become Jeffersonian Republicans (see Smith at 23–25) and was repealed by the Act of Apr. 14, 1802, ch. 28, 2 Stat. 153. The Sedition Act, ch. 74, 1 Stat. 596 (1798), and the Alien Act (or Alien Friends Act), ch. 58, 1 Stat. 570 (1798), were by their terms temporary and expired on March 3, 1801, and June 25, 1800, respectively.

3. The Alien Act authorized the president "at any time during the continuance of this act, to order all such aliens as he shall judge dangerous to the peace and safety of the United States, or shall have reasonable grounds to suspect are concerned in any treasonable or secret machinations against the government thereof, to depart out of the territory of the United States, within such time as shall be expressed in such order ." Alien Act, ch. 58, 1 Stat. 570 (1798).

4. See Richard R. Beeman, The Old Dominion and the New Nation, 1788–1801 186–88 (1972); Adrienne Koch & Harry Ammon, The Virginia and Kentucky Resolutions: An Episode in Jefferson's and Madison's Defense of Civil Liberties, 5 William & Mary Q. (3d ser.) 145 (1948).

5. Malone, note 2 supra at 413; Frank M. Anderson, Contemporary Opinion of the Virginia and Kentucky Resolutions, 5 Am. Hist. Rev. 45, 225 (1899–1900). The Kentucky legislature renewed its protest in a resolution of 1799 but did not repeat or refine its analysis of the defects of the Alien Act at that time. Resolution of Nov. 22, 1799, reprinted in 4 Debates, Resolutions and Other Proceedings, in Convention, on the Adoption of the Federal Constitution 544 (Jonathan Elliot 2d ed. 1836) (hereinafter Elliot's Debates).

6. Beeman, note 4 supra at 210; Koch & Ammon, note 4 supra at 163–64.

7. See Fong Yue Ting v. United States, 149 U.S. 698, 747–48 (1893) (Field, J., dissenting); Hunter v. Martin, 18 Va. 1, 29 (1814) (Roane, J.); South Carolina Exposition, reprinted in 10 The Papers of John C. Calhoun 442 (Clyde N. Wilson & William E. Hemphill eds. 1977) (hereinafter Calhoun Papers); Speech, reprinted in 3 The Works of John C. Calhoun 37–38 (Richard K. Crallé ed. 1853) (hereinafter Calhoun Works) (Senate speech of Feb. 20, 1837, on resolution to purchase Madison's papers); see also H. Jefferson Powell, The Principles of '98: An Essay in Historical Retrieval, 80 Va. L. Rev. 689 (1994).

8. See Smith, note 2 supra at 57–93. The bill had already passed the Senate, but the debates there are not reported. See 7 Annals of Cong. 548–75 (1798).

9. 8 Annals of Cong. 1981 (1798) ("Or will gentlemen say that the Constitution affords a security to citizens which it does not extend to aliens? . . . The trial by jury does not speak of citizens, but of persons."). Actually, Article III speaks of "[t]he trial of all Crimes," and the Sixth Amendment speaks of "the accused," but let that pass.

10. 8 Annals of Cong. 2018 (remarks of Rep. Otis); see also id. at 1984–85 (remarks of Rep. William Gordon) (aliens are not among those for whose use and benefit the Constitution was formed).

11. Debate on Virginia Resolutions, reprinted in The Virginia Report of 1799–1800, Touching the Alien and Sedition Laws; together with the Virginia Resolutions of December 21, 1798, the Debate and Proceedings Thereon in the House of Delegates of Virginia, and Several Other Documents Illustrative of the Report and

Resolutions 34–35 (1850) (hereinafter Virginia Debates) (statement of George K. Taylor); id. at 73 (statement of Archibald Magill); id. at 102 (statement of William Cowan); see also id. at 105 (statement of Henry Lee) ("It was wonderfully kind, he said, in our fathers to devote their time and money to the care of the Turk, Gaul, and Indian, when the proper object was that of their children").

12. Id. at 34.

13. Address of the General Assembly to the People of the Commonwealth of Virgina, reprinted in 6 The Writings of James Madison 332 (Galliard Hunt ed. 1906) (hereinafter Address of the General Assembly); Address of the Minority in the Virginia Legislature to the People of that State; containing a Vindication of the Constitutionality of the Alien and Sedition Laws (1799) (hereinafter Address of the Minority), in American Antiquarian Society, Early American Imprints 1639–1800 (microfiche) (Evans No. 36635).

14. See editorial note in 3 The Papers of John Marshall 498–99 & n. 1 (Charles T. Cullen ed. 1979) (hereinafter Marshall Papers). Lee and Marshall were friends, and partners in the Fairfax lands. 2 Albert J. Beveridge, Life of John Marshall 88 (1916). Marshall was the only major Federalist who publicly criticized the Alien and Sedition Acts, though he called them ill advised, not unconstitutional. To a Freeholder, Sept. 20, 1798, reprinted in 3 Marshall Papers at 503–06; see Beeman, note 4 supra at 196 & n. 34, 205.

15. Address of the Minority, note 13 supra at 9–10. See also Justice Iredell's defense of the Alien Act, in his charge to the grand jury in the notorious treason prosecution of John Fries:

> The clause in the constitution, declaring that the trial of all crimes, except by impeachment, shall be by jury, can never in reason be extended to amount to a permission of perpetual residence of all sorts of foreigners, unless convicted of some crime, but is evidently calculated for the security of any citizen, a party to the instrument, or even of a foreigner if resident in the country, who, when charged with the commission of a crime against the municipal laws for which he is liable to punishment, can be tried for it in no other manner.

Case of Fries, 9 Fed. Cas. 826, 834 (C.C.D. Pa. 1799) (No. 5,126).

16. Plain Truth: Addressed to the People of Virginia, Written in February 1799—By a Citizen of Westmoreland County, (Virg.) 19–21 (1799) in American Antiquarian Society, Early American Imprints 1639–1800 (microfiche) (Evans No. 35723); see also editorial note in 3 Marshall Papers, note 14 supra at 499–500 & n. 4 (discussing Lee's publication of the essays).

17. 9 Annals of Cong. 2987 (1799).

18. Answer of the Commonwealth of Massachusetts to the Virginia Legislature, Feb. 9, 1799, reprinted in 4 Elliot's Debates at 533, 534 (the Alien Act "respects a description of persons whose rights were not particularly contemplated in the Constitution of the United States"); Answer to the Resolutions of the state of Kentucky, Oct. 29, 1799, 4 Records of the Governor and Council of the State of Vermont 525, 528 (1876) ("We ever considered that the Constitution of the United States was made for the benefit of our own citizens; we never conjectured that aliens were any party to the federal compact; we never knew that aliens had any rights among us, except what they derived from the law of nations, and rights of hospitality").

19. See Richard E. Ellis, The Jeffersonian Crisis: Courts and Politics in the Young Republic 164 (1971); Miller, note 2 supra at 139–41. On Addison generally, see The Whiskey Rebellion: Past and Present Perspectives 49–60, 165–82 (Steven R. Boyd ed. 1985); G.S. Rowe, Alexander Addison: The Disillusionment of a "Republican Schoolmaster," 62 W. Pa. Hist. Mag. 221 (1979).

20. Charges to Grand Juries of the Counties of the Fifth Circuit in the State of Pennsylvania, No. 26, in 1 Addison's Reports 590 (A. Addison 2d ed. 1883) (hereinafter Charges). Addison's earlier charge, defending the Sedition Act, drew moderate praise from Marshall, who had received it from George Washington. See id. at 576 (No. 25, "Liberty of Speech and of the Press"); Letter, Marshall to Washington, Jan. 8, 1799, 4 Marshall Papers, note 14 supra at 3. Story cited both No. 25 and No. 26 in his Commentaries. See 3 Joseph Story, Commentaries on the Constitution of the United States 166n. 1 (1833).

Political speeches to grand juries were quite common at this period. See George L. Haskins & Herbert A. Johnson, Foundations of Power: John Marshall 1801–1815, at 221–23 (1981) (discussing the impeachment of Justice Chase, which rested in part on his grand jury charges). Addison himself was ultimately impeached (and convicted) in 1803 due to his interference with a Republican associate judge's attempt to refute one of Addison's grand jury charges. See Ellis, note 19 supra at 164–65 (1971); Trial of Alexander Addison, Esq., . . . Taken in Short Hand by Thomas Lloyd (2d ed. 1803).

21. Charges, note 20 supra at 597. Congress could suspend the writ of habeas corpus as regards aliens whenever it pleased and could convict them of crimes without jury trial. Id. at 591, 599.

22. Alexander Addison, Analysis of the Report of the Committee of the Virginia Assembly (1800), reprinted in 2 Charles S. Hyneman & Donald S. Lutz, American Political Writing during the Founding Era 1760–1805, at 1055 (1983).

23. Id. at 1070.

24. Id.

25. Id. at 1073; see also Charges, note 20 supra at 597–98. It may be remarked that Addison was born in Scotland and emigrated in 1785. See Rowe, note 19 supra at 229. On Addison's xenophobia in the late 1790s, see id. at 245–46.

26. Addison, note 22 supra at 1073.

27. Gordon S. Wood, The Creation of the American Republic, 1776–87, at 68 (1969).

28. See James H. Kettner, The Development of American Citizenship, 1608–1870, at 214–19, 225–30, 236–38 (1978). The Constitution sets both citizenship and residence requirements for senators, representatives, and the president; indeed, the latter must be a "natural born Citizen." U.S. Const. Art. I, §§ 2, cl. 2; id. § 3, cl. 3; id. Art. II, § 1, cl. 5.

29. See, e.g., Smith, note 2 supra at 11–17, 96–104; Beeman, note 4 supra at 134–35, 196–97.

30. Charges, note 20 supra at 601.

31. E.g., U.S. Const. art. I, § 2, cl. 2 ("No Person shall be a Representative"); art. I, § 9, cl. 1 ("The Migration or Importation of Such Persons"); art. I, § 9, cl. 8 ("no Person holding any Office"); art. III, § 2, cl. 1 ("foreign States, Citizens, or Subjects"); art. IV, § 2, cl.3 ("No Person held to Service").

32. 8 Annals of Cong. 2012–13 (1798).

33. Id. at 2012.

34. John Taylor "of Caroline [County, Virginia]," a figure better known to historians than to lawyers, was an agrarian republican whose career included episodes of political activity and episodes of dense writing in political theory. He professed belief in immutable natural rights and viewed the Constitution as a mutable "political law" designed to distribute power so as to protect them. See, e.g., John Taylor, An Inquiry into the Principles and Policy of the Government of the United States 159–61, 413–15, 422–25 (1814); see generally C. William Hill, The Political Theory of John Taylor of Caroline (1977); Eugene T. Mudge, The Social Philosophy of John Taylor of Caroline: A Study in Jeffersonian Democracy (1939); Robert E. Shalhope, John Taylor of Caroline: Pastoral Republican (1980).

35. Virginia Debates, note 11 supra at 27; id. at 24, 25, 116.

36. Id. at 25, 116.

37. Id. at 25, 116. He coupled this danger with the standard republican terrors of corruption, patronage, and standing armies. Id.; see Forrest McDonald, Novus Ordo Seclorum: The Intellectual Origins of the Constitution 77–78 (1985). Taylor retained the emphasis on patronage and corruption throughout his writings.

38. Virginia Debates, note 11 supra at 25.

39. Id. at 116. See also id. at 68–69 (statement of James Barbour, citing Vattel); id. at 88 (statement of William Daniel, Jr.).

40. Id. at 115–16; see John Taylor, Construction Construed and Constitutions Vindicated 279–89 (1970 reprint of 1820 ed.).

41. Madison's Report on the Virginia Resolutions, in 4 Elliot's Debates, note 5 supra at 556.

42. Id. To the contrary, the traditional practice of the municipal law in criminal cases was considerably more generous: "But so far has a contrary principle been carried, in every part of the United States, that except on charges of treason, an alien has, besides all the common privileges, the special one of being tried by a jury, of which one-half may be also aliens." Id. Here he was alluding to the institution of the jury *de medietate linguae*, for which see Lewis H. LaRue, A Jury of One's Peers, 33 Wash. & Lee L. Rev. 841, 847–66 (1976), and Marianne Constable, The Law of the Other: The Mixed Jury and Changing Conceptions of Citizenship, Law and Knowledge (1994) (discussing the history of half-alien juries in England). Madison overstated its prevalence in the United States, although it was still the law in Virginia. See United States v. Cartacho, 25 F. Cas. 312 (C.C.D. Va. 1823) (No. 14,738) (Marshall, C.J., & St. George Tucker, J.); but see United States v. McMahon, 26 F. Cas. 1131 (C.C.D.C. 1835) (No. 15,699) (citing Maryland Act of 1789, ch. 22, § 5 (abolishing mixed juries)).

Madison was under no illusion that jury trial was a natural right; in presenting what would become the Sixth Amendment to the House of Representatives, he had commented:

> Trial by jury cannot be considered as a natural right, but rather a right resulting from a social compact, which regulates the action of the community, but is as essential to secure the liberty of the people as any one of the pre-existent rights of nature.

1 Annals of Cong. 437 (1789).

43. 4 Elliot's Debates, note 5 supra at 557. In an earlier treatment of the issue,

Madison had given the "undefined prerogatives" a fuller republican statement, asking, "[w]ill an accumulation of power so extensive in the hands of the executive over aliens secure to natives the blessings of republican liberty?" and invoking corruption and standing armies. Address of the General Assembly to the People of the Commonwealth of Virgina, 6 Writings of James Madison 332 (Galliard Hunt ed. 1906).

44. 4 Elliot's Debates, note 5 supra at 556.

45. This is a serious weakness in Madison's argument. Putting aside the federalism question, he did not adequately explain how the executive expulsion of alien enemies could be reconciled with separation of powers, due process, or the jury trial guarantee, or why it need not be. Rationalization of expulsion as a nonpunitive civil proceeding could carry over from alien enemies to alien friends, as it ultimately did. See Fong Yue Ting v. United States, 149 U.S. 698 (1893).

46. 4 Elliot's Debates, note 5 supra at 556–57.

47. Id. at 557.

48. Id. at 560.

49. Wood, note 27 supra at 600–01.

50. Wood, note 27 supra at 283; see id. at 282–91, 535–53; Thomas Grey, Origins of the Unwritten Constitution: Fundamental Law in American Revolutionary Thought, 30 Stan. L. Rev. 843, 859–65 (1978).

51. Americans hoped to benefit from both commercial visits and immigration; binding the federal government to ensure the extension of most constitutional rights to visitors and immigrants would encourage such arrivals. See, e.g., Taylor v. Carpenter, 23 F. Cas. 742, 749–50 (C.C.D. Mass. 1846) (No. 13,785); 2 Tucker's Blackstone App. 99 (1803); cf. The Declaration of Independence ("He has endeavoured to prevent the population of these States; for that purpose obstructing the Laws of Naturalization of Foreigners; refusing to pass others to encourage their migrations hither").

52. It may be worth noting some exceptions. Depending on one's view about freedom of expatriation—which Vattel favored but the common law opposed—the alien may have a stronger right than the citizen to leave the country when she feels exploited. See 3 Emer de Vattel, The Law of Nations; or, Principles of Natural Law 146 (1916) (Charles G. Fenwick trans. ed. 1758). There may also be some legal obligations of citizens that the state cannot extend to aliens. Id. The possibility of diplomatic intervention in case of a state's denial of justice to an alien may create an avenue of protection different from those available to citizens. See Stephen Legomsky, Immigration and the Judiciary: Law and Politics in Britain and America 317–18 (1987). These factors may not be compelling, but they impair the neatness of the syllogism if, like Wolff, you have a taste for syllogisms, and they may make a difference at the margin if you have a taste for marginal thinking.

53. This understatement may roughly compensate for the factors in the preceding footnote.

54. See supra note 14. Marshall had also taken a moderate stance—agreeing with the Jeffersonians that federal power over aliens was subject to constitutional limits but disagreeing about what those limits were—in his most famous speech in Congress, his defense of Adams's extradition of Jonathan Robbins to the British. 10 Annals of Cong. 596–618 (1800); 4 Marshall Papers, note 14 supra at 82–109.

55. Smith, note 2 supra at 159–76.

56. See Hunter v. Martin, 18 Va. (4 Munf.) 1, 30–33, 52–53 (1815) (opinion of Roane, J.); Spencer Roane, Hampden No. 4, in John Marshall's Defense of McCulloch v. Maryland 146–47 (Gerald Gunther ed. 1969); Taylor, Construction Construed, supra at 142–48; John Taylor, New Views of the Constitution of the United States 171–73 (1823); Shalhope, note 34 supra at 208–09.

57. 5 U.S. (1 Cranch) 137, 177 (1803); see Cohens v. Virginia, 19 U.S. (6 Wheat.) 264, 380–81, 413–15 (1821); 1 Joseph Story, Commentaries on the Constitution of the United States §§ 338–340 (1833); Marshall, A Friend of the Constitution No. 9, in Defense of McCulloch, supra at 208; see also Elizabeth K. Bauer, Commentaries on the Constitution 1790–1860, at 276–87 (1952); H. Jefferson Powell, The Original Understanding of Original Intent, 98 Harv. L. Rev. 885, 942–44 (1985) (relating rejection of compact theory to Court's interpretive methodology).

58. See, e.g., Fairfax's Devisee v. Hunter's Lessee, 11 U.S. (7 Cranch) 603, 627 (1813); Chirac v. Chirac, 15 U.S. (2 Wheat.) 259, 271 (1817); Orr v. Hodgson, 17 U.S. (4 Wheat.) 453 (1819); Society for the Propagation of the Gospel in Foreign Parts v. Town of New Haven, 21 U.S. (8 Wheat.) 464 (1823); Shanks v. Dupont, 28 U.S. (3 Pet.) 242 (1830). All the foregoing involve property rights.

59. 2 Beveridge, note 14 supra at 202; see G. Edward White, The Marshall Court and Cultural Change, 1815–35 165–73 (1988).

60. Passenger Cases, 48 U.S. (7 How.) 242 (1849); Holmes v. Jennison, 39 U.S. (14 Pet.) 540 (1840) (dictum); but see Mager v. Grima, 49 U.S. (8 How.) 490 (1850) (upholding discriminatory inheritance tax).

61. See In re Kaine, 55 U.S. (14 How.) 103, 141 (1853) (Nelson, J., dissenting from dismissal for writ of habeas corpus on combined bases of jurisdiction and merits) ("[U]nder our system of laws and principles of government, so far as respects personal security and personal freedom, I know of no distinction between the citizen and the alien who has sought an asylum under them"); Taylor v. Carpenter, 23 Fed. Cas. 742, 744 (C.C.D. Mass. 1844) (No. 13,784) ("[I]n the courts of the United States, under the constitution and laws, they are entitled, being alien friends, to the same protection of their rights as citizens"); Society for the Propagation of the Gospel v. Wheeler, 22 Fed. Cas. 756 (C.C.D.N.H. 1814) (No. 13,156).

The Alien Act continued as a subject of academic controversy. St. George Tucker, in his American edition of Blackstone, quoted and paraphrased Madison's Report in condemning the act. 1 Tucker's Blackstone, at 301–04, 306–07. Story's brief discussion of the Alien and Sedition Acts in his 1833 *Commentaries on the Constitution* intimated their constitutionality but did not mention or support the view that aliens lack constitutional rights. 3 Story, note 20 supra at 164–68. Given Story's usual respect for Marshall's views on constitutional issues, and Story's own decisions with respect to aliens, this is not surprising.

62. Scott v. Sandford, 60 U.S. (18 How.) 393, 406, 409–11, 416–17 (1857).

63. Samuel F.B. Morse, Imminent Dangers to the Free Institutions of the United States through Foreign Immigration 23 (1969 reprint of 1835 ed.). Interestingly, Morse was linked to the Francophobia of the 1790s through his father, the Federalist clergyman Jedidiah Morse. See David H. Bennett, The Party of Fear 24–25, 40–41 (1990); Joseph W. Philips, Jedidiah Morse and New England Congregationalism 74–101, 220–21 (1983).

64. See generally Roger Daniels, Asian America: Chinese and Japanese in the United States Since 1850, at 29–40 (1988); Ronald Takaki, Strangers from a Different Shore: A History of Asian Americans 81–115 (1989); Charles McClain, Jr., The Chinese Struggle for Civil Rights in Nineteenth Century America: The First Phase, 1850–1870, 72 Calif. L. Rev. 529 (1984).

65. Lin Sing v. Washburn, 20 Cal. 534 (1862); People v. Downer, 7 Cal. 169 (1857).

66. See Cong. Globe, 39th Cong., 1st Sess. 2891–92 (1866) (remarks of Sen. Conness); see also id. at 497–98 (colloquy regarding exclusion and citizenship for Chinese); id. at 1757 (remarks of Sen. Trumbull on Pres. Johnson's objection to conferral of citizenship on Chinese children).

67. See, e.g., Cong. Globe, 39th Cong., 1st Sess. 1292 (1866) (remarks of Rep. Bingham); Plyler v. Doe, 457 U.S. 202, 214–15 (1982); Raoul Berger, Government by Judiciary 215–20 (1977).

68. Act of May 31, 1870, §§ 16, 17, 16 Stat. 144; see McClain, note 64 supra.

69. See In re Quong Woo, 13 F. 229 (C.C.D. Cal. 1882) (invalidating laundry licensing law, on treaty and other grounds); In re Ah Chong, 2 F. 733 (C.C.D. Cal. 1880) (invalidating statute forbidding Chinese to fish, on treaty and equal protection grounds); In re Parrott, 1 F. 481 (C.C.D. Cal. 1880) (invalidating statute forbidding employment of Chinese, on treaty and equal protection grounds); Ho Ah Kow v. Nunan, 12 F. Cas. 252 (C.C.D. Cal. 1879) (No. 6,546) (invalidating queue ordinance, on equal protection grounds); In re Ah Fong, 1 F. Cas. 213 (C.C.D. Cal. 1874) (No. 102) (invalidating state immigration law, on treaty, statute, and equal protection grounds). Cf. People v. Brady, 40 Cal. 198 (1870) (purporting to hold that refusing Chinese right to testify against whites does not deny them equal protection).

70. 118 U.S. 356, 369 (1886).

71. See, e.g., Brief for Defendant and Respondent at 106–08, reprinted in 9 Landmark Briefs and Arguments of the Supreme Court of the United States: Constitutional Law 17, 134–36 (Philip Kurland & Gerhard Casper ed. 1975). This rambling scrapbook conceded the principle, denied the discrimination, and exhibited the animus.

72. 149 U.S. 698 (1893).

73. 149 U.S. at 748–50 (Field, J., dissenting); id. at 740–41 (Brewer, J., dissenting). See also the earlier invocations of Madison's Report in Chae Chan Ping v. United States, 130 U.S. 581, 583 (1889) (argument of counsel); Passenger Cases, 48 U.S. (7 How.) 283, 513–14 (1849) (Daniel, J., dissenting); id. at 527 (Woodbury, J., dissenting).

74. 149 U.S. at 754. Justice Brewer and Chief Justice Fuller also dissented, on similar grounds.

75. 149 U.S. at 707–09. The majority also invoked John Marshall's defense of executive extradition in the Jonathan Robbins affair to demonstrate the inapplicability of criminal procedure to deportation. Id. at 714.

76. 149 U.S. at 724–25.

77. Wong Wing v. United States, 163 U.S. 228, 238 (1896); id. at 242 (Field, J., concurring in part) ("He owes obedience to the laws of the country in which he is

domiciled, and, as a consequence, he is entitled to the equal protection of those laws. . . . The contention that persons within the territorial jurisdiction of this republic might be beyond the protection of the law was heard with pain on the argument at the bar").

78. Gerald Rosberg called attention to the tradition of alien suffrage in a well-known article in 1977 and urged a return to the practice. At that time, he lamented the absence of an adequate history of the subject. See Gerald Rosberg, Aliens and Equal Protection: Why Not the Right to Vote?, 75 Mich. L. Rev. 1092, 1093–94 (1977). The need for a comprehensive treatment of this important subject still remains, although this chapter and the article from which it derives add some further elements to the story. See also Jamin B. Raskin, Legal Aliens, Local Citizens: The Historical, Constitutional and Theoretical Meanings of Alien Suffrage, 141 U. Pa. L. Rev. 1391, 1441–56 (1993).

79. U.S. Const. art. I, § 2, cl. 1. See The Federalist No. 52 (James Madison). Similarly, in the drafting of the Fifteenth Amendment, proposals for the comprehensive regulation of voter qualifications were rejected in favor of a ban on discrimination "on account of race, color, or previous condition of servitude." U.S. Const. amend. XV; see William Gillette, The Right to Vote: Politics and the Passage of the Fifteenth Amendment 59, 71, 77 (1969).

80. U.S. Const. art. I, § 3, cl. 1; id. art. II, § 1, cl. 2. The Seventeenth Amendment, substituting the direct popular election of senators, made the qualifications for House and Senate electors identical. Id. amend. XVII.

81. U.S. Const. art. V. Article V also envisions other means, such as proposal by "a Convention" and ratification "by Conventions." It does not say who is eligible to elect delegates to the conventions; no proposing convention has yet been held, and the only historical instance of ratification by conventions involves the Twenty-First Amendment, which was proposed after the last state had abandoned alien suffrage. See Laurence H. Tribe, American Constitutional Law 64 n. 9 (2d ed. 1988).

82. See James H. Kettner, The Development of American Citizenship, 1608–1870, at 219–24 (1978).

83. See U.S. Const. art. I, § 2, cl. 2 (representatives must have been citizens of the United States for seven years), id. § 3, cl. 3 (senators must have been citizens of the United States for nine years), id. § 8, cl. 4 (power to adopt uniform rule of naturalization); id. art. II, § 5 (president to be a natural-born citizen of the United States).

84. Compare Chirac v. Chirac, 15 U.S. (2 Wheat.) 259 (1817) (Marshall, C.J.) (power to naturalize exclusive) with Collet v. Collet, 2 U.S. (2 Dall.) 294 (C.C.D. Pa. 1792) (Wilson, Blair, and Peters, JJ.) (power to naturalize concurrent); see Scott v. Sandford, 60 U.S. (19 How.) 393, 405 (1857) (continuing to recognize a state citizenship for internal purposes only).

85. Section 1 of the Fourteenth Amendment provides that "[a]ll persons born or naturalized in the United States, and subject to the jurisdiction thereof, are citizens of the United States *and* of the state wherein they reside." U.S. Const. amend. XIV, § 1 (emphasis added). It does not clarify the status of persons who are not "born or naturalized in the United States, and subject to the jurisdiction thereof." See Rogers v. Bellei, 401 U.S. 815 (1971) (distinguishing national citizenship of children born

to U.S. citizens abroad from Fourteenth Amendment citizenship). Nor does it necessarily forbid the conferral of a local, state citizenship. The Dred Scott decision had emphasized the proposition that a state could legally recognize as its "citizens" persons who were not "citizens of the state" within the meaning of the federal Constitution because not citizens of the United States. See Scott v. Sandford, 60 U.S. (19 How.) at 405. The Fourteenth Amendment could have been read as overturning this proposition, but the Court seems to have assumed its continuing validity in Boyd v. Nebraska ex rel. Thayer, 143 U.S. 135, 175 (1892), and it has occasionally been reasserted in modern times; see, e.g., Crosse v. Board of Supervisors, 221 A.2d 431 (Md. 1966); Jonathan D. Varat, State "Citizenship" and Interstate Equality, 48 U. Chi. L. Rev. 487, 525–27 n. 162 (1981). Distinguishing between local state citizenship and constitutional state citizenship may seem obscurantist because the distinction may have no practical significance at present, particularly because aliens no longer vote in statewide elections and the federal government no longer withholds citizenship from Native Americans.

86. See Elk v. Wilkins, 112 U.S. 94 (1884); Felix S. Cohen, Handbook of Federal Indian Law 520–23 (1st ed. 1942). Congress finally extended citizenship to all Native Americans in 1924. See Act of June 2, 1924, ch. 233, 43 Stat. 253.

For grants of voting rights to Native Americans in particular states, see, e.g., Mich. Const. of 1850, art. VII, § 1; Minn. Const. of 1857, art. VII, § 1; N.D. Const. of 1889, art. 5, § 121(3); Okla. Const. of 1907, art. III, § 1; Wis. Const. of 1848, art. III, § 1.

87. See Vt. Const. of 1777, ch. 2, § 38.

88. Vt. Const. of 1793, ch. 2, § 39. Vermont had finally become a state in 1791, after New York, from which it had effectively seceded, ceased to oppose admission. It is ironic that Vermont lost sight of its own inclusion of resident aliens in the body politic when it defended the Alien Act of 1798 against the Virginia and Kentucky Resolutions. See note 18 supra.

89. See Journal of the Council of Censors, at their Sessions at Montpelier and Burlington, in June, October, and November 1827, at 5–6, 21–22, 31–32, 45–46 (1828) (explaining need for amendment). The Vermont Council of Censors had also recommended denying aliens the right to vote for state officials in 1814. See Journal of the Council of Censors, at their Sessions in June and October 1813 and January 1814, at 28, 48–49 (1814).

90. See Vt. Const. of 1793, amend. I. The 1828 amendment appears not, however, to have precluded aliens who were not freemen from voting in town and school district elections. See Woodcock v. Bolster, 35 Vt. 632, 637–41 (1863).

91. See Va. Act of Dec. 23, 1792, ch. 110, § 2; cf. Va. Code of 1849, tit. 2, ch. 3, § 1; H.R. Rep. No. 520, 28th Cong., 1st Sess. (1844); 1 Hinds' Precedents of the House of Representatives of the United States 1049–50 (1907).

92. Northwest Ordinance, ch. 8, § 9, 1 Stat. 50 ("provided also, that a freehold in fifty acres of land in the district, having been a citizen of one of the States, and being resident in the district, or the like freehold and two years residence in the district, shall be necessary to qualify a man as an elector of a representative").

93. See Orleans Territorial Government Act, ch. 23, 2 Stat. 322 (1805); Michigan Territorial Government Act, ch. 5, 2 Stat. 309 (1805); Mississippi Territorial

Government Act, ch. 28, 1 Stat. 549 (1798); but see, e.g., Missouri Territorial Government Act, ch. 95, § 9, 2 Stat. 743 (1812) (enfranchising white male citizens of the United States and other white male persons already resident at the time of the Louisiana Purchase).

94. See Ill. Const. of 1818, art. II, § 27; Ohio Const. of 1802, art. IV, § 1; Spragins v. Houghton, 3 Ill. (2 Scam.) 377 (1840). It appears that Ohio later reinterpreted the term to exclude alien residents. See id. at 410–13; Rosberg, note 79 supra at 1096–98 & n. 32.

95. See generally David H. Bennett, The Party of Fear: From Nativist Movements to the New Right in American History 39–155 (1988).

96. See, e.g., 12 Cong. Deb. 1007 (1836) (remarks of Sen. Clayton); id. at 4251 (remarks of Rep. Russell). See also 13 The Papers of John C. Calhoun 126–36 (Clyde N. Wilson ed. 1980) (version, of uncertain provenance, of Calhoun's speech on the issue). Alien suffrage was not the only objection to Michigan statehood; the territory was engaged in a border dispute with Ohio and Indiana and had sought statehood without the prior blessing of Congress. See 12 Cong. Deb. at 1008–10 (remarks of Sen. Tipton); id. at 1015 (remarks of Sen. Ewing). In the absence of a congressional enabling act, the territory had made its own definition of the voter qualifications for the constitutional convention and had included alien residents, thus further irritating the nativists. See id. at 4252–53 (remarks of Rep. Russell). To avoid misunderstanding, perhaps I should emphasize that I am not equating opposition to alien suffrage with nativism; Russell's polemics against the Irish and call for a change in the naturalization law go beyond mere opposition to aliens' voting. See id. at 4253–59. A lengthy discussion of alien suffrage in Michigan as a partisan dispute between Whigs and Democrats may be found in Ronald P. Formisano, The Birth of Mass Political Parties: Michigan, 1827–1861, at 81–101 (1971).

97. See Mich. Const. of 1835, art. II, § 1; 12 Cong. Deb. 1008, 1014 (1836) (remarks of Sen. Buchanan). These inhabitants would arguably be naturalized by the admission of Michigan to statehood. See Boyd v. Nebraska ex rel. Thayer, 143 U.S. 135, 167–68 (1892); 12 Cong. Deb. at 4214, 4227–30 (remarks of Rep. Everett). Not everyone in Congress viewed the issue in this light. See id. at 1043–45 (remarks of Sen. Buchanan); id. at 4246–47 (remarks of Rep. Hamer); id. at 4253–57 (remarks of Rep. Russell). A later, superseding constitution of 1850 expanded the electorate to include persons who were unquestionably aliens but had declared their intention to become citizens. See Mich. Const. of 1850, art. VII, § 1.

98. Iowa Territorial Government Act, ch. 96, 5 Stat. 235 (1838); Wisconsin Territorial Government Act, ch. 54, 5 Stat. 10 (1836); Iowa Const. of 1846, art. II, § 1; Fla. Const. of 1838, art. VI, § 1 (admitted 1845); Ark. Const. of 1836, art. IV, § 2. Texas may present a special case. Annexed from foreign territory, its statehood constitution enfranchised persons who had been resident long enough for naturalization but had not taken the required oath of allegiance to Texas at the time of annexation. Compare Tex. Const. of 1845, art. III, §§ 1, 2 (qualifications of electors), with Texas Const. of 1836, General Provisions, § 6 (naturalization). It is unclear whether annexation made these persons citizens of the United States. See 13 Op. Att'y Gen. 397 (1871).

99. Louise P. Kellogg, The Alien Suffrage Provision in the Constitution of Wis-

consin, 1 Wis. Mag. Hist. 422 (1918). The politics of the issue were further complicated by the concentration of immigrants in the eastern part of the future state. Id.
at 425.

100. See Wis. Const. of 1848, art. III, § 1; Kellogg, note 99 supra at 425.

101. See Act of Jan. 29, 1795, ch. 20, § 1, 1 Stat. 414; Frederick Van Dyne,
Citizenship of the United States 62 (1904). The delay between declaration and naturalization was lengthened to five years by the Naturalization Act of 1798, part of the
infamous Alien and Sedition Acts package, but cut back to three years in 1802. Act
of June 18, 1798, ch. 54, § 1, 1 Stat. 566; Act of April 14, 1802, ch. 28, § 1, 2 Stat.
153. The 1906 Naturalization Act modified the procedure so that an alien who did
not petition for naturalization within seven years after filing the declaration would
have to start the process all over again. Act of June 29, 1906, ch. 3592, § 4, 34 Stat.
596. Prior to that time, the declarant could wait indefinitely; some states dealt with
the problem by limiting the declarants' suffrage rights to a period of years sufficient
for naturalization. See Mo. Const. of 1865, art. II, § 18 (five years); N.D. Const. of
1889, art. V, § 121 (six years).

102. Van Dyne, note 101 supra at 62, 66; Rosberg, note 78 supra at 1098. This
fact was emphasized by opponents of alien suffrage. See, e.g., The Attainment of
Statehood 359, 365 (Wisconsin Historical Collections, Vol. 29, Milo M. Quaife ed.
1918) (reprinting debates of second constitutional convention).

103. See, e.g., "Letters of 'Jefferson'—No. 3," reprinted in The Movement for
Statehood 1845–46, at 194–95 (Wisconsin Historical Collections, vol. 26, Milo M.
Quaife ed. 1918).

104. See Act of May 29, 1848, ch. 50, 9 Stat. 233 (admitting Wisconsin); Oregon
Territorial Government Act, ch. 177, § 5, 9 Stat. 325 (1848); Minnesota Territorial
Government Act, ch. 121, § 5, 9 Stat. 405 (1849).

105. See Utah Territorial Government Act, ch. 51, § 5, 9 Stat. 454 (1850); New
Mexico Territorial Government Act, ch. 49, § 6, 9 Stat. 449 (1850); see also Cal.
Const. of 1849, art. II, § 1. I am not sure whether these restrictions have something
to do with the fact that Article 8 of the Treaty of Guadelupe Hidalgo gave Mexican
citizens in these territories one year to declare their election to retain Mexican citizenship, failing which they became United States citizens.

106. See Oklahoma Territorial Government Act, ch. 182, § 5, 26 Stat. 84 (1890);
Wyoming Territorial Government Act, ch. 235, § 5, 15 Stat. 180 (1868); Dakota
Territorial Government Act, ch. 86, § 5, 12 Stat. 241 (1861); Nevada Territorial
Government Act, ch. 83, § 5, 12 Stat. 211 (1861); Kansas-Nebraska Act, ch. 59, §§
5, 23 (1854); Washington Territorial Government Act, ch. 90, § 5, 10 Stat. 174
(1853). Congress initially enfranchised the free white male inhabitants of the Idaho
Territory, but the Revised Statutes restricted the franchise in all territories to citi-
zens and declarant aliens. See Idaho Territorial Government Act, ch. 117, § 5, 12
Stat. 808 (1863); Rev. Stat. § 1860 (1874).

It may be necessary to temper all these observations about voter qualifications in
the territories with the realism expressed by one Senator in the Kansas-Nebraska
debate. See Cong. Globe, 33d Cong., 1st Sess. App. 780 (1854) (remarks of Sen.
Jones of Iowa) ("I have had much experience in territorial elections. . . . I can assure
gentlemen that whether [an alien voting] amendment be adopted or not, every white
male inhabitant of Nebraska and Kansas, above the age of twenty-one years, will not

only be permitted to vote at their first elections, but will be expected, as good citizens, to exercise the privileges always awarded to the sovereign squatter").

107. See Kan. Const. of 1859, art. V, § 1; Minn. Const. of 1857, art. VII, § 1; Neb. Const. of 1867, art. II, § 2; N.D. Const. of 1889, art. V, § 121; Or. Const. of 1857, art. II, § 2; S.D. Const. of 1889, art. VII, § 1; but see Nev. Const. of 1864, art. II, § 1 (citizens only); Wyo. Const. of 1889, art. VI, § 5 (same); cf. Okla. Const. of 1907, art. III, § 1 ("male citizens of the United States, male citizens of the State, and male persons of Indian descent native of the United States"). Montana and Washington limited their prospective enfranchisement to citizens while grandfathering in declarant aliens. See Mont. Const. of 1889, art. IX, § 2 (with five-year transition); Wash. Const. of 1889, art. VI, §1.

108. Illinois, in contrast, imposed a citizenship requirement in 1848, while grandfathering in present voters. Ill. Const. of 1848, art. VI, § 1. The change has been attributed to the Whigs' desire to eliminate a class of voters who overwhelmingly supported the Democrats. See 1 Memoirs of Gustave Koerner, 1809–1896, at 523–24 (Thomas J. McCormack ed. 1909).

109. Ind. Const. of 1851, art. II, § 2; Mich. Const. of 1850, art. VII, § 1.

110. See, e.g., Rosberg, note 78 supra at 1098.

111. See, e.g., Ala. Const. of 1867, art. VII, § 2; Ark. Const. of 1868, art. VIII, § 2; Fla. Const. of 1868, art. XIV, § 1; Ga. Const. of 1868, art. II, § 2; La. Const. of 1879, art. CLXXXV; S. Car. Const. of 1865, art. IV ("an emigrant from Europe, who has declared his intention"); Tex. Const. of 1876, art. VI, § 2. Missouri, also a former slave state, did likewise. Mo. Const. of 1865, art. II, § 18. The Confederacy had adopted the opposite policy and expressly prohibited noncitizen suffrage at both the state and federal level in its Constitution. The prohibition was directed partly at immigrants from Europe and partly at anticipated immigration of Northerners, who would be aliens in the Confederacy. See Marshall L. DeRosa, The Confederate Constitution of 1861: An Inquiry into American Constitutionalism 74–75 (1991).

112. See, e.g., Cong. Globe, 33d Cong., 1st Sess. App. 769 (1854) (remarks of Sen. Seward) ("[T]he right of suffrage is not a mere conventional right, but an inherent natural right, of which no Government can rightly deprive any adult man who is subject to its authority, and obligated to its support").

113. Spragins v. Houghton, 3 Ill. (2 Scam.) 377, 408 (1840). For the political machinations behind this case, which involved a struggle between the Democrats and Whigs seeking to undercut their electoral support, see Thomas J. Curran, Xenophobia and Immigration, 1820–1930, at 31 (1975); 1 John Moses, Illinois, Historical and Statistical 444–45 (1889). The Whigs finally achieved success in the revised state constitution of 1848. See note 108 supra.

114. See, e.g., Henry A. Chaney, Alien Suffrage, 2 Publications Mich. Pol. Sci. Ass'n 130, 132–33 (1894) (quoting from debate at 1850 Michigan constitutional convention); "To Persons of Foreign Birth," in Movement for Statehood, note 103 supra at 439–41.

115. See, e.g., Chilton Williamson, American Suffrage: From Property to Democracy, 1760–1860, at 278 (1960); Ellen Carol DuBois, Feminism and Suffrage: The Emergence of an Independent Women's Movement in America, 1848–1869, at 40–47 (1978).

116. See, e.g., Spragins v. Houghton, 3 Ill. (2 Scam.) 377, 398 (1840); Kirk H.

Porter, A History of Suffrage in the United States 130–31 (1969 reprint of 1918 original) (citing Minnesota constitutional convention); "The Constitution—No. 8," in The Struggle Over Ratification, 1846–1847, at 488, 489 (Wisconsin Historical Collections, vol. 28, Milo Quaife, ed. 1918).

117. See Cong. Globe, 33d Cong., 1st Sess. App. 297 (1854) (remarks of Sen. Pettit) (discussing 1851 Indiana constitution); Chaney, note 114 supra at 134 (discussing 1850 Michigan constitutional convention).

118. Woodcock v. Bolster, 35 Vt. at 640–41. The court also noted that alien parents would be more likely to be supportive of the public education of their children if they were permitted to participate in the management of the schools. Id. at 641.

119. The Senate initially adopted the Clayton amendment to the Kansas-Nebraska bill, excluding aliens from the electorate for the crucial first territorial legislatures. See Cong. Globe, 33d Cong., 1st Sess. 520 (1854). When the Northern-dominated House of Representatives rejected the amendment, all but seven of its supporters in the Senate settled for the bill's other advantages. See id. at 1321; Robert B. Russell, The Issues in the Congressional Struggle Over the Kansas-Nebraska Bill, 1854, 29 J. So. Hist. 186, 208 (1963); cf. Cong. Globe, 33d Cong., 1st Sess. App. 301–02 (1854) (remarks of Sen. Atchison of Missouri) (explicit denial of this motive, followed by offer to permit alien voting if postponed).

See also Cong. Globe, 34th Cong., 3d Sess. 808–14, 849–65, 872–77 (1857) (debate over alien suffrage provisions in the Minnesota statehood enabling act); Eric Foner, Free Soil, Free Labor, Free Men: The Ideology of the Republican Party before the Civil War 256 (1970) ("The vote indicated that most northern anti-Democratic Congressmen were willing to forego nativism to secure the admission of another free state").

120. See, e.g., H.R. Rep. No. 371, 35th Cong., 1st Sess. (recommending bill to bar aliens from voting in the territories); Cong. Globe, 34th Cong., 3d Sess. 864–65 (1857) (remarks of Sen. Crittenden); id. at 874–76 (remarks of Sen. Bell); Cong. Globe, 33d Cong., 1st Sess. App. 775–79 (remarks of Sen. Bayard). For further discussion of this issue in a comparative perspective, see Gerald L. Neuman, "We Are the People": Alien Suffrage in German and American Perspective, 13 Mich. J. Int'l L. 259 (1992).

121. Opinion of the Justices, 7 Mass. 523 (1811). The occasion for the analysis was a request from the House of Representatives for an advisory opinion on the constitutionality of a proposed method of apportionment.

122. 7 Mass. at 525; see also id. at 529 ("that we might not unnecessarily fix on the people an intention of imparting any of their sovereignty to aliens").

123. Id. at 529; see Mass. Const. of 1780, Part 2, ch. 1, § 3, art. 2 (allocating representatives according to number of "ratable polls" in the town).

124. E.g., Ala. Const. of 1867, art. I, § 2; Ill. Const. of 1818, art. VIII, § 2; Ind. Const. of 1851, art. I, § 1; Kan. Const. of 1859, Bill of Rights, § 2; Minn. Const. of 1857, art. I, § 1.

125. In re Conway, 17 Wis. 543 (1863); In re Wehlitz, 16 Wis. 468 (1863); State ex rel. Off v. Smith, 14 Wis. 539 (1861). In the latter case, the court *agreed* with the Massachusetts court's analysis of popular sovereignty and concluded that the state constitution impliedly barred nondeclarant aliens from holding elective office while

conferring "the right of suffrage and privileges of citizenship" on declarant aliens. 14 Wis. at 542–43 (citing Opinion of the Justices, 7 Mass. 523 (1811)).

126. 16 Wis. at 473.

127. 16 Wis. at 470–71 (citing Scott v. Sandford, 60 U.S. (19 How.) 393 (1857)).

128. See State ex rel. Lêche v. Fowler, 6 So. 602 (La. 1889) ("It is, however, difficult to conceive how a person can be an elector and not a citizen of the community in which he exercises the right to vote"); Abrigo v. State, 29 Tex. Crim. 143 (1890). There are also ambiguous decisions from Indiana. See McCarthy v. Froelke, 63 Ind. 507, 511 (1878); Thomasson v. State, 15 Ind. 449 (1861).

129. See Ala. Const. of 1867, art. I, § 2 ("That all persons resident in this State, born in the United States, or naturalized, or who shall have legally declared their intention to become citizens of the United States, are hereby declared citizens of the State of Alabama, possessing equal civil and political rights and public privileges"); see also Ala. Const. of 1875, art. I, § 2 (similar). Alabama phased out declarant alien suffrage in 1901. See Ala. Const. of 1901, art. VIII, § 177.

130. 88 U.S. (21 Wall.) 162, 177 (1874). The case arose in Missouri. The Court's list of examples was incomplete.

131. See, e.g., City of Minneapolis v. Reum, 56 F. 576 (8th Cir. 1893); Lanz v. Randall, 14 F. Cas. 1131, 1133 (C.C.D. Minn. 1876) (No. 8,080) (Miller, Circuit Judge) ("The error has arisen from the same confusion of ideas which induced the advocates of female suffrage to assert, in the supreme court, the right of women to vote").

132. Desbois's Case, 2 Mart. 185, 192–93 (La. Super. Ct. 1812); United States v. Laverty, 26 F. Cas. 875 (D. La. 1812) (Case No. 15,569a) (British and Irish immigrants to the territory cannot be arrested as alien enemies in War of 1812, following Desbois). The Alabama Supreme Court held otherwise in State v. Primrose, 3 Ala. 546 (1842), but the theory of that opinion is not inconsistent with the Louisiana cases (which the Alabama court had heard of but had not read); rather, the Alabama court incorrectly believed that only United States citizens had been permitted to vote on the statehood constitution.

133. 143 U.S. 135, 170 (1892). The doctrine of collective naturalization also entails that grandfather clauses for alien inhabitants of new states may sometimes have been redundant.

134. Id. at 175–77. The case involved a challenge to the eligibility of James Boyd to be governor of Nebraska because he was an immigrant who had never undergone naturalization. Actually, Boyd had never filed a declaration of intent to naturalize either, but the Court held that he was a constructive declarant by virtue of a declaration his father had made in Ohio when James was a minor.

135. See, e.g., Boyd v. Nebraska ex rel. Thayer, 143 U.S. 135, 178–79 (1892); Act of Mar. 26, 1804, ch. 47, § 2, 2 Stat. 292 (when declarant dies before naturalization, widow and children are immediately eligible for naturalization).

136. See Act of Mar. 2, 1907, ch. 2534, § 1, 34 Stat. 1228; Act of Mar. 3, 1863, ch. 79, § 23, 12 Stat. 754; Edwin M. Borchard, The Diplomatic Protection of Citizens Abroad; or, The Law of International Claims 500–02, 567–70 (1915). One famous instance involved the forcible rescue of the Hungarian emigré Martin Koszta from Austrian agents in Turkey. See id. at 570–74; Andor Klay, Daring Diplomacy: The Case of the First American Ultimatum (1957).

137. See, e.g., William W. Fitzhugh, Jr., & Charles C. Hyde, The Drafting of Neutral Aliens by the United States, 36 Am. J. Int'l L. 369 (1942); Charles E. Roh, Jr., & Frank K. Upham, The Status of Aliens under United States Draft Laws, 13 Harv. Int'l L. J 501 (1972).

138. See Act of Mar. 3, 1863, ch. 75, § 1, 12 Stat. 731. The drafting of declarant aliens was added as a floor amendment in the Senate. It was originally proposed by Sen. Doolittle of Wisconsin (a state where declarants could vote), in a form that limited conscription to declarants who had actually voted. The amendment was voted down, but the proposal was successfully reintroduced by Sen. McDougal of California (a state where only citizens could vote) in a form that conscripted all declarants, regardless of whether they had ever voted. See Cong. Globe, 37th Cong., 3d Sess. 991–93, 1001 (1863).

139. See Presidential Proclamation of May 8, 1863, 6 Messages and Papers of the President 168 (James D. Richardson ed. 1899); Act of Feb. 24, 1864, ch. 13, § 18, 13 Stat. 9 ("no person of foreign birth . . . who has at any time assumed the rights of a citizen by voting"); Fitzhugh & Hyde, note 137 supra at 372–73. The problem had already arisen in 1862 with regard to the state militias.

140. Act of May 18, 1917, ch. 15, § 2, 40 Stat. 77; Act of Apr. 22, 1898, ch. 187, § 1, 30 Stat. 361; Fitzhugh & Hyde, note 137 supra at 372–75; see also Selective Training and Service Act of 1940, ch. 720, § 3(a), 54 Stat. 885 (making citizens and declarant aliens liable for service); but see Act of Dec. 20, 1941, ch. 602, § 2, 55 Stat. 845 (extending liability for service to nondeclarant resident aliens); Universal Military Training and Service Act of 1951, ch. 144, § 1(d), 65 Stat. 75 (making aliens admitted to permanent residence and other aliens remaining in the United States more than a year liable for service). I omit here the later history of provisions by which aliens who were willing to renounce the possibility of American citizenship could seek exemption from service.

The declaration of intent was dropped from the naturalization procedure in 1952—see 8 U.S.C. § 1445(f)—and is no longer relevant to selective service law; see 50 U.S.C. App. §§ 453(a), 454(a), 456(a)(1).

141. See Act of Mar. 26, 1790, ch. 3, 1 Stat. 103.

142. Act of July 14, 1870, ch. 254, § 7, 16 Stat. 256; see Cong. Globe, 41st Cong., 2d Sess. 5121–25, 5148–77 (1870).

143. See Gillette, note 79 supra at 56, 90. Senators William Stewart of Nevada (the proponent of the Fifteenth Amendment in the Senate), John Conness of California, and Henry Corbett and George Williams of Oregon successfully opposed Charles Sumner's attempt to have the limitation to citizens struck from the amendment. See Cong. Globe, 40th Cong., 3d Sess. 1030–35 (1869). The Oregon state constitution both permitted declarant aliens to vote and expressly prohibited voting by any "negro, Chinaman, or mulatto." Or. Const. of 1857, art. II, §§ 2, 6. Opposition to ratification of the Fifteenth Amendment in Oregon was based on the view that it might still lead to suffrage for the Chinese, and Oregon gratuitously voted to reject the amendment after it had already been adopted. See Gillette at 153–57.

144. See Act of Dec. 17, 1943, ch. 344, § 3, 57 Stat. 601.

145. See U.S. Const. amend. XIX (sex); amend. XXIV (failure to pay any poll tax or other tax); amend. XXVI (age, if eighteen or older).

146. U.S. Const. amend. XVII (adopted 1913).

147. See, e.g., 2 Official Proceedings of the Constitutional Convention of the State of Alabama, May 21, 1901, to September 3, 1901, at 2721–23 (1940); 3 id. at 3217, 3221–23; Rosberg, note 78 supra at 1099–1100.

148. See John Higham, Strangers in the Land: Patterns of American Nativism, 1860–1925, at 214, 376 n. 50 (2d ed. 1985); Porter, note 117 supra at 252.

149. See Leon E. Aylsworth, The Passing of Alien Suffrage, 25 Am. Pol. Sci. Rev. 114 (1931).

150. See, e.g., Somerset, Md., Charter § 83–21 (1990); Beth Kaiman, Deciding Ballot Rights; Takoma Park to Rule on Non-Citizen Vote, Wash. Post, Oct. 31, 1991, at M1 (listing Somerset, Barnsville, Chevy Chase Sections 3 and 5, and Martin's Additions).

151. See Ill. Rev. Stat. ch. 122, paras. 34–1–1, 34–2–1 (1989) (parents and community residents, without citizenship qualification, eligible to vote and to run for local councils); Ambach v. Norwick, 441 U.S. 68, 81 n. 15 (1979) (alien parents eligible as voters and candidates in New York City community school board elections).

152. See Jamin B. Raskin, Legal Aliens, Local Citizens: The Historical, Constitutional and Theoretical Meanings of Alien Suffrage, 141 U. Pa. L. Rev. 1391, 1462–66 (1993).

153. See Stephanie Griffith, Hispanics Seek Wider Clout in D.C. and Va.; Takoma Park Referendum on Voting Eligibility Spurs Immigrants' Interest, Wash. Post, Nov. 7, 1991, at D6; Melanie Howard, Vote to Extend Voting Rights Seen as Likely to Start a Trend, Wash. Times, Nov. 7, 1991, at B3 (noting both expressions of interest from Texas and California, and opposition of Federation for American Immigration Reform); Howard Jordan, Empowering Immigrants, Newsday, Apr. 7, 1993, at 52.

154. Samuel Orozco, A New Idea for Old Glory, Sacramento Bee, Dec. 13, 1992, at FO1; Deborah Sontag, Noncitizens and the Right to Vote, N.Y. Times, July 31, 1992, at B1.

155. See, e.g., H.R. Rep. No. 9, 103d Cong., 1st Sess. 36 (1993) (minority views); William Raspberry, Motor Voter and the "Them" Problem, Wash. Post, Mar. 19, 1993, at A31; Paul Craig Roberts, "Motor Voter" Registration Bill Is Nothing but a Devaluation of Citizenship, Houston Chronicle, Mar. 18, 1993, at A33. The bill nonetheless became law. National Voter Registration Act of 1993, Pub.L. No. 103–31, 107 Stat 77 (codified at 42 U.S.C. § 1973gg et seq.).

156. See Treaty on European Union, 31 I.L.M. 247, 259 (1992) (Article 8a).

157. See Carlos Closa, The Concept of Citizenship in the Treaty on European Union, 29 Common Market L. Rev. 1137 (1992); Neuman, note 120 supra at 264–66.

CHAPTER FIVE

1. See, e.g., Torres v. Puerto Rico, 442 U.S. 465 (1979); Juan R. Torruella, The Supreme Court and Puerto Rico: The Doctrine of Separate and Unequal (1985).

2. U.S. Const., art. I, § 8. In *The Federalist No. 43*, however, Madison predicted that "a municipal legislature for local purposes, derived from their own suffrages, will of course be allowed them."

3. See generally The American Territorial System (John Porter Bloom ed. 1973); Jack E. Eblen, The First and Second United States Empires: Governors and Territorial Government, 1784–1912 (1968); Laws of Illinois Territory, 1809–1818 (Francis S. Philbrick ed. 1950); J.W. Smurr, Territorial Jurisprudence (1970). The Constitution's only mention of the territory was the ambiguous provision in Article IV, Section 3, granting Congress "Power to dispose of and make all needful Rules and Regulations respecting the Territory or other Property belonging to the United States."

4. Only partial reports of the debates on the ratification and initial implementation of the Louisiana treaty survive. 13 Annals of Cong., passim (1804); William Plumer, Memorandum of Proceedings in the United States Senate, 1803–1807 (Everett S. Brown ed. 1923); Everett S. Brown, Constitutional History of the Louisiana Purchase, 1803–1812 (1920).

5. Johnson v. M'Intosh, 21 U.S. (8 Wheat.) 543, 587 (1823) (Marshall, C.J., no doubt savoring the irony).

6. See, e.g., Brown, note 4 supra at 22–29; Dumas Malone, Jefferson the President: First Term, 1801–1805, at 311–21 (1970).

7. See 13 Annals of Cong. 45 (1804) (remarks of Sen. Pickering); id. at 56 (remarks of Sen. Tracy); id. at 433 (remarks of Rep. G. Griswold); id. at 454–55 (remarks of Rep. Thatcher); id. at 461–62 (remarks of Rep. R. Griswold); Plumer, note 4 supra at 7–9 (remarks of Sen. Plumer). The New Englanders were quite correctly concerned that they would lose influence in national decisions as Western states multiplied across the continent.

8. 13 Annals of Cong. 461–62 (1804) (remarks of Rep. R. Griswold); Plumer, note 4 supra at 7 (remarks of Sen. Plumer).

9. Only John Quincy Adams followed a consistent natural law view, insisting that the consent of the people of Louisiana to the change in government was required and urging self-government for the territory. See 13 Annals of Cong. 66–67 (1804); 1 Memoirs of John Quincy Adams 267–68, 288–90 (Charles Francis Adams ed. 1874); Plumer, note 4 supra at 103–04, 143–46.

10. 13 Annals of Cong. 45 (1804) (remarks of Sen. Pickering); Plumer, note 4 supra at 12 (remarks of Sen. Plumer); id. at 76 (remarks of Sen. White); id. at 107 (remarks of Sen. Pickering); id. at 114 (remarks of Sen. Hillhouse).

11. 13 Annals of Cong. 511–12 (1804) (remarks of Rep. Smilie); id. at 1058–59 (Rep. Eustis); see also id. at 513–14 (remarks of Rep. Rodney, distinguishing between states and territories).

12. See Brown, note 4 supra at 102–44.

13. 13 Annals of Cong. 1129 (1804) (remarks of Rep. G.W. Campbell); id. at 510–11 (remarks of Rep. Jackson); Plumer, note 4 supra at 136 (remarks of Sen. Anderson).

14. 18 U.S. (5 Wheat.) 317 (1820). The arguments are not reported and can be inferred only from Marshall's opinion.

15. Id. at 318. Marshall rejected the claim that the great Revolutionary principle of no taxation without representation deprived Congress of the power to tax the District of Columbia. He admitted that "in theory, it might be more congenial to the spirit of our institutions, to admit a representative from the district," but the actual Constitution too clearly did not authorize such a representative. Id. at 324–25.

16. Id. at 319. Direct taxes, however, were to be apportioned by a different rule,

which, after some textual straining, Marshall construed as flexible enough to permit Congress to include or exclude the District of Columbia and territories in direct taxation at its option. Id. at 319–24.

17. 17 U.S. (4 Wheat.) 316, 408 (1819) ("Throughout this vast republic, from the St. Croix to the Gulf of Mexico, from the Atlantic to the Pacific, revenue is to be collected and expended, armies are to be marched and supported"); see also John Marshall, A Friend of the Constitution No. 4, in John Marshall's Defense of McCulloch v. Maryland 185 (Gerald Gunther ed. 1969).

18. McCulloch, 17 U.S. (4 Wheat.) at 402–05.

19. See, e.g., Don E. Fehrenbacher, The Dred Scott Case: Its Significance in American Law and Politics 100–13 (1978); William C. Wiecek, The Sources of Antislavery Constitutionalism in America, 1760–1848, at 114–16 (1977).

20. 26 U.S. (1 Pet.) 511 (1828).

21. Id. at 515–22. Johnson's opinion is set out as a footnote to the case.

22. 26 U.S. at 533 (argument of Whipple). Daniel Webster also argued on Canter's behalf, to similar effect.

23. Id. at 542. See also Pollard's Lessee v. Hagan, 44 U.S. (3 How.) 212, 225 (1845) ("Every nation acquiring territory, by treaty or otherwise, must hold it subject to the constitution and laws of its own government, and not according to those of the government ceding it") (citing Vattel); Chicago R.I. & P.R.R. v. McGlinn, 114 U.S. 542, 546 (1885) (Field, J.) ("As a matter of course, all laws, ordinances, and regulations in conflict with the political character, institutions, and constitution of the new government are at once displaced").

24. Canter, 26 U.S. (1 Pet.) at 542.

25. Marshall may have disserved the cause of civil liberties in the territories by legitimating the creation of courts with judges lacking Article III tenure protections. But this issue was not directly before him; the American Insurance Company had not complained about the tenure of judges in the territorial court but had argued that the Florida legislature lacked the power to create a court with admiralty jurisdiction at all. As Marshall had previously recognized, however, there was need for courts in the territories beyond those described in Article III, because in deference to the jealousy of the states Article III had created only courts of limited jurisdiction. See Serè v. Pitot, 10 U.S. (6 Cranch) 332 (1810). Marshall had aggravated this need by holding that citizens of the District of Columbia and the territories were not citizens of a state for diversity purposes. Corporation of New-Orleans v. Winter, 14 U.S. (1 Wheat.) 91 (1816); Hepburn v. Ellzey, 6 U.S. (2 Cranch) 265 (1805).

26. See generally Frederic Bancroft, Calhoun and the South Carolina Nullification Movement (1928); William H. Freehling, Prelude to Civil War: The Nullification Controversy in South Carolina, 1816–1836 (1968); John Niven, John C. Calhoun and the Price of Union 134–178 (1988); Merrill D. Peterson, The Great Triumvirate: Webster, Clay, and Calhoun 168–69 (1987).

27. Freehling, note 26 supra at 158; Letter to William C. Preston, in 10 The Papers of John C. Calhoun 431 (Clyde N. Wilson & William E. Hemphill eds. 1977) (hereinafter Calhoun Papers).

28. See 10 Calhoun Papers, note 27 supra at 442; Niven, note 26 supra at 136–37, 158–59. Like Jefferson, he concealed his authorship of this attack on the government in which he was serving as vice president at the time.

29. A Disquisition on Government, in 1 The Works of John C. Calhoun 58–59

(Richard K. Crallé ed. 1853) (hereinafter Disquisition, Calhoun Works). Calhoun's fullest elaboration of his views appears in the posthumously published Disquisition and A Discourse on the Constitution and Government of the United States, in 1 Calhoun Works at 109 (hereinafter Discourse, Calhoun Works). The major elements of the argument are also contained in his Senate speeches and addresses at various stages of the abolition controversy.

30. Disquisition, Calhoun Works, note 29 supra at 7–8.

31. Speech, in 4 Calhoun Works, note 29 supra at 80 (Senate speech of Feb. 28, 1842).

32. Discourse, Calhoun Works, note 29 supra at 119, 131. This was the meaning of the Preamble's phraseology "We the People of the United States of America"— the "United States" were the "States united." Similarly, in declaring that the Constitution was "for the United States of America," they identified the intended beneficiaries as the peoples of the several states. Id. at 128–29, 132–34.

33. Id. at 112–13, 162–68; see also Speech in Reply to Mr. Webster, in 2 Calhoun Works, note 29 supra at 262 (Feb. 26, 1833).

34. See, e.g., South Carolina Exposition and Protest, in 10 Calhoun Papers, note 27 supra at 446–47; Discourse, Calhoun Works, note 29 supra at 244–49, 256–57.

35. See Eric Foner, Free Soil, Free Labor, Free Men 54–58 (1970).

36. See Discourse, Calhoun Works, note 29 supra at 256–57; 4 Calhoun Works at 536 (debate with Webster in the Senate, Feb. 24, 1849).

37. Discourse, Calhoun Works, note 29 supra at 256–57 (emphasis deleted).

38. 6 The Writings and Speeches of Daniel Webster 3 (1903) (hereinafter Webster Speeches) (speech of Jan. 26–27, 1830); id. at 181. The Reply, actually the Second Reply, formed part of a running debate between Webster and Hayne in January 1830. Cong. Deb. 31–93 (1830).

39. 6 Webster Speeches, note 38 supra at 54.

40. Id. at 201.

41. Id. at 210.

42. Id. at 198–99.

43. Id. at 67–68.

44. See Robert A. Ferguson, Law and Letters in American Culture 222 (1984); Peterson, note 26 supra at 177; G. Edward White, The Marshall Court and Cultural Change, 1815–35, at 281–89, 491–93 (1988).

45. Webster served as chairman of the committee that produced the Boston Memorial to Congress on restraining the Increase of Slavery, Dec. 15, 1819, reprinted in 15 Webster Speeches, note 38 supra at 55. See Peterson, note 26 supra at 59–60. Whether Webster drafted the memorial is disputed. See 15 Webster Speeches at 73. Be that as it may, the memorial sets forth Webster's future argument that Congress's power over the territories is legally unlimited and subject only to moral constraints. Id. at 56–57.

46. 26 U.S. (1 Pet.) 511 (1828).

47. 26 U.S. (1 Pet.) at 538 (Webster's argument).

48. See Cong. Globe, 30th Cong., 2d Sess. App. 255 (1849); Fehrenbacher, note 18 supra at 155–57; Peterson, note 26 supra at 448–49.

49. See Cong. Globe, 30th Cong., 2d Sess. App. 273 (1849) (remarks of Sen. Calhoun); cf. id. at 267 (remarks of Sen. Walker) ("If the Constitution will extend

slavery to the land, then let it go. If by that Constitution slavery is extended, I am willing to stand by that Constitution").

50. Id. at 273 ("Is not [the Constitution's] very first principle that all within its influence and comprehension shall be represented in the Legislature . . . ?"). Webster even cited the Canter case as if it supported his position.

51. Id. at 257, 262, 268 (remarks of Sen. Dayton); id. at 270 (remarks of Sen. Hale).

52. For example, Thomas Hart Benton, who lampooned Calhoun's argument as the "new and supreme dogma of the transmigratory function of the constitution in the ipso facto." 2 Thomas Hart Benton, Thirty Years' View 713 (1856). Benton was in any case a longtime enemy of Calhoun.

53. See, e.g., United States v. Minnesota & N.W. R.R. Co., 1 Minn. 127 (Minn. Terr. 1854) (invalidating act of Congress on takings grounds), rev'd sub nom. Rice v. Railroad Co., 66 U.S. (1 Black) 358 (1862); Ponder v. Graham, 4 Fla. 23, 43–46 (1851) (invalidating divorce granted by territorial legislature); Rogers v. Bradford, 1 Pin. 418, 427–28 (Wis. Terr. 1844) (territorial court is not a "Court of the United States" within the meaning of the Seventh Amendment, purporting to follow *American Insurance Co.*); Doty v. Strong, 1 Pin. 84, 88 (Wis. Terr. 1840) (territorial delegate shares constitutional privilege from arrest under Article I); Territory v. Hattick, 2 Mart. (O.S.) 87 (Orleans Terr. Super. Ct. 1811) (criminal jury trial provisions apply only to crimes against the United States); see generally Smurr note 3 supra.

54. See Scott v. Sandford, 60 U.S. (19 How.) 393 (1857) (denying congressional power over slavery in territories); Cross v. Harrison, 57 U.S. (16 How.) 163 (1854) (sorting out customs consequences of acquisition of California); United States v. Dawson, 56 U.S. (15 How.) 467 (1854) (discussing constitutional venue requirements in Indian country); Webster v. Reid, 52 U.S. (11 How.) 436 (1851) (requiring civil jury trial in Iowa Territory); Strader v. Graham, 51 U.S. (10 How.) 82 (1851) (discussing the effect of the Northwest Ordinance on slavery); see also Fleming v. Page, 50 U.S. (9 How.) 603 (1850) (discussing the customs consequences of occupation of Mexican soil).

55. 52 U.S. (11 How.) 437 (1851). It must be recognized that there are serious ambiguities in referring to the "constitutionality" of an act of a territorial legislature, and that the strongest evidence of an "extension" of the Constitution to a territory would be the invalidation of an act of Congress, as in the Dred Scott decision.

56. 56 U.S. (15 How.) 467 (1854).

57. 60 U.S. (19 How.) 393 (1857).

58. Tracing the power to acquire and govern territory to the express power to admit new states, Taney concluded that Congress could not treat citizens in the territories as mere colonists or rule permanent colonial dependencies without restrictions—a neat reversal of the Federalist argument concerning Louisiana. Id. at 451–52. In the spirit of Calhoun's trusteeship argument, he also inferred an implied limitation against preventing slaveholders from migrating with their "property" to any territory. Id. at 450–51.

59. Id. at 450–51.

60. See id. at 542. McLean, the strongest antislavery justice of the period, adopted a version of the moderate antislavery position that though the Constitution

shielded slavery in the states, it did not grant Congress the power to establish slavery in the territories. See Miller v. McQuerry, 17 F. Cas. 335, 336–37 (C.C.D. Ohio 1853) (No. 9,583); Fehrenbacher, note 18 supra at 143; Francis P. Weisenburger, The Life of John McLean: A Politican on the United States Supreme Court (1937).

61. 60 U.S. (19 How.) at 544.

62. Id. at 614. Curtis did not seem to intend a territorial limitation on the scope of constitutional rights; the passage quoted here follows only a few lines after his observation that "Congress has enacted a great system of municipal laws, and extended it over the vessels and crews of the United States on the high seas and in foreign ports, and even over citizens of the United States resident in China." Id. He thus seems to have anticipated the modern geographical scope of the mutuality approach, as in Reid v. Covert, decided exactly a century later.

63. 60 U.S. (19 How.) at 624–27.

64. Not all of Taney's numerous critics, however, limited themselves to Curtis's ground of disagreement. The dying Thomas Hart Benton issued a little book that had some influence later, in which he agreed with Webster that the Constitution protected only the states and that Congress had absolute power over the territories. Thomas Hart Benton, Historical and Legal Examination of that part of the Decision of the Supreme Court of the United States in the Dred Scott Case, which declares the Unconstitutionality of the Missouri Compromise Act, and the Self-Extension of the Constitution to the Territories, Carrying Slavery along with It (1970 reprint of 1857 ed.). See Downes v. Bidwell, 182 U.S. 244, 275 (1901) (opinion of Brown, J.) (invoking Benton's authority); Fehrenbacher, note 18 supra at 631 nn. 54, 56; Edward S. Corwin, The Dred Scott Decision, in Light of Contemporary Legal Doctrines, 17 Am. Hist. Rev. 52, 59 (1911).

65. Elick v. Washington Territory, 1 Allen 136, 140 (1862).

66. Rice v. Railroad Co., 66 U.S. (1 Black) 358 (1862).

67. See Kennon v. Gilmer, 131 U.S. 22 (1889) (jury trial); Reynolds v. United States, 98 U.S. 145 (1879) (same); Wilkerson v. Utah, 99 U.S. 130 (1878) (cruel and unusual punishment).

68. See American Publishing Co. v. Fisher, 166 U.S. 464, 466 (1897); Springville v. Thomas, 166 U.S. 707, 708–09 (1897).

69. See Edwin B. Firmage & Richard C. Mangrum, Zion in the Courts: A Legal History of the Church of Jesus Christ of Latter-day Saints, 1830–1900 (1988); Ray J. Davis, The Polygamous Prelude, 6 Am. J. Leg. Hist. 1 (1962); Orma Linford, The Mormons and the Law: The Polygamy Cases (Parts 1 & 2), 9 Utah L. Rev. 308, 543 (1964–65). There is not enough space here to discuss all the cases, including Miles v. United States, 103 U.S. 304 (1880), Murphy v. Ramsey, 114 U.S. 15 (1885), Clawson v. United States, 114 U.S. 477 (1885), In re Snow, 120 U.S. 274 (1887), and the extreme decision in Davis v. Beason, 133 U.S. 333 (1890) (upholding Idaho territorial statute disenfranchising church members).

70. See Act of July 1, 1862, ch. 126, 12 Stat. 501; Act of Mar. 22, 1882, ch. 47, 22 Stat. 30.

71. See H.R. Rep. No. 2568, 49th Cong., 1st Sess. 7–8 (1886) (recommending antipolygamy amendment to Constitution that would bind states); Firmage & Mangrum, note 69 supra at 127 (discussing Utah's quest for statehood).

72. See, e.g., H.R. Rep. No. 2735, 49th Cong., 1st Sess. 7–9 (1886); H.R. Rep.

No. 83, 36th Cong., 1st Sess. 2–4 (1860); Firmage & Mangrum, note 69 supra at 134–35.

73. 13 Cong. Rec. 1206 (1882) (remarks of Sen. Jones); see also id. at 1162.

74. 98 U.S. 145 (1879). One of Reynolds's wives testified at an earlier trial but could not be found for the later one. Her prior testimony was admitted. Only Justice Field dissented, and only on this issue. See id. at 168.

75. 131 U.S. 176 (1889).

76. Late Corporation of the Church of Jesus Christ of Latter-day Saints v. United States, 136 U.S. 1 (1890).

77. See 136 U.S. at 32–35 (argument); see also Transcript of Argument in 10 Landmark Briefs and Arguments of the Supreme Court of the United States: Constitutional Law 359–61 (Philip Kurland & Gerhard Casper ed. 1975) (colloquy on contracts clause). And in fact Chief Justice Fuller, Justice Field, and Justice Lucius Q.C. Lamar dissented, filing an unhelpfully brief statement that Congress's confiscation of the corporation's assets, without office found, violated "specific limitations in the Constitution" and was in excess of Congress's delegated authority. 136 U.S. at 67–68.

78. 136 U.S. at 44. Cf. Slaughter-House Cases, 83 U.S. (16 Wall.) 36, 119 (1873) (Bradley, J., dissenting) ("But even if the Constitution were silent, the fundamental privileges and immunities of citizens, as such, would be no less real and no less inviolable than they now are").

79. 140 U.S. 453 (1891).

80. 140 U.S. at 464–65. Field mentioned the "impossibility of obtaining a competent grand or petit jury" in a foreign country and pointed out that even the citizen denied these protections was often "the gainer" from being spared subjection to a foreign legal system, which might even involve "extreme cruelty and torture." Id. See also Forbes v. Scannell, 13 Cal. 243, 281–82 (1859) (Baldwin, J., joined by Field, J.); David J. Bederman, Extraterritorial Domicile and the Constitution, 28 Va. J. Int'l L. 451 (1988).

81. See, e.g., Pennoyer v. Neff, 95 U.S. 714, 722–23 (1878); Paul v. Virginia, 75 U.S. (8 Wall.) 168, 180–82 (1868); Fong Yue Ting v. United States, 149 U.S. 698, 754 (1893) (Field, J., dissenting).

82. 140 U.S. at 464 (citation omitted).

83. See id. at 470–80. The case was complicated by the fact that Ross was a British subject on an American vessel, and the British government had protested the trial, but the Court ruled that he was assimilated to the status of an American national during his service on the vessel.

84. Readers who need references on this point may consult, e.g., Charles G. Haines, The Revival of Natural Law Concepts 104–65 (1930); Clyde E. Jacobs, Law Writers and the Courts: The Influence of Thomas M. Cooley, Christopher G. Tiedeman, and John F. Dillon upon American Constitutional Law (1954); G. Edward White, The American Judicial Tradition 95–108 (rev. ed. 1988); Benjamin F. Wright, American Interpretations of Natural Law 298–306 (1931).

85. 182 U.S. 244 (1901).

86. See, e.g., John Dobson, Reticent Expansionism: The Foreign Policy of William McKinley (1988); David Healy, US Expansionism: The Imperialist Urge in the 1890s (1970); Ernest R. May, Imperial Democracy: The Emergence of America as

a Great Power (1961); Stuart C. Miller, "Benevolent Assimilation": The American Conquest of the Philippines, 1899–1903, at 17–19 (1982).

87. See generally Robert L. Beisner, Twelve against Empire: The Anti-Imperialists, 1898–1900 (1968); E. Berkeley Tompkins, Anti-Imperialism in the United States: The Great Debate, 1890–1920 (1970).

88. Scott v. Sandford, 60 U.S. (19 How.) 393, 446 (1857) (Taney, C.J.).

89. U.S. Const. amend. XIV, § 1 ("[a]ll persons born or naturalized in the United States, and subject to the jurisdiction thereof"); but see Elk v. Wilkins, 112 U.S. 94 (1884) (holding that the qualification "subject to the jurisdiction thereof" excluded persons born into Indian tribes). The Insular Cases rendered superfluous an expansion of that exception to cover members of disfavored cultures in the insular possessions. Cf. 8 U.S.C. § 1401–1409 (distinguishing between "citizens" and "nationals" of the United States); Carman F. Randolph, Constitutional Aspects of Annexation, 12 Harv. L. Rev. 291, 309–10 (1898) (predicting such an expansion).

90. See Simeon E. Baldwin, The Historic Policy of the United States as to Annexation, 2 Yale Rev. 133, 156–57 (1893); Thomas M. Cooley, Grave Obstacles to Hawaiian Annexation, 15 Forum 389 (1893); George Ticknor Curtis, The Sandwich Islands: II. Is it Constitutional?, 156 N. Am. Rev. 282 (1893); George S. Patterson, The Constitutional Effect of Hawaiian Annexation upon the Tariff Act of 1890, 33 Am. L. Reg. 309 (1893).

91. See, e.g., Selden Bacon, Territory and the Constitution, 10 Yale L.J. 99 (1901); Simeon E. Baldwin, The Constitutional Questions Incident to the Acquisition and Government by the United States of Island Territory, 12 Harv. L. Rev. 393 (1899); John W. Burgess, How May the United States Govern Its Extra-Continental Territory?, 14 Pol. Sci Q. 1 (1899); Paul Fuller, Some Constitutional Questions Suggested by Recent Acquisitions, 1 Colum. L. Rev. 108 (1901); Paul Howland, The Legal Status of Our New Possessions, 6 Western Reserve L.J. 189 (1901); Paul R. Shipman, Webster on the Territories, 9 Yale L.J. 185 (1900); Edward B. Whitney, Another Philippine Constitutional Question—Delegation of Legislative Power to the President, 1 Colum. L. Rev. 33 (1901); Theodore S. Woolsey, The Government of Dependencies, 13 Annals (Supp.) 3 (1899); cf. Ernst Freund, The Control of Dependencies through Protectorates, 14 Pol. Sci. Q. 19 (1899) (but different rule for protectorate); Harry Pratt Judson, Our Federal Constitution and the Government of Tropical Territories, 19 Am. Monthly Rev. of Revs. 67 (1899) (but many clauses limited to states). The publication date of each of these articles and of those in the succeeding footnotes precedes the decision in the first set of Insular Cases in May 1901.

92. John Kimberly Beach, Constitutional Expansion, 8 Yale L.J. 225 (1899); E.W. Huffcut, Constitutional Aspects of the Government of Dependencies, 13 Annals (Supp.) 19 (1899); C.C. Langdell, The Status of Our New Territories, 12 Harv. L. Rev. 365 (1899); James Bradley Thayer, Our New Possessions, 12 Harv. L. Rev. 464 (1899) (with qualifications).

93. H. Teichmueller, Expansion and the Constitution, 33 Am. L. Rev. 202 (1899).

94. Id. at 210–11; see also Burgess, note 91 supra at 3; Fuller, note 91 supra at 116–17; cf. Shipman, note 91 supra at 206 (quoting Polonius's advice to Laertes).

95. Langdell, note 91 supra at 372–73.

96. Id. at 382; Huffcut, note 91 supra at 32.

97. Charles A. Gardiner, Our Right to Acquire and Hold Foreign Territory, 33 Am. L. Rev. 162 (1899); Thayer, note 91 supra at 467, 469.

98. Gardiner, note 97 supra at 174; Huffcut, note 93 supra at 43–44.

99. Gardiner, note 97 supra at 180, 187.

100. Baldwin, note 91 supra, 12 Harv. L. Rev. at 409–10; Randolph, note 92 supra at 313–15; Teichmueller, note 96 supra at 213–14; cf. Shipman, note 91 supra at 206 (if a territory is permanently unfit for statehood, we must either amend the Constitution or give up the territory); see Tompkins, note 87 supra at 178–82.

101. Abbott Lawrence Lowell, The Status of Our New Possessions—A Third View, 13 Harv. L. Rev. 155 (1899).

102. Id. at 176.

103. See DeLima v. Bidwell, 182 U.S. 1 (1901); Goetze v. United States, 182 U.S. 221 (1901); Dooley v. United States, 182 U.S. 222 (1901); Armstrong v. United States, 182 U.S. 243 (1901); Downes v. Bidwell, 182 U.S. 244 (1901); Huus v. New York & Porto Rico S.S. Co., 182 U.S. 392 (1901); Dooley v. United States, 183 U.S. 151 (1901); Fourteen Diamond Rings v. United States, 183 U.S. 176 (1901).

104. Downes, 182 U.S. at 251 (emphasis deleted); see id. at 285.

105. Id. at 277, 282. However, such legal guarantees would be superfluous, since the Anglo-Saxon character can be trusted to rule justly. Id. at 280.

106. Id. at 285.

107. Id. at 286–87. Furthermore, Congress must have the power to annex land without admitting "savages" as citizens. Id. at 279–80.

108. Justice Horace Gray, who provided the crucial fifth vote, declared himself as "in substance agreeing with the opinion of Mr. Justice White," but his brief concurring statement placed heavy emphasis on the fact that the case involved the temporary government of a territory recently acquired in war. Id. at 345–46.

109. Id. at 289 (White, J., joined by Shiras and McKenna, JJ., concurring).

110. Id. at 293.

111. Id. at 299. The four dissenters, however, ridiculed this purportedly objective test as devoid of meaning. Id. at 372–73 (Fuller, C.J., dissenting); id. at 391 (Harlan, J., dissenting).

112. Id. at 301–02.

113. Id. at 306.

114. Id. at 291. Later in the opinion White rephrased his position as affording unincorporated territories the protection of those "general prohibitions in the Constitution in favor of the liberty and property of the citizen which are not mere regulations as to the form and manner in which a conceded power may be exercised, but which are an absolute denial of all authority under any circumstances or conditions to do particular acts." Id. at 294.

115. Hawaii v. Mankichi, 190 U.S. 197, 220–21 (1903) (White, J., concurring).

116. Chief Justice Melville Fuller wrote on behalf of all four dissenters. He demolished Brown's claims of precedential support for a Websterian membership approach. Fuller mocked the "occult meaning" of White's incorporation theory but had difficulty refuting this mystery in detail. 182 U.S. at 373 (Fuller, C.J., dissenting). He rejected all policy arguments based on the need to accommodate colonialism.

117. Id. at 378 (Harlan, J., dissenting).

118. Id. at 383, 384–85.

119. Id. at 389.

120. 180 U.S. 109 (1901). There the Court had unanimously upheld the extradition of a dishonest American official to Cuba for trial without jury under the military government of General Leonard Wood. Treating the case as extraterritorial, Harlan had written that the jury-trial guarantees "have no relation to crimes committed without the jurisdiction of the United States against the laws of a foreign country." Id. at 122.

121. 182 U.S. at 387–88 (Harlan, J., dissenting). White had invoked *Neely* as precedent on his side. See 182 U.S. at 343–44 (White, J., concurring).

122. Id. at 385.

123. See Twining v. New Jersey, 211 U.S. 78 (1908) (Court holds the privilege against self-incrimination inapplicable to states; Harlan dissents); West v. Louisiana, 194 U.S. 258 (1904) (Court holds the right to confrontation inapplicable to states; Harlan dissents); Maxwell v. Dow, 176 U.S. 581 (1900) (Court holds the right to a jury of twelve inapplicable to states; Harlan dissents); O'Neil v. Vermont, 144 U.S. 323 (1892) (Court holds the ban on cruel and unusual punishment inapplicable to states; Harlan dissents); Hurtado v. California, 110 U.S. 516 (1884) (Court holds the requirement of a grand jury indictment inapplicable to states; Harlan dissents); cf. Patterson v. Colorado, 205 U.S. 454 (1907) (Court does not reach the applicability of First Amendment to states; Harlan dissents); Talton v. Mayes, 163 U.S. 376 (1896) (Harlan notes dissent to a decision holding the grand jury requirement inapplicable to the Cherokee Nation).

124. Hurtado v. California, 110 U.S. 516, 539 (1884) (Harlan, J., dissenting). Unlike his successor Hugo Black, Harlan also found room in the Constitution for unenumerated rights to liberty of occupation, liberty of contract, and expansive concepts of taking without just compensation in such areas as taxation and rate regulation. See, e.g., Adair v. United States, 208 U.S. 161 (1908); Norwood v. Baker, 172 U.S. 269 (1898); Smyth v. Ames, 169 U.S. 466 (1898); Powell v. Pennsylvania, 127 U.S. 678 (1888); see also Lochner v. New York, 198 U.S. 45, 65 (1905) (Harlan, J., dissenting) (finding sufficient basis for the regulation of bakers' hours).

125. See Torruella, note 1 supra at 62–84; Fredric R. Coudert, The Evolution of the Doctrine of Territorial Incorporation, 26 Colum. L. Rev. 823 (1926). Harlan vowed eternal dissent from the theory of the Insular Cases; see Dorr v. United States, 195 U.S. 138, 155–56 (1904) (Harlan, J., dissenting). Harlan continued to dissent until his death, in 1911. See Dowdell v. United States, 221 U.S. 325, 333 (1911); Gavieres v. United States, 220 U.S. 338, 345 (1911); Trono v. United States, 199 U.S. 521, 535 (1905).

126. 258 U.S. 298 (1922). See Torruella, note 1 supra at 85–100; José A. Cabranes, Citizenship and the American Empire: Notes on the Legislative History of the United States Citizenship of Puerto Ricans, 127 U. Pa. L. Rev. 390 (1978). (The island's name was officially misspelled "Porto Rico" from 1898 to 1932.)

127. 258 U.S. at 311.

128. See, e.g., Torres v. Puerto Rico, 442 U.S. 465, 469–71 (1979).

129. 354 U.S. 1 (1957).

130. The decision not only overturned the strict territoriality rule and limited military jurisdiction over civilians, but also resolved recurring uncertainties over the

relationship between the Bill of Rights and the treaty power. See Louis Henkin, Foreign Affairs and the Constitution 139 (1972).

131. 347 U.S. 483 (1954).

132. See Madsden v. Kinsella, 343 U.S. 341 (1952) (upholding the trial by occupation court of an American citizen civilian); Hirota v. MacArthur, 338 U.S. 197 (1949) (finding Allied war crimes tribunal in Tokyo not to be an instrumentality of the United States); Wade v. Hunter, 336 U.S. 684 (1949) (resolving on other grounds a double jeopardy challenge to the court-martial of an American soldier in Germany); id. at 692 (Murphy, Douglas, and Rutledge, JJ., dissenting); Fairman, Some New Problems of the Constitution Following the Flag, 1 Stan. L. Rev. 587 (1949). But cf. Best v. United States, 184 F.2d 131, 138 (1st Cir. 1950) (assuming, in treason prosecution, that the Fourth Amendment applies to a search of a citizen's apartment by the army of occupation).

133. Johnson v. Eisentrager, 339 U.S. 763, 784 (1950). This example provides the context for Jackson's immediately succeeding observation: "Such extraterritorial application of organic law would have been so significant an innovation in the practice of governments that, if intended or apprehended, it could scarcely have failed to excite contemporary comment."

134. See Seery v. United States, 127 F. Supp. 601 (Ct. Cl. 1955) (the use of Maria Jeritza's villa in Austria as officers' club); Turney v. United States, 115 F. Supp. 457 (Ct. Cl. 1953) (the taking of radar equipment in postindependence Philippines).

135. Kinsella v. Krueger, 351 U.S. 470, 475 (1956); Reid v. Covert, 351 U.S. 487, 488 (1956) (following *Krueger*).

136. See Reid v. Covert, 354 U.S. 1, 65 (1957) (Harlan, J., concurring); Krueger, 351 U.S. at 483–85 ("Reservation of Mr. Justice Frankfurter"); id. at 486 (Warren, C.J., dissenting).

137. 354 U.S. at 5–6 (footnotes omitted).

138. 260 U.S. 94 (1922).

139. See 354 U.S. at 8–9, 12 & nn. This was only fair, since White had also conflated them, for the opposite purpose, in Hawaii v. Mankichi, 190 U.S. 197, 220 (1903) (White, J., concurring), and Justice Clark had conflated them in the first hearing of *Reid v. Covert*; see Kinsella v. Krueger, 351 U.S. 470, 474–76, 479 (1956).

140. 354 U.S. at 14.

141. 354 U.S. at 14 ("Moreover, it is our judgment that neither the cases nor their reasoning should be given any further expansion").

142. 354 U.S. at 9 ("[W]e can find no warrant, in logic or otherwise, for picking and choosing among the remarkable collection of 'Thou shalt nots' which were explicitly fastened on all departments and agencies of the Federal government by the Constitution and its Amendments").

143. See, e.g., Adamson v. California, 332 U.S. 46, 70–71, 90–92 (1947) (Black, J., dissenting).

144. 354 U.S. at 6; see Acts 22:25–27. Black's citation ironically recalled the use of the same episode by Justice Jackson to support what Black considered an overemphasis on citizenship in Johnson v. Eisentrager, 339 U.S. 763, 769 (1950); see id. at 798 (Black, J., dissenting).

145. 354 U.S. at 6 (quoting 2 Clode, Military Forces of the Crown); see Barbara

Black, The Constitution of Empire: The Case for the Colonists, 124 U. Pa. L. Rev. 1157 (1976).

146. 354 U.S. at 6–7.

147. John Marshall Harlan (1899–1971) was the grandson of the elder John Marshall Harlan (1833–1911).

148. See, e.g., Rochin v. California, 342 U.S. 165 (1952); Poe v. Ullman, 367 U.S. 497 (1961) (Harlan, J., dissenting).

149. 354 U.S. at 51, 56 (Frankfurter, J., concurring).

150. Id. at 53 (citations omitted).

151. Id. at 75 (Harlan, J., concurring).

152. Id. at 44–45 (Frankfurter, J., concurring).

153. Id. at 75–76 (Harlan, J., concurring). He reiterated this view, with Frank-furter's agreement, in his dissenting opinion in Kinsella v. United States ex rel. Singleton, 361 U.S. 234, 258 (1960) (Harlan, J., joined by Frankfurter, J., dissent-ing).

154. See 354 U.S. at 75 (Harlan, J.); 354 U.S. at 51 (Frankfurter, J.).

155. The same may be said of Chief Justice Burger's recasting, whether deliber-ate or inadvertent, of the test for the applicability of constitutional rights in an unin-corporated territory in Torres v. Puerto Rico, 442 U.S. 465 (1979).

156. 361 U.S. 234, 249 (1960) (Harlan, J., joined by Frankfurter, J., dissenting).

157. See Kinsella v. United States ex rel. Singleton, 361 U.S. 234 (1960) (ex-tending Reid v. Covert to dependents of service personnel accused of noncapital crimes); Grisham v. Hagan, 361 U.S. 278 (1960) (extending it from dependents of service personnel to civilian employees of the armed forces accused of capital crimes); and McElroy v. Guagliardo, 361 U.S. 281 (1960) (extending it to civilian employees of the armed forces accused of noncapital crimes). Clark's opinions do not include the same rhetorical emphasis that Black had placed on citizenship, but neither do they explicitly argue for expanding the coverage of the case to nonci-tizens. Justices Charles Whittaker and Potter Stewart concurred in the dependent case but were willing to treat civilian employees as if they were soldiers and so dissented in those cases; their opinion did call attention to the citizenship of all these defendants. Singleton, 361 U.S. at 259–61.

CHAPTER SIX

1. See, e.g., Act of May 10, 1800, ch. 51, 2 Stat. 20 (forbidding participation by United States citizens and residents in the slave trade from one foreign country to another).

2. See Weedin v. Chin Bow, 274 U.S. 657 (1927); United States v. Wong Kim Ark, 169 U.S. 649 (1898).

3. Reid v. Covert, 357 U.S. 1, 14 (1957).

4. 494 U.S. 259 (1990).

5. See, e.g., Ramirez Arellano v. Weinberger, 745 F.2d 1500 (D.C. Cir. 1984) (due process protection against the military use of property in Honduras), vacated as moot, 471 U.S. 1113 (1985); Powell v. Zuckert, 366 F.2d 634 (D.C. Cir. 1966) (evidence seized under general warrant in Japan is inadmissible in personnel ac-tion); Berlin Democratic Club v. Rumsfeld, 410 F. Supp. 144 (D.D.C. 1976) (First,

Fourth, and Sixth Amendment claims of citizens in Germany). Criminal procedure cases are collected in Stephen Saltzburg, The Reach of the Bill of Rights beyond the Terra Firma of the United States, 20 Va. J. Int'l L. 742 (1980).

6. See, e.g., Cardenas v. Smith, 733 F.2d 909, 915–17 (D.C. Cir. 1984) (leaving open the constitutional rights of nonresident alien regarding U.S. interference with Swiss bank account); Sami v. United States, 617 F.2d 755, 773–74 (D.C. Cir. 1979) (finding no violation of rights in arrest of alien by foreign government at U.S. request, even if such rights exist); United States v. Rubies, 612 F.2d 397 (9th Cir. 1979) (assuming that alien on high seas has Fourth Amendment rights, the search was nonetheless reasonable).

7. See United States v. Toscanino, 500 F.2d 267 (2d Cir. 1974) (finding Fourth and Fifth Amendments applicable to alleged search, interrogation under torture, and abduction of alien from Uruguay by federal agents). One might also so characterize United States v. Tiede, 86 F.R.D. 227 (U.S. Ct. for Berlin 1979) (finding constitutional right to jury trial in prosecution by U.S. authorities in Berlin).

8. See, e.g., Ralpho v. Bell, 569 F.2d 607, 618–19 (D.C. Cir.), reh'g denied, 569 F.2d 636 (D.C. Cir. 1977) (Trust Territory); Canal Zone v. Scott, 502 F.2d 566 (5th Cir. 1974); United States v. Husband R. (Roach), 453 F.2d 1054 (5th Cir. 1971), cert. denied, 406 U.S. 935 (1972) (Canal Zone); Juda v. United States, 6 Cl. Ct. 441 (1984) (Trust Territory); United States v. Tiede, 86 F.R.D. 227 (U.S. Ct. for Berlin 1979).

9. Restatement (Third) of the Foreign Relations Law of the United States § 721 (1987); id. § 722 comment m ("Although the matter has not been authoritatively adjudicated, at least some actions by the United States in respect of foreign nationals outside the country are also subject to constitutional limitations").

10. See Harold Hongju Koh, The National Security Constitution: Sharing Power after the Iran-Contra Affair 208–10 (1990).

11. See, e.g., Restatement (Third) of the Foreign Relations Law of the United States §§ 402–416 (1987); Symposium, Extraterritorial Application of Economic Legislation, 50 Law & Contemp. Probs. No. 3 (Summer 1987).

12. See, e.g., United States v. Robinson, 843 F.2d 1 (1st Cir. 1988) (ex post facto clause); United States v. Ospina, 823 F.2d 429 (11th Cir. 1987) (grand jury); United States v. Gonzalez, 776 F.2d 931 (11th Cir. 1985) (due process notice requirements and ex post facto clause); United States v. Henriquez, 731 F.2d 131 (2d Cir. 1984) (due process and double jeopardy).

13. See, e.g., United States v. Williams, 617 F.2d 1063 (5th Cir. 1980) (en banc); id. at 1090 (Roney, J., specially concurring); United States v. Rubies, 612 F.2d 397 (9th Cir. 1979); United States v. Toscanino, 500 F.2d 267 (2d Cir. 1974); id. at 281 (Anderson, J., concurring in result).

14. 494 U.S. 259 (1990).

15. See 494 U.S. at 275–78 (Kennedy, J., concurring). The other three members of the plurality were Justices Byron White, Sandra Day O'Connor, and Antonin Scalia. Justice John Paul Stevens concurred only in the judgment, finding the search reasonable and the warrant clause inapplicable outside the jurisdiction of the United States "because American magistrates have no power to authorize such searches" and finding broader comment unnecessary. Id. at 279 & n. Justice Blackmun dissented, on grounds relating to the unreasonableness of the search, but he also be-

lieved that the warrant clause was inapplicable. Justice Kennedy addressed the warrant issue at length, but it is difficult to ascertain what position he took regarding reasonableness.

16. 494 U.S. at 265. This argument, which Rehnquist characterized as "by no means conclusive," seems to be a makeweight, and the justices of the plurality seem not to have considered its implications carefully. The idea that "the People" of the Preamble, "the People" entitled to elect the House of Representatives, or "the People" to whom powers not delegated were reserved by the Tenth Amendment includes resident aliens, let alone the broader class described in Rehnquist's opinion, cannot be reconciled with his usual views on aliens' rights. See Toll v. Moreno, 458 U.S. 1, 25–49 (1982) (Rehnquist, J., dissenting); Sugarman v. Dougall, 413 U.S. 634, 649–64 (1973) (Rehnquist, J., dissenting).

17. See 494 U.S. at 267–68 (citing Act of Feb. 9, 1799, ch. 2, 1 Stat. 613); Murray v. The Schooner Charming Betsy, 6 U.S. (2 Cranch) 64 (1804).

18. Moreover, Rehnquist emphasized that Black's opinion in Reid v. Covert was only a plurality opinion, and that Frankfurter and Harlan had concurred on narrower grounds that did not guarantee even a citizen full constitutional rights in foreign territory. 494 U.S. at 269–70.

19. He understandably did not mention the example of mixed law-enforcement and non-law-enforcement activity that could not have been far from the justices' minds—the December 1989 invasion of Panama to topple and arrest General Noriega. See Marian Nash Leich, Contemporary Practice of the United States Relating to International Law, 84 Am. J. Int'l L. 536, 547 (1990) (quoting the State Department's identification of U.S. objectives as "(1) to protect American lives; (2) to assist the lawful and democratically elected government of Panama in fulfilling its international obligations; (3) to seize and arrest General Noriega, an indicted drug trafficker; and (4) to defend the integrity of United States rights under the Panama Canal treaties"). Cf. United States v. Noriega, 746 F.2d 1506, 1531–32 & n. 28 (S.D. Fla. 1990) (following *Verdugo-Urquidez*, treating the applicability of due process as left open but rejecting defendant's standing to claim that the invasion of Panama to effect his arrest violated due process rights of Panamanian citizens killed or injured by invasion).

20. 494 U.S. at 275 (brackets in original). Rehnquist did not explain why the extraterritorial constitutional rights of American citizens might not also hinder these goals. In fact, Rehnquist was quoting from Perez v. Brownell, 356 U.S. 44, 57 (1958) (upholding the involuntary denationalization of U.S. citizens who vote in foreign elections as a rational means of achieving foreign policy goals), overruled, Afroyim v. Rusk, 387 U.S. 253 (1967).

21. 494 U.S. at 269 (quoting Johnson v. Eisentrager, 339 U.S. 763, 770 (1950)). It is by no means clear that Jackson was referring to an ascending scale of constitutional, rather than statutory, rights.

22. 494 U.S. at 275 (Kennedy, J., concurring).

23. Id. at 278.

24. Id. at 277–78 (quoting Reid v. Covert, 354 U.S. at 75).

25. Id. at 278.

26. 494 U.S. at 284 (Brennan, J., joined by Marshall, J., dissenting). He quoted the relevant passage from Madison's Report on the Alien and Sedition Acts, to

which the Court's attention had been called in the ACLU's brief amicus curiae, after a discussion between its author and the present author.

27. 494 U.S. at 297–98 (Blackmun, J., dissenting) (emphasis in original).

28. Id. at 297.

29. It could be argued, for example, that a warrant to search a residence is required only when its issuance can serve the three classical purposes of a warrant: to make the officer's intrusion into the residence privileged (as a defense against civil or criminal liability), to form the basis for an obligation of the home owner not to interfere with the search (typically backed by a criminal sanction), and to safeguard constitutional privacy interests. Cf. Act of July 31, 1789, ch. 5, §§ 24, 27, 1 Stat. 43 (customs warrants); Telford Taylor, Two Studies in Constitutional Interpretation 41–44 (1969) (emphasizing the affirmative character of warrants); 4 William Blackstone, Commentaries on the Laws of England *288 (1979 reprint) ("It is therefore in fact no warrant at all: for it will not justify the officer who acts under it"). Interpreting the warrant clause this way would seem, however, to imply that citizens in foreign countries may also be unprotected, and that both aliens and citizens could still be protected on the high seas and in enclaves for which a true warrant can be issued.

30. A fourth theoretical alternative, treating the people of each country in accordance with their own constitution, has little relevance now that so many countries have constitutions with substantial individual rights guarantees; the United States would not wish to be bound by foreign constitutional rights, and it would not be prepared to extend voting rights to foreign populations in return for the opportunity to apply its own laws to them.

31. Thomas Hobbes, Leviathan 360 (C.B. MacPherson ed. 1985). The third approach may be viewed as a special case of the second approach, with the additional Hobbesian assumption that natural law imposes no constraints in this context.

32. The Federalist No. 41 (James Madison).

33. U.S. Const., art. I, § 9, cl. 8.

34. Id. art. I, § 8, cl. 1.

35. See, e.g., Louis Henkin, The President and International Law, 80 Am. J. Int'l L. 930 (1986).

36. See, e.g., Williams v. Florida, 399 U.S. 78, 118 (1970) (Harlan, J., concurring in part and dissenting in part); Laurence H. Tribe, American Constitutional Law 701 (2d ed. 1988).

37. See Hobbes, note 31 supra at 360; Paul Stephan, Constitutional Limits on the Struggle against International Terrorism: Revisiting the Rights of Overseas Aliens, 19 Conn. L. Rev. 831, 850–51 (1987); see also Thomas Pogge, Realizing Rawls 220–27 (1989) (giving a critical description of the modern world order in Hobbesian terms).

38. See Hobbes, note 31 supra at 272–73, 345.

39. See David Hume, Of the Original Contract, in Essays, Moral, Political and Literary 475 (Eugene F. Miller ed. 1985); see, e.g., David Gauthier, Moral Dealing: Contract, Ethics and Reason 53–57 (1990); Jean Hampton, Hobbes and the Social Contract Tradition 266–79 (1986); John Rawls, A Theory of Justice 12 (1971).

40. As opposed to limits derived from international law, with which Congress is under no constitutional compulsion to comply.

41. Surely the passage of legislation within the United States is not sufficient to trigger constitutional protection unavailable outside its borders; it does not make sense to say that decisions made by executive officials overseas are not constrained by constitutional rights, but that enactment of legislation by Congress including legislation defining the powers of those officials is so constrained.

42. This was true, for example, under the consular court system upheld in *In re Ross*, 140 U.S. 453 (1891).

43. See, e.g., Asahi Metal Indus. Co. v. Superior Court, 480 U.S. 102 (1987); Helicopteros Nacionales de Colombia v. Hall, 466 U.S. 408 (1984); Insurance Corp. of Ireland v. Compagnie de Bauxites de Guinee, 456 U.S. 694 (1982).

44. Verdugo-Urquidez, 494 U.S. at 278 (Kennedy, J., concurring) (quoting Reid v. Covert, 354 U.S. 1, 74 (1957) (Harlan, J., concurring)).

45. See Kinsella v. United States ex rel. Singleton, 361 U.S. 234, 249 (1960) (Harlan, J., dissenting); Reid v. Covert, 354 U.S. at 74 (Harlan, J., concurring).

46. I do not mean, however, to deny the plausibility of a normative argument, independent of American constitutional history, that more protections may be required to justify the exercise of authority over individuals who do not have the right to vote in United States elections, are not the primary intended beneficiaries of United States law, and have no avenue for removing themselves from the class of the governed.

47. Justice Stevens, who concurred opaquely in the result in *Verdugo-Urquidez*, might someday adopt such an approach; on prior occasions he has made unusually clear statements of belief in suprapositive rights. See, e.g., Cruzan v. Director, Mo. Dep't of Health, 497 U.S. 261, 343 (1990) (Stevens, J., dissenting); Meachum v. Fano, 427 U.S. 215, 230 (1976) (Stevens, J., dissenting).

48. This mode of implementation differs greatly from other, subconstitutional modes such as adopting international human rights norms as statutory law binding on the executive, or painstaking voluntary compliance with those norms as international law by Congress. This book is not intended to express any position on subconstitutional modes of implementation of international human rights.

49. See, e.g., Restatement (Third) of Foreign Relations Law § 115 (1987).

50. See, e.g., Stanford v. Kentucky, 492 U.S. 361 (1989) (upholding the death penalty for crimes committed by juveniles); Heath v. Alabama, 474 U.S. 82 (1985) (permitting as many successive prosecutions as federalism requires, despite double jeopardy clause); DeShaney v. Winnebago County Dep't of Social Servs., 489 U.S. 189 (1989) (emphasizing the negative character of constitutional rights); Lindsey v. Normet, 405 U.S. 56 (1972) (no constitutional right to housing); Dandridge v. Williams, 397 U.S. 471 (1970) (no constitutional right to welfare benefits).

CHAPTER SEVEN

1. The first case, Kleindienst v. Mandel, 408 U.S. 753 (1972), scrutinized an executive denial of a waiver of excludability, to protect the First Amendment rights of citizens who had invited the alien to speak in the United States. The second case, Fiallo v. Bell, 430 U.S. 787 (1977), scrutinized immigration legislation that prevented the reunification of illegitimate children with their fathers, in response to

equal protection and due process family right claims. The latter case was not explicit about whose rights were at stake.

2. In immigration procedure, there is no suggestion that the constitutionality of procedures is a political question. Instead, the Court has held that deportation procedure and the procedure for the exclusion of returning permanent residents are subject to normal principles of procedural due process and that other aliens have no right to procedural due process in exclusion. See Landon v. Plasencia, 459 U.S. 21 (1982); United States ex rel. Knauff v. Shaughnessy, 338 U.S. 537 (1950). The inapplicability of procedural due process in exclusion lacks any current justification; earlier explanations in terms of extraterritoriality (which was always partly a fiction, because exclusion takes place within the United States) and the distinction between rights and privileges are no longer tenable. See, e.g., David A. Martin, Due Process and Membership in the National Community: Political Asylum and Beyond, 44 U. Pitt. L. Rev. 165 (1983); T. Alexander Aleinikoff, Aliens, Due Process and "Community Ties": A Response to Martin, 44 U. Pitt. L. Rev. 237 (1983); Hiroshi Motomura, The Curious Evolution of Immigration Law: Procedural Surrogates for Substantive Constitutional Rights, 92 Colum. L. Rev. 1625 (1992).

3. 130 U.S. 581 (1889).

4. The certificate had appeared legally binding on Chae Chan Ping's departure from the United States, on the basis of both a treaty and a federal statute, but in the interim Congress repealed the statute and violated the treaty. The Court held that Congress's most recent expression of will governed.

5. See, e.g., id. at 595 ("It seemed impossible for them to assimilate with our people or to make any change in their habits or mode of living").

6. Id. at 603–04.

7. Id. at 606.

8. 149 U.S. 698 (1893). Field, Justice David Brewer, and Chief Justice Melville Fuller filed separate dissents. Because Justice John Marshall Harlan did not participate, being in Europe to participate in the Bering Sea fur seal arbitration, the decision was that of a bare majority of the Court; correspondence indicates that Harlan would also have dissented. See Alan F. Westin, Stephen J. Field and the Headnote to O'Neil v. Vermont: A Snapshot of the Fuller Court at Work, 67 Yale L.J. 363, 380–82 (1958).

9. See id. at 754 (Field, J., dissenting); see also id. at 738 (Brewer, J., dissenting); id. at 761–62 (Fuller, C.J., dissenting).

10. 149 U.S. at 707.

11. This estimation is not original. The view that the arguments for constitutionally unlimited immigration power do not hold water is nearly universal in modern scholarly opinion. See, e.g., T. Alexander Aleinikoff, Citizens, Aliens, Membership and the Constitution, 7 Const. Commentary 9 (1990); Louis Henkin, The Constitution and United States Sovereignty: A Century of Chinese Exclusion and Its Progeny, 100 Harv. L. Rev. 853 (1987); Stephen H. Legomsky, Immigration and the Principle of Plenary Congressional Power, 1984 Sup. Ct. Rev. 255, 269–70; Martin, note 2 supra; James A.R. Nafziger, The General Admission of Aliens under International Law, 77 Am. J. Int'l L. 804 (1983).

12. See, e.g., Michael Akehurst, A Modern Introduction to International Law

14–16, 70 (6th ed. 1987); Jules Lobel, The Limits of Constitutional Power: Conflicts between Foreign Policy and International Law, 71 Va. L. Rev. 1071, 1110–13 (1985).

13. See Louis Henkin, Rights: American and Human, 79 Colum. L. Rev. 405, 407–10 (1979).

14. See The Movement of Persons across Borders 49–64, 89–97 (Louis B. Sohn & Thomas Buergenthal eds. 1992) (describing international limits on denial of admission to aliens and expulsion of aliens, including requirements of nondiscrimination, respect for family unity, nonreturn of refugees, avoidance of inhuman or degrading treatment, and procedural regularity).

15. See, e.g., John Guendelsberger, The Right to Family Unification in French and United States Immigration Law, 21 Cornell J. Int'l L. 1 (1988); Gerald L. Neuman, Immigration and Judicial Review in the Federal Republic of Germany, 23 N.Y.U. J. Int'l L. & Pol. 35 (1990).

16. See Legomsky, note 11 supra at 269–70.

17. Nishimura Ekiu v. United States, 142 U.S. 651, 659 (1892), and Fong Yue Ting v. United States, 149 U.S. 698, 704 (1893), respectively. Field reacted against this reasoning in the latter case, arguing in dissent that the "government of the United States is one of limited and delegated powers. It takes nothing from the usages or the former action of European governments, nor does it take any power by any supposed inherent sovereignty." Id. at 757.

18. See Head Money Cases, 112 U.S. 580, 591, 600 (1884); Henderson v. New York, 92 U.S. 259, 270–71 (1876); Chy Lung v. Freeman, 92 U.S. 275, 280 (1876).

19. Alexander Addison, Analysis of the Report of the Committee of the Virginia Assembly (1800), reprinted in 2 Charles S. Hyneman & Donald S. Lutz, American Political Writing during the Founding Era, 1760–1805, at 1070 (1983). See Chapter Four.

20. 252 U.S. 416, 433 (1920) ("Acts of Congress are the supreme law of the land only when made in pursuance of the Constitution, while treaties are declared to be so when made under the authority of the United States. It is open to question whether the authority of the United States means more than the formal acts prescribed to make the convention"). That suggestion was rejected in Reid v. Covert, 354 U.S. 1 (1957), which explained the distinction between statutes and treaties as intended to ensure the binding character of the treaties that the United States entered into before the ratification of the Constitution.

21. 299 U.S. 304 (1936).

22. Reid v. Covert, 354 U.S. 1, 5–6 (1957) (plurality opinion) (footnotes omitted). See also United States v. Verdugo-Urquidez, 494 U.S. 259, 277 (1990) (Kennedy, J., concurring) ("[T]he Government may act only as the Constitution authorizes, whether the actions in question are foreign or domestic").

23. 130 U.S. at 595.

24. The 1880 census found 105,465 Chinese in the United States, representing 0.002 percent of the total U.S. population. See Ronald Takaki, Strangers from a Different Shore: A History of Asian Americans 110–11 (1989).

25. See, e.g., Kenneth L. Karst, Belonging to America: Equal Citizenship and the Constitution 179–81 (1989); Hans Kohn, American Nationalism: An Interpretive Essay 8–9 (1957); but see Michael Kammen, A Machine That Would Go of

Itself: The Constitution in American Culture (1986) (tracing the coexistence of cult of the Constitution and ignorance of its contents).

26. I mean not to cast doubt on the constitutional or libertarian allegiances of other countries but simply to leave them out of the present argument.

27. 198 U.S. 253, 263 (1905).

28. See, e.g., Nishimura Ekiu v. United States, 142 U.S. 651, 660 (1892) ("An alien immigrant, prevented from landing by any such officer claiming authority to do so under an act of Congress, and thereby restrained of his liberty, is doubtless entitled to a writ of habeas corpus to ascertain whether the restraint is lawful").

29. See, e.g., Shapiro v. Thompson, 394 U.S. 618 (1969) (interstate travel); California v. Aznavorian, 439 U.S. 170 (1978) (international travel); Aptheker v. Secretary of State, 378 U.S. 500 (1964) (international travel).

30. Act of July 27, 1868, ch. 249, § 1, 15 Stat. 223. The statute was intended to vindicate the rights of naturalized citizens of the United States against the claims of their former countries to their continued allegiance. See Abner J. Mikva & Gerald L. Neuman, The Hostage Crisis and the "Hostage Act," 49 U. Chi. L. Rev. 292, 306–36 (1982).

31. See, e.g., Reno v. Flores, 113 S. Ct. 1439, 1454 (1993) (freedom from institutional confinement); DeNieva v. Reyes, 966 F.2d 480 (9th Cir. 1992) (right to international travel); Sentner v. Colarelli, 145 F. Supp. 569, 580–81 (E.D. Mo. 1956) (interstate travel), aff'd per curiam sub nom. Barton v. Sentner, 353 U.S. 963 (1957).

32. But see Johnson v. Eisentrager, 339 U.S. 763 (1950) (pre–*Reid v. Covert* case denying the extraterritorial applicability of habeas corpus to enemy aliens in the immediate postwar period).

33. See Shapiro v. Thompson, 394 U.S. 618, 629–30 (1969).

34. See Foucha v. Louisiana, 112 S. Ct. 1780, 1785, 1788 (1992); id. at 1804–08 (Thomas, J., dissenting).

35. Haig v. Agee, 453 U.S. 280, 306 (1981); see also Regan v. Wald, 468 U.S. 222 (1984) (upholding the restriction on travel to Cuba as limiting Cuba's access to hard currency).

36. Michael H. v. Gerald D., 491 U.S. 110, 127 n.6 (1989).

37. See, e.g., id. at 131 (O'Connor, J., concurring in part); id. at 136–41 (Brennan, J., dissenting); Planned Parenthood of Southeastern Pennsylvania v. Casey, 112 S. Ct. 2791, 2804–05 (1992) (opinion of O'Connor, Kennedy, and Souter, JJ.).

38. See, e.g., Galvan v. Press, 347 U.S. 522 (1954); Harisiades v. Shaughnessy, 342 U.S. 580 (1952); Kaplan v. Tod, 267 U.S. 228 (1925); Low Wah Suey v. Backus, 225 U.S. 460 (1912); Fong Yue Ting v. United States, 149 U.S. 698 (1893).

39. 194 U.S. 279 (1904).

40. Id. at 292. Nonetheless, Chief Justice Fuller then went on to spend three more pages explaining why advocates of anarchism were sufficiently dangerous that it was not unconstitutional to exclude them. Justice Brewer's concurrence reserved the question "what rights [Turner] would have if he were only what is called by way of differentiation a philosophical anarchist, one who simply entertains and expresses the opinion that all government is a mistake, and that society would be better off without any." 194 U.S. at 296. See also Owen M. Fiss, Troubled Beginnings of the Modern State, 1888–1910, at 340 (1993) ("[T]he status of the speaker in the

constitutional community was not crucial to the Court's thinking [in Turner]. The strong arm of the censor would have been allowed if a citizen had said the same things").

41. A broader implication of the language, that an excludable alien within the United States has no constitutional rights at all, would be inconsistent with Chief Justice Fuller's own dissent in Fong Yue Ting v. United States, 149 U.S. 698 (1893), and the unanimous holding in Wong Wing v. United States, 163 U.S. 228 (1896), and would extend far more broadly than the context called for. Turner was not being criminally prosecuted for his speech, or even deported for anything other than his initial excludability.

42. McAuliffe v. New Bedford, 20 N.E. 517, 518 (Mass. 1892).

43. See, e.g., Richard Epstein, Foreword: Unconstitutional Conditions, State Power, and the Limits of Consent, 102 Harv. L. Rev. 1 (1988); Seth F. Kreimer, Allocational Sanctions: The Problem of Negative Rights in a Positive State, 132 U. Pa. L. Rev. 1293 (1984); Kathleen Sullivan, Unconstitutional Conditions, 102 S. Ct. Rev. 1415 (1989); William Van Alstyne, The Demise of the Right-Privilege Distinction in Constitutional Law, 81 Harv. L. Rev. 1439 (1968); but see Cass Sunstein, Why the Unconstitutional Conditions Doctrine Is an Anachronism (with Particular Reference to Religion, Speech, and Abortion), 70 B.U. L. Rev. 593 (1990) (the constitutionality of conditions should be scrutinized, but there is no need for a separate doctrine of "unconstitutional conditions"). For present purposes, it is interesting to note that some of the Court's earliest struggles with the unconstitutional conditions doctrine involved a state's "exclusion" of "foreign" corporations, i.e., a refusal to allow a corporation incorporated in a different state to carry on business within the state. See Epstein at 31–38; Kreimer at 1303–08.

44. More precisely, the incidental restriction must be unrelated to the suppression of ideas, must further a substantial government interest, and must be more effective than alternative methods that would also further the interest while burdening less speech. See, e.g., Turner Broadcasting System, Inc. v. FCC, 114 S. Ct. 2445, 2469 (1994); United States v. O'Brien, 391 U.S. 367 (1968). If exclusion were conceptualized as a content-neutral "time, place or manner restriction" on speech, then it would also be necessary to ask whether it left the alien ample alternative channels for communication. See City of Ladue v. Gilleo, 114 S. Ct. 2038, 2046 (1994).

45. 408 U.S. 753 (1972).

46. Whether these consequences should be considered incidental instead of intended is problematic, given the complex set of special qualifications, exemptions, waiver possibilities, and forms of relief turning on family relationships in current immigration law.

47. 431 U.S. 494 (1977).

48. 430 U.S. 787 (1977). The opinion does not make wholly clear which of the many factors in the carefully structured litigation justified judicial scrutiny. The statutory discrimination against the relationship between illegitimate children and their fathers involved fundamental due process rights, gender discrimination, and illegitimacy discrimination; the plaintiffs included both citizens and permanent residents, as well as their excluded alien children or fathers.

For an unusual case holding that a departure control order issued to *prevent* an alien child's removal from the country violated his parents' rights, see Polovchak v. Meese, 774 F.2d 731 (7th Cir. 1985).

49. See Reno v. Flores, 113 S. Ct. 1439 (1993) (detention of alien children pending deportation). The Supreme Court's cases on immigration *procedure* also treat deportation as the deprivation of a liberty interest. See, e.g., Yamataya v. Fisher, 189 U.S. 86 (1903); Bridges v. Wixon, 326 U.S. 135, 154 (1945).

50. The liberty of lawful residents to remain would be enough of an innovation that I will not attempt here to construct an argument by which unlawful residence would ripen into a liberty to remain.

51. See, e.g., Harisiades v. Shaugnessy, 342 U.S. 580, 585 (1952).

52. See 8 U.S.C. §§ 1427(a), 1430(a). (There are also further exceptions that shorten the period in special cases.) I am not offering to demonstrate that the current naturalization criteria are perfectly just or flawlessly applied. See, e.g., David S. North, The Long Gray Welcome: A Study of the American Naturalization Program, 21 Int'l Migration Rev. 311 (1985); Ricardo Gonzalez Cedillo, A Constitutional Analysis of the English Literacy Requirement of the Naturalization Act, 14 St. Mary's L.J. 899 (1983).

53. Harisiades, 342 U.S. at 585–87.

54. See, e.g., Ludecke v. Watkins, 335 U.S. 160 (1948) (applying Alien Enemies Act); Narenji v. Civiletti, 617 F.2d 745 (D.C. Cir. 1979), cert. denied, 446 U.S. 957 (1980) (upholding retaliatory investigation of visa status of Iranian students after seizure of U.S. embassy in Tehran).

55. See James A.R. Nafziger, Review of Visa Denials by Consular Officers, 66 Wash. L. Rev. 1 (1991).

56. Treating the limits on the exclusion of aliens as a political question reproduces within the separation of powers Vattel's distinction between "internal" constraints of principle and "external" constraints of enforceable international law. As explained in Chapter One, Vattel contended that a nation was internally bound to admit aliens when it could do so without causing substantial harm to its own interests, but the nation reserved the right to make the evaluation of harm for itself, and so there was no enforceable external norm. Field's argument denied to the internal judiciary, as well as to an external international forum, the authority to override the political branches' evaluation of the need to exclude.

57. 5 U.S. (1 Cranch) 137, 170 (1803).

58. Baker v. Carr, 369 U.S. 186, 217 (1962).

59. See Louis Henkin, Is There a "Political Question" Doctrine?, 85 Yale L.J. 597 (1976). In our example, the third explanation would be that courts might decline to enjoin wars, even unconstitutional wars, for practical reasons, such as the difficulty of extricating troops safely from a war when the enemy knows of the injunction.

60. Id. at 610–13.

61. See, e.g., Thomas M. Franck, Political Questions/Judicial Answers: Does the Rule of Law Apply to Foreign Affairs? (1992); Henkin, note 59 supra; Martin H. Redish, Judicial Review and the "Political Question," 79 Nw. U. L. Rev. 1031 (1985); Michael E. Tigar, Judicial Power, the "Political Question Doctrine," and Foreign Relations, 17 UCLA L. Rev. 1135 (1970).

62. Baker v. Carr, 369 U.S. 186, 211–12 (1962) (footnotes omitted).

63. See Narenji v. Civiletti, 617 F.2d 745 (D.C. Cir. 1979), cert. denied, 446 U.S. 957 (1980) (upholding crackdown on Iranian students); Presidential Proclamation No. 5829, 53 Fed. Reg. 22,289 (1988) (suspension of entry for certain Panamanians).

64. But see Narenji v. Civiletti, 481 F.Supp. 1132 (D.D.C. 1979), rev'd, 617 F.2d 745 (D.C. Cir. 1979), cert. denied, 446 U.S. 957 (1980) ("[T]he reasons advanced for the government's discriminatory actions make it clear they do not serve that interest, there being at best a dubious relationship between the presence of Iranian students in this country, whether legally or otherwise, and the safety and freedom of the hostages").

65. 92 U.S. 275, 279 (1876).

66. See, e.g., Barclays Bank PLC v. Franchise Tax Bd., 114 S. Ct. 2268 (1994) (upholding state franchise tax against foreign commerce clause challenge).

67. See, e.g., Richard B. Lillich, The Soering Case, 85 Am. J. Int'l L. 128 (1991) (discussing ruling by European Court of Human Rights barring United Kingdom's extradition of German national to Virginia because of inhumanity of the "death row phenomenon").

68. 430 U.S. 787, 796 (1977) (quoting from Mathews v. Diaz, 426 U.S. 67, 81–82 (1976)).

69. Michael Walzer, Spheres of Justice: A Defense of Pluralism and Equality 61 (1983).

70. A more difficult question is whether a particular level of numerical limitation on family-based immigration violates familial rights. Outside the immigration field, fundamental rights are rarely subject to explicit rationing. But see Turner Broadcasting System, Inc. v. FCC, 114 S. Ct. 2445, 2456–57 (1994) (describing scarcity rationale for broadcast licensing). Resolving this question could require an estimate of the country's current capacity to absorb immigrants, which might be "an initial policy determination of a kind clearly for nonjudicial discretion."

71. See, e.g., Kaplan v. Tod, 267 U.S. 228 (1925); Low Wah Suey v. Backus, 225 U.S. 460 (1912); Zartarian v. Billings, 204 U.S. 170 (1907).

72. Kleindienst v. Mandel, 408 U.S. 753 (1972).

73. See, e.g., Paul Brest, The Conscientious Legislator's Guide to Constitutional Interpretation, 27 Stan. L. Rev. 585 (1975); Lawrence Gene Sager, Fair Measure: The Legal Status of Underenforced Constitutional Norms, 91 Harv. L. Rev. 122 (1978).

CHAPTER EIGHT

1. See, e.g., [European] Convention for the Protection of Human Rights and Fundamental Freedoms, Nov. 4, 1950, art. 16, 213 U.N.T.S. 221 ("Nothing in Articles 10, 11 and 14 shall be regarded as preventing the High Contracting Parties from imposing restrictions on the political activity of aliens"). Articles 10 and 11 protect freedom of expression, assembly, and association, and Article 14 prohibits discrimination.

2. Cabell v. Chavez-Salido, 454 U.S. 432, 439–40 (1982) (White, J.). A much-discussed series of cases between 1973 and 1984 evolved an equal protection ap-

proach under which the states, though usually forbidden to discriminate against their alien residents, are free to exclude them from a fairly broad category of public employment viewed as closely related to the process of self-government. See, e.g., Harold H. Koh, Equality with a Human Face: Justice Blackmun and the Equal Protection of Aliens, 8 Hamline L. Rev. 51 (1985). The Court summarily rejected a claim that *denial* of the franchise to aliens violates equal protection in Skafte v. Rorex, 430 U.S. 961 (1977), *dismissing appeal from* 533 P.2d 830 (Colo. 1976).

3. Ambach v. Norwick, 441 U.S. 68 (1979).

4. Id. at 81 n. 15; see Chapter Four.

5. The Supreme Court has not recently reexamined the traditional exclusion from the electorate of "insane persons." See Oregon v. Mitchell, 400 U.S. 112, 214 (1971) (opinion of Harlan, J.). It is often omitted from summaries of voting rights law. But see Manhattan State Citizens' Group v. Bass, 524 F. Supp. 1270 (S.D.N.Y. 1981) (disenfranchisement of all involuntarily committed persons overbroad; adjudication of incompetence required).

6. 384 U.S. 641 (1966).

7. Id. at 649; see also Cardona v. Power, 384 U.S. 672, 674 (1966) (remanding case to determine whether ruling on the constitutionality of literacy requirement as applied to persons not covered by the Voting Rights Act can be avoided). The earlier case was Lassiter v. Northampton Election Bd., 360 U.S. 45 (1959).

8. 384 U.S. at 656.

9. Id. at 652.

10. See U.S. Const., art. I, § 2, cl. 2 (representatives must be inhabitants of states from which they are elected); id. § 3, cl. 3 (the same appliesto senators); art. II, § 1, cl. 3 (members of the electoral college must cast one of their two votes for an inhabitant of a state other than their own); amend. XII (same); amend. XIV, § 1 (persons born or naturalized in the United States are citizens of the state wherein they reside); id. § 2 (decreasing representation in House for states disenfranchising inhabitants on certain grounds).

11. Oregon v. Mitchell, 400 U.S. 112 (1970). It is fair to say that the justices' opinions conferred very little of their attention on this aspect of the statute. The government's brief provided a more explicit defense. See Brief for the United States, at 53, 57.

12. See 400 U.S. at 236–39 (opinion of Brennan, White, and Marshall, JJ.); 400 U.S. at 292 (opinion of Stewart and Blackmun, JJ., and Burger, C.J.). Justices Black and Douglas had idiosyncratic reasons for upholding the statute, and Justice Harlan considered it unconstitutional as an interference with state prerogatives. 400 U.S. at 134 (opinion of Black, J.); 400 U.S. at 147–50 (opinion of Douglas, J.); 400 U.S. at 213–16 (opinion of Harlan, J.).

13. See Overseas Citizens Voting Rights Act of 1975, Pub. L. No. 94–203, 89 Stat. 1142 (current version codified at 42 U.S.C. §§ 1973ff to 1973ff-6). Citizens who have *never* resided in the United States, however, are not enfranchised by the statute. See 42 U.S.C. § 1973ff-6(5).

14. See H.R. Rep. 649, 94th Cong., 1st Sess. 5–7 (1975).

15. See Snead v. City of Albuquerque, 663 F. Supp. 1084 (D.N.M. 1987), aff'd mem., 841 F.2d 1131, cert. denied, 485 U.S. 1009 (1988) (upholding extension of

the right to vote on city indebtedness referendum to county residents only if they own property in the city and paid property tax in preceding year); Brown v. Board of Comm'rs, 722 F. Supp. 380, 397–400 (E.D. Tenn. 1989) (extension of municipal franchise to nonresident freeholders is not unconstitutional on its face, but irrational and thus unconstitutional if multiple owners of a parcel of trivial value can all vote). See also Deibler v. City of Rehoboth Beach, 790 F.2d 328 (3d Cir. 1986) (involving qualifications for a city commission candidacy by nonresident property owners); but see id. at 331, 336 (opinion of Ziegler, J.) (doubting that enfranchising nonresidents was permissible).

Another series of cases involves enfranchisement in county service district elections of residents of a city within the county that does not participate in the service district. See, e.g., Sutton v. Escambia County Bd. of Educ., 809 F.2d 770 (11th Cir. 1987) (school district); Creel v. Freeman, 531 F.2d 286 (5th Cir.), cert. denied, 429 U.S. 1066 (1976) (school district); see also Collins v. Town of Goshen, 635 F.2d 954 (2d Cir. 1980) (water service district); Cantwell v. Hudnut, 566 F.2d 30 (7th Cir. 1977), cert. denied, 439 U.S. 1114 (1978) (police and fire service districts); but see Locklear v. North Carolina State Bd. of Educ., 514 F.2d 1152 (4th Cir. 1975) (county residents' vote unconstitutionally diluted by city residents); Hogencamp v. Lee County Bd. of Educ., 722 F.2d 720 (5th Cir. 1984) (finding that city residents had no substantial interest in county school district); Phillips v. Andress, 634 F.2d 947 (5th Cir. 1981) (same).

16. Spahos v. Mayor of Savannah Beach, 371 U.S. 206 (1962), aff'g mem. 207 F. Supp. 688 (S.D. Ga. 1962); see also Glisson v. Mayor of Savannah Beach, 346 F.2d 135 (5th Cir. 1965) (following Spahos). Although Spahos came early in the Warren Court's development of voting rights jurisprudence, the lower courts have not regarded these holdings as outdated. See, e.g., Collins v. Town of Goshen, 635 F.2d 954, 958 (2d Cir. 1980) (Friendly, J.); Brown v. Board of Comm'rs, 722 F. Supp. 380, 398 (E.D. Tenn. 1989); Ortiz v. Hernandez Colon, 385 F. Supp. 111, 115 (D.P.R. 1974), vacated and remanded for consideration of mootness, 429 U.S. 1031 (1977).

17. See Hunter v. Underwood, 471 U.S. 222 (1985) (Rehnquist, J.) (convicted felon disqualification scheme invidiously motivated by a desire to disenfranchise black voters violates equal protection).

18. See Manfred Zuleeg, Grundrechte für Ausländer: Bewährungsprobe des Verfassungsrechts, 89 Deutsches Verwaltungsblatt 341, 347–48 (1974).

19. The quote was dictum in Yick Wo v. Hopkins, 118 U.S. 356, 370 (1886), and more closely informed the result in Reynolds v. Sims, 377 U.S. 533, 562 (1964).

20. Scott v. Sandford, 60 U.S. (19 How.) 393 (1857). Chief Justice Taney contrasted white women and children, who were members of the sovereign political community without being entitled to vote, with aliens and free blacks, who in some states were entitled to vote without being (in his view) members of the sovereign political community.

21. Congress has not done so yet. The National Voter Registration Act of 1993, though it requires attestation of "each eligibility requirement (including citizenship)" in its registration provisions—42 U.S.C. §§ 1973gg-3(c)(2)(C), 1973gg-5(a)(6)(A)(i), 1973gg-7(b)(2)—does not appear to preclude states from affording alien suffrage in federal elections. First, the quoted language should probably be

interpreted as meaning "(including citizenship, if applicable)" (and under current state laws, it is always applicable), because the statute is concerned with procedures for registering eligible voters, not mandating eligibility criteria. Second, the statute expressly declares its procedures to apply "in addition to any other method of voter registration provided for under State law." 42 U.S.C. § 1973gg-2(a).

22. Conversely, the federal government's powers would probably support a national policy extending voting rights in state and federal elections to aliens who would be qualified but for their alienage. This extension might be accomplished by reciprocal treaty, as a means of facilitating international travel for trade in goods and services. Alternatively, Congress might act unilaterally under its power to "enforce" the Fourteenth Amendment; restoring the franchise to resident aliens in order to help them protect themselves from discriminatory action by state and local governments would be consistent with the Supreme Court's analysis in Katzenbach v. Morgan, 384 U.S. 641 (1966). I am referring here to the uncontroversial "remedial" branch of the enforcement power, not the controversial "interpretive" branch. See Laurence H. Tribe, American Constitutional Law 341–43 (2d ed. 1988). The history of invidious discrimination against aliens and the Supreme Court's own recognition of alienage as a suspect classification for equal protection purposes would make it easy to distinguish Oregon v. Mitchell, 400 U.S. 112 (1971), where the majority rejected the idea that enfranchisement of eighteen-year-olds could be justified as a means of protecting them against discrimination.

23. Cf. Gerald M. Rosberg, Aliens and Equal Protection: Why Not the Right to Vote?, 75 Mich. L. Rev. 1092, 1110 (1977) (referring to all resident aliens).

24. I do not mean to ignore the racial qualifications imposed for most of United States history. The point is that naturalization generally followed as a matter of course for those who were not openly disqualified from the outset, then as now.

25. These are among the standard arguments for considering resident aliens members of the national community. See T. Alexander Aleinikoff, Citizens, Aliens, Membership and the Constitution, 7 Const. Commentary 9, 23 (1990); David A. Martin, Due Process and Membership in the National Community: Political Asylum and Beyond, 44 U. Pitt. L. Rev. 165, 201–03 (1983). Rosberg, note 23 supra, uses similar arguments in reaching toward the stronger conclusion that aliens are constitutionally entitled to vote.

26. See, e.g., Carlisle v. United States, 83 U.S. 147 (1873).

27. U.S. Const., art. I, § 2, cl. 3; id. amend. XIV, § 2; Aleinikoff, note 25 supra at 21; T. Alexander Aleinikoff, The Census and Undocumented Aliens: A Constitutional Account, 33 Law Quadrangle Notes 26 (Winter 1989). In the debates leading up to the Fourteenth Amendment, Roscoe Conkling opposed a proposal to change the basis of apportionment to voters, on the grounds that it would give states an undue incentive to enfranchise aliens. Cong. Globe, 39th Cong., 1st Sess. 356–57 (1866).

28. After the Civil War, the United States was able to negotiate a series of treaties to ensure recognition of the changed nationality of naturalized citizens. Even today, United States naturalization law requires only an oath of renunciation of other allegiances, not the legally effective abandonment of former nationality. See 8 U.S.C. § 1448(a)(2).

29. See Vance v. Terrazas, 444 U.S. 252 (1980) (elaborating standard of volun-

tary relinquishment of citizenship); Parness v. Shultz, 669 F. Supp. 7 (D.D.C. 1987) (applying standard in naturalization context); 8 U.S.C. § 1481(a) (codifying standard).

30. See, e.g., William S. Bernard, Cultural Determinants of Naturalization, 1 Am. Soc. Rev. 943 (1936); Louis De Sipio, Social Science Literature and the Naturalization Process, 21 Int'l Migration Rev. 390 (1987); Philip Q. Yang, Explaining Immigrant Naturalization, 28 Int'l Migration Rev. 449 (1994).

31. Such opportunities may arise especially rarely in local elections. Once a state has made resident aliens eligible to vote in state legislative elections, the Constitution entitles them to vote for senators and representatives, but it also bars them from running for Congress or the presidency.

32. See Salyer Land Co. v. Tulare Lake Basin Water Storage Dist., 410 U.S. 719, 730 (1973) (observing, but not adjudicating, this circumstance).

33. Alien Act of 1798, ch. 58, 1 Stat. 570. The act expired by its own terms in 1800.

34. See Chapter Two.

35. See Chapter Two.

36. See David M. Rabban, The First Amendment in Its Forgotten Years, 90 Yale L.J. 514 (1981).

37. Act of Mar. 3, 1891, ch. 551, § 1, 26 Stat. 1084; William Mulder, Immigration and the "Mormon Question": An International Episode, 9 W. Pol. Q. 416 (1956). The 1891 act excluded "polygamists." Later statutes clarified or expanded this ground to include belief in or advocacy of the practice of polygamy. Act of Feb. 20, 1907, ch. 1134, § 2, 34 Stat. 899; Act of Feb. 5, 1917, ch. 29, § 3, 39 Stat. 875. The 1952 act's exclusion of aliens who "are polygamists or who practice polygamy or advocate the practice of polygamy" was not repealed until 1990; since then only immigrants seeking to enter the United States to practice polygamy remain excludable. See Immigration and Nationality Act of 1952, ch. 477, § 212(a)(11), 66 Stat. 182; 8 U.S.C. § 1182(a)(9)(A).

38. Act of Mar. 3, 1903, ch. 1012, 32 Stat. 1213; see Mitchell C. Tilner, Ideological Exclusion of Aliens: The Evolution of a Policy, 2 Geo. Immig. L.J. 1, 19–31 (1987). The exclusion of aliens for anarchism was repealed in 1990, but aliens who advocate or teach opposition to all organized government remain ineligible for naturalization. See 8 U.S.C. § 1424(a)(1).

39. Act of Feb. 5, 1917, ch. 29, §§ 3, 19, 39 Stat. 875–76, 889.

40. Act of Oct. 16, 1918, ch. 186, 40 Stat. 1012.

41. Act of June 5, 1920, ch. 251, 41 Stat. 1009.

42. See Tilner, note 38 supra at 46–47.

43. See Alien Registration Act of 1940, ch. 439, § 23, 54 Stat. 673; Kessler v. Strecker, 307 U.S. 22 (1939); Tilner, note 38 supra at 53. See also Harisiades v. Shaughnessy, 342 U.S. 580, 582 (1952) (upholding the deportation of an alien who had abandoned the Communist Party in 1929, at the age of twenty-five).

44. Act of Sept. 23, 1950, ch. 1024, § 22, 64 Stat. 1006.

45. See id.; Act of June 27, 1952, ch. 477, § 212(a)(27), 66 Stat. 184; Tilner, note 38 supra at 60–65.

46. See, e.g., Steven A. Shapiro, Ideological Exclusions: Closing the Border to Political Dissidents, 100 Harv. L. Rev. 930 (1987); Tilner, note 38 supra at 81–85; Judy Wurtzel, Note, First Amendment Limitations on the Exclusion of Aliens, 62

N.Y.U. L. Rev. 149 (1987); Philip Monrad, Comment, Ideological Exclusion, Plenary Power, and the PLO, 77 Calif. L. Rev. 831 (1989). The Supreme Court's opportunity to address this conflict was squandered when the justices split three to three. See Reagan v. Abourezk, 484 U.S. 1 (1987).

47. 8 U.S.C. § 212(a)(3)(D)(i). If the alien shows that she is not otherwise a threat to the security of the United States, termination of membership two years before applying for a visa suffices, unless the party in question is governing a totalitarian dictatorship at the time. Id. § 212(a)(3)(D)(iii). The statute also makes an exception for "involuntary" members and permits a waiver for close relatives of U.S. residents. Id. § 212(a)(3)(D)(ii, iv). There is no corresponding deportation ground.

48. 8 U.S.C. §§ 212(a)(3)(A)(iii), 241(a)(4)(A)(iii).

49. 408 U.S. 753 (1972).

50. Id. at 762.

51. Id. at 767.

52. Id. at 769.

53. See Harvard Law School Forum v. Shultz, 633 F. Supp. 525 (D. Mass. 1986) (so holding), vacated, 852 F.2d 563 (1st Cir. 1986).

54. 395 U.S. 444 (1969).

55. An additional government justification, the protection of important foreign policy interests, is not discussed here. Current law permits the government to exclude aliens because their admission would have potentially serious adverse foreign policy consequences but also limits the government's authority to base this conclusion on "past, current, or expected beliefs, statements, or associations" that "would be lawful within the United States." 8 U.S.C. § 1182(a)(3)(C). If this provision is as sparingly applied as Congress intended—see H.R. Conf. Rep. 955, 101st Cong., 2d Sess. 129–30 (1990)—it would not cover the indiscriminate exclusion of Communists.

56. One of the sources of controversy over the Supreme Court's decision in Rust v. Sullivan, 500 U.S. 173 (1991), upholding the "gag rule" that prohibited organizations receiving federal family planning funding from discussing abortion with their clients, was the majority's acceptance of family planning counseling exclusive of abortion counseling as the purpose of the program. Some have contended that by accepting such a gerrymandered purpose, *Rust* eviscerated the unconstitutional conditions doctrine.

57. Rust v. Sullivan, 500 U.S. 173, 194–95 (1991); Seth F. Kreimer, Allocational Sanctions: The Problem of Negative Rights in a Positive State, 132 U. Pa. L. Rev. 1293, 1367 (1984).

58. To be precise, under current law most categories of immigrant admissions are subject to annual numerical limitation, and some categories are exempted from such limitation in the knowledge that demand in those categories is limited; nearly all categories of nonimmigrant admissions are numerically unlimited. Although the details change frequently, this basic contrast has been true since the adoption of quantitative limits on permanent immigration in the 1920s.

59. See 8 U.S.C. § 1101(a)(15)(B).

60. For example, the INS estimated 17.6 million nonimmigrant entries in fiscal year 1990, although this number includes repeated entries by the same alien. The Visa Office issued nearly 6 million nonimmigrant visas that year, and the INS esti-

mated more than 4.8 million entries by nonimmigrants for whom the requirement of a visa was waived. See U.S. Dept. of Justice, Immigration and Naturalization Service, 1990 Statistical Yearbook of the Immigration and Naturalization Service 117, 128 (1991); U.S. Dept. of State, Bureau of Consular Affairs, Report of the Visa Office 1991, at 13, 85 (1992).

61. See 8 U.S.C. § 1153(b)(1).

62. The apparent motivation for the diversification policy was the concern that existing criteria did not permit a higher level of immigration from Ireland. How this legitimately benefits the United States, aside from increasing the utility of the groups that lobbied for it, remains obscure. Compare Walter P. Jacob, Diversity Visas: Muddled Thinking and Pork Barrel Politics, 6 Geo. Immigr. L.J. 287 (1992), with Patricia I. Folan Sebben, U.S. Immigration, Irish Immigration and Diversity, 6 Geo. Immigr. L.J. 745 (1992).

63. See Jerold H. Israel, Elfbrandt v. Russell: The Demise of the Oath?, 1966 Sup. Ct. Rev. 193, 219 (identifying these as interests commonly alleged). Israel also noted a third interest, "elimination of persons who, aside from any question of danger or fitness, simply are not considered deserving of a government position because they oppose the basic principles on which the government is founded"; I will discuss this interest later in terms of national self-definition.

64. See 8 U.S.C. § 1182(a)(1)(A)(ii)(II) (the likelihood of future harmful behavior based on a history of physical or mental disorder), 1182(a)(2)(A) (past conviction of crime), 1182(a)(2)(C) (past trafficking in controlled substances), 1182(a)(2)(D) (prostitution within past ten years), 1182(a)(3)(i)(I) (past terrorist activity).

65. See, e.g., Dawson v. Delaware, 112 S. Ct. 1093 (1992) (membership in racist prison gang, without more, not relevant evidence of character in capital sentencing proceeding); Elrod v. Burns, 427 U.S. 347, 365 (1976) (new superiors cannot impute lack of motivation to members of losing party).

66. See United States v. Robel, 389 U.S. 258, 266 (1967).

67. See Elrod v. Burns, 427 U.S. 347, 367–68 (1976); Rutan v. Republican Party of Ill., 497 U.S. 62, 70–71 & n. 5 (1990).

68. Pickering v. Board of Educ., 391 U.S. 563 (1968); see Rankin v. McPherson, 483 U.S. 378 (1987) (noting that if petitioner had had law enforcement duties, her remarks about an assassination attempt might have justified her discharge); McMullen v. Carson, 754 F.2d 936 (11th Cir. 1985) (clerical employee in sheriff's office properly discharged after publicly disclosing membership and recruitment activities for Ku Klux Klan); Lawrenz v. James, 852 F. Supp. 986 (M.D. Fla. 1994) (prison employee properly discharged after publicity concerning his wearing of White Power T-shirt with swastika).

69. See 8 U.S.C. §§ 1182(a)(3)(D), 1424. Indeed, a separate provision makes excludable aliens who are reasonably believed to be entering the United States to engage in any activity that has the overthrow of the government as a purpose. Id. § 1182(a)(3)(A).

70. See John A. Scanlan, Aliens in the Marketplace of Ideas: The Government, the Academy, and the McCarran-Walter Act, 66 Tex. L. Rev. 1481, 1492–95 (1988).

71. See Aleinikoff, note 25 supra at 9; Martin, note 25 supra at 199–202, 211.

72. Lamont v. Postmaster General, 381 U.S. 301 (1965); cf. Meese v. Keene, 481 U.S. 465 (1987) (denying that the label "foreign propaganda" on foreign government materials substantially burdened access to them).

73. See, e.g., Lawrence H. Fuchs, The American Kaleidoscope: Race, Ethnicity, and the Civic Culture 32–34 (1990); Kenneth L. Karst, Belonging to America: Equal Citizenship and the Constitution 100–01 (1989).

74. See Karst, note 73 supra at 196–97; Rogers M. Smith, The "American Creed" and American Identity: The Limits of Liberal Citizenship in the United States, 41 W. Pol. Q. 225 (1987).

75. Afroyim v. Rusk, 387 U.S. 253 (1967), overruling Perez v. Brownell, 356 U.S. 44 (1958).

76. United States v. Robel, 389 U.S. 258, 264 (1967).

77. United States v. Eichman, 496 U.S. 310, 321 (1990); see also Texas v. Johnson, 491 U.S. 397, 421 (1989) (Kennedy, J., concurring) ("[T]he flag is constant in expressing beliefs Americans share, beliefs in law and peace and that freedom which sustains the human spirit").

78. Texas v. Johnson, 491 U.S. at 415. The statement reads in full as follows: "If there is any fixed star in our constitutional constellation, it is that no official, high or petty, can prescribe what shall be orthodox in politics, nationalism, religion, or other matters of opinion or force citizens to confess by word or act their faith therein." West Virginia v. Barnette, 319 U.S. 614, 642 (1943).

79. United States v. Eichman, 496 U.S. at 321 (Stevens, J., dissenting); Texas v. Johnson, 491 U.S. at 436–37 (Stevens, J., dissenting) ("A country's flag is a symbol of more than 'nationhood and national unity.' . . . It also signifies the ideas that characterize the society that has chosen that emblem. . . . So it is with the American flag. . . . It is a symbol of freedom, of equal opportunity, of religious tolerance, and of goodwill for other peoples who share our aspirations").

80. Texas v. Johnson, 491 U.S. at 429 (Rehnquist, C.J., dissenting).

81. See Sanford Levinson, Constitutional Faith 94–99 (1988) (discussing the notion of an "American creed").

82. Texas v. Johnson, 491 U.S. at 418.

83. Compare U.S. Const. art. V with Grundgesetz (Constitution) art. 79(3) (Germany); see United States v. Schneiderman, 320 U.S. 118, 137–39 (1943). The U.S. Constitution does rule out amendments that deprive a state of its equal representation in the Senate without its consent; even this is not a fixed principle, but an unusually strict supermajority requirement. Some U.S. authors have argued for implied limitations on the amending power. See, e.g., Akhil Reed Amar, Philadelphia Revisited: Amending the Constitution Outside Article V, 55 U. Chi. L. Rev. 1043, 1045 n. 1 (1989); Walter F. Murphy, An Ordering of Constitutional Values, 53 S. Cal. L. Rev. 703 (1980); see generally Responding to Imperfection: The Theory and Practice of Constitutional Amendment 163–236 (Sanford Levinson ed. 1995) (essays by Walter F. Murphy, John R. Vile, and Mark E. Brandon arguing for and against implied limitations).

84. See Grundgesetz art. 21(2) (prohibiting parties that seek to impair or abolish the free democratic basic order of the Federal Republic of Germany, even by peaceful means); Gregory H. Fox & Georg Nolte, Intolerant Democracies, 36 Harv. Int'l L.J. 1 (1995).

85. Gitlow v. New York, 268 U.S. 652 (1925) (Holmes, J., dissenting).

86. See, e.g., United States ex rel. Turner v. Williams, 194 U.S. 279, 293–94 (1904) (explaining dangerous tendency of anarchistic views). Similarly, in Harisiades v. Shaughnessy, 342 U.S. 580 (1952), the majority relied on the then-recent decision in Dennis v. United States, 341 U.S. 494 (1951), upholding the conviction of leaders of the Communist Party for conspiracy to advocate the overthrow of the government, as making it easy to reject the First Amendment challenge to the deportation of party members.

87. See, e.g., Bridges v. Wixon, 326 U.S. 135, 148 (1945); Bridges v. California, 314 U.S. 252 (1941); Schneider v. State, 308 U.S. 147 (1939).

88. Bugajewitz v. Adams, 228 U.S. 585, 591 (1913) (Holmes, J.) (deportation is "simply a refusal by the Government to harbor persons whom it does not want").

89. Whether returning to such conditions is more painful than failing to flee them in the first place may depend on other circumstances; in this respect, exclusion may sometimes be harsher than deportation.

90. See 8 U.S.C. § 1251(a)(4); Woodby v. INS, 385 U.S. 276 (1966) (adopting clear and convincing evidence standard as statutory burden of proof in deportation proceedings).

91. See, e.g., Harisiades v. Shaughnessy, 342 U.S. 580 (1952) (deported aliens immigrated at ages thirteen and sixteen); Galvan v. Press, 347 U.S. 522 (1954) (deported alien immigrated at age seven).

CHAPTER NINE

1. Kennedy v. Mendoza-Martinez, 372 U.S. 144, 159 (1963).

2. See, e.g., Vance v. Terrazas, 444 U.S. 252 (1980) (lawfully conferred American citizenship can be lost only by voluntary renunciation); Ng Fung Ho v. White, 259 U.S. 276 (1922) (requiring the judicial resolution of claims of citizenship in deportation proceedings); United States v. Schwimmer, 279 U.S. 644 (1929) (pacifist ineligible for naturalization), overruled by Girouard v. United States, 328 U.S. 61 (1946).

3. Scott v. Sandford, 60 U.S. (19 How.) 393 (1857).

4. Although children born to U.S. citizens abroad are not constitutionally guaranteed citizenship, Congress has extended citizenship to them by statute. See 8 U.S.C. §§ 1401(c,d,g), 1409.

5. Peter H. Schuck & Rogers M. Smith, Citizenship without Consent: Illegal Aliens in the American Polity (1985).

6. Id. at 9.

7. 7 Co. Rep. 1b (1608); see 9 W.S. Holdsworth, A History of English Law 73–91 (1926).

8. See Schuck & Smith, note 5 supra at 25–26.

9. Id. at 27–28, 43–48.

10. Id. at 37.

11. Id. at 50–54.

12. Id. at 72.

13. See Act of Apr. 9, 1866, ch. 31, § 1, 14 Stat. 27 ("[A]ll persons born in the United States and not subject to any foreign power, excluding Indians not taxed, are hereby declared to be citizens of the United States").

14. Schuck & Smith, note 5 supra at 85.

15. Id. at 117–18.

16. Id. at 118–19.

17. Id. at 98–99.

18. Id. at 99.

19. Id. at 103–15.

20. Id. at 94. The authors later clarified that they were undecided on whether eliminating birthright citizenship for the children of nonimmigrants and undocumented aliens would represent sound public policy. Peter H. Schuck & Rogers M. Smith, Membership and Consent: Actual or Mythic? A Reply to David A. Martin, 11 Yale J. Int'l L. 545 (1986). In 1995, Prof. Schuck argued against eliminating it.

21. See Arthur Helton, Book Review, 19 N.Y.U. J. Int'l L. & Pol. 221 (1986); Joseph H. Carens, Who Belongs? Theoretical and Legal Questions about Birthright Citizenship in the United States, 37 U. Toronto L.J. 413 (1987); David A. Martin, Membership and Consent: Abstract or Organic?, 11 Yale J. Int'l L. 278 (1985); David S. Schwartz, The Amorality of Consent, 74 Cal. L. Rev. 2143 (1986).

22. Schuck & Smith, note 5 supra at 86.

23. Schuck & Smith, note 20 supra at 546.

24. Cf. United States v. Wong Kim Ark, 169 U.S. 649, 668 (1898) ("Nor can it be doubted that it is the inherent right of every independent nation to determine for itself, and according to its own constitution and laws, what classes of persons shall be entitled to its citizenship"). The Court coupled this positivist assertion, however, with a holding that the Fourteenth Amendment had put it beyond the power of Congress to withhold citizenship from children born to Chinese aliens residing in the United States.

25. Cong. Globe, 39th Cong., 1st Sess. 2890 (1866) (remarks of Sen. Howard).

26. Cong. Globe, 39th Cong., 1st Sess. 2891 (1866). See also id. at 500 ("I am not prepared to say whether or not the contingency may come upon that coast when our people will have to assert their dominion by depriving that race which is now making inroads upon them of even the natural rights which usually belong to men in society").

27. See Cong. Globe, 39th Cong., 1st Sess. 2890–92 (colloquy of Sens. Cowan and Conness regarding the Fourteenth Amendment) (1866); id. at 498 (colloquy of Sens. Trumbull and Cowan regarding Civil Rights Bill). Sen. Conness of California recalled the depredations against the Chinese in his state in recent years and declared himself ready to accept equal rights for the children of Chinese parents.

28. Schuck & Smith, note 5 supra at 132, 136–37.

29. Although the fragile decision in Plyler v. Doe, 457 U.S. 202 (1982), struck down a state's exclusion of undocumented alien children from the public schools, it suggested that federal discrimination, most state discrimination against undocumented adults, and other forms of discrimination against undocumented children would be judged only by the rational basis test. Where that is the applicable test, decreasing undocumented aliens' incentive to stay would seem to provide a rational basis for virtually any discrimination.

30. Schuck & Smith, note 5 supra at 117.

31. Wong Kim Ark, 169 U.S. at 693; Elk v. Wilkins, 112 U.S. 94 (1884).

32. Schuck & Smith, note 5 supra at 154 n. 46; see Wong Kim Ark, 169 U.S. at

682; Inglis v. Sailors' Snug Harbor, 28 U.S. (3 Pet.) 99, 126, 155–56 (1830). The example repeatedly used in the congressional debates was the children of ambassadors. See, e.g., Cong. Globe, 39th Cong., 1st Sess. 2897 (1866) (remarks of Sen. Williams).

33. See, e.g., Cong. Globe, 39th Cong., 1st Sess. 2895 (1866) (remarks of Sen. Howard); see also Elk v. Wilkins, 112 U.S. 94 (1884).

34. See U.S. Const. art. I, § 2, cl. 3; id. amend. XIV, § 2; Elk v. Wilkins, 112 U.S. at 102–03.

35. See Elk v. Wilkins, 112 U.S. at 102.

36. See Wong Kim Ark, 169 U.S. at 680–86.

37. Schuck & Smith, note 5 supra at 86.

38. Id. at 118.

39. Id. at 102.

40. 169 U.S. 649 (1898).

41. Id. at 707–09, 724–26, 731–32 (Fuller, C.J., dissenting). The dissent followed consensual logic even further; it would have limited citizenship at birth under the Fourteenth Amendment to children of citizens.

42. 169 U.S. at 694, 701.

43. Id. at 693, 657, 697–98.

44. Schuck & Smith, note 5 supra at 79, 118. They also suggested that Congress accepted birthright citizenship for the children of resident aliens in the belief that its effects would be *de minimis*. Id. at 78–79. This disparagement rests on a confusion of the relevant categories; even if it were true that Congress accepted birthright citizenship for children born in the United States to Chinese parents in the belief that their numbers would be de minimis, Congress could not have thought that the number of children born to unnaturalized European immigrants would be de minimis. The latter children had always been considered U.S. citizens, and the Fourteenth Amendment was not intended to change that practice.

45. Acceptance of *Wong Kim Ark* is also inconsistent with an odd suggestion that the authors made in passing, that the relevant notion of jurisdiction may require complete absence of allegiance to any other sovereign. Schuck & Smith, note 5 supra at 83, 86. If that is what jurisdiction means, then *Wong Kim Ark* and the authors are wrong, and only the children of citizens (and maybe not dual citizens!) are entitled to citizenship.

The notion derives from the remarks of Senator Trumbull, who stated as his personal opinion that Indians maintaining tribal relations were not fully "subject to the jurisdiction" of the United States for two reasons: (1) because they owed allegiance to the tribe as well as to the United States, and (2) because (in his opinion) the independent lawmaking authority of the Indian nations left them not fully subject to the legislative power of Congress. Cong. Globe, 39th Cong., 1st Sess. 2893–94 (1866). Other senators, including Senator Howard, the draftsman of the citizenship clause, associated themselves with Trumbull's second reason but not his first. Id. at 2895 (remarks of Sen. Howard); id. at 2897 (remarks of Sen. Williams).

46. Coke had been explicit on the status of children born to aliens temporarily within the realm in Calvin's Case, 7 Co. Rep. 1b, 6a ("[F]or [the alien] owed to the King local obedience, that is, so long as he was within the King's protection; which local obedience being but momentary and uncertain is yet strong enough to make a

natural subject, for if he hath issue here, that issue is a natural born subject"); see also Holdsworth, note 7 supra at 89.

47. Not only was naturalization restricted to "free white persons" until 1870 (see, e.g., Act of Mar. 26, 1790, ch. 3, 1 Stat. 103), but in 1870, after a bitter debate with much vilification of the Chinese, the Senate rejected Senator Sumner's effort to eliminate racial qualifications for naturalization and extended eligibility only to "aliens of African nativity and to persons of African descent." Act of July 14, 1870, ch. 254, § 7, 16 Stat. 256.

48. See Chapter Four.

49. See, e.g., 169 U.S. at 655 ("aliens in amity, so long as they were within the kingdom"); id. at 658, 687 ("residing"); id. at 674, 688 ("native-born children of foreign parents"); id. at 693 ("children here born of resident aliens").

50. See, e.g., Cong. Globe, 39th Cong., 1st Sess. 2891 (1866) (remarks of Sen. Conness) ("Those persons return invariably, while others take their places, and, as I before observed, if they do not return alive their bones are carefully gathered up and sent back to the Flowery Land"); Ronald Takaki, Strangers from a Different Shore: A History of Asian Americans 31–37 (1989); but see id. at 10–11 ("Initially many Asian immigrants, probably most of them, saw themselves as sojourners. But so did European immigrants").

51. See Chinese Exclusion Case, 130 U.S. 581 (1889); Fong Yue Ting v. United States, 149 U.S. 698 (1893).

52. Schuck & Smith, note 5 supra at 44–45, 147–48 n. 9.

53. 2 Jean Jacques Burlamaqui, Principles of Natural and Politic Law 214 (Nugent trans., 4th ed. 1792). In the original French: "Or de cela seul, que les enfans des Citoyens, parvenus à un âge de discretion, veulent vivre dans le lieu de leur famille, ou dans leur patrie, ils sont par cela même censés se soumettre à la Puissance qui gouverne l'Etat, & par conséquent ils doivent jouïr, comme membres de l'Etat, des avantages qui en sont les suites." Jean Jacques Burlamaqui, Principes du droit politique 19 (1763 ed.) (bound with Principes du droit naturel).

54. Burlamaqui, Politic Law, note 53 supra at 213. In the original: "pourvû néanmoins que ces Descendans parvenus à l'âge de raison, voulussent de leur côté se soumettre au Gouvernement & reconnoitre l'autorité du Souverain." Droit politique, note 53 supra at 19.

55. Burlamaqui, Politic Law, note 53 supra at 214. In the original:

Les Sujets d'un Etat sont quelques fois appellés Citoyens; quelques-uns ne font aucune distinction entre ces deux termes, mais il est mieux de les distinguer. Celui de Citoyen doit s'entendre de tous ceux qui ont part à tous les priviléges de l'association, & qui sont proprement membres de l'Etat, ou par leur naissance, ou d'une autre maniére: Tous les autres sont plutôt de simples habitans ou des étrangers passagers que des Citoyens.

Droit politique at 20; orthography as in original.

56. Cong. Globe, 39th Cong., 1st Sess. 2890 (1866) (remarks of Sen. Howard); see also id. at 3031–32 (remarks of Sen. Henderson) ("[T]his section will leave citizenship where it now is. It makes plain only what has been rendered doubtful by past action of the Government"); Wong Kim Ark, 169 U.S. at 688.

57. Schuck & Smith, note 5 supra at 95.

58. Id. at 92, 95, 129–30.

59. Id. at 155 n. 3.

60. See Henderson v. New York, 92 U.S. 259 (1876); Chy Lung v. Freeman, 92 U.S. 275 (1876); Act of Mar. 3, 1875, ch. 141, 18 Stat. 477 (1875); Chapter Three.

61. Moreover, the earliest use of the term that LEXIS or WESTLAW turns up in a judicial opinion occurs in Waisbord v. United States, 183 F.2d 34 (5th Cir. 1950), which is itself not a masterpiece of decorum. The term *undocumented alien* is even newer.

62. *Illegal alien* does appear as a defined term in both 8 U.S.C. § 1365(b) and 29 C.F.R. § 500.20(n), but the two definitions are context driven and inconsistent. The former specifies a category of aliens who were unlawfully in the United States at the time they committed a felony, and the latter reduces to aliens without employment authorization.

63. For example, some forms of unauthorized presence involve criminal violations, and others do not; some nonimmigrants render themselves deportable by violating the conditions of their admission, and others do so by passage of time; some aliens enter without inspection, even though they are legally entitled to enter. Some aliens who have been paroled into the country pending decision on a request for admission are thought of as illegal aliens, even though they are not unlawfully in the country at all. Permanent resident aliens who commit acts rendering them deportable are not normally thought of as illegal aliens. The Immigration and Nationality Act recognizes that one may fail to maintain lawful status "through no fault of his own or for technical reasons." 8 U.S.C. § 1255(c).

64. An alien's presence may be tolerated as a matter of administrative discretion under the rubric of deferred action; an alien may apply for asylum or for temporary protected status; millions of aliens were permitted to apply for legalization under 8 U.S.C. §§ 1160, 1255A; an eligible alien may apply for adjustment of status under 8 U.S.C. § 1255.

65. The parallel fades almost completely, however, in a legal regime that relies solely on bond posting and commutation fees. One might view such a regime as authorizing the entry of all immigrants and merely trying to shift public costs onto the carrier. Still, the regime can operate as an immigrant-screening system if the state imposes charges high enough to affect carriers' behavior. Then carriers could select passengers at ports of embarkation, either directly or by setting ticket prices that impoverished emigrants could not meet, or carriers could decide after arrival and official inspection that it would be more profitable to return a passenger to Europe than to pay the charges. Immigrants who could formally comply with the requirements would be authorized to enter, even if they later imposed costs on the state—in a broader sense they may have been "undesired," but it does not seem accurate to consider them illegal. Immigrants who evaded the system by fraud or by landing in secret, however, might be comparable to modern-day illegal entrants, whether or not the legal system imposed a sanction on them directly.

66. Bugajewitz v. Adams, 228 U.S. 585, 591 (1913). This definition was intended to contrast with an understanding of deportation as punishment, which would subject immigration regulation to a series of constitutional limitations from which it is presently exempt.

67. See, e.g., Reno v. Flores, 113 S. Ct. 1439 (1993); Plyler v. Doe, 457 U.S. 202 (1982).

68. See Schuck & Smith, note 5 supra at 99.

69. Cf. 8 U.S.C. § 1182(l) (providing for nonimmigrant visa waiver program in Guam).

70. See Chapter Two. The example of federal registration laws is made particularly interesting by the fact that the Supreme Court relied on the modern federal registration laws as the basis for its argument that the exclusionary rule should be inapplicable in deportation proceedings because it would permit an illegal alien to continue to commit the crime of unregistered presence. INS v. Lopez-Mendoza, 468 U.S. 1032 (1984).

71. Act of Mar. 2, 1807, ch. 22, 2 Stat. 426 (effective 1808); see U.S. Const., art. I, § 9, cl. 1 (delaying until 1808 Congress's power to ban the importation of slaves into existing states willing to receive them).

72. This traffic was repeatedly brought to Congress's attention. See, e.g., Cong. Globe, 36th Cong., 1st Sess. 2216 (1860) (resolution of Rep. Wells); Cong. Globe, 35th Cong., 1st Sess. 1362 (1859) (remarks of Rep. Covode); but cf. S. Exec. Doc. No. 1, 36th Cong., 1st Sess. 5 (1859) (Annual Message of the President) ("After a most careful and rigorous examination of our coasts, and a thorough investigation of the subject, we have not been able to discover that any slaves have been imported into the United States, except the cargo of the Wanderer, numbering between three and four hundred"); see generally W.E.B. DuBois, The Suppression of the African Slave Trade to the United States of America 1638–1870 (1896) (1969 reprint); Warren S. Howard, American Slavers and the Federal Law 1837–1862 (1963).

73. See, e.g., Act of Mar. 3, 1819, ch. 101, 3 Stat. 533 (requiring the safe return of seized slaves to Africa); Act of Mar. 15, 1820, ch. 113, 3 Stat. 601 (increasing the penalty for importing slaves to death); Act of June 16, 1860, ch. 136, 12 Stat. 41 (seized slaves to be returned to Africa after captured vessels are brought to port in the United States). See also Act of Feb. 19, 1862, ch. 27, 12 Stat. 340 (prohibiting the "Coolie Trade").

74. See C. Vann Woodward, American Counterpoint 82 (1971); see also 1 Robert W. Fogel & Stanley L. Engerman, Time on the Cross 23–25 (1974). If the statutes for the suppression of the slave trade were underenforced, if enforcement efforts were underfunded, if a segment of the population encouraged the illegal migration in order to benefit from the slaves' labor, then the parallel with undocumented aliens today is merely all the stronger.

75. See, e.g., DuBois, note 72 supra at 121, 187.

76. "It is enough to say that whatever the proper reach of the consent principle may be, it cannot logically be applied to include the native-born children of illegal aliens, to whom the nation's consent has been expressly denied"; "[C]itizenship at birth would not be guaranteed to the native-born children of those parents—illegal aliens and 'nonimmigrant' aliens—who have never received the nation's consent to their permanent residence within it." Schuck & Smith, note 5 supra at 96, 118.

77. Neither the Civil Rights Act nor the Fourteenth Amendment conferred citizenship on former slaves who had been born abroad or on free black immigrants. As early as 1867, Senator Sumner's attention was called to the plight of an alien black

who had been in the country for decades. See Cong. Globe, 40th Cong., 1st Sess. 728 (1867). But Sumner's efforts to extend naturalization to blacks did not succeed until 1870.

78. Cong. Globe, 39th Cong., 1st Sess. 497 (1866).

79. Elk v. Wilkins, 112 U.S. 94, 102 (1884) ("Persons not thus subject to the jurisdiction of the United States at the time of birth cannot become so afterwards, except by being naturalized"); Wong Kim Ark, 169 U.S. at 702–03. It was also the rule at common law that a natural-born subject must be within the king's protection at the time of birth. Inglis v. Sailor's Snug Harbor, 28 U.S. (3 Pet.) 99, 126 (1830).

80. I will not rely here on the systemic harm to U.S. constitutionalism arising from the very fact that the Fourteenth Amendment would be amended. See Note, The Birthright Citizenship Amendment: A Threat to Equality, 107 Harv. L. Rev. 1026, 1039–40 (1994).

81. H.J. Res. 117, 103d Cong., 1st Sess. (1993).

82. H.J. Res. 129, 103d Cong., 1st Sess. (1993).

83. H.J. Res. 340, 103d Cong., 2d Sess. (1994) ("No person born in the United States after the date of the ratification of this article shall be a citizen of the United States, or of any state, on account of birth in the United States unless the mother or father of the person is a citizen of the United States, is lawfully in the United States, or has a lawful status under the immigration laws of the United States, at the time of birth"). Although this proposal, from a North Carolina congressman, is the only one that would preserve birthright citizenship for children born to nonimmigrants in lawful status, the discussion here will focus on children of undocumented parents, who are the principal target of the controversy. There are similar arguments to be made about children who are born and grow up in the United States during the lengthy stays of their parents as lawful nonimmigrants or during lawful nonimmigrant stays that turn into unlawful overstays.

84. See Note, note 80 supra, at 1027 n. 12. Under current interpretations of statutory law, however, children born to foreign diplomats in the United States become permanent residents at birth. This results less from deliberate policy than from practical accommodation to a gap in the statute. See Nikoi v. Attorney General, 939 F.2d 1065 (D.C. Cir. 1991); Matter of Huang, 11 I. & N. Dec. 190 (Reg. Comm. 1965). The amendment proposals might lead to a similar gap at first.

85. See Schuck & Smith, note 5 supra at 110–14; 139 Cong. Rec. H1005–06 (daily ed. Mar. 3, 1993) (remarks of Rep. Gallegly) (citing Schuck and Smith and paraphrasing their book at length).

86. See Wayne A. Cornelius, Leo R. Chávez, & Jorge G. Castro, Mexican Immigrants and Southern California: A Summary of Current Knowledge 53–68 (1982); Schuck & Smith, note 5 supra at 113; Peter L. Reich, Jurisprudential Tradition and Undocumented Alien Entitlements, 6 Geo. Immigr. L.J. 1 (1992); Deborah Sontag, Illegal Aliens Put Uneven Load on States, Study Says, N.Y. Times, Sept. 15, 1994, at A14. Unfortunately, the politics of the situation are inflamed by the fact that the federal government derives disproportionately more revenue from illegal immigration than the states, relative to the services provided.

87. See Acosta v. Gaffney, 558 F.2d 1153 (3d Cir. 1977); Bill Piatt, Born as Second Class Citizens in the U.S.A.: Children of Undocumented Parents, 63 Notre Dame L. Rev. 35, 40–41 (1988). De facto deportation occurs when deported parents

choose to take their minor citizen child with them, rather than leaving the child behind in the United States.

88. Actually, there are two situations that satisfy this description. One is suspension of deportation under 8 U.S.C. § 1254(a), a very substantial form of relief but with extremely strict eligibility requirements, including a minimum of seven years' prior residence. See Piatt, note 87 supra at 41–46. The slim prospect of being granted that relief cannot have a significant effect on the rate of illegal entry. The other form of relief is the exercise of prosecutorial discretion, a very minimal version of lawful status that the executive can retract at will. The knowledge that the INS does not trouble to deport every undocumented alien it catches probably does have a significant effect on illegal immigration, but this policy is not limited to aliens with citizen children.

89. Schuck & Smith, note 5 supra at 94.

90. See 139 Cong. Rec. H1006 (daily ed. Mar. 3, 1993) (remarks of Rep. Gallegly on his proposed amendment).

91. Martin, note 21 supra at 281–82.

92. See Matt Moffett, Border Midwives Bring Baby Boom to South Texas, Wall St. J., Oct. 16, 1991, at 1.

93. Los Angeles County, Internal Services Department, Impact of Undocumented Persons and Other Immigrants on Costs, Revenues and Services in Los Angeles County 15, 23 (1992). The estimate of the number of citizen children was based on applying a fertility multiplier to the number of undocumented women.

94. See Schuck & Smith, note 5 supra at 95, 156 n. 17. This figure was based on an extrapolation from births recorded in Los Angeles County hospitals.

95. See United States General Accounting Office, Benefits for Illegal Aliens: Some Program Costs Increasing, but Total Costs Unknown (1993) (testimony before the Task Force on Illegal Immigration, Republican Research Committee, House of Representatives, GAO/T-HRD-93-33); Private communication from Andrew Sherrill, General Accounting Office (computer runs on which the testimony was based). The GAO numbers were 103,146 and 89,340, respectively. The estimated total federal, state, and local cost for the 103,146 households was $479 million.

96. See U.S. Dept. of Justice, Immigration and Naturalization Service, 1991 Statistical Yearbook of the Immigration and Naturalization Service 37 (1992). The legalization program, enacted in November 1986, required continuous unlawful status since January 1, 1982.

97. Robert Warren & Jeffrey S. Passel, A Count of the Uncountable: Estimates of Undocumented Aliens in the 1980 United States Census, 24 Demography 375, 382 (1987). This does not include aliens who were *uncounted* by the census.

98. See General Accounting Office, Illegal Aliens: Assessing Estimates of Financial Burden on California 3, 9–10 (1994) (noting INS and Census Bureau estimates ranging between 3.4 and 3.8 million for 1992 and growing by 200,000 to 300,000 annually).

99. 457 U.S. 202, 218–19 (1982) (footnotes omitted).

100. Id. at 230.

101. See id. at 224–26; id. at 242 (Burger, C.J., dissenting).

102. See Martin, note 21 supra at 283.

103. See Hartmut Esser & Hermann Korte, Federal Republic of Germany, in European Immigration Policy (Tomas Hammar ed., 1985); Marilyn Hoskin & Ray C. Fitzgerald, German Immigration Policy and Politics, in The Gatekeepers: Comparative Immigration Policy (Michael C. LeMay ed., 1989).

104. Rogers Brubaker, Citizenship and Nationhood in France and Germany 171–74 (1992).

105. See Jurgen Fijalkowski, Aggressive Nationalism, Immigration Pressure and Asylum Policy Disputes in Contemporary Germany, 27 Int'l Migration Rev. 850 (1993); Gerald L. Neuman, Buffer Zones against Refugees: Dublin, Schengen, and the German Asylum Amendment, 33 Va. J. Int'l L. 503, 511–16 (1993). The killings in turn prompted an extraordinary series of antiracism demonstrations.

106. Linda S. Bosniak, Exclusion and Membership: The Dual Identity of the Undocumented Worker under United States Law, 1988 Wis. L. Rev. 955, 992–97, 1003–04.

107. See Jenifer M. Bosco, Undocumented Immigrants, Economic Justice, and Welfare Reform in California, 8 Geo. Immigr. L.J. 71, 74–76 (1994).

108. See Proposition 187, in California Ballot Pamphlet, General Election, November 8, 1994, at 91–92. Most provisions of Proposition 187 were preliminarily enjoined from taking effect by a federal district court in January 1995. See League of United Latin American Citizens v. Wilson, Nos. CV 94–7569 et al. (N.D. Cal. Jan. 17, 1995), appeal pending sub nom. Gregorio T. v. Wilson, No. 95–55192 et al. (9th Cir.).

109. 457 U.S. 202 (1982). The proponents of Proposition 187 understood that its education provisions were clearly inconsistent with *Plyler* and sought to have that decision overturned.

110. United States v. Verdugo-Urquidez, 494 U.S. 259, 272–73 (1990); see, e.g., Toll v. Moreno, 458 U.S. 1, 25–49 (1982) (Rehnquist, J., dissenting); Sugarman v. Dougall, 413 U.S. 634, 649–64 (1973) (Rehnquist, J., dissenting).

111. The government can rebut this evidence of citizenship by showing that the parents were foreign diplomats. It is a long time since invading troops last occupied U.S. soil.

112. See United States Commission on Immigration Reform, U.S. Immigration Policy: Restoring Credibility, Executive Summary at 12–17 (1994) (proposing a central database of all citizens and aliens authorized to work in the United States); Andrew M. Strojny, Papers, Papers . . . Please: A National ID or an Electronic Tatoo?, 72 Interp. Rel. 617 (1995).

113. See Bosniak, note 106 supra at 1013–17; Kitty Calavita, Employer Sanctions Violations: Toward a Dialectical Model of White-Collar Crime, 24 L. & Soc. Rev. 1041 (1990); Peter H. Schuck, The Emerging Political Consensus on Immigration Law, 5 Geo. Immigr. L. J. 1, 10–12 (1991).

CHAPTER TEN

1. See NLRB v. Jones & Laughlin Steel Corp., 301 U.S. 1 (1937); Wickard v. Filburn, 317 U.S. 111 (1942).

2. Katz v. United States, 389 U.S. 347 (1967).

3. 357 U.S. 1 (1957).

4. McCulloch v. Maryland, 17 U.S. (4 Wheat.) 316, 407 (1819) (emphasis in original).

5. 494 U.S. 259 (1990); see also Johnson v. Eisentrager, 339 U.S. 763, 796 (1950) (Black, J., dissenting) ("It would be fantastic to suggest that alien enemies could hail our military leaders into judicial tribunals to account for their day-to-day activities on the battlefront").

INDEX

Adams, John, 60
Adams, John Quincy, 38, 238n
Addison, Alexander, 55, 56, 122
admissions: guest theory of alien admission, 121; immigrant and nonimmigrant, 154–57; to United States as form of subsidy, 153–54; to United States as privilege, 125. *See also* entry into United States; exclusion of aliens
Alien Act (1798): debates related to, 52–60, 62; expiration (1800), 60; Federalist position on, 52–53; Federalists' defenses of, 54–56, 122; as ideological restriction, 40–41, 149; Jeffersonian Republican position on, 53–60
Alien and Sedition Acts (1798), 40–41, 52–53
Alien Enemies Act (1798), 40–41, 58
aliens: citizenship for children of, 165; dilution of nation's independence and identity by, 123–24; distinction between permanent resident and nonimmigrant, 133, 173–74; drafting of, 69; First Amendment rights, 162; illegal, 177–79, 183–86; in social contract theory, 10–12. *See also* constitutional rights; deportation; exclusion of aliens; rights of aliens
aliens, declarant: defined, 65; enfranchisement, 146; factors in decision not to naturalize, 147–48; federal government treatment of, 69; suffrage for, 65–66, 68–69
aliens, nondeclarant: defined, 146; suffrage for, 146–47
aliens, resident: deportation on ideological grounds, 161–64; enfranchisement of, 143–49; exclusion from certain public employment, 140; freedom to remain, 131–33
alien suffrage: constitutionality of, 63, 139–49; declarant and nondeclarant aliens, 65–66, 146–49; decline of, 70–71; history of, 63–66, 70–71; under Maastricht Treaty, 71; selective exclusion from, 69–70; significance of, 66–70; state and local level status of, 64, 70; in territories, 64–66. *See also* electorate, optional
amendments to Constitution. *See specific amendments*

American Insurance Co. v. Canter (1828), 75–76, 79

Balzac v. Porto Rico (1922), 88, 89
banishment of aliens, 22–23
Beilenson, Anthony C., 180
Benton, Thomas Hart, 86, 241n, 242n
Bill of Rights. *See* constitutional rights
birthright citizenship. *See* citizenship clause
Black, Hugo, 89, 91–92, 103
Blackmun, Harry, 108
black people, free: federal law restricting entry of, 36, 38, 42, 48; objections to migration of, 35–37; state laws related to movement of, 34–40
Boyd v. Nebraska ex rel. Thayer (1892), 68
Bradley, Joseph, 81–82
Brandenburg v. Ohio (1969), 152, 162
Brennan, William: dissent in *Verdugo-Urquidez*, 107–8; on political question doctrine, 124–36
Brown, Henry Billings, 86
Brown v. Board of Education (1954), 89
Buchanan, James, 38–39, 41
Burger Court, 104
Burlamaqui, Jean Jacques, 167, 174–75
Burlingame Treaty (1868), 39

Calhoun, John C., 36, 76–78
Calvin's Case (1608), 166, 268n
Canter. See American Insurance Co. v. Canter (1828)
Chae Chan Ping v. United States. See Chinese Exclusion Case (1889)
Chinese Exclusion Case (1889), 44, 51, 118, 119, 134, 136, 151
Chy Lung v. Freeman (1876), 45, 48, 51, 137
citizens: constitutional rights of U.S., 4, 100–103; in core electorate, 141–43; impact of alien exclusion on, 130, 133–34, 138; prohibition against disenfranchisement, 69
citizenship: emphasis in *Reid v. Covert*, 91–92; *jus sanguinis* rule of, 165; *jus soli* rule of, 147, 165–66, 181–87; of native Americans, 171–72; relationship between state and federal, 64; revisionist interpretation of Fourteenth Amendment, 166–80; rights under Fourteenth Amendment, 84, 165–

About the Author

GERALD L. NEUMAN is Professor of Law at Columbia University.